HAROLD GASSON'S
STEAM DAYS

HAROLD GASSON'S STEAM DAYS

A Railwayman's Journey
from Footplate to Signal Box 1941-1957

Harold Gasson

A Goodall paperback
from
Crécy Publishing Limited

Harold Gasson's Steam Days
Copyright © HH Gasson 1973-1981

FIRING DAYS
Copyright © 1973
FOOTPLATE DAYS
Copyright © 1976
NOSTALGIC DAYS
Copyright © 1980
SIGNALLING DAYS
Copyright © 1981

This combined edition Copyright © Crécy Publishing Ltd 2020

ISBN 9781910809679

Front cover image: No 6953 'Leighton Hall' on down side station pilot duty at
Reading. *KJR collection*
Rear cover image: The terminus at Lambourn. Harold would work here on the
one Sunday train from Didcot via Newbury. He has fond memories, and stories,
from his association with the branch. *KJR collection*

Printed in Malta by Melita Press

A Goodall paperback
published by

Crécy Publishing Limited
1a Ringway Trading Estate, Shadowmoss Road, Manchester M22 5LH
www.crecy.co.uk

Contents

FIRING DAYS

Introduction

This Book is an attempt to re-capture the happy days of Steam. I was fortunate enough to serve with a most Honourable Company of Gentlemen — the Enginemen and Shed Staff of Didcot Locomotive Department.

During the 1939-45 War, Didcot, as a Main Line Shed in the London Division, was in a unique position. The locomotives of all the other Companies, including the U.S.A. Army Transportation Corps, were serviced and worked by Didcot Enginemen. After working these 'foreign locomotives' we were delighted to find that a fact was confirmed, we were indeed working on "God's Wonderful Railway".

The locomotives of Messrs. Dean, Churchward, Collett, and Hawksworth were the finest in the world.

Didcot Locomotive Shed is now a living Steam Museum, but it is with pleasure I find that the Great Western Preservation Society have re-captured the atmosphere of a past age, even to including 6106 Tank, an original locomotive stationed at Didcot during my cleaning and firing days.

H.H. Gasson. 1973

DIDCOT, NEWBURY, SOUTHAMPTON LINE

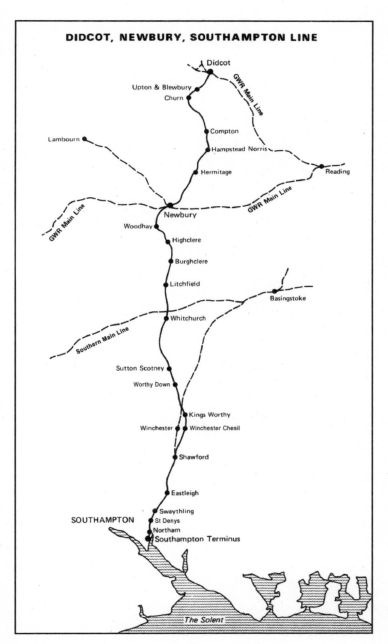

No. **47806**

IDENTIFICATION CARD

GREAT WESTERN RAILWAY

The undermentioned person is authorised to be on the Lines and Premises on the Great Western Railway Company while in the execution of his duty. This card is valid until cancelled or withdrawn.

NAME IN FULL *GASSON Harold Henry*

DEPARTMENT *L. M. E. A.*

GRADE *Fireman*

STATIONED AT *Didcot*

SIGNATURE OF HOLDER *H. H. Gasson*

This Identification Card must be signed in ink by the holder immediately he receives it, and be carried by him until further notice when engaged in work on the Railway. It must be produced at any time on request, and the holder must, if required, sign his name as a proof of his identity.

Signature of Issuing Officer

H. Henry

General Manager.

Chapter One
Early Days

My introduction to the Great Western Railway steam locomotives at Didcot and my subsequently joining the ranks of the enginemen working those engines all started through a chain of events begun by my Aunt Annie in 1905. Annie Gasson lived in a farm cottage with her parents, four brothers, and two sisters. The cottage was situated in the small hamlet of Charcotte, just outside Tonbridge.

As was expected of young girls in those day, she left home and entered 'service' and by 1910 she had obtained a position of Cook to a household in the Banbury Road, Oxford. While working in this house she was to meet a young man who was to become her whole life until she died in July 1972. This young man was working as an Engine Cleaner at Oxford Locomotive Shed at this time, and was one Albert Edmonds, normally known as Bert. His journey to and from the shed took him up and down the Banbury Road twice each day, and with an eye for a pretty girl it was not long before he spotted Annie, and being an enterprising young man, as were all Great Western Cleaners, he took steps to make her acquaintance at St. Giles' Fair. That they were made for each other was evident from the start, for the courtship blossomed. Annie took what was later to prove a vital step in my life; she took Bert home to meet the family, where he was accepted with open arms. What his thoughts were of the South Eastern and Chatham Railway between Reading and Penshurst Station as he, a Great Western man, made the journey with Annie are not recorded, but the locomotives must have made a profound impression, as we shall see.

After the introductions had been made, and Bert settled in, Annie did not see a lot of him for the rest of that weekend, as two of her brothers, William and Harold, found that they had a lot in common with him. They were both spellbound by Bert's description of the Great Western Railway, and any comment of the South Eastern and Chatham was quickly dismissed in true Great Western pride. Bert talked long and ardently about Armstrong and Dean engines, and particularly about Mr. Churchward's three French engines at Oxford, 102 *La France*, 103 *President*, and 104 *Alliance.*

After Bert and Annie had returned to Oxford, Bill and Harold started to take more interest in the local railway. On the way to work they had to go through the level crossing at Penshurst Station, and up to this point they had considered it an inconvenience to be held up by the locked gates; they would pass the time of day with 'Old Joe' the Signalman, but never take much notice of the locomotives. However, Bert's visit had changed all that. They began to take an almost professional interest in the 4-4-0 Jumbo's, 0-6-0 Stirlings', and the tall chimney 0-4-4 Tanks.

There were long conversations in bed until the small hours, about railway work, until Dad Gasson told them to shut up and go down to Tonbridge Shed in the morning and try their luck, as it was quite evident now that neither of them were going to muck out cow sheds, milk cows, or scare crows much longer.

They cycled into Tonbridge to have a look, but there was no *La France* on Tonbridge Shed. Bert had done his work well; the seeds of future Great Western Enginemen had been sown, and were soon to bear fruit. They both decided that a better and more exciting life lay in the direction of Oxford, so they promptly packed their few possessions together and set off. The South Eastern and Chatham's loss was to be the Great Western's gain, as both lads were to have a long and distinguished career as members of an elite group of men on the locomotive staff of 'God's Wonderful Railway'.

They set off from Penshurst Station in the late afternoon on a Sunday, changing at Redhill for Reading, which landed them up at the terminus of the South Eastern. At Reading General they found that the last train to Oxford had gone, so after a meal and a walk round the town, they returned to the station to await the first morning train. It never occurred to either of them that Reading might have a locomotive shed; all they could think about was Oxford and all those engines that Bert had talked about. At 4.00am a kindly Guard gave them a lift to Oxford on a milk empty, where they arrived in time for a quick wash in the toilet. Bert had talked about 6.00am start, no hardship for two farm boys, but they didn't want to arrive late, even if there was no job waiting for them.

At 6.00am, with no job, little money, and that queasy feeling in the stomach, they knocked on the door of 'Jobber Brown' the Foreman of Oxford Locomotive Shed.

At the curt bid to enter, they took a deep breath and walked in to meet a most formidable man wearing the Great Western badge of office, the bowler hat.

The fact that Harold could charm the birds off a tree, and that Bill could take over when his brother dried up, coupled with Bert Edmond's name, must have impressed Mr. Brown. Here in his office he had two lads, who had scorned the South Eastern and Chatham, and had come all the way from Kent to join the Great Western at Oxford, and what's more, they could tell him why it had to be the Great Western and no other.

'Jobber' did not relish the idea of refusing them a chance to become members of his staff, so he sent them to see Mr. Swallow the Foreman Cleaner. This gentleman found he had on his hands a situation that he was unprepared for, but he too was impressed by the two lads and their story, so he solved the problem in the one way he knew how. While he collected his thoughts together, he gave them a large cardboard box full of lengths of coloured wool and told them to sort the wool out into piles of the same colour. He said he would return later to see how they were getting on.

What this could have to do with steam engines neither could figure out, but with Father's advice to keep their eyes open and mouths shut they got on with the job.

The difficulty was that so many predecessors had handled the wool with grubby fingers that the colours were much about the same. However, small piles of wool began to grow larger on the table. They were not to know that this was the Great Western's way of testing for colour blindness, a method which was to continue for a long time to come.

Mr. Swallow returned, looked at the piles of wool, then swept them all back into the cardboard box. He gave them an envelope addressed to a Doctor in High Street, and told them to report there at 10.00am for a medical examination. This Doctor was the medical officer retained by the Great Western to deal with staff when they arrived in the Oxford area. They both had a stiff medical examination; (as Bill said "for everything except Foot and Mouth!"). One thing which did puzzle them for a time was when they were both given a glass jar and instructed to fill it with water. In vain they looked round for a tap, until the Doctor informed them in no uncertain terms on how to fill the jars! However, they were sent back to the Loco Shed with the news that they had passed.

For a second time that day they knocked on 'Jobber Brown's' door. Mr. Brown read the contents of the envelope they had brought back from the Doctor, and with a smile told them that they were both accepted as Cleaners and could start next morning, but in the meantime they should have a look round the Shed and meet some of the other Cleaners.

As it was now mid-day there were not many engines on Shed except those in the boiler washout, but to the brothers' delight 102 *La France* was one of them. No thoughts were given to clothing as they clambered aboard her, where they found everything Bert had told them was true. Gleaming copper pipes, brass fittings, and that wonderful aroma of steam, hot oil, and the quiet gentle noise of a large steam engine at rest.

A very loud shout aroused them from their day-dreaming, with the firm order to get down from that so and so engine. It was 'Old Swallow', as they were to get to know him. They came down as ordered, and were promptly told to get back up again and this time to come down the right way. They did not know, of course, that to come down from the footplate with their backs to the steps was not only almost impossible but highly dangerous.

Mr. Swallow then took them round the Shed, explaining the duties of a Cleaner and the need to be at all times punctual, obedient, and sober; he then went on to explain that they would receive 12/0d a week for a twelve hour day, working six days a week alternating with a twelve hour night duty. Sunday would be a day off, and he expected to see them in church. Lodgings had been found for them in Hythe Bridge Street at 11/6d a week, so in their wisdom the Great Western had made sure of two things; they would surely remain sober on sixpence a week pocket money, and would not lead a riotous life so far from home.

Bill and Harold soon settled down to the life of a Cleaner, and as members of a regular gang they became adept with scrapers, tallow, and cleaning rags. Each gang of half a dozen lads were allocated several locomotives which became their responsibility, so there was much rivalry between gangs as to who had the cleanest engine.

Bill and Harold had 103 *President* as the "number one engine", but, such was the standard of cleaning, there was not much to choose between any of the engines on Oxford Shed; in any case, 'Old Swallow' saw to that. Mr. Swallow was a good Foreman Cleaner. His standards of cleanliness took on an elaborate form of inspection, whereby he would produce from his pocket a steel foot rule which he would poke between the frames, and then would wipe the rule on a clean piece of linen; if this showed any trace of grime Mr. Swallow would show his displeasure in the form of a fine, usually a half-hour loss of pay, so on a pay rate of 12/0d there were some very clean engines! A cabin was provided for meal breaks, known as 'The Black Hole' (a term that needs no description), but the day shift were far too busy to use it, and the night shift found that an empty firebox with a flare lamp perched on the brick arch was a safe place to disappear for the odd half an hour.

They both, of course, saw a lot of Bert and Annie, but Bert did confess that life was a little difficult for a few weeks until Annie had got over the shock of Bill and Harold turning up in Oxford. With Annie a Cook in a big house, food was no problem, and they were the best fed lads in the Shed.

A very happy year passed, then Bert's expected promotion to Fireman came up, which meant a move from Oxford as he was posted to the Main Line Shed at Cardiff. It was time for a wedding, so all four of them went home to Penshurst for a week.

As they walked up the wooden platform at Penshurst Station and passed the engine, Bill and Harold had some very caustic remarks to make about the South Eastern and Chatham loco stock but, as Bert could see the fireman reaching for a coal pick, he very wisely kept his mouth shut.

The wedding took place in the little church just up the hill from the station, and in a way it was a true railway wedding, because as they waited to go over the level crossing a 'Jumbo' came by and gave them a blast on the whistle; the gesture returned by Bill and Harold gave no doubt that a Western whistle would have been preferred.

Bert and Annie left for Cardiff at the end of the week, and Bill and Harold prepared to return to Oxford. When their train ran into Penshurst they both crept into the coach without any comment about South Eastern

Locomotives, for it was the same crew that had brought them down and discretion was the order of the day.

They started back on the night shift and were in trouble at once through a silly prank. All Cleaners get up to some kind of mischief, but this one is still remembered by some of the retired Enginemen at Oxford. In Hythe Bridge Street some few houses up from their lodgings lived a gentleman whose occupation was to convey cakes from a famous Oxford cake maker to the Station. His transport for this job was a box tricycle, and to allow him to make an early start he would ride the machine home at night, parking it outside his house.

In the early hours of the Tuesday morning following their return, Bill and Harold 'borrowed' thirty feet of old signal wire, then crossed the main line, went through the North Western Railway Yard and the Oxford Coal Yard and out into Hythe Bridge Street, where they proceeded to wire the tricycle's pillar to a nearby lamp-post.

Soon after 6.00am all the night shift lads, and some of the day shift, were gathered just round the corner of the coal yard, looking up Hythe Bridge Street waiting to see the fun. Sure enough the inevitable happened. The portly gentleman came out of his front door, with great ceremony placed his cycle clips in position, and mounted the tricycle. They thought for a moment that he had noticed the wire; but portly gentlemen do not just ride off — there was a period of adjustment. Then he set off down the slight fall of the road towards them, with the wire uncurling behind him, and by the time he had travelled the thirty feet he was going a fair old lick.

He came to a very sudden stop, (in railway circles it is known as a 'rough shunt'); he sailed over the top of the tricycle, still in a sitting position, and landed in the middle of the wet coal slurry and cart ruts in the gate-way of the coal yard.

There was a mad scramble, reminiscent of a rugby forward line on the move, back to the safety of the Shed but Bill and Harold were recognised. They sat in the 'Black Hole' for an hour waiting for things to settle down, then crept back to their lodgings. At 9.00am a day shift Cleaner fetched them out of bed, with orders to report to Mr. Brown within the hour. As they walked to the Shed both discussed the possibility of dismissal, and the shame of returning home, so it was with a tremulous feeling that they knocked on the office door.

Mr. Brown was waiting, sitting behind his desk, with Mr. Swallow at his side; both gentlemen were wearing their bowler hats, so Bill and Harold knew this was the moment of truth. A complaint had been received from that most eminent of persons, 'a Member of the Public' against the Great Western Railway, dishonour had been brought to the Locomotive Shed by two young ruffians, and the punishment must be swift and severe.

They stood there and took it all, not saying a word, as did Mr. Swallow, but both lads noticed that 'Jobber' had some trouble in keeping a stern expression on his face. They were fined one loss of duty, being told not to report that night, while the rest of the nightshift would lose one hour. They said "Thank you very much Sir, it won't happen again Sir, we are very sorry Sir, three bags full Sir," (well, almost the last phrase), and with gratitude in their hearts backed out of the office. As they closed the door, thankful for getting off so lightly, they heard an explosion of laughter from inside the office, but they did agree on one thing — no more interviews of that nature again, the only misdemeanours to arise would be the night swimming in the canal behind the Shed.

In the summer of 1915 they were promoted to Firemen at Didcot, and this association with Didcot Enginemen was to last many years. Mr. Brown and Mr. Swallow saw them on their last day at Oxford, and said that they were two of the best lads they had had through their hands; but then they said that to every Cleaner when the time came to leave. Although both gentlemen were strict and insisted on a job well done, they were sentimentalists at heart. Bill and Harold left Oxford with a clean record, and the incident with the tricycle was not recorded; it certainly would not be forgotten, but added to the folklore that builds up over the years as a little bit of the history of Oxford Shed.

At Didcot they found lodgings at the March Bridge Cottages, with Mrs. Keats, a war widow. The cottage was opposite the bridge itself, which carries the main line from Paddington to Bristol and South Wales; indeed, their bedroom window was the same level as the rails.

Bert and Annie were notified of the move, and as Bert was now firing on the vacuum fitted goods and the occasional South Wales expresses, a 'Crow' (four short and one long blast on the whistle) was a signal that he was on his way through. There was no mistaking Bert on the footplate, even when he was promoted to Driver. He was a well-known figure, with a red handkerchief tied cowboy fashion round his neck and a briar pipe permanently in his mouth. If that pipe was smoking well, then so was the chimney; it only went out when Bert was having a rough trip for steam.

The lodgings with Ada Keats turned out to be a real home from home, particularly in Bill's case, as he became very attached to Ada. She responded likewise so they decided to get married. Harold moved on to other lodgings and settled down with Jackie Wilkins, a well known and respected Driver in the Didcot passenger link, and remained there until he too gave up the bachelors life in 1922.

In 1924 I arrived as his only son, and much to his dismay, Mother registered me with the local authority with the same name of Harold. She waited until he was on a double home turn to do it, so the foul deed was over when he arrived back home. He hated the name to such an extent I can never remember him using it; it was always 'mate' or 'son'.

Two Harolds in the household was a bit confusing at times, especially when visitors were present, so Mother arrived at a typical woman's solution, Harold number one became Big Harold, Harold number two became Little Harold. The 'Little' bit stuck to me, even when I topped the old chap by a good six inches.

Bill and Harold were on the long slow haul through the links, which were in effect a prolonged apprenticeship to the status of Driver before I began to appreciate that my Dad was someone special.

As a very small boy, I can remember Mother taking me to the Hagbourne Road bridge to see Big Harold come down the bank from Newbury with his Driver, Jim Brewer, on 3454 'Skylark' of the Bulldog class, and visits to the old wooden Shed that stood at the top of the steps which now lead to the present Shed. In 1930 engines began to take hold of me.

There was no collecting names and numbers, that was for amateurs, for I had access to the real thing. In a railway town there was no status at school in being a footplateman's son, but there was considerable rivalry between the Traffic and Locomotive Departments, so the Great Western was well equipped for future recruits.

The house seemed always full at weekends with locomen; on Sundays mornings it was Mutual Improvement Classes in the front parlour, so I was on familiar terms with eccentric rods, lifting links, lap and lead; and in the afternoon it was band practice. Dad loved music, he was a cornet player of some repute, and as Didcot Silver Band was made up almost exclusively of railwaymen, I soon knew every member of Didcot Loco Shed.

About this time, Bill and Harold moved up into the double home link, so I did not see much of either of them, as they were always in bed or away from home. In common with most Western Sheds, Didcot men's working was similar to the spokes of a wheel. They went north to Wolverhampton and Birmingham via Stratford or Banbury, East to Paddington, West to Swindon and Gloucester, and South to Westbury via Reading, and to Southampton over the Didcot-Newbury Branch. They spent two years doing this, then both moved up into the passenger link as Passed Firemen.

This was the time I really began to enjoy steam, as Big Harold was now doing driving duties from time to time. He still had a regular driver, and a regular engine, 3454 *Skylark* of my early years.

One Sunday morning in 1932 he was Shed Pilot Driver, shunting engines from the Ash Road and Coal Stage, turning them, and placing them in the Shed in the order of dispatch. The Shed was brand new, and it was arranged that I should visit it at 10.00am and spend the rest of the turn with Dad.

Builders' materials were still laid about, but what a change from the gloomy old wooden Shed. This was a day I shall never forget, for I really worked that morning, up and down from engine to engine, but the highlight came in the early afternoon, when we had to turn *Skylark*.

She was standing just inside the Shed on No. 1 road, and I was allowed to drive her. I backed her gently over the points, wound the reversing lever into forward gear while Big Harold turned the points, then drove her down to the turn-table. We had her balanced so finely that I could move her unaided; then I drove her back up past the lifting shop and shed offices, over No. 1 points again and back to stop near the sand drier. There I had a surprise, as waiting to prepare her for a Sunday passenger working was Dad's regular driver, Joe Beckenham.

Joe Beckenham was a typical example of the Great Western passenger driver, being rather small in stature and inclined to stoutness, wearing clean overalls bleached almost white, with brass buttons and shoes sparkling, a heavy white moustache, rosy complexion, cap-peak polished, and a Gold Albert across his stomach; in fact, the very essence of the top link driver. He climbed up on the foot-plate, and with great ceremony placed on my head a new Engineman's cap. This cap, I believe, was the last issue to carry on each side of the peak the two small brass buttons showing, in relief, Lord of the Isles. The cap is long worn out of course, but I still have those two buttons in my collection of Great Western treasures, one up I think on Swindon Museum, as I have looked there in vain for replicas.

All this fun had to come to an end when Bill and Harold were made Drivers, as Bill was sent to Aberbeeg, the main Shed in the South Wales Western Valleys, which handled all the coal traffic there, and Big Harold was sent to Moat Lane Shed in Mid Wales for the summer service.

In the summer of 1933 they both had another move, Bill to Barry Dock Shed, and Harold to the Neath and Brecon Shed. Both thought at the time that the move was to be permanent, so the families were moved to South Wales, but, as an insurance, both applied for a return to the London Division, with Didcot as first choice and Reading as second.

By a twist of fate, just as the two families settled in Wales, Bert and Annie moved to Acton. Bert was promoted to Driver at Old Oak Common Shed, so he now found himself on the right hand side of the 'Twenty-Nines' and 'Castles'. The change for Bert was one of Sheds, more than of work, as his knowledge of the main line between Paddington, Bristol, and South Wales was considerable, so he soon found himself on the 'runners' again, the only difference being that he now had a chance to handle a 'King'.

Bert Edmonds and a 'King' in good order were a formidable combination. He soon became known as a member of a small group of men who had that little extra which enabled them to get the best out the 'King' Class in the most adverse conditions. I've seen him go through Didcot and down Savernake Bank doing the magic Ton, and he didn't exactly hang about on the 'Castles'. Like Bill and Harold, he was loved by the Firemen, always taking a turn on the shovel, and never expecting a Fireman to do more than he was prepared to do himself.

During this time I did not see much of engines, except for one visit to Neath and then Barry Dock Shed. Somehow this seemed different from the brand new Shed I had known at Didcot, but then I suppose I was too busy growing up in a strange environment. But in 1936 everything changed again.

The long arm of 'Jobber Brown' reached out over the years and touched Bill and Harold. On that first day long ago he decided that as Bill was the eldest by one year, he would be senior, so when a vacancy came up in the London Division, Bill filled it. This was at Reading, which was to be the last move, and within a month a vacancy arose at Didcot which brought Harold back home again. Both brothers had been happy in South Wales and were prepared to see their time out in the Valleys, but their wives could not settle down so it was back to old friends again. Harold was most upset, not that he didn't welcome the return to his old Shed, but he loved the Welsh people, and nothing pleased him more in later years when I met and married a girl from those same Valleys.

As a child I had spent odd weekends back where it had all begun at Charcotte. This was a wonderful place to go to, as when one left Penshurst Station to reach the cottage, the footpath led across the perimeter of the aerodrome, where flying was always in progress. The aircraft were Avros and Sopwiths, and the pilot would give a friendly wave to a small boy as he swished overhead, with magnetos cut and engine spluttering, to make a bumpy landing on the grass.

During the period spent in South Wales the annual one week's holiday was spent at Charcotte. I was now old enough to take interest in the 'other railway' and its locomotives, and I cultivated the friendship of the Signalman at Penshurst Box. The amount of different engines passing up and down between Redhill and Tonbridge was amazing. There were engines of all shapes and sizes and there was nothing standard as I was used to seeing on the Western. I spent hours in that small signal box, and looking back on it now I can see that my friend the Signalman was very indulgent to the critical remarks I made about what was by now the Southern Railway; very bad manners on my part, but such is the way of inexperienced youth.

There was plenty of leg-pulling from Grandad Gasson about how there was one more future professional water boiler in the family, but he was a grand old man who never showed his disappointment in the fact that only one son stopped on the farm. He would talk about how he remembered his grandfather living in the cottage, so quite a few small Gassons had trod the brick path up to the front door.

The rest of his family were connected with railways, as the two remaining girls had married Southern men — Elsie was married to George Young, a goods Guard at Tonbridge, and Mabel was married to Fred Holman, Signalman at Minster — so the topic of conversation at the table was certainly not about heifers or milk yields.

His youngest son, Arthur, was a disappointment to us, although he thought he had the best job out of all the Gasson Clan. He was a Green Line bus driver, which he said was the only job to sort out the men from the boys; this statement only came when he was on his way out through the door. How can a petrol engine compare with Steam? Ugh ...

Dad told me once that the Valleys were very much like working the Didcot to Winchester Branch, except that whereas he could spell Upton, Compton, etc, the Welsh names had him beat. However, at Moat Lane and at Neath he had Welsh-speaking Firemen, so he was able to manage.

Bill's move to Reading was the result of a retirement, but Harold's came as a result of a tragic accident, which led to the death of a brother-engineman, Ernest Edmonds. Ernie was a well-loved and respected man, he was a local J.P., an Alderman, and the branch secretary of the A.S.L.E.&F. He was preparing a Dean Goods, and had just got up between the front of the firebox behind the big ends to remove the corks for oiling, when a 'Bulldog' in front moved back a few inches and buffered up to Ernie's engine. The big ends moved, and crushed Ernie. His injuries were too severe for him to recover. It was an accident that affected me also, as I had known Ernie Edmonds since I was a very small child, and I had never given it a thought that my beloved engines could hurt anyone.

Now that Harold was back, I started where I had left off, spending every Saturday or Sunday on the footplate when he was on a local shunting job. Looking back over the years I wonder how I ever got away with it, as I never once saw a Foreman; there are two possibilities — they either kept out of the way as they could see a future engineman, or, the 'old chap' took care to see that I was only allowed on the Shed when no Foreman was about. All I know is that I had the time of my life, and couldn't wait until I was old enough to officially join the Great Western.

I had to wait until I was sixteen however, so I filled in the time after leaving school as a messenger boy at R.A.F. Benson, starting at 6.45am after a ten mile cycle ride, which was at least good training for getting up in the morning. One thing struck me as ironic about the job; I was paid 12/0d a week, not much progress from Bill and Harold in 1910, and although Fairey Battles and Hampdens had a certain amount of glamour, they didn't work by steam, and certainly were not worth twelve bob a week with a twenty mile ride thrown in. My sixteenth birthday came in August 1940, and in early September I received a letter to report to Park House, Swindon, for an examination for Locomotive Cleaner. Eureka! Here I come at last!

Chapter Two
Cleaning Days

On September 6th 1940 I stood at Didcot Station on the Down Main Platform opposite West End Signal Box, waiting for the 5.30am Paddington. I had a free pass in my pocket made out to one H.H. Gasson, Didcot to Swindon Return. My orders were to report to Park House at 9.00am, and I did not intend to be late.

It was a typical September morning — thick fog, with the promise of a fine day. Fog held no problems for a train starting only 53 miles away with A.T.C. to guide it, and right on time 6026 *King John* rolled in and stopped near me. I could hear the "whoosh" of the vacuum brake as she came to a stand, and as I opened the carriage door, the large ejector was opened up to blow the brakes off again. At last I was on my way to join the two gentlemen up front. It was 6.40am and we were away, clearing the fog at Challow, so when I arrived at Swindon I had plenty of time for a cup of tea before walking down the road. When I arrived at Park House I found only two lads there, but by 8.30 our total had grown to seven, and, with the familiarity of boys forced with each other's company, we soon knew all about one another's hopes and fears. The Woodbines were handed round and with the nervousness we all felt it did not take long to fill up the ash tray. Out of the seven, one other lad had railway connections as I did. His father was a Driver at Severn Tunnel Loco Shed so with this common bond the two of us were a little condescending to the others.

At 9.00am the examination started, with some simple arithmetic and dictation. We were then given the Medical such as Bill and Harold experienced 30 years before; it was as Bill had said, for everything except Foot and Mouth, but when given the glass jar and told to fill it with water, I did not look for a tap. Such is progress. When this was all over and we were dressed again, we were taken to another room for the eyesight test. This was something we were familiar with at school — the card on the wall, first cover the right eye, then the left; but it was not to end there, for a cardboard box was brought in and placed on the table. This was a very old box, patched all round the corners with medical tape, and on the side, almost faded away with age, was the crayoned word, "Oxford". Inside this battered old box was the most motley collection of coloured wool I have ever seen.

I burst out laughing and was very sharply informed that it was no laughing matter, for this was a serious examination to determine if I could distinguish one colour from another, and particular attention would be taken over my selection.

My little pile of coloured wool was examined piece by piece, then put back into the box which was taken out, to disappear from my life for ever. Could it have been the same box of wool Bill and Harold had gone through 30 years before?

We were told to settle down for ten minutes, so out came the Woodbines again while we held an inquest on our possible progress. We just had time to suck them down before the door opened, and the Severn Tunnel lad and myself were summoned to another room.

The gentleman who sat behind the desk was the same person who had conducted the wool test. On the coat hanger was a bowler hat, so we both knew we were in the presence of a man of some consequence. He informed us that out of the seven lads examined, we were the only two who had passed. He then enquired into my disgraceful behaviour during the test, so I told him the story about Bill and Harold. This caused as much merriment on his part as it had on mine, and he had to agree that it could be the same box of wool, as he had been using it for years. Seven years later, Bill's son, Ted, followed my footsteps to Park House, and he too found that a battered old cardboard box full of wool was still in use. There should be a place of honour in Swindon Museum for that cardboard box; it must be one of the original relics of the Great Western Railway Locomotive Examination Board. So I was through, with orders to report at Didcot Loco Shed for cleaning duties on Monday, September 27th 1940.

That first morning I walked through the station subway, up the steps and down the cinder path by the coal stage excited by the thought that in a few minutes I would be climbing all over steam engines, and getting paid for it. However, I was quickly disillusioned when I reported to Ernie Didcock, the Chargehand Cleaner.

In the chain of command from Cleaner to Shed Foreman I was right at the bottom, so for starters I could clean out the ashes and light the fire in the Foreman's office. Disposing of ashes was no problem — one simply tipped the bucket onto the nearest pile of locomotive ashes — and filling the bucket with coal was not a challenge to your ingenuity for you climbed up one-handed on to the nearest engine and filled the bucket. I found that it was not easy to climb down from the footplate of a Saint with a bucket of coal in one hand so, since the small Tankies carried the same brand of coal, I filled up from them without having to struggle to get down so far, and losing half the load in the process.

Once the fire was alight, I had to go into the stores and assist there, weighing up cotton waste in ¼ lb balls, issuing oil to Enginemen, and generally helping to do all the hundred and one jobs in a busy locomotive shed stores.

The Storeman was Reubin Hitchman, who was the kindest of men, so my time as the junior Cleaner was spent in very pleasant company. He went out of his way to help all the lads as they passed through his hands, so that when one moved on, out into the Shed, it was an easy transition.

The night duty was one that I did enjoy, as from midnight I was out on the streets of Didcot calling up crews, (the junior Cleaner was, in fact, the call boy.) I started at 10.00pm by helping Reubin in the Stores until 11.30 pm, then I copied the names of all the Drivers and Firemen who were on duty from 1.00am until 5.45am, and then the fun started. You would call in order of booking on, standing outside the customer's house shouting as loud as possible, "Driver Jones, Driver Jones", until an answer was received, and then you shouted out the duty and the time of booking on.

This was all right as long as the man concerned woke up at once, but if he was a heavy sleeper and you had to keep on calling, the neighbours got a little upset. Dad's Fireman, Bill Yaxsley was the worst one to have to wake up; I could call and call, without result, and then a neighbour would open the window and start casting doubts on my ancestry. I would abuse him back and eventually the front door would open and a strategic withdrawal had to be made — in other words, you got on your bike, and went like hell! The neighbour would then take action by getting Bill up, to stop me from returning and starting it all over again. I still see Bill and have a laugh over old times, as he now drives a stinking old diesel shunting engine for British Leyland at Cowley.

Jim Brewer, Dad's Driver of my childhood days, had a better method of being called. He had fixed up a bell push on his window-sill, which he connected to the bell on his bed headboard. It worked satisfactorily for years, until I brought some sticky tape from the first aid box with me one morning and taped the button down.

This led to my first interview with Bill Young, the Shed Foreman. Bill was a little man, never without his bowler hat, and, as we shall see later, he had a soft spot. As this was my first offence, I got off with a warning.

There were 'perks' to the callboy's job; we soon got to know which Enginemen's gardens had ripe apples and there was always the Nestles chocolate machine on number 5 platform.

The War had not been on long enough to affect supplies, so the chocolate machine was kept full. One good kick and a snatch at the draw-handle would produce a bar of chocolate every time. It was a secret handed down from callboy to callboy, and never shared with the station staff, such was the rivalry between the Locomotive Department and the Traffic Department, although we did condescend to share a pot of tea in the Porters' Room between calls. They were a good lot on the Station, but conversation was kept at a neutral level, as the rivalry between departments was something to be believed. A Southern Engineman would argue against a Western man on locomotives, but all Enginemen would close ranks against the Traffic side!

At the end of January 1941 another lad started cleaning, so I was no long the baby of the Shed, and it was time to move out of the stores.

About this time I was issued with an identification card and a brass check, two items I still have and treasure. I was one step nearer to the Main Line.

In the issue of the brass check the Great Western were very wise in the ways of Engine Cleaners. The Drivers and Firemen were gentlemen — they merely shouted to the time clerk to be booked on and that was that — but the Cleaners had to have some physical proof that they were indeed on duty, so they handed in this brass check when booking on, and collected it when booking off. The check was also used for collecting one's pay. I 'lost' my check when promoted to Fireman, but I kept it to prove that I was not a gentleman at least at one time in my life. The check measures 1 in x ½ in and is stamped G.W.R. Loco. Dept., and in the middle is the number 262. I was a mere number!

The identification card was issued for my protection against trigger-happy soldiers, or so we were told. It was in the days when German paratroops were landing in France dressed as nuns, so the Great Western thought they could just as easily land dressed as railwaymen. We looked to the sky for our German Cleaner — we would have been only too pleased to show him how to rake out a full engine ashpan on a windy day.

My card is 3" x 4", coloured pink, bears the G.W.R. badge, the number 47806, and reads thus:

The undermentioned person is authorised to be on the Lines and Premises of the Great Western Railway Company while in the execution of his duty. This card is valid until cancelled or withdrawn.

Name in Full	Gasson Harold Henry
Department	C M E
Grade	Locomotive Cleaner/Fireman
Stationed at	DIDCOT LOCO

The Identification Card must be signed in ink by the holder immediately he receives it, and be carried by him until further notice when engaged in work on the Railway. It must be produced at any time on request, and the holder must, if required, sign his name as a proof of his identity.

To Didcot Loco I was a number, to the Management I existed; honour was satisfied.

Cleaning engines in 1941 with the War well and truly on became very much a secondary occupation, and we Cleaners were pressed into covering every job in the Shed. There was an acute shortage of labour in those days, so we washed out boilers acting as boilersmith mates, assisted the fitters as mates, dropped fires, and coaled engines, but it was all good training in the running of a busy locomotive shed. One job we all hated was coaling engines, as it meant shovelling coal out of a 20 ton wagon into tubs, then tipping the contents of the tub into the tender waiting below. It always seemed to me that whenever I was detailed to work at the coal stage it was blowing a gale; consequently one was covered with coal dust in the first hour. One duty that gave light relief was damping down fires on the ash road. This was necessary because the glow of dropped fires during the night gave away the position of the Shed to German bombers, so a Cleaner was detailed to use a hose pipe to damp down the glowing coals as the firebox was being emptied.

The blackout was complete to such an extent that one had to use a hand lamp to get about the Shed, and poor old Jack Jacobs was no exception. He was a ponderous man, very bad on his feet, and never without his badge of office, the foreman's bowler hat. To see a hand-lamp appear from the Shed and come slowly towards one was a signal that Jack was on his way. We would judge the pace and distance, then lift the hose pipe just a fraction, and Jack would get a wet bowler every time. In the blackout he could never find the culprit.

I once received a right old wigging and the threat of being sent home, from Bill Young the Senior Foreman, for a prank I should have had more sense than to try. I was detailed to assist George Giles, the senior Boilersmith, in washing out the boiler of 'Bulldog' 3376 *River Plym*. George was in the firebox tapping stays, so I stuck a hose pipe in a tube at the smokebox end and turned the tap on! George crawled out of that firebox wet through, and proceeded to play hell. Now I had to face the music. Bill Young to his credit did not tell the 'Old Chap', but of course he soon heard of it, so I had a second session when he came home. I had the good sense not to remind him of the box cycle incident in Hythe Bridge Street years before.

A cold dismal morning in early February of 1941 found me in the fire-box of 5935 *Norton Hall* equipped with flare lamp, short pricker, and handbrush. It was not such a bad place to be as she still had 40 lbs showing on the steam gauge and was pleasantly warm. She was booked in for washout and tubes, so my task was to hook the 'corks' of clinker out of the tubeplate, then brush off the brick-arch. At 7.00am I was well on my way to completion when I heard banging on the steel footplate and my name being called. I stood up, with my head and shoulders sticking out of the firebox doors to see the shift Foreman, Jack Jacobs, calling me. He informed me that the Fireman on the West End Pilot had gone home sick and I would have to take over the duty. I quickly climbed out of the firebox, handed in my tools to the Chargehand Cleaner, picked up my box from the Cleaners' cabin and made my way to Didcot West End Box. I was also careful to check the "time". This was important to a Cleaner, as, if a firing duty was 6½ hours or over this counted as a firing turn and was not only paid as such but went towards counting in seniority when one became a Fireman. The duty was booked until 2.00pm so this would be my first turn as a Fireman.

I crossed the carriage sidings, the up yard and centre yard to west yard, and there, in all her grime and glory, stood 0-6-0PT 907. Built in 1875 she still retained the open cab but had fitted to her the spark arrester chimney for working in the Didcot Ordnance Depot. To me at that moment she could have been King George V. I climbed aboard her and saw that my mate for the day was Joe Withers, one of the senior enginemen at Didcot and who was now on pilot driving work because of poor health. Joe was one of the true 'characters' of Didcot Shed, a very tall thin man addicted to the habit of taking snuff. Joe greeted me warmly, enquiring as to my skill in handling the shovel. I confidently assured him that I knew where the injectors were and what to do, but that morning I was to learn a great deal more of life on the footplate of a steam engine.

The steam pressure was at 100lbs so I fired her all round the box until she came round almost to her blowing off point of 165lbs. The water in the glass was thick with chalk and only about an inch was showing, so I put on the left hand injector and brought it up to three-quarters full. On Great Western pannier tank engines it was always the left hand injector which was used, simply because the water feed was up in the Fireman's corner; the right hand injector water feed was the Driver's side, also up in the corner, but young Firemen never disturbed the sanctuary of the Driver's side. I have known some Drivers draw a chalk mark down the middle of the floor boards and in such circumstances it was not wise to cross the line. Looking back over the years it would seem that the right hand injectors were as good as new because they were never used except for a test run when the engine was prepared for duty.

No. 907 was in quite a state. She smelt like a steam laundry, she also leaked steam and water from every gland, both right and left live steam unions on the injectors dripped, the regulator handle was the old single pushover type which kept up a steady weep of steam, and when a shunting movement was called for fog emerged from her leaking spindle glands. But she was my first engine and I forgave her many faults.

As I have said, Joe liked a pinch of snuff so when he offered me a pinch I accepted with innocence, always ready to try something once. Joe's idea of a pinch was a fistful and on his instruction to hold out my hand he poured on the back of it a small mountain of brown powder. I was then told to place it near my nostril and sniff hard. At that point I thought the end of the world had come; my nose was on fire, my eyes streamed, I spluttered and coughed, and in a welter of tears I filled up the bucket with cold water and stuck my head in it. I can still hear Joe's laughter, but I had learnt one lesson in life that morning — don't take up the snuff habit.

Lesson number two came soon afterwards, when Joe enquired if I had a gauge glass and rings in my box. I was proud of that box, as it was one of the genuine enginemen's boxes manufactured by Dukes of Grimsby; indeed, I still use it as a tool box. The small brass plate on it pronounced that the owner was H.H. GASSON. Inside I had my sandwiches, and a pint of cold tea in an empty whisky bottle, as this was before the days of the tea can and the footplate brew-up. As Joe had enquired about a gauge glass I slid back the small bolt of the drop-down lid. Being a keen lad I had everything, a rule book, the appendix to the rule book, a copy of Arthur Hathaway's *The Locomotive, Its Peculiarities, Failures, and Remedies*, Algy Hunt's *Descriptive Diagrams of the Locomotive*, five detonators, a red and green flag, and last but not least one gauge glass complete with two rubber rings. Joe viewed all this with quiet amusement and then enquired if I had ever changed a gauge glass. The answer was, of course, 'No'. Then to my horror Joe took of the gauge frame and calmly smashed the glass with a spanner. The result was almost indescribable as steam and water roared into the cab. I felt for the gauge frame handle, found it and shut off the steam by pulling it down, then lifted the blow-through cock. At last there was peace in the cab again, with Joe sitting on his seat taking a pinch of snuff and making comments on what a nice fine day it was to learn how to change a gauge glass.

Joe produced from his pocket a key ring which contained the weirdest collection of tools I had ever seen. All were about four inches long, made of heavy-gauge wire. There were spikes, hookers, corkscrews, and probes, everything for removing stones from horses' hoofs, and, most important, old rubber rings from gauge glass frames. It was a lesson well learnt. I was never worried about a gauge glass breaking again, for if at any time I found a suspect one on an engine it was changed at once, so I never did have one go on me when on the road. I found also that twenty Players to a Fitter was a respectable price to pay for a similar set of instruments on a key ring such as Joe had lent me on that first day as a Fireman.

Much to my delight, Joe's Fireman was off sick the rest of the week, so I had a full week of firing duties to my credit by Saturday, but not all on 907, as she was long overdue for a boiler washout, and was changed for 2076 on Wednesday. This was a far nicer engine to work on as the cab was enclosed and she was in good condition, not long back from a complete overhaul at Swindon. It was a pleasure to brush up the new floor boards, and clean off her front boiler in the cab. With no spark arrester as with 907, and valves perfectly set, she gave out that crisp Great Western bark when moving a heavy transfer load from the centre yard, and she would steam with a candle in the firebox. It was just as well she was so free with steam, as will be seen later, for I had another reason to be grateful to that little Pannier Tank 2076.

Firing turns became more frequent now, mostly on the yard pilot duties, and of course Didcot Ordnance Depot, which was turning out vast supplies for the Army. We would book on at 4.45am for the 5.45am Depot jobs, book off Shed at 5.30am and couple up five engines at a time at the Shed signal. The Great Western had a simple system for preparing engines, from a Pannier Tank up to a Collet 22XX class. The allowance for such engines the size of 6106 Tank was three-quarters of an hour, any engine above that was allowed one hour. It was just not possible to do the preparation in the time, unless one was prepared to go off Shed half-ready, so everyone came on at least a quarter to half-hour early, if only to leave the Shed in a complete state of readiness.

The Depot engines would shunt all day returning to Shed at 6.00pm. The loaded wagons would be brought up to the hump yard for marshalling on the last trip, all five engines pushing the day's work into the Long Road, then leaving via Foxhall Junction. One engine would remain to shunt the day's work into trains ready for dispatch; this was the Hump pilot, which would pull 60 or 70 loaded wagons out of the sidings up the spur towards the rear of Foxhall box, then slowly creep back, while the shunter would uncouple for the different roads required. It was on this night Hump pilot job that I came unstuck with 2076, and it was with good reason that I was to be grateful for her steaming.

About 1.30am a goods train ran through the catch points on the up relief line at Foxhall derailing half a dozen wagons, which meant that we were blocked in until the line was clear. We had completed the work to be done at that point, so the shunters, my Driver and myself, decided to get our head down in the Shunters' cabin, an old converted coach. I filled up the boiler on 2076, shut the dampers, and then made myself comfortable with my mates, until 5.30am when the telephone rang to inform us that the line was now clear for us to leave. I climbed up on 2076, saw that we had half a glass of water, then opened the firebox doors and found that, next to dropping a lead plug, I had committed the unforgiveable sin — I had let the fire out. There was 90lbs of steam in the boiler, so I had a quick look round for anything that would burn, old bits of sleepers, branches off the trees, and grease out of the wagon axle boxes. She had been out of the Shed for 24 hours, so the firebox was full of ash and clinker, but that little engine responded splendidly to the unusual fuel, for she began to creep up on the steam gauge until I had 120lbs showing, so I was able to put on the injector and get a glass-full, but at the cost of knocking her back again to 90lbs. We crept out of the Depot with the regulator just open and with black smoke pouring out of the chimney, for all the world the first oil-burner on the Western. Foxhall Box set us for the Up Relief, which meant going through the station, instead of letting us round the West Curve; by going the latter way we could have slipped into Shed unnoticed. With our fingers crossed we made it over the points at Didcot East Junction and then we had to stop. There were 20lbs of steam on the clock when the points changed over to let us on Shed, and by all the rules 2076 should not have been able to move, but very slowly she began to creep forward and as soon as she passed the ground frame she came on to the slight fall down to the ash pit. I stopped her on the handbrake, gently buffering up to the engine in front, with no steam showing on the clock. Then my mate and I gathered up our belongings and nonchalantly climbed down and walked to the Shed to book off. We kept very quiet about that incident, but somehow it got out, because for months afterwards I was constantly being offered a lighted flare lamp and the enquiry made as to my need for a light. The 'Old Chap' at home made no reference to it, other than when he had occasion to make up the fire for Mother, when he would make some very pointed remark about "keeping the home fires burning". Poor little old 2076, I suppose she has been cut up long ago, but she remains one of the Engines I shall never forget.

The next week I was back on the Shed doing every kind of work except cleaning engines; (funnily enough I never did get to be Boilersmith's mate again — perhaps George Giles had something to do with it). Bill Miles the Senior Foreman Fitter kept me busy, and I had the job of packing the spindle glands on 907. I've no doubt that Bill had heard about the hose pipe down the tube and the "fire out" episode, but he never once mentioned it, he just kept me so busy there was no time to dwell on anything except work.

By the May of 1941 I had eighteen firing turns to my credit, all on shunting duties in either the Didcot Yards or the Ordnance Depot, and had prepared most of the engines for those duties, so I was beginning to get the hang of things, or so I thought.

Because of War commitments there was a rapid build up of crews at Didcot. These were mostly lads from the Welsh Valleys. Firemen made up to Drivers, or Cleaners made up to Firemen, and with accommodation rather sparse in the town, they were housed in sleeping coaches stabled on the end of No. 7 and No. 8 Roads outside the Shed. A kitchen coach was also provided, with a main line chef, and this arrangement was to remain until the hostel was built. The shortage of crews was acute, and led to my first firing turn outside shunting.

As I was leaving for home one Monday afternoon, Bill Young called me into his office. As this was usually for a 'Wizzer' I tried to think back on what I should have done but hadn't or what I had done but shouldn't, but he asked me to sit down, so I knew something was on.

He then asked me if I felt ready to try a bigger firing job, so I accepted at once without question. He explained how tight he was for crews; he had had to take a Passed Fireman off his job for a driving duty for the rest of the week, and I could take over if I felt ready for it. The Driver was willing to give me the chance, so it was up to me. The duty in question was the 7.37am Didcot to Southampton, not exactly the Torbay Express but quite an exacting task for a young Cleaner. As I left the office Bill Young's parting words were "Don't let the fire out Boyo", and as I passed his window I could see that he was grinning like a Cheshire cat; so he *had* known about that little episode with 2076.

Booking on time for the Southampton was 6.30am, off Shed at 7.15am, but I was there at 6.00am; I wanted more than three quarters of an hour to prepare an engine for this job. The engine booked was 3376 *River Plym*, a 'Bulldog'. I knew her tubes were clean as I had done them one week before, and she was tight at the front end, so I should have no trouble about steaming, and I knew I should want plenty of that before I saw the Shed again.

My Driver was Fred Essex, a man I had known all my life, and the father of one of my mates in the cleaning gang, and I was fortunate in going out with one of the kindest men it was my privilege to work with. I had known Fred as Mr. Essex for years, but he told me to cut out that nonsense; I was to refer to him as "mate", and so he was in every sense of the word.

When I climbed up on 3376, she was just right for preparing, with a nice bit of fire in the firebox, half a glass of water in the boiler, and 80 lbs. on the clock, so I could spread the fire over the box and build it up without using the blower. As engine preparation is a team job, I filled the oil feeder for Fred and placed it on top of the boiler to warm; then when he went under the motion, he would check the ashpan for me — little things that made the job so much more pleasant.

I went round the framing, checking the sand box on the left hand side, then opened the smoke box, found all the plates secure, tightened the smoke box again and swept off the ashes with the hand brush, then round the right hand side to the other sand box, then back to the footplate.

While I had been busy with this Fred had arrived, collected the oil cans, drawn his requirements from the stores, and was on the footplate to greet me. He thanked me for filling his feeder and said he would check the ashpan, and if I would pull the sand levers he would check the pipes. I was off to a good start. By the time I had the fire made up well and the coal broken up and stacked on the tender, the footplate was almost clean, so I had a look over the side to see where Fred was. He was up front oiling the front coupling of the side rod, so I shouted to him that I was going to wash off the boiler front and footplate, and check both injectors. A Fireman always checks where his mate is before using injectors to avoid a blast in the face with boiling water. Both injectors were working, so I shut off the left hand one, then found my little bit of copper pipe. Most Firemen had this small bit of quarter-inch pipe, slightly flattened at the end, and pushed up into the coal watering pipe, so that cleaning off the footplate and boiler front could be done with high pressure. We were now ready to fill up with water, wash our hands, and go up to the Shed signal on time.

I called up Didcot East Junction ground frame on the telephone and informed them that we were the Southampton standing at the Shed signal. They in turn passed it on to the signal box, so that before I had time to get back on the footplate I could hear the points being set; then as I mounted the last footstep, the signal came off with a bang.

This was a busy time at East Junction Box, and to get us from the Shed signal to the Newbury branch meant a movement of 118 levers, so Fred opened out *River Plym*, and we clattered smartly through the crossovers, over the up relief, down relief, up main, down main, and onto the branch. He gave 'crow' on the whistle to let East Junction know we were over the points, then the road was changed to let us drop gently back onto our train in No. 1 east bay.

Fred buffered up to the first coach, put the brake on and then came down on to the platform to see how I was getting on in coupling up. I managed that like an expert, having no trouble with the vacuum or steam pipes, so much so that he complimented me. What he didn't know was that on the way home after the interview with Bill Young the afternoon before, I had run into Harry Lane the passenger shunter, and on the promise of a couple of pints in the "Prince of Wales" I received half an hour of very instructive tuition on the art of tying a steam engine to a coach!

Our guard was the one and only Walter Beard, the most senior of Western men at Didcot, immaculately turned out as usual, with his white winged collar, black bow tie, and flower in his button hole. He expressed surprise and pleasure on seeing me saying how it seemed only yesterday that I was a schoolboy. Thus we had on the train that morning a very senior Driver and Guard, and neatly in the middle, a right 'sprog' of a Fireman.

The load was five coaches and two horse boxes, a total of 215 tons — not much compared to the 400-odd the 'Kings' pulled away with, but with 38 stops and starts there and back, the 114 miles over the switchback gradients of the Didcot, Newbury, Winchester, Southampton Branch would mean a wet shirt and a few tons of coal moved.

River Plym was all ready to go; the fire was burning through well, I had a glass full of water in the boiler, and pressure was just on the point of blowing off at the safety valve at 200lbs.

Walter Beard consulted his pocket watch, blew his whistle, waved his green flag, and we were away, collecting the single line token at East Junction for the Upton section.

This was before the building of the double line between Didcot and Newbury, so there would be a lot of tokens to exchange. Fred was in no hurry until we passed over the bridge near the milk depot, then he gave her a bit more on the regulator and began to link her up, but not too much as the climb was 1 in 106. I now began to work in the Western manner; the fire box flaps had been removed because of blackout regulations, so each movement meant opening the fire hole doors. It was a case of open doors, shovel in coal, swing round, coal into fire box, close doors. Although a complicated method to describe it could be carried out with a sweetness that had to be seen.

As Fred shut the regulator to run into Upton, I eased on the blower to stop any blow-back and put on the right hand injector, and we came to a stop level with the end of the platform. I now found I had experienced something new in locomotive running, and that was the smell of hot brake blocks. It was an acrid smell and one that I was to become used to over the years, but after shunting jobs it was a surprise that blocks become so hot.

We exchanged tokens with the Signalman for the Compton section, Walter blew his whistle and we were off again up the long drag to the top of the Berkshire Downs at Churn, and it was up this bank and on the sweep down into Compton that a characteristic of the 'Bulldog' Class endeared them to me. At Didcot we had 3376 *River Plym*, 3408 *Bombay*, 3448 *Kingfisher*, and 3407 *Madras*, and they were all very free steamers, but up the banks they had a galloping stride, with the side rods going round in such an easy manner that when they came to a level bit of road or a slight fall, such as we came to through Churn, they literally flew, riding as steady as a coach.

I was beginning to enjoy myself, but on the pull up from Hampstead Norris to Hermitage steam pressure began to drop. The water level dropped also, but Fred was not worried as we had the long drop down into Newbury with the regulator shut and plenty of time to fill the boiler. He knew what had gone wrong, but kept quiet so that I should learn a valuable lesson. I had been a bit over enthusiastic with the shovel and had 'blacked' the fire in; it was a solid mass up to the brick arch.

We ran into Newbury on time, then after the passengers had gone and the station work was completed we pulled up over the main line points, and backed into the bay to wait for a connection.

I got the pricker down and gave the fire a good pull through until it was thick and level all over the box, then as we departed for the Winchester branch, Fred gave *River Plym* half regulator with 35% cut off to Enborne Junction, where we collected the token for Woodhay.

I did not touch the fire, but had a look in the firebox when we ran into the station. It was one great incandescent mass, the steam pressure had come round to the point where she was blowing her head off with the injectors on, and I had so much steam I didn't know what to do with it. I had learnt another lesson; all that work further back down the line just to make steam to blow out of the safety valve! From then on I kept the back-end of the firebox packed tight and let the fire slope gently down to the front end. Fred never said a word, bless him; he knew the value of learning by mistakes. We arrived at Winchester dead on time, sliding out of the tunnel so quietly that we caught the station staff on the hop. We left Winchester over the long 40ft high Shawford viaduct to Shawford Junction, to join the old London and South Western Railway, by now the Southern, and ran down into Eastleigh where we were booked for ten minutes. Fred and I gazed at the many strange locomotives, and I saw both the most horrible locomotive and one of the most beautiful engines that morning.

Up the main line towards us came one of Mr. Bulleid's indescribable 'Q1' Class. Later I had a chance to go aboard one and came away most impressed.

Leaving Eastleigh Fred set the regulator just off the jockey valve so that we would drift past a place he knew I would want to see just at the end of the platform—Eastleigh Works and Shed. It covered a large area reminiscent of Swindon, with sidings full of engines of every shape and age, and I remember that I fervently wished I could have a look round it all, but that time was in the future, I was later to get to know Eastleigh Shed very well.

At the Shed signal, waiting to come out, was one of the most beautiful steam locomotives I had ever seen—a compliment, indeed, for a Great Western man to make, but it was deserved. She was so graceful, her green paint work had a deep transcendent lustre, proof of much loving care; her side rods sparkled in the sunshine and looked so delicate that they reminded me of photographs I had seen of La France; even the copper pipes from the cylinder drain cocks had been burnished. She was 2333 *Remembrance*. I wrote the name and number down, determined to find out more about her at the first opportunity.

When we arrived at Southampton Terminus I uncoupled, and the coaches were drawn back by the station passenger pilot engine. We followed the train as far as the platform edge while the train carried on clear of the points. The road was set to allow us onto the turn-table, then while we turned *River Plym* our train was propelled back into the station, where the pilot engine came off. We were all ready to start the long haul back.

I coupled up again, then got up on the tender and brought the coal forward, while Fred went round oiling the bars and glands. This completed, we had our sandwiches, a drink out of the tea bottles, and then Fred settled down to make his log ticket up to date, for we had twenty minutes to spare. I told Fred that I was going over to the Southern pilot engine for a few minutes, as I wanted to know a lot more about the engine we had seen at Eastleigh.

I asked permission to climb up on the footplate of the T9 and was made most welcome by the driver and fireman. Both were middle-aged, and seemed surprised by my youth. When I mentioned that beautiful engine I found I was in the company of two gentlemen who knew all about her. I was told that she was a former London, Brighton, and South Coast Railway engine; she was one of four locomotives designed and built as 4-6-4 express passenger tanks by Mr. Billinton for the LBSC Railway, and later re-built as tender engines. The one I had seen at the Shed signal at Eastleigh was named *Remembrance* in memory of the railway lads who had died in the Great War.

Both the Southern men were very enthusiastic about these engines, and appreciated the fact that I was so interested in them. The Fireman said that they were free-steaming if fired all over the box, and that they would run like the wind.

This bit of information was to come in handy in 1942, because 2330 *Cudworth*, 2331 *Beattie*, 2332 *Stroudley*, and 2333 *Remembrance* were transferred on loan to the Great Western to help out an engine shortage, together with three of Mr. Urie's Moguls 496, 498, and 499. We all had a bit of a surprise when we did get our hands on them; to our chagrin we found that the Southern engines were very good.

At 11.30am we began the long drag back home. From Southampton to just this side of Burghclere it was a steady climb. We stopped and started so many times I began to wonder if we should ever see Didcot again.

One interesting incident came our way as we were between Eastleigh and Shawford Junction, where we saw the first of Mr. Bullied's "Merchant Navy" Class Pacifics, *Channel Packet*, tearing down towards us. We had heard rumours of this locomotive which could show our "Kings" a thing or two, but she went flashing by at such a speed she was just a blur of slab-sided metal, with no exhaust audible but just the roar of the coaches. From Fred's side I looked back along our train to see her last coaches swaying and rapidly diminishing in the distance. We were both very impressed.

We plugged away on towards home until Compton was reached. There I pushed the fire all over the box, splashed a bit round her, and put the shovel down for the last time; it was downhill now, and with *River Plym* going to Shed there was enough in the firebox to see her through.

I swept up the footplate, then sat down on the tip-up seat. A feeling of utter exhaustion came over me, my back and legs ached, the palm of my right hand was sore and bruised from the hundreds of times I had hit up the live steam injector handle. I was a very tired sixteen year old boy. The glamour had gone, and I just wanted to curl-up and rest.

The chatter from the chimney softened as Fred linked her up, then I felt his hand on my shoulder. He pointed out a hare running level with us in a field; he gave me a squeeze and said I would be better tomorrow, as I would know the road and engine, and that the first time was always the worst. He was pleased with the way I had handled the job and said he would tell Bill Young so, and that he would insist that I remained with him all the week. With a wink he said I had not let the fire out once.

It was the encouragement I needed. I looked over the side and watched that side rod go round and round with the regularity of a clock and felt a great satisfaction in knowing it was my efforts which had made it possible. At a rough guess I had shovelled 3½ tons of coal, and boiled away over

3,500 gallons of water to keep that side rod moving. I placed a pad of cotton waste in my hand and hit up the injector handle for the last time as Fred shut off to run into Didcot east bay. I felt a lot better.

Relief was waiting for us when we stopped. As we walked down the platform towards the Shed to book off, the solid surface of the platform seemed strange after the movement of the last few hours. I looked back towards *River Plym* with affection; she had responded to an amateur perfectly, and I would never forget her.

The next few day were as Fred had predicted. Things were a lot better, for I could anticipate him shutting off for station stops, I had a 'feel' for the engine working, and could sit down at intervals of easy running. I was beginning to get to know the Didcot, Newbury, and Winchester Branch; in fact the time was to come when I knew every rail-joint, bridge, bank, and person, throughout the whole length of the line. It saddens me now, when on a fine summer Sunday I have a run down to Southsea in the car and see the broken bridges, deserted signal boxes, and the air of desolation over the miles of ballast, empty of rails. To me and all the old Didcot steam enginemen, it is a loss keenly felt.

Saturday came, and with it my last trip over the Branch for some time, for when I eventually did become a Fireman there were the pilot and goods links to go through first, with only the occasional passenger job to cover.

This last day also brought a change of engines. We were given another "Bulldog", 3448 *Kingfisher*, because *River Plym* was due for a boiler washout. I felt a little peeved about this as I had come to regard her as my regular engine, and could now understand the feelings of enginemen who had their own engines in the old days. I had a look round the Shed for her, and found her at the bottom of No. 4 road standing 'dead'.

I climbed up on footplate and could feel the coldness about her. It was an alien atmosphere, devoid of the warmth and life of the previous days; her footplate was covered with coal, clinker and ash from where her fire had been dropped, she reminded me of a very old lady caught with her teeth out. I felt like a stranger, she had abandoned me. I searched round for her shovel and found it under the fire irons in the rack on the tender. I had become attached to that shovel so I swopped it for the one off *Kingfisher*.

Kingfisher, if anything, was a better locomotive than River Plym; her steaming was about the same, and although the exhaust had a crisper bark she did not burn as much coal. This was due to the work of Bill Miles the Foreman Fitter. He had just released *Kingfisher* from his lifting shop and he had set the valves to perfection, and the results of his labours were evident in the way she lifted the train up the banks.

I had time to admire the scenery on that lovely early spring morning; the green of the Downs, the gentle rolling countryside, and the swoop down the bank between Highclere and Burghclere.

I always enjoyed that little bit of the Winchester Branch. Leaving Highclere the road dropped to 1 in 106 into Burghclere. We would tear down the bank, shoot through the bridge and up the other side like riding a roller coaster at the fair.

Two other places to enjoy were the drop down from Litchfield into Whitchurch, with the town stretched out on our left hand side looking like a model township in the morning sunshine; and crossing the 2,000-odd feet of the 40ft high Shawford viaduct across the valley from St. Catherine's Hill down to Shawford Junction.

The other side of the picture was, of course, the punch back up again on the return journey; but who cared, on a sunny day with the engine steaming well, good Welsh coal in the tender, and a Driver who had not only a gentleman but a Great Western engineman who had a complete understanding of his engine and of his young Fireman.

Thank you Fred Essex, you were a great man to know, and I look back with nostalgic memories of those happy days with you on *River Plym* and *Kingfisher*.

The next week I was back to earth with a bump, on nights coaling engines, and sure enough it was blowing a gale from the north straight into the coal stage, so that every tub of coal tipped into the tender waiting below sent up a cloud of dust. Within an hour I was as black as any miner who had dug that coal out. A shovel and 20 tons of coal from a common bond between miners and steam locomotive Firemen.

Between the odd jobs of coaling, fire dropping, ash loading, and all the other dirty, filthy jobs connected with the turn-round of steam engines, I had the firing turns cropping up more frequently on the many yard pilots and Didcot depot pilots, so in turn I fired for every Driver at Didcot. Some of the older men were a bit grouchy—and so I expect I should be if I were nearly 65 years old and had to get out of bed at 4.30 in the morning—but on the whole they were not a bad lot.

The younger Drivers would let me have a go on the regulator and I soon became skilled in shunting a load of 70 wagons with a pannier tank engine, all good training for enginemanship.

The months crept on until the last weekend of August, and on my birthday, August 28th, I was notified that I had been appointed Fireman at Didcot; my Registered Number for seniority was 27297. I was at last a Great Western Steam Locomotive Fireman.

Big Harold and I went home to Charcotte that weekend where I had great satisfaction in informing Grandfather Gasson that I was a professional now.

Chapter Three
Firing Days

I booked on duty that first day as a Fireman at 5.45am with a sense of pride, and looking back on it now I still feel proud that the Great Western considered me competent enough to entrust me with their locomotive boilers. I had now come up from junior Cleaner to junior Fireman, a system that ran to junior Fireman in the relief link, number three link, number two link, to the passenger link; then, good fortune prevailing, one became a Driver, junior of course, and started the whole process again.

Now it was my turn to catch out the junior Cleaner with requests that he go to the stores for a tin of vacuum dust to rub on the brake blocks, and a key for the smoke-box door, or for good measure to see if they had in stock a left handed shovel or coal pick. We all fell for it in our turn, but it was good clean fun.

One thing I could never understand was the system of priorities applicable to all enginemen, whether they be G.W.R., L.N.E.R., L.M.S. or Southern, compared to other occupations. In a young man's world you have pilots, racing car drivers, speedway and racing motorcyclists, all with the reactions and state of mind that goes with youth, yet the average express passenger driver was a solid man in his early sixties, undoubtedly a grandfather, who would get out of a warm bed, cycle a couple of miles to the Shed, light a smoking dirty old flare lamp, and crawl about in a pit oiling a great steam locomotive. He would make a thorough job of preparation, back it on to a train of coaches with a dead weight of 400 tons, then proceed to nurse it, coax it, love it, and sometimes swear at it, but with all the aplomb of the youths listed above he would then go tearing off at 90 to 100 miles an hour; the top link man in steam days was without doubt a special breed of man.

It was to be some months before I had a regular Driver, as I was one of several 'spare' Firemen to be found in every Shed, a dogsbody to be at the whim of the shift Foreman's command, which usually meant engine preparation which was a thankless task when all the work was for another Fireman, and after the fourth engine one began to feel a sense of injustice; but all loco men had it in their turn so it was not so bad as it felt at the time.

Mr. Mathews, the Chief Clerk, would write out the duty list in his beautiful copperplate handwriting and place it in the glass panels in the booking-on hall where I would sometimes find my name on it as a Fireman to one of the shunting turns. It would list the time of booking on, time off shed, engine number, Driver and Fireman's name, and the duty, e.g. up yard pilot, or Moreton yard pilot, but usually I would find I had been booked 'as required' or 'shed assisting'. Both jobs were about the same, but Mr. Mathews had a great sense of humour, he thought I would like a change now and again! He was a very tall, gaunt man who came to work on a large double-framed bicycle of great antiquity; he also wore a trilby hat and raincoat that were equal in age.

The very large wicker basket on the handle-bars contained his paper and lunch; if ever there was a 'ringer' for a retired Bishop then Mr. Mathews was that, he could have made a fortune in the film industry. But looks are deceptive; Mr. Young might be the Shed Foreman in charge, but Mr. Mathews ran it, he was very much the Chief Clerk with all the authority the Great Western gave to such a position, but he was always a gentleman in every sense of the word.

The duty 'shed assisting' had its lighter moments, as this enabled one to do the odd spot of driving, helping the Shed Driver to turn and stable locomotives, but it also had its hazards.

Moving engines after they had the fire cleaned and had been coaled meant they were short of steam—the most one could expect was 80lbs in the boiler—so judgement of stopping distance and careful control of the hand brake had some hairy moments. Even so, I can remember only one incident that was a disaster, although it was a laugh at the time.

We had on loan from the L.N.E.R. some of the old Great Central Robinson's R.O.D. engines, still in original condition, and like the engines of this class the Great Western had bought, horrible lumps of machinery. The original engines had the horizontal regulator which was pulled towards one, but they had a fault which I expect the North Eastern men were fully aware of, but which the Great Western men did not find on a Swindon boiler; if the water in the gauge glass was over three-quarters full you could open the regulator all right but you could not shut it again, which of course led to complications when it came to stopping.

Standing first under the coal stage ready to be turned was one of these R.O.D. engines, L.N.E.R. No. 6265.

Four of us clambered up on her footplate to take her down to the turntable and then place her in the 'field' as we termed Nos. 7 and 8 roads. She had a glass full of white water, indicating the need of a long overdue boiler washout, and 80lbs showing on the steam gauge, just enough steam to complete the movement.

Once on the footplate we found it rather restricted, as both sides of the cab were built up with two raised wooden platforms, leaving a narrow well for the Fireman to work in, so we could see that care would have to be taken when swinging a shovel to avoid tearing skin from one's knuckles. The fireman elected to driver her was a diminutive little Welsh lad, so he stood up on the raised platform and gave the regulator a tentative pull towards him but nothing happened; then he placed one foot up against the boiler casing and pulled hard with both hands.

The old R.O.D. gave a lurch and slipped with a roar, sending up a great column of dirty water from her chimney as she primed, showering the whole area with fine wet soot, but the regulator would not close completely. There was a sound from the regulator valve like a fish-frier, and at walking pace she began to move with a clank, clank from each side rod as it came round, and with the regularity of a pile-driver.

With the weariness of an old lady she clanked her way towards the turn-table. I rode on the bottom step and dropped off near the lifting shop to change the point for the engine already on the table, expecting to hear the soft beat of the exhaust stop as the regulator was shut. Instead I saw two of my mates jump off her with some urgency and saw her remorselessly clank on to the inevitable end.

The turn-table was half-way round with a Collett 0-6-0 2226 on it when the old lady reached the end of the rails. Both Driver and Fireman of 2226 had a look of utter disbelief on their faces as that old R.O.D. dropped over the well of the table and buried her nose in the ballast. She stopped then, all right, shearing off both front cylinder cocks which clouded her in steam and emptied the boiler in the process.

We forgot the seriousness of the situation and burst out laughing, for she looked so ridiculous sitting there with her nose in the ground, cab tilted up over the tender, but bad news travels with the speed of light in a locomotive Shed and within minutes the whole Shed staff were gathered round, with Bill Young making noises that all Shed Foremen make when things go wrong.

There was plenty of advice on how to get her out, some of it good, some of it a bit hare-brained, but all well intended and all of which Bill Miles ignored—a Foreman Fitter has his own ideas on how to tackle such a situation, and as soon as the dust had settled he gathered his lads together with blocks and jacks and set about getting her out.

The turn-table was out of action for the rest of the day, so all engines that had to be turned were coupled together and sent off shed to turn via West Curve and Foxhall Junction.

Orders came out reminding us of the rule book that in future only Passed Firemen and Drivers were to move engines, but it only lasted a few weeks. The War was on and every engine had to be serviced and back on the road as soon as was possible, so it was a question of all hands mucking in, and as long as incidents such as the one just related were few and far between then the job got done.

The R.O.D. engine and the Western counterpart were not engines that were loved. Along with Webb's 26XX Class, the 'Aberdares', and Mr. Riddle's 2-8-0 'Austerity' Class, we referred to them as members of the bovine species, except that they did not give milk!

The R.O.D. and the Aberdares were fine engines in their day but by the time my generation of Firemen laid hands on them they were long past their best. The Austerity Class did some good work, they were without frills, and easy to maintain, but as every Great Western engineman knew, Mr. Riddles need not have gone to all that trouble to design and build them; all that he needed was a set of drawings from Swindon of the 28XX Class, for they could do all that was required for freight working, Mr. Churchward had seen to that in 1903.

Later on honour was satisfied to some extent when the War Office sanctioned the building of Sir William Stanier's Class 8F for the L.M.S. The Swindon-built engines started at 84XX and as the designer had worked for many years at Swindon with Mr. Churchward we found we had a part-Great Western Engine after all.

A lot of Swindon was built into them and they proved to be fine locomotives with plenty of room in a comfortable cab. Unfortunately, the injector handles were large heavy brass wheels with a spoke sticking out of the side, designed to make a whacking great blister in the palm of one's hand. When they were shut off the spindle would expand so that the adjustable spanner was always to be found on the tray over the fire-hole door, and at the last resort the coal pick was brought into use. I could never understand why the Great Western injector handle was never made standard on these engines; this was made of wood on a steel spindle, it was cheap to produce and easily replaceable, particularly as brass was at a premium in those days.

At this period of time our main preoccupation was the lack of tools. It was a nightmare to prepare engines, as overnight coal-picks, headlamps, gauge-lamps, hand brushes, shovels and even deflector shields disappeared. It got so bad that we made up the fire as best we could with our bare hands then went searching the other engines on shed to rob them of their tools. It deteriorated to such an extent that the only way to obtain the items needed to go off shed was to go back up the ash road and meet engines as they came in for service. At one period when we had the same engine all the week and took her off shed and returned with her, my Mate and I would tie all the tools with strong twine and lower them into the tank of the tender, making sure we had allowed the water level to drop well down! It was demoralising to see Drivers and Firemen creeping about in pits, either looking for tools or hiding them to use the next day; we were being turned into a band of scroungers and thieves. Morale was at a very low point when this came on top of long hours on duty with bad coal and engines in urgent need of repair, but we carried on and made the best of it; we were still Great Western and proud of it.

At the end of October I was teamed up at last with a regular Driver in the pilot link, and I was in luck. The first Driver a young Fireman has as a

Mate can make a profound impression on him, and my time with Ben Foxwell was a happy one. Ben was one of three ex-Cardiff main line men I was fortunate enough to have as Mates and from each one I was to learn something valuable. I don't think it was possible to upset Ben, he was a very quiet man, kind and considerate, completely unruffled under any set of circumstances that came along.

I was inclined to get a bit agitated when the engine would not steam as it should, but Ben would look in the firebox, offer some good advice, and all would be well again. From him I learned to have confidence in myself and the need for patience. I know that he was worried about his family enduring the bombing of Cardiff, and for his sake I was hopeful that his application to return to his home shed would be soon, but he freely gave his help to me when I needed it most.

The greater part of my time with Ben was shunting Moreton Yard. This had just been built but no water supply had been connected, so we were given tender engines to shunt the many trains that called there, but what engines they were. They were little old L.M.S. 0-6-0's of 1885 vintage, (the numbers I have in my diary are 3103, 3485, and 3196) about the same size as a Dean Goods Engine; but there any resemblance ended, for they couldn't pull the skin off a rice pudding. I have read that pre-war the L.M.S. enginemen ran passenger trains with them, but the thought of it makes me shudder, those engines were an abomination.

There was a set procedure to go through when attempting to re-marshal a train from the goods loop. We would couple on to the first wagon with a full boiler and a full head of steam, then back away up the spur towards the bridge to clear the yard points, but this was done with a great deal of slipping, panting and groaning that was torture to hear, and by the time we had cleared the points we had no steam or water, so we had a 'blow up' before starting to shunt. This called for fog working, because the spindle glands were leaking so badly that once the regulator was opened the whole front of the engine was enveloped in steam, and the shunter could not be seen!

It was in such un-dignified circumstances that Ben's old Driver found us one day. He came tearing along the up main line on a South Wales express, blasting away on the whistle and making gestures, half hanging out of the cab of his 'Castle' to attract our attention. He got in return the shrill blast of an L.M.S. whistle and the victory sign, but not in the way Mr. Churchill meant it. From then on, every up or down South Wales express went through the same performance and received the same reply. As I have said earlier, on a family railway such as the Great Western news travels very fast indeed, and to see Ben, an ex-main line man, messing about on a worn-out old Midland engine was too good to be true. The news went round Cardiff Shed with almost the speed of light.

They were a good lot though. Cigarettes were hard to obtain in the Didcot area, but the Cardiff men would throw a packet of twenty out of the cab and always with a message of good cheer wrapped round the packet. It did Ben good; he did not feel so far from home, but he did look a bit wistful at the last coach disappearing in the distance.

In the New Year of 1942 the water was connected up to the water columns at Moreton and we lost the little L.M.S. engines to the local pick-up jobs. We now had the proper tools for the job, our 57XX and 36XX pannier tanks. Those engines would lift a load of 60 twenty-tonners out of the up goods loop with an angry aggressiveness that was a joy to see. Moreton Yard proved to be such a success that it was extended out into a cornfield, but with the second yard the cutting was not dug out; instead it was graded to make a hump yard. We had three pannier tank engines working hard 24 hours each day by the end of 1943.

1942, however, saw a small revolution in the habits of footplate staff—it was the year of the Tea Can. Because of the lack of canteen facilities we were allowed a small ration of tea and sugar. The firebox brew-up was born and the pint whisky bottles were thrown away; no more cold tea. With this revolution was also born a very enterprising business. It was possible to buy commercially made tea cans holding a pint, but two cups each are not enough for thirsty loco men. However loco boilersmiths could make and supply two-pint cans.

These cans were made of heavy-gauge tinplate and were a joy to behold, the soldering was sheer artistry while the base was a good solid one; the lads who made the oil cans could certainly turn their hands to other things, they knew the requirements of the customer, and at 3/6d a time those tea cans were value for money.

There were three main supply points in the area, the boiler-smith's shops at Old Oak Common, Banbury, and Wolverhampton, and you placed your order with whoever you were relieving on the road at that time, but it was recognised that the Wolverhampton-manufactured can had the edge on the other makers and was worth waiting for.

Once acquired the can was cherished and protected with all the love given to a young wife. It was a symbol of cheer in those dreary days, and to be offered a cup of tea out of another man's can was a mark of comradeship. The art of making the tea was a performance equal to anything seen in the kitchen. The first movement was to protect the can, and this was done by plastering the bottom and sides up to the water line with thick oil, then it was placed on the fire using the handle of the coal pick through the handle of the can.

On big engines the fire was built up over the firebox ring in true Great Western fashion, so a little platform was dug out and the can placed on the red hot coals. By the time one had got the tea out of the food-box the water was boiling; the can was then lifted out and the tea thrown on top, the lid placed on, and then put on the firebox tray where the oil was wiped off. The result was a perfect cup of tea.

One thing we did learn quickly was to keep the lid on. It was known to get eight cups of a six-cup can, particularly at night, and this phenomenon could always be traced to a leaking regulator valve! We would eat a cheese sandwich in the dark with a perfect finger and thumb print in the corner of the bread quite cheerfully, but tea topped up from a dirty boiler was another matter.

The main requirement was, of course, clean fresh water, but at a push we would use boiler water if we had nothing else. The second requirement was knowledge of the road. It was a regular manoeuvre on a long run—regulator shut, can in, then two minutes of coasting and out with the can. The right measure of tea went in and the regulator was opened again with only a slight drop in running time.

On a passenger train, if the guard noticed a momentary pause he would book 'signal check', the passenger might think 'one in front', but to the two men on the engine doing all the work it was our tea break.

It was also quite a work of art to pour out a drink when on a fast-running train without spilling any, but we became experts. There was always the regular spot when we knew it was possible for the brew-up; my favourite place was on the Berks and Hants Line going down. My Mate would shut off as we cleared the top of Savernake Bank, then it was downhill all the way to Westbury, with plenty of time to enjoy a drink and clear it all away before Heywood Road Junction signals came into view.

One thing we had to come to a clear understanding on, was the drink we were going to have. We had stopped for signals on a dirty wet night and on this occasion my Mate decided he would like a cup of Oxo for a change—very nice so long as he had told me of this important change in plans. I placed the can on the fire and as soon as it reached boiling point I turned round to get the tea, but while I was engaged in this my Mate had lifted the can out and put in two Oxo cubes. The tea went on top, was given a stir and then placed on the firebox tray to brew.

It was after the second cup that my Mate made a remark about his Oxo tasting queer, and I said the tea tasted a bit off, but we got the rest of it down. A couple of hours later we both made a quick dash to the toilets.

Some members of the traffic department had what is known as "fringe benefits" coming with the introduction of the tea can; these members were the signalmen. There was no contract between locomotive men and signalmen but by mutual agreement a fair rate of exchange was soon arrived at—one can of boiling water from the signal box kettle was equal to half a ton of coal in the signal-box bunker.

Rule 55, which requires the Fireman to go to the signal box to remind the signalman of the presence of the train at his signals, was carried out with a regularity that would gladden the heart of any Inspector. There were no cold signalmen or thirsty footplate men, and it was an agreement that lasted until the end of steam. When the last steam engine ran on British Railways the tears in the eyes of signalmen were not just nostalgic ones.

At the end of February I was working my last week with Ben. A new link had been formed to relieve the many goods trains now running and I was to go up into this link, so I would be on the main line at last.

Ben read a bit in the newspaper that still makes me chuckle when I think back on it. The Ministry of Food had issued a statement that all juveniles up to the age of seventeen years and six months engaged on war work and/or shift work and without the facilities of a canteen were to be allowed hot cocoa between the fourth and fifth hour of work. Ben dared me to try it on Bill Young, so I took him up on it just for a bit of fun.

I made a formal application to see the Shed Foreman on a domestic matter, and at this stage I would not request the presence of my Union representative. I was notified to book on duty half an hour early the next day, when the Foreman would see me.

The next day I knocked on Bill Young's door and walked in. He was sitting behind his desk with a neutral look on his face; poor man, he hadn't a clue as to what it was all about.

I showed him the newspaper cutting which he read, then I asked him what time would it be convenient for him to prepare my hot cocoa. Bill sat there very quiet for several seconds, in fact I can still remember the loud ticking of the clock in his office and the dust dancing in a shaft of sunlight across his desk; it is referred to I think as a 'pregnant pause'. Bill very slowly and carefully tilted his bowler hat further over his right eye, gave it a tap to make quite sure it was on firmly, then he with great deliberation said just two words in Welsh.

Now Welsh is a language I am not conversant with, but I was in no doubt about the two words Bill had spoken; even in Hindustani they would have been understood. I got out before Bill did himself an injury. Ben paid up like a gentleman, I collected twenty Woodbines for that little episode, but kept out of Bill Young's way for a couple of weeks. When I did see him again he gave me a grin and called me a 'cheeky bugger'.

On reflection Bill could see that he had been taken for a gentle leg pulling session and the Gassons had a reputation for this sort of incident, but he did have a couple of pints in the Prince of Wales on the strength of the story.

In the new link I was again Mate to another Cardiff man, Leonard Judd. Len was a short stout man, bubbling over with life. He scorned the engineman's cap for a cloth cap pulled down over his left ear, and from Len I learnt how to fire the big engine. He had been an expert on the main line expresses, and he showed me every trick of the trade. To see him swing a shovel was an exhibition of a master craftsman at work.

Len loved being a Driver, but he had one regret on leaving the ranks of the Firemen, for he had to leave behind his beloved 5020 *Trematon Castle*. This engine was one of the regular engines Len had fired when he was on the 'runners' and according to him there was not another 'Castle' like her, she was perfection, and every engine on which we worked was compared to her—Len never missed the opportunity to relate some story about 5020. We would see her sometimes when we were running on the up relief line between Didcot and Reading. She would come sliding up alongside on the up main line with that beautiful easy gait of a 'Castle' in tip-top condition, with just a wisp of steam coming from her safety valve, her copper cap and paintwork gleaming in the sun. She was a credit to Cardiff Shed.

There would be a shouted conversation between us as she slowly crept by, and if it was Len's ex-driver some good natured advice on how to drive a steam engine would be shouted across the gap between us; then her greater speed would take her on and away.

Apart from the many 'Halls', 'Manors', 'Granges', 43XX, 28XX, and other classes we had a few big engines, 4082 *Windsor Castle*, 4038 *Queen Berengaria*, 4062 *Malmesbury Abbey*, 4045 *Prince John*, to name but a few, and most of the 'Saints' still in service. Each one was compared to *Trematon Castle* with unfavourable remarks from Len.

I shall never forget my first trip on a 'Saint', or a 'Forty'. Those great 6ft.8½in wheels would begin to revolve so slowly when the regulator was opened, then they would start to run like a race horse.

If ever there was an engine to be compared to a lady of breeding then the 'Forties' were that; for the first time I could really appreciate the genius of Mr. Churchward. It was sacrilege to work them on a goods train, which was the only time we had a chance to handle an engine of quality, but to work them back to their home shed was the economic way with the shortage of engines. We looked after them with special care.

Wednesday March 18th was a very special day in the life of Len and myself. We booked on at 10.00am and were given a job straight away, to relieve the 4.30am Avonmouth to Acton standing at Didcot West Box. When we saw the engine I could hardly contain myself. It was 2333 *Remembrance*, the former London, Brighton, and South Coast engine I had seen and admired so much at Eastleigh the year before. Len was pleased for me as I had talked almost as much about her as he had about *Trematon Castle*, and he welcomed the chance to try a Southern express engine.

She was not in the pristine condition of a year ago, but she was still a fine looking locomotive. We climbed aboard and had a look at our unfamiliar surroundings. Everything was recognisable, if in a different place, so we would manage.

There was a Locomotive Inspector with the engine to see how Western men could handle a strange engine, but I cannot remember his name. He was a South Wales man and on first name terms with Len. The Swindon men we relieved were not too impressed with *Remembrance*; the Fireman said she was a bit shy in steaming, and this was confirmed by the Inspector.

When they were gone I had a look in the firebox. The fire was built up in Great Western manner, right up to the firebox ring. The firebox door was a strange contraption—it worked like a baker's oven door, swinging back on a hinge. When in the closed position there was a small flap in the middle that could be lifted up and secured by a ratchet. With a small narrow shovel the Southern men used it would be possible to fire her through this flap, but not with the Great Western shovel, or with the large Welsh steam coal.

I remembered what the Southern fireman had told me the year before about firing all over the box, so I got the long pricker out of the tender rack and pushed the fire about until it was level, then, as she started to lift her safety valve, I had a test run on the injectors. Both picked up at once with a sweet singing, higher pitched than the Western injector but with a clear healthy sound. Len and I were satisfied, we gave a short 'toot' on the whistle and at once the home and distant signal dropped.

We had a load of 48 banana vans all loose-coupled, so as soon as I had unwound the tender handbrake, Len opened the ejector, blew the brakes off and eased open the regulator.

She moved forward with a soft 'whoof, whoof' from the chimney, so unlike the crisp bark of the Great Western exhaust, but by the time we were half-way through the station she was beginning to speed up and Len had to wind her up to shorten the valve travel. We had a clear road, which was a change. I left her alone until we were passing Moreton, then I opened the firebox door, leaving it open and started to fire her all over the box. I could smell scorching and could see Len edging away, for with the door open Len's overall trousers were beginning to steam. I had her on the boil all right! Len made sure he was standing well back when he saw me reach for the shovel. He found that the tender running plate was the coolest place.

Remembrance was not shy of steam, the needle stood still on the red line even when the injector was on. At each signal box we passed the Signalman was looking out of the window to see this great Southern locomotive on Western metals, and each signal box was a sign for the Inspector to make an entry in his pocket book. I had a quick look over his shoulder to see what it was all about and could see a list of passing points and the words 'boiler pressure constant'.

It was a morning to remember, for except for a check through Reading we ran all the way to Acton Yard. Going through Reading, though, we saw a Southern engine at Reading East Main waiting to come out of New

Junction. They blasted away on the whistle and waved their caps, and as we returned the compliment *Remembrance* lifted her safety valve with a roar as if to show she was in good hands.

We took her to Old Oak Common Shed from Acton Yard, and placed her on the ash road with regret. Even with the fire run down she still steamed; we were very impressed with a fine locomotive. All three of us walked away from her chatting about some incident on the trip up, and I felt on top of the world. Not only had I had a wonderful morning on a strange engine and had made her steam where others had failed, but a real live Locomotive Inspector was referring to me as 'son'. I felt I had arrived, I was a Main Line Fireman.

Before the year was out I had fired all of her sister engines, each in the same manner, and each one was a good locomotive, but *Remembrance* was more than a name to me now. Even Len, with all his affection for *Trematon Castle*, had to admit she was something special.

We had our tea and sandwiches at Old Oak Common, in the engineman's mess room, then reported to the Shift Foreman who, like all Shift Foremen, had a job all lined up for us. Now a Locomotive Shed Foreman is a man of manners; he uses etiquette unless he is dealing with a Cleaner. He does not give a direct order but suggests, and he suggested that we make our way to the carriage sidings where we would find a train of empty coaching stock for Newport. He also suggested that if we had reported to him earlier we could have taken the engine off shed. We both thought he had a point there but to show that we were good chaps at heart, and not the rogues he thought we were, Len informed him that we knew the road right through and he could tell Control no relief was required. There was an ulterior motive to this of course, but we did not want to spoil his day; Newport is but a stone's throw from Cardiff and Len could see a night at home if we used a little finesse.

We set off from the shed before the Foreman could change his mind, for from the look on his face we could tell that he knew something was not all that it could be, and in our obvious haste we took the wrong path between the lines of coaches and had to walk some distance to get to our train.

We had turned the corner of the long line of coaches towards the train which we were to work back when Len stopped so suddenly that I nearly knocked him over. There facing us was a 'Castle', and on the red painted buffer beam was the number 5020. It was his beloved *Trematon Castle*.

For Len at that moment it was Christmas, birthday, holidays all rolled into one; he gave a little jig, put his arms round me and nearly squeezed my ribs in, and half-walked, half-ran towards her. It was a reunion with a very dear friend.

The Old Oak Common driver began to explain what preparation he had carried out for the journey, and I could see that Leonard was assuming an act of extreme nonchalance while underneath he was seething for these two men to leave. He wanted a few minutes to himself before blowing up for the signal. *Trematon Castle* had failed that morning on the up Fishguard with vacuum trouble; the Old Oak fitters had repaired her and as Cardiff wanted her back quickly Control decided to work her back with the empty coaches.

With a South Wales engine working home they had not coaled her. There was no point in transporting coal all the way from the Welsh pits just to take it back again, so all they had done was to clear all the coal from the back plate of the tender to the front, and a right old mixture it was too.

Len climbed down to do the bars and glands, but this was just an excuse to have a look round her, since the Old Oak driver had already oiled her. I had a look over the side and saw Len wipe her slide bars with cotton waste. It was a caress, contact with a happy past re-established. I climbed down to join him and placed one hand on his shoulder and together we walked slowly round her without speaking; there was no need for words, it was sufficient to drink in the magnificence of this beautiful locomotive.

Our load was a mixed bunch of coaches; we had 14 on ranging from Webb clerestory's to Collett 35 tonners so our total weight behind the tender was about 500 tons.

Len and I climbed back on to her footplate. His eyes were moist as he opened the large ejector to blow off her brakes, and the twin needles climbed up the vacuum gauge and stopped level on the train pipe and reservoir at 25 1bs. He shut the ejector, the needles dropped to 22lbs and held. She was all right. I blew the gauge glass through to check the water level, nodded to Len, and we were off; he opened the regulator just enough to glide down to the signal. The 'dummy' came off and we eased out on to the down relief, looking back to see the last coach go through the points, then Len gave her half regulator, knocked down the locking handle on the screw reverser and began to slowly wind her back, letting her take her own time and pace. I started to fire her as Len had taught me, while he began to gently tap down the regulator until she was just off the jockey valve. The cut-off was at 25% and she was beginning to move like a turbine running.

There was no need to hurry. As we came in sight of each distant signal it would be at caution, then as Len raised his finger to cancel the A.T.C. warning buzzer the distant would drop and the shrill ring of the bell would sound in the cab as the shoe under the frame rode over the ramp. We were content to amble along at a steady 35mph so as to avoid catching up the signal in front. It was uncanny the way she rode, each rail joint could be heard under the wheels and the gentle 'slap slap' of the vacuum pump on Len's side.

Between Ealing Broadway station and starting signal I opened the left hand water feed and gave her a full turn on the exhaust injector. It picked up at once, the sound synchronising with the exhaust from the chimney, undulating almost as a symphony with the vacuum pump and wheel beats.

Leonard was happy, he sat there with his arms folded, legs crossed and swinging under his seat, singing 'Saspan Fach' but in English for my benefit. Only one thing was missing, and that was his old shovel.

Most of the Firemen on the 'runners' had their own shovels, not because the standard shovel was at fault, but the artiste demanded a special tool for a specialised job, so they would get a fitter to 'breathe' on one. The sides would be ground down from the middle to the facing edge in a taper, then a little ground off the corners. The result was a sharp cutting tool that was balanced to a nicety and that would cut through coal like a knife. Len's shovel had been so doctored, but to compensate for his short reach they had fitted a longer shaft for him. He had said goodbye to that shovel when he was made Driver and posted to Didcot, but life has many surprises to offer to the unsuspected, and one big surprise was to come up and help complete a perfect day.

Passing through Slough I was back in the tender with a coal pick moving out some choice lumps to help with the duff. I had cleared out behind the tool box and was scraping away under the fire iron rack when I spotted a shovel handle. It was not possible to move it as it was jammed in under two prickers, a fire bar and fire dropping shovel, so I came out from my hole, lifted out all the fire irons on to the tender then went back behind the tool box for another go.

This time I was successful and was able to remove a rusty, dirty old shovel.

Somehow I had a feeling about that shovel. I placed it behind the tool box then splashed a bit more duff round *Trematon Castle*'s firebox. Even at our easy pace she had to be attended to, and the Fireman's motto is 'a little and often'.

The fire taken care of, I returned to the discovered shovel, giving it a good swill-off with the coal watering pipe, then wiping the shaft with some cotton waste, and sure enough I found burnt into the shaft the initials "L.J."

Leonard had viewed all this activity with detached interest. He was deep in his own thoughts enjoying a sentimental return of a golden age, his Mate had found a dirty old shovel and from the preparations he had made in cleaning it off he intended to use it.

With my long reach I found that I could slide that shovel with its extended shaft into the coal, lift it out and place the coal in the firebox while sitting on my seat; not that it could be carried out for long, but long enough to make a point. We were near Maidenhead and Len was on the second verse of 'Men of Harlech' when he noticed how I was firing. The singing came to an abrupt stop, he shot off his seat, grabbed that shovel, and with amazement written all over his face he kept repeating "You've found my bloody shovel, you've found my bloody shovel!". Truth is indeed stranger than fiction.

Len was absolutely delighted. If a signalman had looked into the cab as we ran under his window he would have thought there were a couple of lunatics on the footplate; we were holding hands and dancing round and round.

With the discovery of that shovel I was informed that as I was completely familiar with the road between Reading and Swindon I would be the Driver of *Trematon Castle*, and God help me if I knocked her about.

We carried on towards Reading on the down relief line and at Reading East Main the Distant signal was at caution and remained so, the Home Starting signal dropping as we approached. Our speed had dropped to walking pace as we drifted through the station, with the 3.55pm Paddington to Fishguard roaring through on the down main, but surprise, surprise, as the express cleared Reading West Junction the points came over and our signals came off for the down main line. We were going to have a run at last.

Len came over to my side his fingers itching to get hold of his old shovel, while I crossed to the Driver's side and took over. The cut-off was at 45% where we had drifted through the station, so I gave her a little steam and then looked back along the line of coaches to see the last one through the crossover. My moment of glory had come. I was 17 years and a few months, on the main line driving not just any old 'Castle', but the pride of the stud, 5020 *Trematon Castle*. I opened her on to the second valve of the regulator and from the feel of her running I began to slowly wind her back a half turn at a time until she was back on 25% valve cut-off.

No ambling along now, this was the real stuff, and she began to get into her stride as only a 'Castle' can, the speedometer swinging from side to side until it settled at a steady 50mph.

Len came over and had a look; he advised a bit more on the regulator and to wind her back another couple of notches. Within a mile the speed had climbed to 60mph, we were beginning to fly. Len had removed his cloth cap and overall jacket; he was out of condition after six months as a Driver, but he was still an expert with a shovel; the steam pressure was steady at 225lbs and the exhaust injector singing away as in the old days. We swept through Pangbourne and on to the water troughs at Goring picking up 2,000 gallons in one minute, then we began to draw alongside a goods train running on the down relief, the train that had held us back between Old Oak Common and Reading.

This train was rattling along at a good pace so we ran side by side for some miles, and as we drew level with the engine I could see that they were Didcot men on board. It was time to make a noise—I could see that the Fireman was Big Harold's Mate.

To meet my 'Old Chap' out on the road was always a pleasant encounter but to pass him while driving a 'Castle' was a treat not to be missed. Both whistle chains were pulled, making the most unholy row and as he looked across we held up a piece of string; the implication was plain enough—we could give him a tow!

My being his son made no difference, the reply was two fingers in the Churchillian manner! We had been rebuffed, our display of good manners rejected, but what else could you expect from a common old goods train?!

Big Harold picked up the coal watering pipe and tried to squirt water over the gap between us but the wind pressure was too great and much to our delight, he received some of it back. We gave him a final blast on the whistle, then swept majestically on.

Approaching Moreton we could see the Distant signal for Didcot East Junction at caution, and with this situation in sight I at once could feel all the frustration the main line men endure from a signal check. Here we were, running like the wind behind an express and some 'nit' of a signalman had decided to allow a movement across the junction in front of us. We pulled long and hard on the whistle chain, as if by doing so we could blow the signal off, but it remained at caution.

I closed the regulator, knocked down the clip on the reverser and wound her down to the 45 mark, then gave her a short sharp touch on the vacuum brake. The result was instantaneous, as 124 brake-blocks bit into the wheels; it was as if a giant hand had caught hold of the last coach and was holding us back. The speed dropped so quickly I had to open the large ejector and blow the brakes off again.

As they came off the inner Distant signal dropped off and we were away again, but the run had been knocked out of her. We were working hard as we passed Didcot East Junction Box. We gave them a blast on the whistle but in such circumstances signalmen remain shadowy figures behind the glaze of the windows: we were ignored. This came home to me in later years when I too was a signalman in a large box, but that is another story. *Trematon Castle* settled down again in her unflurried manner and the miles sped by until we sighted the Distant signal at caution for Highworth. It looked as if our fears were right; we ran on towards Swindon down the middle road and came to a stand at the end of the platform.

A Severn Tunnel Junction crew were waiting to relieve us and take the train on to Newport, then *Trematon Castle* would run 'light' to Cardiff Shed. Leonard decided to remain with her and spend a night at home. It was a shame Control had taken us off as we had looked forward to going through Severn Tunnel together, but there was another day. I said my farewells to Len and with reluctance climbed down from that lovely engine to catch a train back to Didcot.

The sequel came the next day when we booked on. Len told me that after I had left *Trematon Castle* he placed the shovel up in the corner so that the new Fireman had to use the original shovel. Just outside Cardiff Len's shovel 'accidentally' fell off, right opposite his allotment, and he had to get his old bike out to go and see if it had damaged any of his spring cabbages. That shovel ended up in a good home.

The rest of the week we came down to earth with a bump, covering local goods and shunting jobs, and on the Saturday we were shunting out Wantage Road Station goods yard when Big Harold came by on a brand new engine just out of Swindon Works. We were on a little 0-6-0 L.M.S. Engine; it was time to hide. The 'Old Chap' was never one to let things pass, he could remember as far back as Wednesday and he had a very long length of string ready. It was coiled round and knotted and, as cool as a cucumber, he slowed right down and tossed it right on to our footplate. The French have the right word for such a situation, "Touché!"

Number four link continued to increase in numbers of crews with the war traffic building up so that the number of men away from home was equal to the 'home grown' product. It was decided to make number four link into a weekend link to give the lads a chance to get home more frequently. We were all working long hours and to give up a few rostered free weekends was little enough to help our mates. It meant I would have to leave Leonard, but he was due to return to Cardiff soon anyway, so I moved up into number three link.

This link covered much the same as number four in the way of goods working, but it also had the Didcot, Newbury, Winchester and Southampton Branch, both passenger and goods working. Now this Branch was either loved or loathed, and I loved it, taking to it like a duck takes to water. I was fortunate also to know it before the alterations that began in August came about, and doubly fortunate in my Driver Ralph Painton.

Chapter Four

The week before I was to join Ralph I filled a sick vacancy in the passenger link. This was the 3.45pm Didcot to Paddington, returning with the 7.50pm Paddington to Didcot. It was a nice little turn stopping all stations to Slough, then fast to Paddington; the return was much the same, fast to Slough then all stations to Didcot. Booking on time was 2.30pm for off shed at 3.30pm, but I was climbing up on our engine at 2.00pm. I liked plenty of time in preparation.

The engine booked was 6923 but without name-plates — (she was named *Croxteth Hall* after the War) — due to a shortage of brass, so it was said; perhaps the brass was needed for those great injector handles on the L.M.S. Class 8F they were building at Swindon. With or without a name she was a fine engine, and just as well too; my Mate for the week was Bill Darby, and he had a reputation of being a 'hard hitter'.

With this in mind I built up a good fire so that when we backed on to our ten coaches on Number 5 Platform I had plenty of steam, fire, and water. The Guard was on Bill's side, so he would take the 'right away'. At 3.42pm the road was set "up relief" to Didcot East Junction, then "up main line". The signals dropped off, and we were ready to go.

I expected Bill to lift the regulator with his left hand when we started off, but not a bit of it; he walked over to my side, turned his back on me, caught hold of the regulator in both hands and pushed it right up into the cab roof. Only a Great Western "Hall" would stand such treatment; she took off like a scalded cat without one trace of a slip, and my carefully prepared fire had great holes torn out of it.

Passing Moreton I began to fire her as Bill wound the lever back, but he snapped down the clip at 35% cut off. It was going to be a hairy trip. My small lumps of coal never touched the fire, they went over the brick arch, through the tubes, out of the chimney and back down onto the tender again! The blast from the exhaust was something to be heard; I half expected to see the bricks fly out of Moreton Bridge as we passed underneath.

He shut off early for Cholsey, so I had a chance to regain on the boiler. There was only one way to fire for Bill and that was to keep piling it in, and if the lumps of coal were big enough to go through the fire hole so much the better, at least they stopped in long enough to burn. For all that, though, Bill was a kindly man, even if his method of driving made sure of no unemployment in the South Wales coal pits, and I was to enjoy my week with him.

I can remember with pleasure that first short, sharp, burst of fast-running between Slough and Paddington. We came up to Southall with the chimney kicking up one hell of a racket, hanging on the whistle chain as we approached the long bridge preceding the station. Passengers packed on the platform receded like waves on the sea-shore as we burst under the bridge, and we looked back along the train to see the dust and newspapers flying, with hands grasping desperately at hats of all shapes. Bill looked over at me with a grin on his face, he knew what was making me laugh, he had seen hats go flying before.

We ran into Paddington on time, where my education into the so-called 'weaker sex' was to begin. I was a well brought-up simple country boy who had been taught that ladies were ladies. I knew there were the other kind, but being a clean living lad I had no contact with that other kind. My innocence was to be shattered by an accident.

I lit the flare lamp and walked around the frame to light the headlamps. This job done I blew out the flare lamp and jumped down on to the platform with one headlamp in my hand to place on the tender bracket. I had timed it just right; the passengers we had brought with us were tearing past like they do at Paddington, always in a hurry.

One of these passengers was a young lady of ample proportions; she had a bosom that made the lads look twice, and covering this bosom was a spotless white blouse.

As I landed on the platform the dirty charred paraffin soaked stump of the flare lamp went right across that white-covered bosom leaving a long black streak. She stood quite still for a moment, looked at me, then at her blouse, then that bosom started to heave as bosoms do under stress, but the sound that issued from her mouth was nothing like a lady should use! She sounded off like a factory hooter, using words that were quite unbecoming! I got the impression that she was upset, and when she started to question the validity of my parents being married I knew she was upset. Poor Bill hung over the cab window helpless with laughter. The coaches were drawn off our engine so Bill blew off the brakes ready to follow; it was time to make a move. One more bit of indignity came my way; this distraught young lady(?) said that she would report me to the Midland manager, and me a Great Western man! I was shattered. She swung round on her heels to leave and the string bag she had in the crook of her arm clouted the heavy headlamp I still had in my hand. There was a tinkle of glass and half a pint of gin cascaded on the dusty platform.

Bill, bless him, was quick off the mark. He had already started to move back. I flung the headlamp onto the footplate and leapt after it—this was one time to leave Paddington for Ranleigh Bridge turntable without a lamp on the tender bracket!

For the rest of the week when running into Paddington we took precautions not to be recognised, in railway language, 'From Tuesday to Saturday inclusive'. When we stopped at the buffers Bill would take off his cap, take out his teeth, and put on a pair of black horn-rimmed reading glasses. Each day that young lady would have a look up into the cab, but she would see an almost bald man with sunken cheeks wearing glasses and bent over a book. Bill, of course, picked this time to bring his train journal up to date. And Fireman? Well, he was standing on the frame with his back to the boiler on the blind side of the platform, so she never did see him again. That was the week I decided to grow the moustache I still wear, 30 years later.

It was a good week, and although Bill liked to hear the chimney bark he was a good Mate. Each day he would pass a remark about stopping on the return journey on the down relief at Maidenhead, and each day he would make the same mistake. We had a long train on the 7.50pm and to get it all on the platform we had to run to the extreme end. The A.T.C. ramp was positioned there, and as we were booked 10 minutes for Station work, to stop on the ramp would mean the A.T.C. bell ringing in the cab all that time. Bill never missed, much as he tried to! We would ram cotton waste round the rim of the bell, then go and sit on the platform bench. Bill would leave the small ejector open, then two minutes before departure we would climb back on board, but even two minutes with that bell ringing was a lifetime.

The only embarrassment was on the Friday evening when a small boy came along. All enginemen at some time or another meet these small boys. They were not only 'spotters' but they could give one information about the engine that even the designer did not know, such as how many times the wheels went round between Paddington and Plymouth, and how many times the engine exhausted in a mile, and this boy was no exception. He informed us with all seriousness that we had stopped on the A.T.C. ramp and did we know that the bell was ringing. Bill looked very sad, then beckoned the lad forward and whispered in his ear. He took off up the platform as if his tail was on fire, leaving Bill with a satisfied smirk on his face! I never did find out what he said, but I can guess. I recently saw a photograph in a railway book showing two enginemen sitting on a platform bench on the down relief at Maidenhead. The caption under the photograph was 'Resting'. True, very true. Perhaps the photographer was deaf.

I joined Ralph Painton as his Fireman on the Sunday night, and straight away was into another spot of fun. We booked on at 11.00pm for relief duties, on one of those nights that sometime crop up in May. It was like mid-winter, driving rain with a gale blowing. We were ordered to relieve a Swindon to Bordsley goods standing at west curve, so we walked down the centre yard between the wagons to escape the weather until we arrived by the shunters cabin, and there stood our train. One look and we almost turned back; the engine was a Westernised version R.O.D., No. 3007. She looked a stinker true to her class. To her credit she steamed, but not only in the boiler. Like her sisters she leaked steam everywhere; the cab dripped with condensation, and just to rub it in the coal was a mixture of dust and ovoids. We started off with the gait peculiar to the "Thirties". As described earlier, each revolution of the wheel produced a loud clang from the side rods and with each beat from the exhaust the engine would go forward, pause, then forward again; the result was that with the slackness between the engine and tender a perpetual backwards-forwards motion would set up. With all the time and money spent on designing self-trimming tenders the only true self-trimmer was on these monstrosities.

We clanked our way wearily towards Oxford spilling ovoids all over the track and covered in dust before we had reached Radley. No amount of water would keep it down, but at Oxford our discomfort was to be shared.

We pulled up the middle road after being checked by Distants from Hinksey, to receive a red light from Oxford Station North Box. Ralph stopped outside while I climbed down with the gauge lamp in my hand and set off to see what was wanted. As I entered the signal box the first person I saw was an R.A.F. Squadron Leader. The signalman explained that this officer had missed the last train to Heyford and asked if we would give him a lift.

Against regulations of course, but there are not many enginemen who have refused to give a serviceman a helping hand in wartime, and besides, he was such a picture in his number one uniform. I was sure he would fully appreciate our version of a Wellington bomber!

I helped him over to the engine with the feeble light from the gauge lamp, and guided his feet onto the steps and up on to the footplate. Introductions and explanations were made, then he produced an expensive cigarette case and handed it round; he was obviously a well brought up young man. We in turn showed good manners in offering him a light from our cigarette lighter, the gauge lamp. The little door was unclipped and the lamp turned towards him, and to show him that we, too, were gentlemen we advised him not to let the cigarette come in contact with the wick or it might spoil the taste of the smoke. He thanked us, accepted the light, then burnt his nose on the hot metal case of the gauge lamp! We were off to a good start.

To make him feel at home, Ralph and I went through a pre-take off check, opening and shutting the blow-through cock and generally creating an atmosphere of great things to come; then we set off. I settled him down on the seat on my side and started work, and by the time we had reached Wolvercote Junction we were beginning to pick them up a bit. We clattered over the Junction with our Squadron Leader looking a bit apprehensive. By the light of the fire I could see that the shine on his polished shoes was beginning to dim with coal dust. I gave the footplate and his toe-caps a wash down at the same time, then Ralph gave her a bit more on the regulator ready for the long pull up Tackley Bank.

The old engine began to shake and rattle as only a "Thirty" can. I opened the firebox doors, got down the long pricker and gave her a good pull through. When I withdrew the pricker it was almost white-hot from the tip to half-way up the handle. The R.A.F. trouser began to steam. She lifted her safety valve and blew off hard just as we passed under Kidlington road bridge. For one moment Ralph and I thought we would lose our passenger as we roared through the station. He was on the point of bailing out, but it would have been a bit foolhardy without a parachute! As we topped the bank at Tackley the gale caught us straight into the cab, and whipped his cap off into the night! He gave a cry of despair. Conversation had not been possible because of the noise, but I gave him a Woodbine, patted him on the knee and managed to convey to him that worse things happen at sea! Once over the top, Ralph shut off and we drifted down the other side of the bank to come to a shuffling halt in Heyford Station.

In his eagerness to leave us our Squadron Leader put his foot under the damper handle, ripped the upper from the sole and landed face-down in the mixture of ovoids and wet dust! We picked him up and wiped him down with cotton waste, then helped him onto the platform.

He looked very forlorn standing there in the driving rain. He was covered in coal dust, he had lost his cap, somewhere he had lost one beautiful tan leather glove and he had a scorch mark on his trousers. He was no longer the immaculate officer who had joined us at Oxford, but true to tradition he was an officer and a gentleman.

With a very refined public school accent he courteously thanked us for the lift back to his station, then he said he now had two ambitions in life where before he had only one. The first was to survive his flying operations and the war; the second was to get Ralph and myself into the air with him for just ten minutes! Somehow we got the impression that he had not enjoyed steam traction, and we watched him flap his way out of the station gate, with his shoe opening and closing like a crocodile's mouth. I expect he by-passed the guard room at Heyford R.A.F. Station and used the hole in the fence to get in. No self-respecting guard would have believed his explanation for the state he was in.

Two weeks later Ralph and I were chugging gently along between Kingham and Charlbury on an old "Dean" 2676 towards Oxford. We had had a rough trip from Honeybourne up through the tunnel to Campden and were enjoying the Spring sunshine as we ambled along. A flight of Wellington bombers were making a long sweep round on the horizon, then lining up for the approach to Heyford in the east.

As they passed overhead one at a time we idly followed their progress. They were only about 200 feet up, so they were close enough for us to see them in detail. One by one they all disappeared behind the contour of the land on our left except one; we watched him gain height and circle away, then turn towards us, gradually dropping down to about 50 feet. He flew along level with us then pulled away to make a second run, but this time he throttled right down at about the same height as the first run but much closer. The small window in the pilot's cabin was open. We could see an arm extended and two fingers in the 'V' sign moving up and down, both front and rear gun turrets were pointing in our direction; our Squadron Leader was paying a call on us! We gave him a long blast on the whistle, knowing he could not hear it, but he would see the long column of steam.

It gave us a nice feeling to know he had not forgotten us, and we both hoped that he did survive the hard days ahead.

Most of the next few months were spent on the Didcot to Winchester Branch. It gave me an insight of single line working, but not for long between Didcot and Newbury, for the Branch was closed in August and the re-building began. When it re-opened for traffic in April 1943 it was double line as far as Woodhay.

This part of my firing days had three advantages. Ralph knew every inch of the Branch and as I was an apt pupil he soon had me loving it too. I found I could change a train staff at 45 to 50 mph with complete confidence, even on the darkest night. Regulation 23 states "10mph" but you can't mess about on a bank at that speed!

I was introduced to the modern version of the Dean Goods Engine, Mr. Collett's 22XX Class, and with the re-building I literally walked every inch of the Branch between Didcot and Winchester.

The "Twenty Two's" were, I think, the best engine we had for local Branch work. We had a large stud of them at Didcot loco shed, and each one of them was a good engine. There was one only that was disliked, but not because of the engine alone—that part of her was alright. This was 2282, and she was mated up with an old R.O.D. tender. The result was ridiculous, the overall picture was completely out of proportion and spoilt a fine engine.

The first trip I had with Ralph over the 'lingering die', as the Branch was known to the Didcot men, was on a Sunday morning with a special goods for Winchester.

Our engine was the old *Comet*, Number 3283, one of the "Duke of Cornwall" Class, she still retained the outside frames, a very narrow cab with a great screw reverser taking up most of the Driver's space, but for an old engine, like her sister 3254 *Cornubia* she was a good one.

Boiler pressure was only 180lbs but she would steam like the proverbial kettle, pull like a cart horse, and run like a deer. The firebox was low down on the footplate, so firing her was a bit awkward. It was almost as if one threw the coal in a hole in the floor; you had to miss the damper handles with the left hand when swinging round with the shovel, and miss the Driver's ankles with the blade.

Ralph now and again would try an old trick Drivers liked to play. Just as the shovel swung round for a planned shot to the front corner of the firebox he would stick out his foot. The result would be coal scattered all over the floorboards. Retribution would come when next the floorboards were washed down—the coal watering pipe would stray—so as soon as Ralph saw me pick up the pipe he would sit up on the reverser with his feet on the tip-up seat. Who would have thought that 20 years later Ralph would be the Driver of the last passenger train over the branch? They were happy days, but with the amount of engineering material we began to transport it was obvious that the alterations about to begin were to be major ones. The Branch was to become part of a planned strategy for the invasion of Europe.

In August 1942 we began working engineering trains until we were sick of the sight of them. Our old Branch was being ripped apart, and it was a pleasure to have a week away on the main line, although even that could be spoilt as a result of the 'block'.

With air raids going on it was a common occurrence to be blocked back by Control, so that it sometimes took as much as 10 to 12 hours to work a train from Didcot to Reading. Engines were on the road weeks overdue for boiler washout, superheaters and tubes leaked, the coal was bad, and duties of sixteen, eighteen and twenty hours were worked frequently; but enough has been written about the bad days, this is a book written about the good days, and human nature being what it is it is better to recall days that gave pleasure.

The year 1942 gave us a new and exciting engine to work, with the introduction of the 2-8-0 Freight on loan from the U.S.A. Transportation Corps. The Great Western locomen took them straight to their hearts; they were great ugly locomotives, sporting a maze of plumbing all over the boiler and with every bit of motion exposed, and were the direct opposite to the clean lines of a Western engine. Perhaps it was the fact that they were so opposite that gave them their charm, and perhaps, too, it was the comfort.

I can still remember the wonderment on climbing aboard one for the first time. The first impression was one of greatness, everything looked twice as large; it seemed a massive boiler front which extended back into a large cab, but each side of that boiler was an armchair upholstered to such a degree that it was obvious they were meant to be sat in. This was something new indeed after the tip-up wooden seat we were used to. We tried them for size and found them very comfortable, but the proof would be in the eating. The crew we relieved explained the controls to us, but with the adaptability of all enginemen we could see that we would have no trouble in handling this monster.

We stood on the up middle road at Swindon Station. A large crowd of passengers had gathered on the platform to examine this strange new engine while we waited for signals, and they were in for a surprise! I opened the firebox doors and splashed half a dozen shovelfuls of coal round that great square box, and as the needle climbed up to blowing off the end of the world came! Instead of a gentle whisper at the safety valve to warn one of pressure about to escape, those valves lifted with such a roar that we both thought for one moment that the boiler had exploded. I had never heard such a roar of escaping steam before, and then as suddenly as they had gone off the valves closed with a 'pop'.

I looked over to Ralph to see the colour come back into his face. He looked as shaken as I did, I could hear my heart thudding. We had been taken for a ride! I thought that the draught was a bit fierce in the firebox, and I could now see why—the Swindon Fireman had given the blower half a turn! Ralph and I looked over the side; there was not a passenger left on the platform near us, the last one was still running towards the far end! And the Swindon crew? They were about four wagons back, the Driver with a grin on his face, but the Fireman was sitting on the ground absolutely helpless with laughter!

Well, two can play at that game. We would try it on the next crew, and so it would go on until everyone was initiated to the peculiarities of the Yank engines.

The gauge glass was a flat Pyrex effort set in a frame showing the water black. She was three quarters full, so after one experiment with the injector we were ready to 'blow up' for the signal. Ralph gave a pull on the whistle and we had our second surprise. It was a full-blooded, honest-to-goodness American railroad bellow. In that one moment we were transported away from the flat plains of green England to the vast expanse of the great American West. We were the Baltimore and Ohio, the Union Pacific all rolled into one. On shutting one's eyes one could almost see the arrows flying and hear the whoops of the Indians.

We pulled gently away to get the feel of her, Ralph set the regulator on the ratchet and let her take her time as he linked her up, and passing Highworth Box I placed a dozen shovelfuls round her firebox.

It was then that I found that the arm-chair on the Fireman's side was to be used after all. I sat down all the way to Challow, where I put a bit more round her again and put the injector on for a bit, then sat down again to Didcot. We had never seen anything like it; there seemed no end of power in that boiler, and at such little effort.

With a light load and with the up road from Swindon in our favour it did make for an easy trip, but later as we had more and more Yanks allocated to the Great Western we found them to be capable of any task set for them. There was the unfortunate accident at Honeybourne, where one of them blew a main steam pipe, killing the enginemen, that gave us all a few moments of concern, and as they aged they got a bit rough on the motion, but for all that we were well satisfied with them. The one part of them I did dislike was the sand box. This was situated on the top of the boiler between the whistle and chimney, and I can well remember topping one up with sixteen buckets of sand. How many buckets they took when empty was an experience I was happy to forego.

However, this first trip was a very pleasant one. I ran the boiler down a bit as we passed between Wantage Road and Steventon so that I could put the injector on and keep her from blowing off as we waited for relief. It was now our turn to scare the pants off the unsuspecting enginemen!

Our relief came almost at once, and we climbed down leaving the engine in the up loop at Foxhall Junction. Needless to say, the blower was left on half a turn!

We had just crossed over the Junction when we heard the bellow of her whistle, and were walking up the foot-path between the up relief and the provender stores sidings towards Didcot West Box when she came creeping by. Like Ralph at Swindon, this Driver was taking her away gently to get the feel of her. Her Fireman was standing on the running plate between the engine and tender with a cup of tea in his hand when she blew off; he dropped the cup as if was red hot, and the Driver jerked back his head and thumped it against the back support of the cab! Like the crew we had relieved at Swindon, Ralph and I hung on to each other, helpless with laughter. Vengeance is sweet.

These safety valves proved somewhat of a problem during the next few months, causing damage to the elaborate overhang of some stations, and blowing out signal lamps all over the system. I had one blow off on the up main line coming through Banbury Station, which took half of the footbridge with it. (Banbury needed a new station, so part of the demolition took place a little early). Orders were soon distributed to all locomotive sheds, drawing attention to the rule book whereby the emission of smoke or steam is prohibited. The message from Management was plain enough—knock it off boys, you've had your fun.

The winter of 1942 saw us hard at work on the Winchester Branch with the engineering trains. I say hard at work with tongue in cheek to some extent; there were of course some hard duties but the majority of the work was very undemanding.

There were up to eight ballast trains working between Didcot and Winchester taking three crews to each train. The early shift would prepare the engine and leave with a ballast train for the site, or go light engine; the middle shift would go by bus to the site, and relieve the early shift who would return by bus; the late shift would relieve the middle shift, then take the engine back to shed.

All shifts had a bus ride either coming or going, but the 'plum' job was the middle shift, particularly if the work was south of Whitchurch, as this meant a three hour ride over the Berkshire Downs and into the Hampshire countryside, five hours on the engine, then a nice ride home on the bus again.

As all the train services in this area were suspended, the travelling public used the buses, but there was one unpublished goods train in each direction early morning and late at night. Working this train had its moments, as at some places the single line token was suspended as total occupation was in force, at others the points were clipped and we shuttled over from up to down, or crossed over where none existed a few hours before. However, in spite of all the difficulties throughout a long winter the re-building was completed without any accidents—well, almost.

At Burghclere, before the alterations, the signal box was on the Down side, and the single line instruments in the booking office on the Up Side. The Signalman would place the token in the post for the next section then retire to the office. It was then the practice of Firemen to pick up the new token and by skilful aim throw the old token through the doorway of the booking office, where the Signalman would place it in the instrument without getting up from his chair. Ralph had taught me how to throw this token, and being a darts player I soon found I could throw this heavy piece of metal through the door each time without adding any more marks to the scarred door post.

On the very last day of the old working before the new signal box was brought into use, the inevitable happened. I threw the token as the Signalman walked out of the door! For a man in his sixties he moved quicker than he had moved for years—he would have done credit to that most eminent of dancers, Fred Astaire. His footwork was a work of art, but his language was not, it was most unbecoming for a man who I knew was a sidesman in the local church!

My diary shows that from Monday October 5th to Saturday October 10th I was with Ralph on the Winchester ballast. "Booked on at 7.15 am, bused to Winchester; worked with 'Bulldog' 3448 *Kingfisher*, then bused home, booked off at 6.15 pm." So it was an 11 hour day and a 66 hour week. My pay was £3.19.3d.

On this middle shift that week we had one driver who was working the Whitchurch section. He was an expert in catching rabbits, and with the meat ration on the short side he was in demand. To meet this demand he would bring to work with him a couple of nets and a ferret, and set to work on the banks of Larks Barrow Hill Cutting. He was a fat man, so with the assumption that a couple of pounds extra to his figure would not be noticed, he would undo a button on his shirt, pop the ferret in, tighten up his belt and sit down. He always chose the back seat of the bus, so the little ferret would lie along his stomach, warm and comfortable, and go to sleep. At Newbury we were joined by a large overbearing lady passenger who made it quite clear that the railway was going to the dogs when passengers had to share a public vehicle with dirty old engine drivers. She sat opposite our mate, viewing him with distaste all the way to Litchfield, until the back wheel of the bus dropped into a hole in the road and woke up little Fred. He stuck his sharp little nose out the shirt front, his whiskers on each side of his dear little face twitching with anticipation. The large lady and ferret looked into each other's eyes for some seconds, then she let out a screech that sounded just like a hot axle box! Fred disappeared back into the warm like quicksilver. From her description of the animal she had seen it could have been a kangaroo. It took us all the way to Whitchurch to convince her that she had suffered an illusion, probably due to something she ate, and the jerking of the bus had brought it on! We advised her to see her doctor.

As the work progressed we could see that the freight trains we would be handling in the next few years would be of main line proportions, for we noticed the length of the passing loops, and this would mean big engines on the Branch. At times, the engineering work would allow us to be stationary for lengthy periods, so we would take it in turns to leave the engine and go and examine our new Branch. In this way, little by little, we walked the whole distance between sections.

We both looked at the drop down from Litchfield to Whitchurch with some misgiving. The ruling gradient was 1 in 106 falling, to end up with some throw off points just to the south of Whitchurch Station. It did not take long to work out that a Twenty Eight, L.M.S. 8F, and the big Yank engines would be loaded with up to 46 Number Ones, and with a 20 ton brake van at the back we should be running down that bank with best part of a thousand tons on the move, with every chance of landing up in the road leading to Whitchurch Town.

A mental note was made to make sure we had full sand boxes when the crunch came.

By the middle of April 1943 it had all been completed, we were ready for anything, and it was not long in coming.

The American Army and Air Force arrived at Newbury and Sutton Scotney via courtesy of the Great Western Railway and the Didcot — Winchester Branch. We ran troop trains for weeks, filling up the South of England with Yanks, and with them came a new invention—instant coffee. Whenever we arrived at the discharging station, we would be loaded up with 'K' rations, long waxed cardboard boxes stamped 'Breakfast' or 'Dinner'. Inside these was a wealth of food, cheese, biscuits, tinned meat, four Chesterfield or Camel cigarettes; and half a dozen little packets of brown powder, with instructions to empty one packet into a cup, add boiling water and stir; the result was coffee such as we had never tasted before. In these 'K' rations were also a dozen soft toilet tissues, to be used for obvious reasons. They made a pleasant change from an old service book cut in half, drilled in one corner for the string, and hung in a corner. It was said that the Yanks had ice cream too, but we did not see any; we were very satisfied with powdered coffee and nice soft toilet paper.

We ran one American troop train that summer with our old *Comet*. The train of eight coaches arrived in the up gully at Didcot East Junction from Birkenhead Docks, the engine came off and we backed on, to ribald comments from the troops watching the operation.

From their point of view I suppose we did look a bit comic backing on to couple up, with our tall chimney, steam dome, and curved splashers joining the small open cab. There were many comparisons made between *Comet* and the *General Grant*, so Ralph and I set out to show these Yanks a thing or two. All troop trains were allowed plenty of time in running, (in fact main line running was restricted to a shadow of pre-war years), and we might be called "That little old locomotive" in a deep Southern-state American accent, but they would change their minds by the time we arrived at Sutton Scotney.

We pulled away and clattered over the junction towards the Branch, letting her take her time until we were under the Hagbourne road bridge and into the bank heading for Upton. I had a deep solid bed of fire, so she had plenty to bite on.

Normally Ralph would have started to link her up, he was the most gentle of Drivers, but we were both a bit upset, and if Ralph wanted to work her hard that was all right by me. We stormed up that bank so fast that the Upton signalman was standing on the steps of the box to watch us. Through the station we roared and pounded on up the bank. By the time we had reached the three-arch bridge and three-quarters of the way to the top, we had made the fastest time ever. I had had the exhaust injector on all the way from Didcot, and had not once stopped firing. Then we were over the top and on the way down the drop as far as Hampstead Norris. We rocketed through Compton, and bucked and swayed through Hampstead Norris at such a speed that the 1 in 106 climb to Hermitage was a mere pimple, but we had to ease down a bit for the drop down the bank into Newbury—we had made such fast time there might be some questions asked if we arrived there too early.

We were booked for water at Newbury, so after we had stopped on the middle road I put the bag in the tank, then nipped into the signal box for a quiet word with the signalman.

We arranged for him to telephone ahead to all boxes as far as Sutton Scotney to have the single line tokens placed in the racks, and not for the signalmen to stand on the end of the platforms with them as they normally would do. Hand-exchange of tokens had become custom and practice with the leisurely life of the Branch, but the staff were in for an example of main line running to brighten up the quiet stations. Ralph's instruction during the past months were soon to bear fruit; I had a heavy leather glove all ready to place on my left hand, for there would be no 10mph on these token exchanges.

We 'blew up' for the road, the home and starter dropped and we were away, building up speed towards Enbourne Junction. Ralph eased down a bit as we turned left off the main line, but as soon as we had passed Enbourne Box he opened her up again for the 1 in 106 climb to Woodhay.

We were now on the last bit of double line. I collected the token at Woodhay as we climbed at 30mph towards Highclere. The exchange was made there for Burghclere, and even at 30mph the heavy hoop stung through the leather glove. Then came that little bit of road described in my first firing trip over the branch; we swooped down the bank, shot through the bridge at the bottom and were away up the other side.

News of our record run had brought half the population out to see us through Burchclere but speed was not so high, for we still had a short bit of bank to climb. It was about a mile south of Burghclere that the real run of speed would begin, right down to Sutton Scotney ten miles further on. Through Litchfield we were on a falling gradient of 1 in 106, and we went through like the "Bristolian". The token which I threw onto the post went round and round like a spinning top, and when I picked up the token for the Whitchurch Section the speed was such that it flew back, hitting the tender with such a thump that it knocked out a great lump of paint, but I hung on to it much to Ralph's relief; he told me later he thought he had overdone it a bit through Litchfield.

Down into Whitchurch we flew, but Ralph gave her a touch on the brake, the exchange was made, and we tore on towards the next station, Sutton Scotney. The old *Comet* stood there sizzling, while the American troops piled out. Ralph was going round placing his hand on the axle boxes; the *Comet* had been run faster than she had ever run before, but all was well. She started to blow off as if to tell us she could do it all over again.

One of the American sergeants came along to us and said he would never have believed it possible for an engine such as ours to run like that unless he had been on board. He told us that we had achieved something that would go down in the Regimental History Book; we had stopped the game of 'craps' in his platoon, and instead they were laying bets on me missing the next token, and whether or not the side rods would fly off. He himself was an ex New York Central man, so he had some previous knowledge of locomotive running. He patted his tunic pocket with appreciation, for he had backed me catching all the tokens, then he handed over a carton as a gesture of thanks—a few cigarettes, as he termed 500 Chesterfields.

An officer came up and told him to get a move on. The reply was to shock us; the 'Lootenant was to stop beating his gums'. No salutes, no recriminations, in fact the 'Lootenant' looked chastened for disturbing us. Our Sergeant did eventually get a move on as requested, but only just in time to scramble up on the tailboard of the last lorry pulling out of the station yard. No God-dammed Officer was telling him what to do!

We were booked to run to Winchester with the empty coaches, and then turn the engine back to Didcot, but as it was a nice day we decided to run round the train and go back tender-first. We were in no hurry, in fact we were very pleased with ourselves, and anyway, Winchester turntable was no picnic. It was fitted in the days of small engines, so the only way to turn was to run the engine over the table, lift up some heavy ramps with a crowbar, and then back the tender up these ramps. It was impossible to balance an engine perfectly, but once she was on, the table was moved by turning two great mangle-wheels round and round. It was the most efficient method of stripping off waistcoat buttons I have ever seen; sooner or later everyone was caught by those handles. They would come round and under, then up inside the garment, and then it was either over the top with you, or lose the buttons! Thank goodness for weak cotton!

We ambled back, smoking our Chesterfields and discussing the run. The Yanks now had a different outlook on Limey enginemen, but they were a good lot of lads, and generous to a fault.

South of Newbury was a restricted area right across the south coast, and security was tight. All troop movements were top secret, and even we did not know until booking on where we would be sent when handling these trains. But in spite of all the precautions taken to ensure secrecy there was a leak in the system. The local children knew all. Their intelligence service must have been the envy of every army commander; they would line the fields each side of the station, and as soon as they were spotted by the Yank lads the windows would come down and a shower of sweets, chocolate, chewing gum and tins of Spam for Mum would come flying out, to the delighted shrieks of the children. I can't ever remember an American troop train leaving without the children being there. How those Yanks loved our kids.

Ralph and I saw the start of the heavy freight traffic to Southampton on the Branch, then the Management formed a special link of twenty Drivers and Firemen to work these supply trains. I was one of the Firemen who applied to be in this link, while Ralph took on a job he richly deserved—he was appointed to Shift Foreman on the Shed.

I kicked about for several weeks waiting to be mated up with another Driver, and spent that time on loan to Newbury.

There was no shed there; instead half a dozen sets of men worked Engines supplied by Didcot. It was my good fortune to spend the first week on night duty on the Newbury Town pilot engine with a real gentleman for a Mate, Charlie Darrle-Smith who in later years became a Locomotive Inspector. I keep coming across his name in railway literature, and read of his exploits with interest, although I expect he is now retired and I hope in good health.

The second week was spent as a member of the American Army, firing a diminutive little tank engine on Newbury race course for a very large Driver. The Americans had turned the race course into a vast supply depot, with miles of railway lines laid down. They were short of Firemen, so I had a wonderful week with them. I have the very cherished memory of passing the winning post up the straight opposite the grandstand on Newbury race course on a steam locomotive!

That week I used to go home loaded with all the food I could carry. My American Driver had taken one look at my brown wartime bread with its thin sliver of cheese and had thrown it in the firebox. Then he had taken me off to the canteen for 'chow'. The first meal was an eye-opener; the ham on the plate was a quarter of an inch thick, covered with two eggs 'sunny side up'. To go with it were waffles, or as we would call them pancakes, topped with a thick brown syrup, and then to wash it all down was a pint of American coffee. Each evening he would load me up with tins of Spam, sausage-meat, butter, and cheese, and at the end of the week my underclothes, shirts, and boots ended up in the firebox and I was kitted out with my American Army clothes. I had two pairs of boots which lasted for years. They were made of soft leather, uncoloured and in their natural state, so they could be dyed black or brown. As for cigarettes, I had enough to last me for months.

I can't remember that Driver's name now except that his first name was Charlie, and that he was a locomotive man from Milwaukee, but I can remember he couldn't bring himself to call me "Harold" or "Mate"; I was 'Al'.

At the end of that fortnight I was back at Didcot and all ready to start on the Southampton run, but it was a gradual build up for there was still plenty to do on the Main Line.

I had another week spare and spent it in Foxhall up loop in charge of trains blocked back. There would be as many as four or five trains in the loop, all with engines in steam at the head of each one, and by the time I had worked my way back to the last one, topping up the boiler and firebox, it was time to walk back to the first one and start all over again.

I had on one of the trains an old friend, 2330 *Cudworth*, one of the "Remembrance" Class from the old London, Brighton, and South Coast Railway. As she was so low on coal and water I threw out her fire; she was so full up with muck from being on the road for so long that it took me all night to complete the job in between looking after the other engines, but it was nice to be able to take care of an old friend.

The next week I had a Mate again, Jack Thomas, one of the Welsh Drivers. No more messing about spare, now we could get on with the job of running trains again.

Chapter Five

Jack had been at Didcot for some time, so he was no stranger to the area covered by Didcot Shed. He was proud of the fact that he had started his career in railway work with the old Taff Vale Railway, and although now a Great Western man the Taff held pride of place. Thus the Winchester Branch held no problems, for Jack had been weaned on banks and heavy coal trains up and down the Welsh Valleys.

I worked with him from May 1943 until February 1944 and found, like all the Welsh lads, he was a grand person to know.

With Jack I never used the tender hand-brake, as he was a master with the vacuum brake and on our first trip together he asked me to leave all the braking to him. The normal practice was for the fireman to wind on the hand-brake when the Driver shut off and bring the buffers of the wagons up together, and then, as the speed began to fall off, to gently unwind again; on bank working, however, the hand-brake went on hard as soon as the engine stuck her head downhill. But Jack would give the engine five inches of vacuum and take the train down the steepest bank with a nonchalance that had to be seen.

He never worried about anything. We had our rough trips like other men, with poor coal, dirty fires, and leaking tubes, the steam pressure could be down so low we would just be able to keep going, and the water level in the boiler bobbing in the bottom nut, but Jack would give a grin, hand me a cigarette, and somehow we would get over the situation. If it did get too bad, then we would do the same as all the others — stop for a brew up. Then, as soon as we had recovered steam pressure and water level, we would be off again. We always reckoned that if the engine needed a rest then so did we, so the tea can went in the firebox as soon as we had stopped.

Our first week on the Branch went off with a bang — literally! We were booked on the 4.30 am. Didcot to Winchester Goods. This duty was a double-headed job. Two of Collett's "Twenty Two's" were coupled with a full load for Newbury where the front engine would come off and work at Newbury as the pilot engine, while the second, or train engine, would carry on with a reduced load as far as Burghclere or Litchfield, and change over with the Winchester stopping passenger and work back to Didcot, the Winchester men going forward with the Goods. It was a pleasure to have this duty, as we had regular engines and we could be sure of an early finish, which made a change from some of the twelve and fourteen hour duties of the previous weeks.

That 4.30am start out of Didcot up yard was a sight to see. We would pull gently away until we were clear of Didcot East Junction points, then both engines would be opened up.

A Twenty Two worked with a small regulator opening and short valve cut off could make quite a racket from the chimney, but two working together was enough to wake up the whole town!

On a clear summer morning as we passed through Upton station we could look back down towards Didcot and see where we had left the Yard for there would be a smoke trail for about four miles, then we would be into the cutting and going hammer and tongs towards Churn, showering sparks and cinders high into the air.

Hampstead Norris was the worst place, as if the train was a long one it would be on four levels between the north of the station and the start of the bank, so we would both ease down until we felt the slight tug as the guard wound his brake on, (this would indicate that all the couplings were tightly stretched out and there was no fear of a division in the train), then we could open up again and blast our way up to Hermitage.

On the Tuesday we had the aforementioned Bang. Our train engine was 2222, and the front one a Didcot "Dukedog", 3208. We coupled up at the Shed signal on a wet morning, and as the signal came off made our way up towards the stop blocks to clear the points into the yard. Speed was only walking pace, but when our mate on the front engine applied the brakes that old "Dukedog" picked up her feet on the wet rails and we slammed into the blocks. With a combined weight of around 180 tons it was a hell of a wallop; it brought the coal tumbling down all over the floor boards. My first thought was for the brick arch, but that was all right. Jack was swearing because our can of tea had gone flying.

We climbed down and went forward to see what damage was caused. The chaps on the front engine were all right, and a look round both engines showed that they, too, were undamaged; but the stop blocks were a sorry sight, as both fishplates were broken, the wooden beam of the block was a mass of firewood, and we had shifted the whole lot forward about three feet.

We backed down the yard on to our train, leaving the mess for the platelayers to clear up, then carried on with the business of belting away up towards Upton.

Although late away by about half an hour over the stop block incident, we made good time, and with only a little station work at Newbury we left early and got as far as Whitchurch before meeting the stopper and changing over. We had a normal run back, arriving in the No. 1 bay platform on time. Looking over to our right we could see that while we had been away the platelayers had been busy; they had rebuilt the shattered stop block, and were putting the final coat of red paint on to the block. Our station work completed we backed right over to the Newbury bridge on the branch and waited for the road to be set for the carriage sidings. Then, after a down main fast had gone through, we made our way over the junction.

Once in the sidings the station pilot came on the back and pulled our coaches off, and we were ready for Shed.

Back up the sidings we crept, towards the stop blocks where the platelayers were packing up their tools and wiping the paint brushes. We had no vacuum, as the pipe had not been placed back on the plug when the coaches were drawn off, so Jack operated the steam brake as we drew near to the blocks. There was a loud bang from underneath the engine, and at once we both knew what had happened—the steam pipe had broken. There was no time to wind on the tender hand brake: we slammed into those stop blocks, and all the hard work of the last few hours by those platelayers was undone!

The ganger in charge was a churchman like the signalman at Burghclere who had jumped about so smartly when I had thrown that token, but he did not swear until Jack made an undiplomatic remark when we were examining the damage we had caused. All that Jack had said was that we were the only engine at Didcot that had two nice red buffers! The paint was still wet, and the buffers did look smart with a shiny coat of paint on them, but that statement was the straw that broke the camel's back. The Ganger used words that he thought he had forgotten: Jack and I agreed afterwards that he must have spent his youth in the Navy, and in foreign ports!

Looking back on it now, I can see he had good reason to swear. It had been a dirty wet morning, and we hadn't helped matters by knocking down his stop blocks. It should have been done in the afternoon for then he would have been paid overtime for the repair, which would have made the job sweeter!

The rest of the week went off as it should with no incidents. Then we found that we would be back on the Branch the next week, as we were booked relief for the Southampton supply trains.

At 11.00am on the Monday morning we relieved a Long Marston to Eastleigh in the up gully. The engine was 2818, now preserved in the Bristol City Museum. She was one of the originals without the outside steam pipes, having been built in 1905 and somehow escaped some of the modifications that had been applied to a lot of the "Twenty Eights". She was in fine fettle, just out of Swindon Shops after a heavy overhaul. We used to refer to the type of repair she had undergone as 'soled and heeled'. The repairs carried out at Swindon were major, so the engine was as good as new, except that no paint-work was renewed, the smokebox and chimney only receiving a coat of black paint.

We pulled out of the gully and across the junction without any trouble with a full load of 46 number ones, all open coal wagons full of jerry cans filled with petrol. Jack put his left foot on the large bolt that comes right through the reverser quadrant and pulled back on the great reversing lever to notch her up, but she was so tight on the valves that he had to shut off before he could move the lever. It was a good sign, she was steam tight everywhere. The exhaust injector began to sing with a sweetness that was a joy to listen to as I put it on to maintain the boiler. I fired her for about a mile, then sat down on the seat to enjoy the view.

We went spanking up the bank towards Upton. It was going to be one of those perfect days. Little did we know what was in store for us before we reached Compton.

We were halfway up the bank when we ran into a sudden rain shower. Our "Twenty Eight" picked up her heels and slipped; Jack shut off at once, then opened her up again. She slipped, again Jack shut off, then opened her up, and again she slipped. The regulator was tight so Jack had to use both hands, but try as he could he found it impossible to get her to hold the road. The exhaust injector blew out with the regulator being opened and shut, so I closed it and gave Jack a hand. As he opened her up, I worked the sand levers, but nothing would stop her slipping. It looked as if we would have to stop and part the train, and go to Compton with the front portion, then return for the rear on a Guard's wrong line order form, but there must be an answer to this persistent slipping, so I climbed down the foot-steps and had a look as Jack worked the sand levers. There was no sand on the rails.

I climbed back onto the running plate, then worked my way along the frame to the sand boxes, lifted the lid of the left-hand side box and found it full of wet sand. The right hand side was in the same condition; no wonder we couldn't stop slipping.

Our speed had now dropped to walking pace. It was touch and go. With only half a mile to the top of the bank, Jack had closed right down; we had stopped slipping, but as soon as he tried to give her a bit more steam she would pick up her heels again.

I gave her a good dozen shovelfuls of coal to keep her firebox up. Then we thought we would try just one more thing to help her to the top. I climbed down with the shovel in my hand, ran ahead of her and started to shovel earth, ballast, chippings, and anything else that was handy, scattering it all over the rails in front of her. She followed me along, scrunching the rubbish under her wheels, but she kept going. That half a mile seemed like two, but we made it. I climbed back aboard just before we reached the top; it had been a near thing. If she had been a worn out old engine I don't think we would have made it, as the boiler and fire would have needed too much attention. We had been lucky.

Jack shut off as we passed through Churn. It was a gentle drop down now to Hampstead Norris, and we had time to take a breather; the tea can went in the firebox in double quick time. That was one of the best cups of tea we had enjoyed for a long time, and a cigarette to go with it which we both felt was well-earned.

We had no more trouble with slipping. Hampstead Norris bank was dry and she sailed up, but we were very careful descending a wet rail into Whitchurch later on. It started to rain as we ran through Litchfield, so as soon as we started the drop towards Whitchurch I wound on the tender hand-brake and when I felt her start to bite I screwed it down as far as I could. Even then we began to increase speed, so Jack had to give her a whiff of vacuum to hold her back, but we made it without ending up in the road at the bottom of the bank.

We ran without any further incident to Eastleigh goods yard, then to Shed to turn; for once the Southern Control had no back-working for us and we could go home light engine.

It was the first time we had been on Eastleigh Shed with an engine, although Jack had had a look round when he was learning the road. The planning of the Shed was first class. There was no need to go on the table as a triangle had been provided, so we used it, pulling up behind three Southern engines at the Shed signal.

I say signal, but in fact it was a ground dummy. There was no telephone to the signal box but instead a route indicator let the signalman know where the departing engine was to go.

This was a new procedure to me, so I went forward to see the Southern Fireman operate it and explain it to me. I found it a simple and straightforward piece of equipment to use and thought that it could be of some advantage on our Sheds: in fact, it was a bit of a shock to find another railway with something better than the Great Western! I knew we had the best locomotives, but this really was something.

The indicator was in a large box. When the door was opened you were confronted by a clock with one hand. Instead of numbers the positions on the clock face showed the lines on which you could go, such as "up main", "up platform", and so on, all round the clock face. On the outside of the clock all round the rim and opposite the names on the face were small levers, all in the locked position except one, and that would be where the preceding engine had gone.

The drill now was to pull back the lever that was out, watch the hand go round the clock face, then push the lever opposite the line indicated where one wanted to go. This would be repeated on a duplicate clock in the signal box, so the signalman would know exactly where one engine at the Shed was bound for without calling him to a telephone.

The only snag I could see was that although both signalman and enginemen knew where they were heading, one dummy coming off took one to any of a dozen routes; you could come off Shed right into the path of a down express tearing through Eastleigh Station, or so it seemed, then at the last minute turn away on another line, but there was a moment of doubt when one wondered if a slip-up had been made.

Who would have thought when we left Eastleigh Shed that day on 2818 that nearly thirty years later she would be the one "Twenty Eight" chosen for preservation, and that she would return to Eastleigh for overhaul! From photographs I have seen of her since preservation they made a good job of her at Eastleigh. I am not surprised, for they are a grand lot of lads on the Southern, and on the next trip down I found that to be true.

Jack was off sick, and I had an Eastleigh trip with another Driver. This time we had one of the big American engines, Number 2573, the same number as a Dean goods engine we had at Didcot, but what a difference in engines! We had a good run down to Eastleigh Yard, then orders to take the engine to Shed, leave her there and return home.

My Mate had relations living in Southampton, so he went off to visit them, leaving me to make my own way home. It was an opportunity not to be missed. Here was a Great Western Fireman, for once with time on his hands on a large Southern Shed, and in those days Eastleigh Shed was full of every type of locomotive they had.

I knew if I just wandered round on my own I should soon be spotted, so to avoid any trouble I reported to the Shed Foreman and explained the circumstances to him. I told him how we on the Great Western had the "Remembrance" Class, and what fine engines I thought they were, and how much I would like to look round the Shed.

That Foreman was kindness itself; he gave me a free hand to go where I liked. The obvious first choice was to the "Merchant Navy" class *Channel Packet* being prepared for the road. She was a beautiful locomotive, even if the Fireman did refer to her as a 'spam can' but he was proud of her, even as I was proud of our "Kings" and "Castles".

The two parts about her I did like were the electric lights in the cab and the steam pedal for operating the firebox doors, but I could not work the pedal with comfort when trying my hand with the shovel, for the engine was left-hand drive, which to a Western Fireman used to right-hand drive meant firing 'cockie handed' or about-face. But what a firebox, it looked big enough to steam the Queen Mary!

One part of her I should have to remember to tell my Mate about, was the absence of a flare lamp. The Southern Driver took round with him an electric inspection lamp, and simply plugged it into points on the frame. I should have liked the chance to fire her on the road, but it was not to be. After a good look round I reported to the Shed Foreman again and thanked him for giving me the chance to look round his Shed.

He walked with me to the top of the Shed, and in our conversation he pointed to a sand bin in the corner of the Shed. It was kept there usually full of sand to deal with incendiary bombs. He told me that a few weeks previously he had been caught outside the shelter during a heavy raid, and he had dived into that sand bin for protection. The funny part about it was that he was on the large side and the bin was not all that big, and he had since tried to get into it again but without success; such is the incentive for self-preservation.

I made my way home with much to think on, but nothing would shake my faith in the Great Western engine. We might not have steam-operated firebox doors or electric lights in the cabs, but we had the best engines.

Like all railways in wartime, we were grossly overloaded, but we managed to deal with whatever came our way. I used to marvel at the way the 43XX Class would handle a heavy goods train. Had Mr. Churchward allowed for this kind of work when he first designed them, or was it one up his sleeve for future requirements? The early built ones were unchanged when I had to work on them. We had three allocated at Didcot 4326, 5379, and 6397. They were kept in good condition by the Shed fitters, but 4326 was an outstanding engine.

The "Forty-Threes" we had on the road were not quite so good. They were not only 'common users' but were on the road for long periods without the care and attention they should have had. If any one of our three was missing, Bill Young would soon make enquiries round the Division to get it back.

Pulling out of the up gully at Didcot East Junction or from the west curve across Foxhall Junction were the places to see their brute power at work. As each cylinder took a charge of steam they would rock from side to side, for all the world like a ship rolling in heavy seas, but once they had got their teeth into the load and it was possible to link up a bit they would start to run. Like all the Great Western engines, on a firebox of good Welsh steam coal to bite on they would perform prodigiously, moving tons over the limit.

The end of February 1944 came, and with it my association with Jack. He was moving back into Number Four Link, which would give him a few more weekends to get home. I should miss him as I had missed all my Drivers when it was time to part.

A Driver and Fireman work very much as a team, each depending on each other and I had been very lucky, all of my Mates were good chaps. So who should I fall in with next? I knew I should have a short period spare. I never did find out how it worked, but there was never a clean change-over for the Fireman, he always kicked about the Shed on his own for a couple of weeks, but this time I was in for a surprise. I followed the duty sheet down the list of names to see who or where I was booked for the next week, and when I found my name I could hardly believe my eyes, "1.45am Thatcham, Engine 6106. Driver: H.G. Gasson. Fireman: H.H. Gasson". I was to fire to the 'Old Chap' for a week! To see 6106 in Didcot Shed now, beautifully preserved by the lads of the Great Western Society, brings back many happy memories, not only because I worked on her with my father for a week, but because also I have worked her for thousands of miles. She is truly a Didcot engine, home where she belongs and in steam, not cold and silent in a museum gathering dust along with *Lode Star* and *City of Truro*.

The duty was a nice little round trip; leave Didcot yard for Thatcham paper mills, put off the wagons in the mill yard, then on to Newbury with the rest of the train; this dispensed with we would run down to Newbury race course, stand on the blocks over the turn-table until 8.00am, return to Newbury Town station, run a fast passenger train to Reading, then back to Didcot with a stopping passenger train.

On the outward journey we were routed up main line to Reading West Junction, then round on the Berks and Hants Line, so we could go sailing past the sluggards puffing away on the up relief.

The 'Old Chap's' policy was to drive only one way. He not only liked to keep his hand in with the shovel, but he used to say that if a Fireman was to become a Driver then the only way to learn was to let him drive. I soon found that he meant it.

We walked down the road to the Shed together not saying much. I think he was a little bit excited, as I was, at the thought of father and son working together. We prepared 6106 inside the Shed, then pulled outside and filled her tank.

I had cleared out all the large lumps of coal in the bunker in making up the fire, and had broken up the rest into small pieces so that it would pass through the hole in the cab. There is nothing more awkward when on the run with a tank engine than to find one's firing impeded by a large lump of coal jammed in the hole. There isn't room to swing a coal pick, and while one is poking, prodding, levering, and swearing to clear the obstruction, the fire and boiler are getting lower and lower.

We washed hands, made our can of tea, and then Father informed me that I was the Driver on the outward trip, and to show that he meant it he handed me his pocket watch, note book, and train journal. If I was going to drive then that did not mean just lift the regulator, it meant doing the lot. I was also informed that the big lever on the right hand side was not just for going forward and backward, it was put there to shorten the travel of the valves, and if he had to shovel more coal than was necessary

then I would get a wet shirt when it was my turn to swing the shovel. Point taken.

We pulled out of the yard, across the junction and on to the up main line; I started to pull the lever back a bit at a time until she was on the last notch and almost in mid-gear. The 'Old Chap' looked up at me with a grin, and reminded me that I had a pocket watch and a note book, and it was time to get the pencil out and use it. I had forgotten all about booking. We swept along with the regulator just open until I sighted Scours Lane

Distant on, then it was a case of shut off, lever into the 45 notch and let her run so that we took the Junction at just the right speed; then, as we passed over the Oxford road bridge, open her out again and on to Thatcham and Newbury. We detached our half-dozen wagons in the yard, carried on to Newbury Town yard, then light engine to the race course for our breakfast. Father would be the Driver on the passenger work, and a good job too for I don't think I would have had the confidence to run 6106 to Reading like he did. That engine will run with the speed of a "Castle", but it is not the fast running so much as stopping at the other end, and that is what the skill of handling a steam locomotive is all about.

We ran into Reading No. 1 bay dead on time, but our lady passenger guard made a point of informing us we were half a minute late. Father looked down at her from the height of the cab, tilted his cap over his eyes, and in all seriousness told her that we had miscalculated the wind resistance of the two headlamps we carried on the front buffer beam! She strode up the platform quite satisfied with the explanation.

It was a wonderful week and one I shall never forget, and I found the answer to something that had puzzled me for a long time. As a small boy I had owned an air pistol, and with the aptitude of small boys I had become somewhat of an expert shot with it. Our garden backed on to the gardens of the houses on the other side of the block, and one day a neighbour was in his garden at the bottom of ours doing some weeding. The sight of that big backside was a temptation too great to bear; as he bent down I let fire from my bedroom window. He gave a yelp, put both hands on his backside, and looked round for the culprit. I was down under the window frame. The day afterwards my air pistol disappeared, never to be seen again, and I was wise enough not to make any enquiries about it. It was on the last trip with Dad and we were rattling along over the river bridge just east of Cholsey station when he came over to me and asked me if I remembered owning an air pistol. When I nodded my head he pointed to the river and told me that was where it had ended up. The 'Old Chap' had taken it to work and tossed it over the side. I gave him a grin and said it was better than having my block knocked off.

The next week my new Mate came into the picture, and with all respect to the other Mates I had worked with, Ted Hurle was the greatest man next to my Father. We hit it off right from the start; I was to have a wonderful time with him. Dear old Ted, who gave so much pleasure with his company, and who passed away the day after he had retired.

Chapter Six

Ted had come up from Llanelli Shed to Didcot but he was not a Welsh lad, having started out from the small village of Edington and Bratton, just outside Westbury; after service life in the Great War he had settled down in Wales and joined the Great Western.

Most of his firing had been on the 43XX Class, or the 52XX and 72XX Tanks; it used to grieve him to see how we carried on with the two big tank engines, but we were the victims of circumstance, and with every chance of there being hours between any water supply we had to take drastic measures to ensure we were full.

The 52XX Class had a capacity for 1,800 gallons in the tanks, the 72XX Class a little more with 2,500 gallons, but both were far short of the 3,500 to 4,000 gallons we were used to, plus the fact that with the tank engines we could not top up on the water troughs, so when we filled up we also filled the boiler.

We would fill those tanks to the last quarter of a pint, but the boiler, (I look back on it now and shudder), was filled so full that it was a wonder that the cylinder ends were not blown off. Those pistons could no longer be propelled by steam, we must have been working on the hydraulic principle! The problem then arose on the first movement, and on no account could the engine be allowed to blow off or else she would blow water to the moon! The regulator had to be opened so carefully that she crept forward with just enough power to move until the water level in the boiler had dropped. This was the time for the piece of chalk to come in handy—no self-respecting Fireman was without a piece of chalk in his pocket to be used on the water feed.

When the injector was put on the water feed handle was pulled open and the live injector handle turned on, then the water feed handle was tapped back towards the stop, while an eye was kept on the overflow pipe under the foot steps until any surplus water stopped running. The injector was then taking all the water, so we would place a chalk mark on the feed handle and also on the supporting bracket, then the next time the injector was used the feed handle would be opened only to the chalk mark. We not only saved a lot of water, but at night time it saved hanging over the side with a torch or the gauge lamp to watch the overflow.

We arrived at a sensible arrangement with these big tank engines. I would open the water feed to the chalk mark and Ted would give the live steam handle a turn, so we used every drop without waste.

If ever there was a man with a sense of humour it was Ted; he could laugh when other men would have given up in despair. One of his favourite parts of the Division was between Didcot and Reading, particularly when we had a "Forty Three" Class engine with the open cab. Ted, like my 'Old Chap', thought that the Fireman should take a spell on the regulator, so we would start off up relief to Reading and by the time we had reached Moreton we would be spanking along. This would be where Ted could start to enjoy himself. He would look back towards the up main line waiting for the first express to show, then as the train drew near he would go into action. With our train running at 45mph and the express at 70mph there would be several minutes where we would be running side by side.

In those days the corridors of the coaches would be packed, and passengers would watch with interest the working of the engine running along with them. Ted would go up into the corner of the cab, remove his cap, and place on his head a large coloured handkerchief knotted in each corner; he would then take out his teeth and place them in his pocket. He was now ready to perform. He would pick up the shovel and get stuck in, firing her with a great show of exhausting labour, then he would slide the shovel into the coal, stagger over to my side, place one hand on my shoulder and the other hand on the water scoop handle for support and start panting. Then he would remove the head-gear revealing a large expanse of skin, wipe off the perspiration, pick up the shovel and start firing again. I would be sitting on the seat all this time, with my arms folded and a very stern look on my face, and the second time he stopped firing and staggered over for another breather I would pick up the shovel, place it in his hand, and make gestures to him to get on with it.

The passengers in the corridor would be looking at me with loathing. That poor old man having to work like that while the young one sat there and watched him. When the train had passed us Ted would give a grin and say, "That's given the buggers something to think about!" I used to think that one day someone would write to the Management about old men being exploited, but nobody wrote to the 'Times'. If they had done so Ted would have been delighted. One day, after this performance, a very large sailor dropped down the window and started hurling abuse. Ted opened his mouth and showed the sailor a row of pink gums in a caricature of a grin, so I took off my cap and cuffed him with it!

The sailor nearly went mad with rage. I thought we had perhaps gone too far with our joke, but we heard nothing more of it. Ted, however, could not stop laughing; I only had to take my cap off and make out that he was going to be cuffed again to start him off!

He used to tell me about his mate in the trenches during the Great War. They had gone through the lot together, but had lost touch over the years. Ted knew that his mate had joined the Great Western but did not know where, but when he told me his name I knew where he was; it was one up my sleeve to give Ted a surprise in a few weeks' time. This old mate of

Ted's was a Driver at Winchester, named Tommie Keoghon. In a couple of weeks we would be working on the Branch, and I had worked it out that when we were working the 3.35pm Didcot to Winchester passenger we would change over trains with the Winchester goods on the Branch somewhere, and the Driver would be Tommie Keoghan.

Ted hadn't bothered to learn the road to Southampton, as he knew I had worked every inch of the line and knew it backwards; it was nice to know he had that much confidence in me. It was worth holding on to that bit of information to see those two old mates meet again after so many years. We ran into Burghclere to stop opposite the engine on the Winchester goods; it was just a matter of stepping over the space between the two engines. Ted looked over and saw Tommie at the same time as Tommie saw Ted. They just stood there for a moment not saying anything, then the penny dropped, there was a whoop of delight from both of them, they hugged one another, danced the footplate in each other's arms, and completely ignored the whistles and flag-waving of the Guard. There was so much to say and no time to say it, but it was Monday afternoon and we would change over each day for the rest of the week so there was plenty of time to make arrangements for the future. Ted really appreciated that surprise, but the pleasure was mine also. I had a Mate I would do anything for; we were a good team.

The Southampton supply trains really came into their own now, so hardly a day went by without our being on the Branch. The engine power was the good old "Twenty-Eight" or "Thirty-Eight", the American Transportation Corps engines, or the L.M.S. "8F"which proved to be a very good locomotive. The latter were all numbered from 8400 and bore a small plate on the frame which read 'Built Swindon', so that was something even if the tender proclaimed L.M.S.

We would run out of Winchester Chesil station and over Shawford viaduct to see on the Winchester by-pass the largest collection of armoured vehicles ever known. There were tanks, self-propelled guns, and amphibious 'Ducks' nose to tail as far as could be seen, and on each side of the by-pass the tents and supplies for this great Army.

We carried every kind of weapon, from boxes of small arms ammunition to large calibre shells and depth charges, all in open wagons, and to look back along the train to see some of those shells, nose up, oscillating with the motion of the wagons made one wonder if we would ever arrive without the whole lot going up with a bang.

On one of those trips we arrived in Southampton Old Docks behind the Ocean Terminal building late in the evening, and just in time to coincide with an air raid.

We left our train in the sidings, but before we could make our way out of the docks the German airmen very unkindly blew a great hole in the rails. Ted and I spent the night under the tender watching the biggest bonfire we had ever seen as the dock buildings burnt down; then when it was all over we had to wait until the hole had been filled in and the track repaired before we could leave. We were on duty for 36 hours on that trip.

The run into Millbrook Docks had its hazards also, not so much going in as coming out. We would come through Southampton Central station, through the tunnel, and head for Eastleigh and home. Just outside the tunnel, however, was a brick retaining-wall so close to the cab that it was unwise to stick one's head out. At the top of this wall were some houses with very small back yards. They must have been small, because one lady living there would empty her tea pot over the wall and down onto the line.

She did just that one day, and as I was in the tender pulling some coal forward I had the contents of her tea pot right down my neck! Ted roared.

The old saying of he who laughs last laughs longest was to be very true. We had a train of empties on the return journey so were routed to Winchester Junction and over the new single line connection to Worthy Down and on to the Branch again.

We made signs of drinking when passing Whitchurch Box to let the signalman know that we were stopping at the end of the passing loop for water; not that we really required water, but at the bottom of the embankment was a smallholding, and the other lads in the link had told us that it was possible to obtain eggs and tomatoes there.

I climbed onto the tender and pulled the water column round—we might as well top up as we had stopped. Ted slithered down the embankment and through the wire fence. I watched him walk up a gravel path and disappear between two greenhouses. He had hardly gone out of sight when he reappeared, running back towards the fence, and behind him came a large black Labrador dog going like a greyhound! His tail was out straight, and a row of white teeth could be seen under his curled-up top lip, he was grinning in the excitement of the chase. Ted reached the fence first, and for a small man he did a vault that would have been a credit to an Olympic competitor, one hand on the top wire and over he came.

I sat on the seat helpless with laughter. One emptied tea pot was worth seeing Ted clear that fence! We both agreed to keep quiet about the incident, as it was obvious that we were victims of the old 'con trick'.

After the 'D-Day' landings in Normandy we were very busy running troop trains from Newbury and Sutton Scotney to Southampton Docks, returning with the empty coaches for a second and third trip before being released. Then, as the advance built up, we had train-loads of German prisoners for either Newbury or Banbury.

It was quite a shock to see some of the early captures; the black uniforms and silver braid worn by S.S. men, they did exist after all. But as time went on we took no notice of them; they began to look a scruffy lot, not a bit of 'master race' about them.

The difference in guards on these prisoner of war trains was amusing. The American trains would have armed guards patrolling the corridors, but the British trains would have one guard sitting on a kit bag at the end of the corridor, his rifle standing in the corner behind him while he read the "Daily Mirror".

As the Allied advance pushed further into France we started to run Leave Trains from Southampton, and for once we were able to indulge in some long non-stop runs. These were usually from Southampton Docks to Banbury, where we came off and the G.C. engine would take over.

Although it had been years since the Great Central had been lost in the formation of the L.N.E.R. it was still the G.C. to Western men and would remain so until British Railways came into being.

Ted and I booked on one morning in late September to prepare one of our Didcot engines, a Churchward Mogul 4326, for one of these leave trains. We collected our 10 coaches from the sidings and set off south, empty to Southampton.

We had a good run down with no need to hurry as the timing was liberal, but as usual when a good start was made we were in for one of those days where things start to happen.

As we drifted down the bank from Worthy Down a Hurricane fighter came in from the south towards us, banked over our head, and dived down on to the Naval Air Station behind and started to fire his guns. The return fire from the aerodrome was too late to hurt him, but he climbed out of his dive, banked over and came back towards us. As he passed overhead we could see that our "Hurricane" was in fact a Messerschmitt 109; he had no black cross underneath, which we thought was a bit unfair. When he made a long low sweep to the east we could see that he was turning and coming back. Ted and I both thought that if he had any ammunition left he might take a crack at us—it was time to get a move on.

Now the drop down into Kings Worthy is 1 in 106 so we were beginning to move when we sighted the signalman. He was standing on the platform with the token all ready to make a hand exchange, and expecting our speed to drop. All credit to him, he stood his ground when he saw that we were not going to slack off. I lobbed the Worthy Down token on to the post, and snatched the Winchester one out of his hand — in fact he was almost on the point of dropping it but I caught it just in time; we must have been touching 70mph. I looked back to see him bent forward against the wind pressure of our passing, then we were in the protection of the cutting. We were still way above regulation speed when we hit Winnall gas works siding; our old 4326 gave a lurch, then we were in the tunnel, the flanges of the engine wheels squealing in protest as we took the curve. Ted was braking hard, but we shot out of the tunnel and almost ran past the signal on Winchester platform.

The Winchester signalman said that he had just had time to acknowledge 'Train on Line' on his block instrument and book the time when we shot out of the tunnel. It was the quickest time ever between Kings Worthy and Winchester, but then, we had had an incentive to push that old engine along. I rang up the Kings Worthy signalman to see if he was all right. He was, of course, but a bit shaken. I see him sometimes now, and he still talks about seeing the great engine thundering towards him that morning.

The Messerschmitt 109? We never did see him again, but we both felt a bit exposed as we rounded the curve of St. Catherine's Hill and swept over the long Shawford viaduct. The Observer Corps had nothing on Ted and I as we searched the sky!

We ambled along to Millbrook Docks, uncoupled along-side a ship, ran round the coaches, coupled back up again, and waited for our American friends. It was time for a brew up. After I had poured Ted a cup we had a good omen for the return run. Ted stood his tea on the tool box to cool, where it was bombed from a great height by a seagull. The top of the tool box looked as though it had just been painted white, except for a small circle where Ted's cup had been!

Although I washed that cup out with boiling water and steam, Ted refused to drink out of it again, so we had to share my cup. It proved a point, however, as I explained to Ted—a seagull has a tighter turning circle than a Messerschmitt, but Ted's indignant answer was that it was a British seagull not a bleeding German one!

While we waited for the American troops to board, the guard and the officer in charge came up on the footplate. There was a good deal of laughter when the story of our dash for safety was told, then we pointed out a hazard on the coach behind the engine. We had no blank on the corridor. The guard said he would lock the sliding door so it would be safe enough, then they both walked back to the guard's compartment, the American officer stopping to have words with two cigar-chewing American soldiers sitting in a Jeep. They tore off into the Docks to return within a few minutes with an enamel jug of steaming coffee, 500 Camel cigarettes, and a box of biscuits. They handed it all up to us with the compliments of the captain. The situation was typical of American generosity.

We chuffed gently away from the quayside and out of the docks, round the corner where it rained tea leaves, and headed north with plenty of time. We were not booked much faster than a goods train, so it was just a question of setting the regulator and letting her take her time. I took the token at Shawford Junction by hand and again at Winchester, but when we got to Kings Worthy it was in the bracket of the pick up post. I shouted "Windy!" as we passed the signal box and received two fingers in reply. I think that the down trip had put the signalman off us somehow. It was a good run to Newbury, then we had to open up a bit as the timing was much tighter to

Banbury. It seemed no time at all and we were sweeping down from Upton and clattering over Didcot East Junction heading north to Oxford. For once we had a clear road through Oxford. Ted and I were enjoying the run, but we were both getting a bit anxious about the water. We had started out with 3,500 gallons but we should make the water troughs at Aynho all right. Every now and again the corridor door would slide back, and an American serviceman would stick his head out, then finding he could go no further the door would be shut. Our Guard had evidently forgotten to lock it, but we both forgot to check that door at Aynho—the last person had left it open.

Ted took the water troughs fast. We needed 3,000 gallons to fill the tank, and I wound down the scoop and watched the level indicator climb up the gauge; as it neared the "Full" position I started to wind the scoop back up again, but our speed was too high, and the scoop too low, and I could not budge it. We were only half-way across the troughs so we knew that we could be in for a drenching. We therefore lifted up the running plate between engine and tender, so that any water gushing out of the vents would now run down into the track. But we had forgotten about that open corridor door.

At the 3,500 gallon mark the water lifted the tender flap and it went up in the air like a Texas oil gusher. Then wind pressure caught it and drove it through the corridor door and into the first coach.

When we ran into Banbury station we had run non-stop from Southampton. I climbed down onto the platform, then down between the engine and coaches to uncouple, as the G.C. Engine was waiting to take the train on.

I did notice a little water seeping from the coach door on the platform side, then I remembered about the missing blank on the corridor end. I climbed back up onto the platform and had a look inside the first coach. Our American passengers were sitting with their feet up on the seats; there was about six inches of water all through the coach, and any article left on the floor was swamped. But worse was to follow. A hulking great American marine was sloshing his way up the corridor with an automatic rifle clenched in both hands across his chest; he was making a lot of noise, and saying how he was going to shoot those "God-dammed engineers". It was time to depart friends, and in a hurry.

A Messerschmitt on the way down, a seagull when we got there, and a blood-thirsty marine at the end; we had had enough for one day! We dropped in Banbury Shed, turned 4326, and made for Didcot light engine. It had been a long hard day.

The week after, Ted was away on his annual week's leave, but I had no respite from the Branch. I was covering a Fireman who was also on leave, working the 3.35pm stopping passenger to Winchester, changing over en route, and returning with the goods. It was a good week although I did miss Ted, except that on the Saturday I had the biggest fright of my footplate career.

We were coming back from Newbury where we had been made up to a full load. The engine was 2226 and one I had fired for many miles; she was a Didcot engine and no stranger to either of us.

It had been a bit of a struggle from Hampstead Norris up the long drag to Churn, but as soon as she stuck her smokebox downhill for Upton the work was over.

I screwed down the tender handbrake, felt the blocks begin to bite, then placed my foot on the back plate and screwed the brake down as hard as I could. It was a long drop down into Didcot and with that heavy load we would have to be on top of it right from the start.

My Mate began to give her a bit of steam brake, and with each application I was able to give another quarter of a turn on the tender brake. About a half a mile down the bank my Mate made a full application of the steam brake. She held for a moment, then a loud bang came from underneath the footplate. The steam pipe had blown out, but this time there were no stop blocks to hit as I had done with Jack Thomas the year before. As we passed under the three arch bridge it was obvious we had lost the train; she was rapidly gaining speed. We rocketed through Upton, bucking and swaying over the crossover, the tender brake blocks were glowing red, showering a stream of sparks which tumbled and swirled away under the wagons. We blasted away on the brake whistle alternating with the train whistle, a frightful, urgent, desperate sound to be lost in the thunderous roar of the run-away train.

Upton signal box was just a flash of soft light and blurred windows with the silhouette of the helpless signalman at the window. Between the starting signal and the public stile the brake whistle snapped off at the stem, hit the boiler casing, bounced down onto the frame, and rolled down the embankment.

It was time to take drastic action. My Mate wound her into reverse and gave her some steam, and her free running changed almost at once; she began to labour and groan. As he opened and shut the regulator I worked the sand levers back and forth. She was beginning to respond, her speed was falling, but we were tearing the very heart and guts out of her.

My Mate placed her in mid-gear so that she ran a little sweeter, but as we passed the distant signal for Didcot East Junction it was obvious we would not stop at the home signal. We had one more course of action to take to try and stop her mad rush to disaster; we would have to abandon her. We both climbed down on to the bottom foot step on each side of her. As I let go and hit the ground I tumbled over and over hearing the wheels of the wagons clattering past my head. I picked myself up and ran alongside the train, lifting up and dropping down the hand brakes on the wagons as they passed. Somehow, my Mate had also survived the jump and he was just ahead of me dropping down brakes on the other side.

As the brake van passed us we could see the Guard swinging into his brake with both hands, the blocks squealing in protest. But she was slowing rapidly; we had won.

We walked up the now stationary train to find the engine standing quietly near the home signal. I went to the telephone to let East Junction know that the emergency was over, then climbed back on board. My Mate would not move her with only the tender hand brake in use, so he made out a 'Wrong Line Order' form and I walked to East Junction Box with it. They were a bit shaken up in the box to receive the 4-5-5 ('Train running away on Right Line') on the block bell from Upton, but obeying Regulation 23 they had stopped all traffic until I had telephoned in. The signalman countersigned my 'Wrong Line Order' form, then I walked over to the station pilot engine with it and gave it to my old mate Jack Thomas. We went back up the wrong line, coupled up to our train engine and pulled engine and train into the yard at Didcot North, then 2226 was drawn back to the Shed.

Both my Mate and I were shaken up. I could not stop shivering, but a hot cup of tea in the engineman's cabin with a Woodbine soon had me feeling better. It had been a nasty half an hour and not one I should want again, although had it been in the daylight it may not have seemed so bad. Standing on the bottom footstep and then letting go had been the worst bit.

The next day we booked on for the same job, changed over trains again at Burghclere with the Winchester men and onto 2226 again. The return load was not so heavy, but when we stuck her nose down that bank at Churn it was with some misgiving; we both had our fingers crossed when we applied the brakes, but this time it was all right; it always is, but there is one time at least in every engineman's life when the moment of truth comes. You win some and lose some, and we had been lucky.

The Newbury line is now lifted, only the earthworks remain, but somewhere down the embankment past the position of the old distant signal is the brake whistle from 2226. I know to within 200 yards where it should be, and if circumstances allow it I shall return one day with a metal detector and find it. Polished up and mounted on an oak stand it will remind me of a day in the life of a Didcot Fireman.

Ted returned from his holiday and was most upset to hear of the runaway incident. He said that he couldn't leave me for just a week without me getting into trouble, but he knew what a runaway is like, as he had experienced one a few years before when he was firing. A 52XX Tank with a full load of coal wagons had got the better of him and his Mate, and they had landed up on their side at the end of a sand drag, with three wagons in the street below.

Before the winter set in, however, we were to have three wonderful runs. The first one started out innocently enough—we ran a battered old

43XX Mogul to Swindon for shopping, then reported to Control for orders.

There was a derailment at Chippenham, and an empty coaching stock train for Westbury on the way from Gloucester to be run via Reading West and Newbury. We were ordered to relieve and proceed.

The train ran up the middle road and stopped. We licked our lips in anticipation—ten coaches and at the head 4045 *Prince John.*

The "Twenty Nines", "Forties", "Castles", and "Kings" were the only locomotives fitted with a speedometer, so we enjoyed our occasional run on them for the pleasure of that one instrument, and it was one of those days that Ted and I enjoyed; we were both in the right mood to have a go. Thank God the powers-that-be turned a blind eye now and again. It was not often we had our hands on a main line "Forty" in 'good nick', and she was in perfect condition, nicely warmed through from her run from Gloucester.

Ted eased her away, letting her take her time to build up speed, and as we passed under Stratton Park bridge she began to take on that long, easy stride of the greyhound she was. The speedo began to wave back and forth 30, 35, 40, 45. I put on the exhaust injector and began to fire her, the exhaust turning colour with each shovel-full, the distinctive pungent aroma of good Welsh steam coal burning drifted back into the cab, and the pressure stood still at 225lbs, with just a wisp of steam from the safety valve.

At Shrivenham she began to run, Ted had set the regulator with the second valve just open and cut off at 30%. He wound her back half a turn to 25% and snapped down the reverser clip. It was now a case of letting her run, but run is not the right word, for she began to fly, speed climbing slowly from 70 to 75 mph. Between Uffington and Challow she touched 80, and the 'ton' was in sight. We slipped through Challow station so fast it was like the passing of the wind. We were in trouble now, as speed was far in excess of wartime running, but we had to get away with it. Mr. Churchward would have understood; it was as if he was there with us, as she kept climbing until the speedo wavered between 85 and 90mph. I had both hands on Ted's shoulders watching that needle, and it was with surprise that I saw him reach over and shut off. We were through Steventon and running too fast to go through Didcot without someone reporting us, and it was time to drop down.

We had all the distants off through Didcot, but Ted let her run to Moreton before opening her up again. We ran at a steady 60mph until he shut off at Scours Lane, then we drifted sedately round the corner at Reading West and headed towards Newbury.

I began to fire her more frequently now. She needed more to bite on for the drag up to Savernake, but Ted did not punch her for she was a lady even if the name-plate was masculine. I topped up the water on Aldermaston troughs as she settled down to a steady 60mph then sat down as tar as Newbury to enjoy the running.

We swept majestically through Newbury middle road, and at Enbourne Junction we gave the signalman a toot on the whistle; for once, we were not turning left for Winchester.

At Bedwyn I fired her for the last time, for she would go to Shed at Westbury, and fire droppers do not appreciate a firebox full of glowing coal. As Ted shut off at Savernake, I closed the exhaust injector, opened the firebox doors and sat down. I could now enjoy the long sweep down through the Wiltshire countryside.

Ted came over to my side as we ran down through Edington and Bratton, pointing out places he had known as a boy. It was a scene worthy of a painter, the green of the fields, the russet colour of the trees, and this beautiful green and copper-topped locomotive gliding down, a blue haze just visible from her chimney, a feather of steam whisking away from her golden safety valve, and the quiet echo of her vacuum pump slapping away. We could have gone on for ever, enjoying the sheer beauty of that moment. If ever there was a heaven for enginemen then this surely must have been it.

Regretfully we climbed down from her at Westbury. For a short time she had not been a Great Western-owned engine but was ours, and she had given us a gift that would remain forever, long after the passing of steam; she had given us perfection between man and machine.

We had for once enjoyed a high speed run, even if it was only for a short distance. That 90mph between Challow and Steventon would never be recorded except in our memories, and we would never again have the same chance. For one brief moment of time we had experienced immortality. The sedate pace at 60 for the remainder of the run was just routine running.

We did the next year run 2915 *Saint Bartholomew* up to 95mph but that was 'light engine' and she was so rough on her boxes that it was impossible to fire her after she had reached 75mph so we never did touch the 'ton'.

Early November was to see Ted and myself engaged in another run of some distinction—distinctive to a couple of goods men anyway. We booked on duty at 8.00pm, relieved the crew of the 1.15am Aberdare to Old Oak Common at Didcot West Box and set off in fits and starts for London. Our engine was 3822, and she had been on the road for 19 hours so was past her best. However no running was required, as the fog was so thick we could not see her chimney and it was just a question of "keep moving". We crept from signal to signal all the way to Reading, with distants on and the A.T.C. buzzer sounding each time we hit the ramp. It was a miserable journey, both of us were chilled through from leaning out of the cab to find the home signals, and neither of us were looking forward to the approach to Old Oak Common. The country fog we could bear with, but London fog was another matter; it was so thick and clammy you could almost walk on it. How the Old Oak men could put up with it I could never understand, but thank heaven for A.T.C., at least we could run with confidence when the distants were off and the bell was ringing in the cab.

At Reading goods yard we topped up the tank, as speed over Goring troughs had been too low to pick up water, but that short stop gave the train in front of us a chance to get away. We pulled up through the station and received our first bell with Twyford distant off; it was to be a clear run to Slough, then we caught up with that train and the pattern was repeated until we pulled into Acton Yard. It was 4.00am, we were tired out, eyes red-rimmed with the constant searching for signals. We left the train and groped our way on to the ash pit at Old Oak Common Shed, then climbed down from 3822 and made for the warmth of the enginemen's cabin. It was time for a cup of tea and a chance to relax for a while. When the Shift Foreman came in we reported to him, and as we had been on duty for eight hours he told us to make our way home. We walked over to the carriage sidings and caught a lift to Paddington in a train of coaches, arriving just in time to catch the 5.30am. As we walked up towards the engine we saw the Fireman climb down holding his hand, and from the look on his face he was not too happy. As we drew near we could see why, the blood was dripping through his fingers onto the platform. He told me he had crushed his thumb when the tool box lid had slammed down on it. I told him to go and get some attention to his injured hand, and to inform the Locomotive Inspector that the Didcot Fireman would see the train through to Swindon.

Looking over his shoulder I could see the number of the engine — 6000 *King George V*. Didcot men never had the chance to work a "King" for they were all stationed at Old Oak Common, Wolverhampton, and Laira, and as tired as I was I did not intend to miss this chance if the Driver would take me.

Ted had never been on a "King" either, so we both climbed aboard, and with departure time one minute away the Driver was most pleased to see us. I can remember that his name was also Ted, and that he was a very small man, in fact when he sat on the tip-up seat his feet dangled underneath. So we had on the footplate two small Drivers to one very large engine, with a tall lanky Fireman in between.

Ted looked back along the train to catch the 'right away' from the station staff, while I placed the shovel in the firebox to deflect the smoke and gasses so that I could examine the fire. *King George V* had a perfect fire prepared by an expert. Boiler pressure was just below blowing off at 250lbs and the gauge glass was full; she was as ready to receive the attentions of a country boy as she would ever be. I looked into that great 11 ft.6 inches of firebox, and began to wonder if I should ever ring the bell on the front framing.

There is a story about ringing that bell. It has been suggested that if a Fireman could throw the coal hard enough to reach the front end of the Firebox it would ring the bell, and to some extent this story was true, but

VI

only for the benefit of young Cleaners and Apprentices at Swindon Works. They would be victims of a leg pull. The bell would be rigged, a long length of string being tied between the clapper and the damper handles, passing along the framing into the cab. A Cleaner or an Apprentice would then be invited to try his luck in throwing a shovel-full of coal up against the front end of the firebox, but try as they could they would not be able to ring the bell. Then of course the Fireman would show them how to do it; he would loop his left foot through the string, then as he swung round to place his shot up the front end, his movement was to get the audience to watch the coal going in the clang just as the coal hit the firebox front. The object during this movement was to get the audience to watch the coal going in the firebox so that they could see for themselves that there was no dirty work afoot, just as long as they didn't see that length of string. I wonder if the lads at Hereford have ever tried it now that they have *King George V* in their care.

Dead on time at 5.30am my Ted gave Ted No. 2 the 'right away'. I looked up from the firebox and saw that we were in the presence of a 'master'. Ted No. 2 was a "King" Driver all right; he had donned a dirty old black beret, and placed over his eyes a pair of motor cycle goggles, then he lifted the regulator up about two inches, and *King George V* glided out of Paddington as if she was powered by electric.

I walked over to my Ted, placed one hand on his shoulder and had a look out. I could see along a massive boiler, long and fat-looking after our usual nondescript "Forty Threes" and "Twenty Eights", and on top of this great boiler was a squat chimney exhausting with a crisp sharp bark so characteristic of the Great Western engines; then we were into the fog.

Fog, I had forgotten all about it in the excitement of climbing up on 6000, I would not have much time to worry about it, for I would be far too busy. The A.T.C. bell began to ring with regularity, Ted No. 2 gave her a bit more 'stick' and began to link her up, I put on the exhaust injector which picked up with that sweet familiar singing, and got down to the serious business of firing this famous "King".

My Ted stood up in the corner out of the way, now and again nodding his head for me to look over at Ted No.2. He sat there swinging his feet under him, head stuck just round the corner of the cab, completely unconcerned with the fact that we were hustling along best part of 600 tons in a fog so thick it was like a solid wall, and on board with him were two men who had never been on a "King" before.

I fired her just the same as the "Castles", "Halls", "Granges", and "Manors"; under the firebox door, with the back corners packed tight, then straight down the middle. And she responded, holding pressure at 240lbs with the exhaust injector on, until we were passing through Slough, when she began to drop back a bit. I placed the shovel in the firebox and with the deflection I could see a hole in the fire on the right and left hand side

89

of the firebox about half way up. I quickly filled both holes then looked round for the reason. The back damper and back middle damper were open as they should be, but the front middle had worked open, as it was not pegged down on the ratchet. This was attended to by wedging it shut with a piece of slate I had found in the coal. No more trouble from that quarter. She soon came round to 240lbs again.

When the buzzer on the A.T.C. went off as we hit the ramp for Reading East Main it came as a bit of a shock. I had been so busy and so full of the novelty of firing *King George V* that I had no idea we were so close to Reading. With the nonchalance of the top engineman he was, Ted No. 2 eased himself off his seat, cancelled the buzzer and quietly closed the regulator all in one unhurried movement. He knocked down the reverser clip, wound her forward to the 45% cut off mark, let her run a few minutes, then gave the vacuum brake a short sharp burst. As the vacuum pump pushed the twin needles up again, he would give her another short burst. We dropped down in speed so gently one would have thought it was a clear summer day with visibility perfect. Then we were coasting into Reading down main platform with the fog swirling in behind us; one more application of the brake, this time a long one, and we were at a stand, dead on time.

He had a look in the firebox, patted me on the shoulder, then shut off the steam-heating to the coaches. All the slight leaks in the system on the train slowly disappeared and we could now see well back along the platform. Ted No.2 opened up the large ejector and blew off the brakes ready to leave, while my Ted gave me a Woodbine, pushed me up into the corner, and told me to stand well back; he didn't see why I should have all the fun, for he wanted to try his hand in firing a "King".

Whistles blew and green lights waved from back along the platform, so we gave a toot on our whistle and were off again.

Ted No.2 gave me a wink, and pointed at my Ted with the shovel in hand, then he opened up *King George V* full regulator and blasted her out of Reading.

The blast from the firebox was so fierce when my Ted bent down that he had to make a grab at his cap. Between Reading West Main and Scours Lane Ted No.2 was still hammering her, and my Ted was shovelling as fast as he could and looking very unhappy.

Ted No.2 eased her down and wound the reverser back to 25% cut off, then he burst out laughing. It had been an incident he couldn't resist, one Driver taking the 'micky' out of another Driver, but in the nicest possible way. He had my Ted worried for a moment.

Ted enjoyed the firing as much as I had, but it was not all over yet, and as he was busy I wound down the scoop at Goring and filled the tank, then stood behind Ted No.2 to watch *King George V* at work.

The speedo stood at 60mph as if it was fixed in that position, without any alteration to the regulator or cut off. It was an example of controlled precision running that was the hall-mark of an ace engineman. This remarkable man just sat there with his arms folded, legs swinging, peering round the side of the cab. He would come back inside every now and again, pull out a battered old tin, roll a cigarette as thin as a matchstick, light it, then stick his head out of the cab again. Not once did he alter the setting, not once did he consult his watch, yet when we ran into Didcot we came to a stand again dead on right time.

Going up in the early hours Ted and I had been chilled through, but Ted was now glad to wipe his brow; free-steaming as that engine was, she still needed a lot of work to keep her going.

I handed Ted his jacket and picked up the shovel, only to have it taken out of my hand by Ted No.2, while my Ted was gently led over to the Driver's side and told to get on with it.

The grin on his face went from ear to ear. I had fired her, Ted had fired her, and now he was invited to drive her. And drive her he did, with all the aplomb of the other Ted. If my Ted had been a regular "King" Driver, he would have been a cracker of a main line express man. The way he handled that engine was a joy to behold, and Ted No.2 was his equal with the shovel. All together, for the three of us, it was a trip we shall never forget; we parted at Swindon, making promises to write and get together again, but we never did. He did seek out Bert Edmonds and tell him that his nephew at Didcot had now got the rudiments of boiling water!

We all had a cup of tea after being relieved, and travelled back up to Didcot as passengers, leaving Ted No.2 to carry on to Bristol. We would sometimes see him when on the road, and when that encounter took place the blast on the whistles would send the cows in the fields running.

That run was an example of Great Western locomotive comradeship, with each man ready to help out in an emergency, and the world was a better place for it. The end of steam was the end of a special relationship. How can a diesel engine compare with the living beauty of steam?

The third run to remember came in the first week of December, and was quite the opposite to the two main line runs. We had a bad outbreak of flu at Didcot Shed, so Ted and I found ourselves covering a passenger link duty together, on the 7.37am Didcot to Southampton. On Monday and Tuesday we had Collett 2222 as motive power, and expected to have her all the week, but fate took a hand in our lives, plus the sentimentality of Bill Young the Shed Foreman. We were both walking away from the Shed between the coal stage and the carriage sidings, making our way home, when I glanced over towards the ash road. There was the usual collection of locomotives waiting for their fire to be dropped, but I could see a "Bulldog" half hidden under the banking and half of a word on her nameplate. All I could see was '*lark*' but it was enough, Ted and I were round that banking in a flash, and there she stood, 3454 *Skylark* of my boyhood days.

She was not in the pristine condition of pre-war days, showing some signs of wear and age, but she was still the same old *Skylark*.

Ted knew of my affection for this engine, so the proposal I made to him had his full backing. Back to the Shed we went, knocked on Bill Young's door, and bowled in, with the request that could we please have *Skylark* on the Southampton tomorrow. The answer was "No". What did we think he was running, a locomotive Shed or a private locomotive hire firm? But he hadn't allowed for the eloquence of Ted, my Ted who was Welsh by adoption, talking to a full blooded Welshman. Had he no soul? Had he no romance?

Had working with the English driven out all that was held dear in the Valleys? Had he no compassion? He stuck it for some time, then he said "yes" to get a few moments peace before Ted started again. There had to be a reason for this impassionate speech by Ted, he had conducted this appeal with all the virtuosity of a great criminal barrister defending his client at the Old Bailey. So, after Bill had said yes, the next question was "Why? And it had better be good".

I related the story of years ago when this locomotive was my 'Old Chap's' regular engine, and how I held her dear to my heart. I was, in fact, beginning to pick up where Ted had left off.

Bill held up his hand; enough had been said, we could have *Skylark* tomorrow, and to show us both that under the bowler hat was a brain full of compassion we had alleged he was so sadly lacking, my 'Old Man' would be taken off spare duties for one day and booked "Learning the road to Southampton". I asked Bill if I should kiss him now or when we came back, then beat him in reaching the office door and the safety of the Shed outside. It was a beautiful little bit of skulduggery to brighten up those wartime days.

When I arrived home and told Father he was learning the road to Southampton in the morning with Ted and myself, his first reaction was that a mistake had been made. He had worked the Branch for 20 years and knew it better than either of us. Then the grey matter started to work; after all, he was the father of the son. Something was afoot and he tried every way to prise it out of me, but I was the son of my father; in skulduggery we cancelled each other out.

The next morning I was in the Shed long before Father woke up. He did not have to book on until 7.15am, just time enough to walk from the Shed to the station to catch the train, and in any case, I wanted to spend some time on *Skylark* apart from the normal preparation duties.

I had a look over the top of the brick arch before I started on the fire. Her tube plate had corks of clinker all over it, so I borrowed a tube rod from Ernie Didcock, the Chargehand Cleaner, and cleared her tubes, ramming the rod right through until it cleared the firebox end. There was evidence of a superheater seepage, but at least she would start with clean tubes. Ted arrived just as I was closing the smoke box door, and we set about getting her ready. Bill Young was a real old sentimentalist after all; he must have left orders with the night shift, for from somewhere they had scraped together a couple of Cleaners to give Skylark a wipe down—not cleaned as she had been in pre-war days, but wiped over with some oily rags so that she shone in the winter sunshine.

As we took water before leaving the Shed, I climbed along the boiler with an oily rag in one hand and some sand in the other and gave the safety valve casing and her copper band round the chimney a good scouring. It was the finishing touch, she looked a beauty.

We backed on to the coaches in the bay platform and waited for Father, and as soon as his short familiar figure appeared up the station steps and headed towards us we both took up a position of studied innocence. Even then he didn't know what was going on. He climbed on to the footplate, and looked at Ted and me without saying a word, waiting for something to happen. Ted examined the finger nails on his right hand, blew on them, polished them on the lapels of his jacket, and then suggested that Harold senior had better have a look at the name plate of the engine.

The 'Old Chap' jumped down onto the platform and had a look. He turned round to us with an expression on his face that covered everything—surprise, wonderment, enjoyment, shock, and extreme pleasure, they were all there. He was at a loss for words for some moments, then he could only say two words, and for a man who did not use profane language those two words had a depth of affection, "You buggers, you buggers!" For once in my life I had taken the wind right out of my old. Dad.

Ted said cheerio and disappeared into the first compartment of the coach behind the engine. Father, Son, and *Skylark* were reunited after so many years, but it was not to be the perfect run as planned. The years of neglect and age had taken their toll from that old engine, for all my efforts at cleaning the tubes, and even with a clean fire she was shy on steam. We had to nurse her like a baby, mortgaging the boiler for steam on the banks, then letting her free-wheel down the other side to fill her up again, but we made it, having a wonderful day. Dad drove her to Newbury, I drove her to Winchester, then he took over to Southampton. We reversed the procedure on the way back. And Ted? He enjoyed the day of a gentleman, lounging back on the cushions watching the world go by!

Page 49 of Mr. R. C. Riley's 'Great Western Album Number 2' shows a very fine photograph of Skylark on October 24th 1951, just before her withdrawal from service, and the poor old lady looks as if she has had enough. I regret now that I did not make a bid for one of her name plates, but she's gone the way of so many fine engines; far better to be broken up in the early days than stand for years in a scrap yard to be cannibalised for her brass and copper fittings.

The winter drew on, with the problems of severe weather. Most people think that a locomotive footplate was a warm haven on a cold day, but this was not the case. It was a cold and draughty place to work, the only part of your body to be warm were the legs when the firebox door was open for firing, and even then they were scorched. In an open cab the icy wind could be vicious; hands would split open with the constant contact with water, and to lean out of the cab in a driving snow-storm to exchange single line tokens was a pleasure to forgo at any time.

It was a time, too, when we had trouble with injectors. I've read of the "A4s" on the East Coast expresses having injector failures, (something that was unheard of with the Great Western injector), but in the winter we would have the water feed-pipe freeze, and there was only one answer to that. We would stop, wrap some cotton waste round the pipe, soak it in paraffin set light to it and hope for the best. It was a bit drastic but it never failed.

Ted, being a thin man, used to suffer with the cold, particularly his bottom, and each time we stopped he would open the firebox door, lift up his coat, and back up to the glowing heat. Then, as the heat penetrated and the smell of scorching cloth filled the cab, he would let out a long drawn out 'Ahhhhh' and quickly nip back to his seat and sit down to conserve the warmth. Being a young man I would pull his leg about it, but I am older now, and I too enjoy backing up to a fire. This method of warming is hereditary in the male, and all stems from Noah and his Ark; when Noah had a hole in his Ark he had to sit on it to keep the water out.

The suffering of Ted did not stop at the cold. He suffered from an insidious craving for gorgonzola cheese. I say insidious because I could not stand the sight of it, and the 'aroma'—phew! Ted, though, would eat it for every meal if he could get hold of it! I always knew when he had that cheese, because of the metal box. Normally Ted would carry his food in an old gas mask haversack, but when he had this gorgonzola cheese he would bring it in a little metal box. This box had a hasp and staple attached to it. Ted would place it on the floor boards in my corner, tie a piece of string through the staple, then tie the other end to the handrail. He would then place large lumps of coal all round the box, building up a wall between the box and me. I then would receive instructions to watch it, and if it moved I was NOT to hit it with the shovel, but to talk kindly to it, and coax it back behind the wall! What a great mate he was, never a dull moment with him, life was too short and it was to be enjoyed to the full.

His other talents were that of a matchmaker. Over the years I fired to him at every opportunity he would bring up the subject that it was time I settled down and got married, and that a very attractive young lady who worked in the Great Western Hostel would be a most suitable wife for me—and best of all, Boyo, she can cook like a dream.

He was right, of course, he always was. I met this young lady, courted her in the proper manner, and to Ted's delight married her. We have our Silver Wedding Anniversary in 1974, so Ted made an excellent job of matchmaking.

Ted and I stuck together until the end of 1947 when my seniority took me up into a higher link. Even on the last day together Ted refused to be down-hearted, but we were both upset. We had shared so much together, not once a harsh word between us, and if the roster clerk tried any move to part us during those years either Ted or myself was in to see Bill Young at once. The only time we were away from each other was at holiday time, for then we had no choice.

The shock was softened to some extent when I found who was to be my new mate. To say that the Lord moves in mysterious ways is something of an understatement; the vacancy for a Fireman in number two link was with a Driver I knew well, very well indeed. I was to be Fireman to Harold George Gasson himself, the 'Old Chap', the 'Old Man'. Father of the Son no less!

Chapter Seven

As Fireman to Father, household life took on some degree of sanity. Mother could arrange meals for all of us together, social functions could be enjoyed as a family for once, we both left for the Shed together, and returned home together.

We were both darts players of some standing in the London Division Staff Association, and playing together we were almost unbeatable. There was a time during this period that whenever the two Gassons walked into the Staff Association hut, or any of the local pubs, dart playing came to an end! We had wiped up all the opposition, and could not get anyone to play against us.

But it was more than father and son; as I had grown from boyhood to manhood the bond of affection between us had matured to a point where we knew each other's thoughts, and this bond reflected itself on the footplate. We both knew it could not last, for it was against Great Western policy to allow father and son, or two brothers, to work on the footplate together for any prolonged period of time. There was nothing personal about this, but it did reduce the possibility of the entire males of a family being lost in the event of any accident.

The only answer to this situation before the Management insisted that we were parted was to make the most of it. And we did. We ran trains as they had never been run before. The sight of the two Gassons walking towards a train to relieve the crew was the time for the local signalmen to look at the clock and begin to think of margins between the other traffic.

As soon as we 'blew up' for the signal the points would come sliding over, the signals would drop off one by one, and we would be given a run on the tightest of margins in front of booked expresses.

The signalmen knew us both, and could afford to take the chance for we wouldn't let them down. It was a wonderful time, but we did have a few cracks to put up with. Signalmen would lean out of the box windows and shout 'Fix!' or 'Wangle', and our own shed mates would suggest good-naturedly that Bill Young wouldn't need to buy any cabbages for some time. But we accepted all the compliments with the Gasson grin, and got on with the job.

To the 'Old Man' I was just another Fireman. We worked perfectly together, as we would have done with any other Mate. The only thing I had to watch was that I didn't 'bash' the engine when I was doing a spot of Driving, because if I did have a little go, when Father came to the Driver's side he'd drop the lever down a notch and say "Come on boy, it's my turn now, head down, backside up!" On the second week together we had the Incident of the cats and as usual this incident started from the most unlikely source.

The 10.30pm Banbury to Westbury goods had been brought forward four hours and routed over the Newbury Branch because of a derailment at Southcote Junction. We booked on at 9.00pm and relieved her in the up gully at Didcot East Junction. The engine was 2858 and in fair-to-middling condition, in other words, she would steam her head off with the regulator shut and get a Fireman on his hands and knees praying up the banks in between the times he was standing on tip-toe trying to see the water in the bottom nut of the gauge glass. She was, in fact, the common run-of-the-mill goods engine. We had worked on better engines and worse engines, this was nothing new; the object was to get the best out of her.

The fire was a bit dead as she had been standing for a while, so I got out the long bar from the fire-iron rack and gave it a good lift up, then levelled it all over with the pricker. We now had a bed of fire to build on. I clambered up on to the tender, and with the light from the flare lamp picked out some nice choice lumps and threw them forward, while Dad Gasson built the fire up in Great Western fashion, right up to the firebox ring. On the back plate of the tender I found a fire bar. This went across the tool boxes, and then I shovelled coal forward until it was up over the boxes in a great pile. We should need it all before we closed the regulator at the top of Savernake bank.

I used the telephone to East Junction to let them know we were ready, and, as usual, when they heard my voice they were ready. The signal came off and the 'Old Chap' had started to move before I could get back onto the footplate. I waved the gauge lamp back and forth until the Guard answered with his hand lamp. We were complete. We gave a toot on the whistle to confirm, then we started to open her out for the long drag to Churn.

As the Banbury Fireman had predicted, she began to lose steam pressure, dropping back a little bit at a time, and without the injector on, but honour would not allow me to fail for steam with Father. Halfway between Upton and Churn I had to put on the injector. The water level was dropping and with her head up hill I should soon uncover the lead fuseable plug. I began to get a bit concerned.

The 'Old Chap' came over and had a look. We had 120lbs of steam and quarter of a glass of water, but the fire was perfect even if the exhaust did sound a bit queer. Father solved the dropping steam pressure in his usual unconcerned manner; he placed his cap over the steam gauge, stood on his seat so that for once he towered over me, and said he would knock my block off if I had a peep under that cap. But it was obvious that all was not well at the front end, so we would stop at Compton, not for a 'blow up' but to examine the engine.

We eased down past the signal box and shouted to the signalman that we were stopping in the station to examine the engine, then as we came to a stand Father put the blower on, shut the firebox doors, and told me to open the smoke box. It was as he had expected, the jumper ring on the blast pipe was jammed on one side.

Twenty minutes were spent on cleaning that jumper ring with the sharp end of the coal pick, a couple of pocket knives, some cotton waste, and a few softly-spoken swear words, (although I did hear one loud word when Father lost some skin from his thumb). I filled the buckets of the signal box with coal, wetted the tea in the can from the signal box kettle, and had to admit that I still had something to learn about locomotives. Father knew what was wrong as soon as he heard the blast of the exhaust and the steam pressure began to drop, but he didn't think it would do any harm to let the 'Old Boy' sweat a bit! From then on 2858 steamed as she was built to. I had a job to keep her from blowing off and we ran all the way to Westbury without any more trouble.

The return trip was on a locomotive that was a favourite with all Great Western enginemen, one of the seven 47XX Class, No. 4701 that Mr. Churchward built in 1919. The chance to work on one did not come very often, as they were used between the West Country and Paddington Goods for most of the time. What locomotives, almost as big as a "King", they were just a little under the all-out power of a "Twenty Eight". They would run like a "Castle" on the vacuum fitted goods, and were used with some regularity on express passenger services. This one was not long out of Swindon following an overhaul. She ran so sweetly that each rail joint could be heard. It was my pleasure to drive her, as far as Reading anyway, (as much as I enjoyed the regulator I did not fancy threading my way into Acton Yard). It was always the same when we had a free steaming engine; it was my turn to drive, while the 'Old Chap' sat there with firebox doors open and the engine blowing her head off. He used to say that the Devil looked after his own, but that was not fair, the Devil sat with him.

We put 4701 away at Old Oak Common Shed with just enough time to get up to Paddington and catch the 4.45am newspaper train home. The Driver had started to move before he saw us running, and being a good chap he shut off so that we could dive into the first vehicle, a parcel coach, and into the Incident of the Cats.

There was a distinctive and unpleasant smell in that coach, a heavy, clammy, and sickly smell that even outweighed Father's pipe; and that's saying something, because when he reached the bottom that old pipe sounded like a man in wellington boots walking on gravel! If we had to stick this all the way to Didcot then we were entitled to know what was causing it.

We tracked it down to a large wickerwork laundry basket. On closer examination there was no doubt; it stank, but not a sound came from it. There was no label evident to identify the destination. We discussed the possibility of a murder, it could be a body in the stages of decomposition. Two tattered straps and buckles stood between us and the answer; it was more than we could stand, so we undid the buckles and lifted the lid. It was not a body we had uncovered, but ten cats with one thought in their minds, escape—and before we could shut the lid they were out.

There then started a hunting expedition that would have done credit to a big game hunter. We used all the craft and guile, the sneakiness and cunning of the old time horse traders to catch those cats. The soft, sweet, calling of 'Pussy, Pussy' ended by the pussy being grabbed by the scruff of the neck and stuffed back into that basket, and each time a pussy was pushed in, another popped out.

Leaving Reading we decided we had caught them all, no more cats were to be seen. In the final check-round we found the label, "Ten Cats consigned to Kidderminster". It was agreed that we should make one more check. Father lifted the lid an inch while I shone my torch inside; twenty-two eyes glared back at us. We had them all safely back inside, down went the lid, and the straps were secured as the brakes were applied for Didcot.

Both of us were covered with perspiration and cat's hair, and we had worked harder in the last hour than all the night put together.

On the way home the 'Old Chap' suddenly stopped and asked me how many eyes I had counted in that basket, and when I said twenty-two he agreed. But the label had stated "Ten Cats", twenty eyes; where had the other two eyes come from? Father thought back on that label again, and remembered that it had read 'Ten Female Cats'. What if we had stuffed in a Tom with them? The consequences of such an action was too awful to contemplate.

When we opened the back door at home and walked in the old dog bounded forward to meet us with his usual greeting, then stopped short, turned round with a disgusted look and went back to his bed. He faithful masters had been consorting with cats! He was used to the smell of coal, steam, and oil, but this was the aroma of the enemy. We were duly punished, he ignored us for a week!

During this time with Father we relieved Uncle Bert Edmonds a couple of times, and of course he told Aunt Annie about it, and as Annie knew her brother very well nothing would convince her that it had not been a 'fix'. There had been some jiggery pokery between her Bert and her two brothers back in 1910, which resulted in them both turning up in Oxford, and although she loved them both she knew their capabilities; they were rogues, and her Bert was a rogue too for he had started it all with his brain-washing! Bert would suck on his old pipe and grin, he had heard it for years.

I think the situation did strike home one day at Reading. There was an engineman learning the road from Paddington to Swindon, and he had joined Bert Edmonds at Acton. Bill Gasson had relieved Bert at Slough, where the family news was exchanged, then the 'Old Chap' and myself had relieved Bill. All within two hours this poor man had been in the company of the Old Oak Branch, the Reading Branch, and now the Didcot

Branch of the family! He was well aware that the Great Western was proud of the fact of being a family railway, but this was ridiculous! It was a situation Father relished.

A week later we had a Locomotive Inspector on the footplate with us. We were working a Divisional inspection special with 1334, the old Midland and South Western Engine kept at Didcot for working the Lambourn Branch. We stopped at Winchester for the top brass to take lunch, where the introductions were made; please meet Mr. Harold Gasson the Driver, please meet Mr. Harold Gasson the Fireman. Very important eyebrows were raised, very important heads were put together. As we climbed respectfully out of that inspection coach some very important muttering could be heard.

The Locomotive Inspector was most apologetic; he thought he was in the company of two Harolds, nothing more, but he knew as we did, the damage was done. We had got away with it for four months, and probably would have done so for much longer, but it was the end; a week later I had to exchange places with another Fireman, and with that exchange I would see the end of my firing days.

It was a quick and simple swop, Fireman Jones to Driver Gasson, Fireman Gasson to Driver Champ. Bill Young had us both in and explained the position. Orders had come from above. He was more upset about it than we were, but we had survived together longer than we had expected, and with Bill Champ as a Mate I had a lot to be thankful for.

Bill was one of those big burly men, and in common with men of his size he was as gentle as a lamb. He had one trick that used to amaze me with his strength; he would hold out two hands that were as big as a couple of shovels, catch hold of a Fireman in each hand—and I was usually one of them—and pick us up clear off the ground. He was full of practical jokes, and when he found I would jump if my knees were pinched it was fraught with danger to pick up the shovel! He would wait until I had started to swing with a full shovel, then make a grab for me. The result was coal all over the footplate. There was only one way to retaliate, and that was through his 'nose warmer'. The only time Bill was without his pipe was when he was eating. The stem was so short that it literally was a nose warmer, and sooner or later he would lay it down. I was all ready to 'doctor' it when he did so. I had cut a little rubber from the coal watering pipe, chopped it up fine, and had it all ready. I had to wait nearly a month before the chance came, and that was when Bill went to the stores, leaving his pipe on top of the reverser. I emptied out some of the tobacco, tipped in the chopped up rubber, then packed the tobacco back in.

Bill smoked that pipe-full without turning a hair—I think he even enjoyed it! His tobacco was like rubber anyway; he would cut it from a little black block, rub it in his hands and stuff it in his pipe. (It had its merits, for we never had a fly or wasp on the footplate, and if we were sent home as passengers we had the compartment to ourselves in a very short time).

Bill was of the same seniority as my Old Dad and his brother Bill. They were all Firemen together, and I heard stories about those two that would fill another book, especially when they were all together in a double home lodge. For all the tricks I had got up to, I found that my 'Old Chap' in his time had been as bad!

The time spent with Bill was a happy one. He was an excellent Driver, in fact a good man to know and work with. I only saw him upset once.

We were spanking along on the down relief between Twyford and Reading on 7202, one of the big tank engines, when Bill sneezed and away went his beloved pipe, to bounce along on the ballast. Poor Bill was inconsolable. We were running much too fast to stop, and we could not stop in the section. Bill had his second-string pipe, of course, so he wouldn't be without a smoke, but it was only ten years old and by his standards just 'run-in'.

He hardly spoke a word for the rest of the day, so something drastic had to be done. We telephoned the signalman at Twyford and asked him to get the ganger for that section to have a look for the pipe when he walked through the next morning, then we set about making arrangements at our end.

The next day we put out feelers in the right quarter. The man in charge of the Control Office at Reading was Bert Povey, a Didcot traffic man who knew us both well. Now Bert Povey more than anyone else in the Division could appreciate the importance of that missing pipe, so with a little connivance on his part he had us relieve an up goods train at Didcot, work it to Reading West Yard, engine to shed, then orders to make our way home. He did not add "via Twyford", but the old saying "a nod is as good as a wink" applied here; we were off on the next up stopper to Twyford! That walk back to Reading was the only time I ever enjoyed searching a section. All enginemen at some time during the year search a section, usually for cattle on the line, or if a passenger falls out of a train, and always at Christmas time when some nit of a Christmas club treasurer finds he can't balance his books and throws himself over a bridge, so for a change we were not looking for bits and pieces of the human anatomy. We found Bill's pipe, a little battered about the bowl, but otherwise in good condition. The Great Western Locomotive Department could now breathe freely again, and Bert Povey collected a well-deserved pint in the Staff Association.

At the start of the summer we had a new duty added to the Didcot roster. A new goods train was formed to run from Moreton Yard to Feltham Yard on the Southern; we would work it to Reading New Junction, then return light engine to Moreton for the second and third trips. It was quite a heavy duty for a night's work, around 110 miles of running, and to work this duty a request was sent out to the South Wales Divisions for three 7200 tank engines.

A request of this nature is manna from heaven to a Shed Foreman. It gives him a chance to get rid of some lame ducks, so the three 72XX Tanks we received were some right old tubs.

We received 7202, (the engine Bill had lost his pipe from), 7208, and 7228; out of the three 7202 was about the best.

Bill Miles, the Foreman Fitter, and his lads got stuck into them and made a very good job out of a bad bargain, but we disliked those big tank engines, I think simply because we were used to working on the open footplate of the tender engines so much. We had 6106, our own tank engine, but she was a Didcot engine and well looked after.

The 7200 Class were stretched-out versions of the "5200" tank engines, but to me they were "Twenty-Eights" with side tanks nailed on. Although the tractive power was slightly below the "Twenty-Eight" it would have been a good man who could find the difference; the power produced was sheer brute strength. It was most noticeable because of the lack of movement between any cab or tender. The "Seventy-Two" was just over 92 tons of solid dead-weight on the move, one great lump of steam locomotive pounding remorselessly on. This dead weight reflected in the way they rode, for there was no movement except forward, and the same applied, of course, when running bunker first. This was the whole idea of having them on this new duty, as it was basic economics to avoid the need for turning for the light engine trip back to Moreton Yard. Some bright boy on the management staff had worked it all out; let's bring in the "Seventy-Two" Tanks for this new duty, then we can get three trips each night out of the devils!

I only wished we could have had him on the footplate with us on a hot summer night, for firing those big Tanks was like working in an inferno; the heat must have put the temperature up to well over the hundred. We suffered, as we were gentlemen enginemen in the London Division, and not used to this type of locomotive. It was all right for the Welsh lads, they were brought up on tank engines. We changed our mind about them when the winter set in, for there was a sliding steel plate each side of the cab, and when this was drawn back we were cocooned in a warm little world of our own. We took back all that we thought of economic experts, (and at least they were Great Western engines, and anything Great Western was better than those Austerities!)

Bill and I did have one bit of fun that summer. We were running on the down relief between Reading and Didcot, and as we passed through Cholsey the signalman noticed that we had a wagon on fire about half-way back along the train. So he had us stopped at Aston Tirrold intermediate box, and the signalman there sent to Moreton for another engine to come on the up relief line and stop near the burning wagon and deal with the fire.

I rode back with this engine, taking our bucket with me. When we stopped at the burning wagon we could see that it was a wagon-load of farm manure. By this time the Station Master, Mr. Fouracre, had arrived from Cholsey, resplendent in a new uniform with gold-braided cap, and he set to work with enthusiasm. The object was to get to the heart of the fire, so he borrowed the coal pick from the engine, hit up the clips on the side of the wagon, and dropped the flap down.

This was excellent reasoning from a man of responsibility, but he had missed out one little thing, co-ordination, he hadn't informed me of his intentions as he dropped the flap on that wagon and poked his head over the top of that stinking burning manure. I was on the back of the tender with a bucket-full of water I had drawn up out of the tank, and at the precise moment that Mr. Fouracre stuck his head over the top of that manure, my bucket of water hit that manure about a foot in front of him!

Needless to say, the fire was soon out, but no farm worker mucking out a cow shed had ever got in the state that poor man was in. He was plastered in manure from head to foot. At arm's length, we wiped him down with cotton waste, then stood him on the tender while we ran him back to Cholsey. We couldn't place him on the footplate near any heat, as he smelt bad enough on the tender! In later years when he was Station Master at Culham, and I was District Relief Signalman covering Culham Box for a day, he brought his wife out of the Station house and pointed me out as the only man to cover him with manure and get away with it.

I think that incident was the only time I have seen my mate Bill let his pipe go out. He started to laugh, and it went on for hours. He would go quiet for a little time, then it would cross his mind, and he would start all over again. There was more to steam locomotives than shovelling coal!

It was a good time, but the last few years of Great Western steam were drawing to a close. Nationalisation was upon us, and with it the identification of being a true Great Western Engineman was to be lost for ever in British Railways. The locomotives were in need of repair and gradually getting worse, I had a talk with a Chief Inspector I knew very well at Paddington one day, and although nothing definite could be said, it was evident that with my seniority I could count on only a few years as a Steam Driver. I searched my soul for many hours before coming to a decision, but I did not want to be present at the end of steam; I wanted to leave as a Great Western Fireman, not a B.R. man.

The 'Old Chap' agreed with me. I had seen the best of the old days. His brother Bill's son, Ted, had just been made Fireman at Reading, so there would still be a Gasson firing in the Division. He told me later that it was a bad time when the decision was made to replace steam with diesels. The introduction of the Standard engines softened the blow to some extent, but except for the brilliant work done by Mr. Sam Ells at Swindon, the common user engine began to fall rapidly into a state of disrepair.

The lads at Reading had some hairy trips out of Redhill with the old 45XX class during the summer service in those last few months, but I think every man on the footplate at that time opened the eyes of those above; Great Western Steam went down with full honours.

I applied for a transfer to the Traffic Department as a Signalman. I had spent a few off-duty hours in the local boxes, and was fascinated by the work at the big junctions, so after a couple of weeks my application for a transfer was granted. I was sent to Reading Signal School for a three month course in signalman's training. My off-duty hours of study paid off; I passed the examinations and was out of the school in three weeks, and landed a Class Three Box at Milton. Three years later, and a lot of hours spent in study with the inevitable exams at the end, I was appointed to Class One District Relief Signalman, covering 22 signal boxes in the Didcot and Oxford District.

I think that probably the years on the footplate made me a better Signalman for they gave me an understanding of conditions and working of the steam engine that allowed me to operate a busy junction box much more effectively. The ordinary Signalman would wait for the Driver to blow up for the signal, but when I heard the ejector being opened I was setting up the road, and had the signal off before the whistle blew. Little things, but added together they made the working of a busy box much easier.

The Oxford lads soon got to know when I was at Kennington Junction. There was no need to hang the single line token from Cowley on the post, and they would sweep down off that branch at a speed no other Signalman experienced, holding up the token for me to take at the end window. I never missed—the Winchester Branch had taught me all about single line tokens.

Regrets? There were many, but if I have in this book re-captured some of the atmosphere of Great Western Steam, and the work of the enginemen, then all is not lost.

FOOTPLATE DAYS

Introduction

During my years on the footplate I experienced many many situations, some amusing, some serious, some awkward and some routine. In my first book "Firing Days" I tried to recapture some of these moments and in this book I shall try to relate to you even more experiences of my footplate days and tell you stories of the engines I loved which I shall remember with nostalgia for the rest of my days.

After writing "Firing Days" I received many lovely letters from people I had never met who said that I had also brought back many memories for them. From these letters I acquired a large number of new friends who often wrote telling me of their experiences when they themselves were working in the steam days. They brought back memories for me that made me realise that there were many more stories that I had forgotten to relate in "Firing Days", enough in fact to write another book. However, I found that it was far easier to fire an old 43XX or a Manor than to make my fingers find the right keys on the typewriter!

Since my first book was published I have had offers to fire locomotives such as *Lydham Manor* and *King George V*. The thought of having the opportunity to work these Great Western locomotives made my heart beat twice as fast with excitement. I recalled standing in my garden at Kennington in May 1973 long after steam had finished and seeing the immaculate *King George V* flash past on the "Royal Giants Rail Tour" blowing her whistle through Radley and I was as excited as all the small boys around me. As it was some years since I had fired a steam locomotive I wondered whether I would still be able to slide coal up to the front end of the King firebox. When the time came, however, I realised that nothing had changed and I felt completely at home, experiencing one of the most memorable days of my life. They did me proud at Hereford that day and I shall never forget their kindness. I think that day at Hereford, in conjunction with the letters I received pleading with me to write another book, was the inspiration for me to write "Footplate Days".

Writing the book has taken the best part of 300 hours, stealing an hour here and there during evenings and weekends, so I must thank my dear wife Betty for tolerating my disappearing acts into the back room to work on the book.

Chapter One

The advent of Nationalisation brought little noticeable change to the newly-formed Western Region for some time: 'God's Wonderful Railway' carried on as it had done for 113 years; Great Western locomotives crewed by Great Western Enginemen ran on Great Western metals completely oblivious of the existence of a British Railways Board. But change was in the air. It started innocently enough with the next issue of uniform—gone were our woven red cap badges with 'G.W.R.' and in their place we were issued with a metal badge; which was held in the cap with a long split pin which proclaimed 'British Railways'.

The overalls also lost the bright red G.W.R. badge. Thus we felt naked and rubber-stamped into anonymity, but we still had our locomotives. They too had to suffer the indignity of losing the 'Great Western' from their tenders, to be replaced by a lion mounted on a wheel. At first, it was noted that the lion faced towards the rear of the tender which brought many ribald remarks from the enginemen especially owing to the position the lion had taken up, being most uncomfortable at speed. The management, however, must have sensed this, as in no time whatsoever all the lions were changed to face forward. Fast running of the trains was of a nature not seen since the pre-war years, not because of nationalisation, but because it was the nature of Great Western men to give of their best. The Enginemen of the other three old Companies were the same. There was a feeling of uncertainty as to which future engine would be supplied before the great slab-sided diesels took over from steam.

A standard locomotive was in the offing, and with its introduction the complete loss of individuality of each company's locomotives was envisaged.

The first standard locomotive to be offered as a competitor in the inter-region trials was a beautiful little 2-6-0 tender engine entered by the London Midland Region. It was designed by Mr. Ivatt and was to work on lines restricted to the large locomotives and replace some of the antiquated engines then operated by the other companies. Working on the maxim that if it looks good it must be good, the Midland must have felt confident that it would meet all the requirements demanded of it. However, they overlooked one thing: the Great Western had had 'standard' steam locomotion in operation for forty-five years due to the foresight of George Jackson Churchward, which was carried on by Mr. Collett and Mr. Hawksworth. There was the little 0-6-0 22XX class built by Mr. Collett in 1930 which complied with all the requirements for the new standard, and out of the large stud at Didcot Nos. 2222 and 2221 were outstanding. But such was the confidence at Swindon that it was thought unfair to enter such a modern engine which had been built to take the place of the Dean Goods, so to give the opposition a chance, there was a search for an old Dean Goods engine to compete against the Ivatt 2-6-0.

At Didcot we had No. 2579 still in the livery of the Great Western, 50 years old and, except for the fitting of superheaters, much the same as when William Dean built her. Despite her age she was a wonderful little engine. The lads at Swindon must have rubbed their hands together with glee as No. 2579 was just the engine they were looking for. They had her in, tuned her up, lined her out in smart black paint, and sent her into battle.

With her tall chimney, dome, and flower-pot safety-valve cover she looked a really smart old lady done up for a day out as she crept unpretentiously up to the shed signal, her single push-over regulator was eased open, and she chuffed her way into immortality. She had every right to be proud, as it was not long before the railway jungle-telegraph began to filter through the news that the old lady was not only doing well in the trials but beating the newcomer. Much to the discomfort of the Railways Board she was steaming better, using less water and coal, and producing a greater tractive effort than Mr. Ivatt's engine could do. Bad coal was mentioned, (and to be truthful it was some foul stuff we were burning), but facts speak for themselves and our old 2579 was the better engine. In her old age she had gone out into the world to uphold the honour of the Great Western and was to return home after "tanning the pants off" the newcomer.

When she dropped on to the ash road it was to the accompaniment of the whistles of every engine in steam on the Shed; she had something about her that is hard to describe, almost the brazenness of an aged Madam who had just married into the aristocracy. We did not gloat over the discomfort of the Midland Region, for Mr. Ivatt's engine would be the one to set the standard after some slight modifications, but we did have a feeling of exhilaration over the performance of our little engine.

I have fired her for miles, and if fired all round her square firebox, shaping the fire like a saucer, she would steam like a tin kettle. She still had the old-type live steam injector handles, and small wheels bound round with steel wire projecting out from the boiler front on thin spindles. It was advisable to turn them with a pad of cotton waste in the palm of the hand because they not only became hot but also the steel wire was inclined to bite, but we forgave small faults, since old ladies are allowed to show a little bit of temperament.

As enginemen, we could not understand the need for this so-called standard locomotive. William Dean started a standard in Victorian days, and George Jackson Churchward had perfected it. We had standard cabs and fittings, interchangeable wheels, boilers, side-rods and we could step down from a small tank engine and on to a 'King' to find all the fittings in the same place. They were all right-hand drive, and all that was needed was to build a few more 'Kings', 'Castles', 'Halls', and 'Twenty-Eights' and the job was done. I don't expect the Southern, Midland, and Eastern Region enginemen would have liked it much to start with for we all thought we had the best steam power, but that was part of pride in the job and I am sure Bill Hoole and his 'A4' and Sam Gingel on his 'King Arthurs' would have loved the 'Castles' and 'Kings' eventually, and the Midland men would have taken to them even sooner since most of their own engines were built by Mr. Stanier, who was a Great Western man. But the powers that be had to have a new standard locomotive for all types of working, so intensive trials with other Regions' engines were carried out.

To their credit some fine locomotives emerged from Swindon, Doncaster, Crewe, and Eastleigh, to live a short life, but the writing was on the wall, starting with the Brown Boveri Gas Turbine on the Western and ending with the introduction of the Diesel locomotive.

The Western went mad for a time, painting 'Kings' and 'Castles' light green and blue, and at first they looked most attractive after the grime of the war years but with oil streaks and coal dust on a background of light blue paint, a 'Castle' did not look quite right, and when the change back to the deep Brunswick green was made the real regal magnificence of the Great Western locomotive could be appreciated.

It is interesting to note that during this period of paint experimentation, a walk down the cycle racks at Swindon works could be an education. It was the 'Mecca' of cycles as there was not a rusty one to be seen, they were all light blue or green, and the lining out would have done credit to the lads who lined out the boilers and cylinders. It was sheer artistry, and professionalism with the brush at its best.

When the change-over from steam was made it came with a swiftness almost reminiscent of the weekend change-over from broad gauge. For weeks we had seen the odd live engine pulling a couple of dead ones, and Didcot Shed was packed from end to end with every class. But when the day arrived for almost every train to be powered by a Diesel we were quite unprepared for it.

The slaughter of the steam locomotive was on a scale of complete extermination and was the execution of an age, comparable to the days when sail gave way to steam at sea.

At this time we thought the main line steam locomotive was gone for ever, and the few that did slip through the net would be banished to the quiet of the museum to keep company with the other cold exhibits, to be looked on with wonder by a new generation.

The last steam runs were made with much publicity and with such runs the preservation societies were born; the steam locomotive would not be allowed to die.

Two years after the end of main line steam, a visit to Barry scrap yard filled me at first with nostalgia, soon changing to revulsion and disgust. Every example of Great Western engines stood buffer to buffer, line after line, in various stages of decay. It was a warm summer day, but to walk between the rows of dead engines one felt the chill of a massacre. There was the 'King' I had last seen roaring through Didcot at 90 mph on the 'Bristolian', now rusting with the paint peeling from her boiler casing; the 'Castle', which I had seen drifting along the sea wall at Dawlish with a train packed with people on their way to the seaside, now had groundsel and chickweed growing out of her floorboards. There was the little pannier tank I had blasted round Didcot West curve into the depot, now covered in bird droppings standing there forlorn and forgotten, her spindle glands still filled with the packing I had rammed in years before, over-shadowed by the great bulk of a Bulleid "Pacific" on the next road. The 'Halls', 'Twenty-Eights' and 'Forty-Threes', engines to which I had given life, were now in a state of decomposition, all of them stripped of cab windows, safety valve covers, injector pipes, and main steam pipes.

One engine was to shock me more than any other. She had been a 'Forty-Three' which I had fired on many occasions. I had boiled many a can of tea in her firebox, nursed her with a dirty fire, and nosed her through thick fog. She had lived by fire, and now she was dying by that same fire. Her side-rods had been cut through with an acetylene torch leaving the stumps hanging on the coupling pins. She had been cut through from the front of the boiler to just behind the smokebox saddle, leaving her with a cab at one end, and smokebox with chimney still on the main frame at the other end. A pile of tubes lay on the ground in mute evidence of her destruction. She had been gutted and one last small touch added to the pathos of this assassination. Almost unreadable with the ravages of the weather was the chalk mark on her cabside. 'Washout 10/10/66'. The poor old lady would receive no more shed service.

No. 6024 *King Edward I* stood there, stripped of window frames, cab fittings, and safety valve cover, her paint peeling from her boiler, keeping company on one side with a pannier tank and a Bulleid "Pacific", and on her other side a 'Hall' and a 'Twenty-Eight'. The ironical point about it all was the condition of her stabling, for she was in mid-gear, with the tender handbrake hard on. To the end, the regulations for leaving a locomotive had been adhered to.

To fully appreciate the enormity of Barry was to stand on the bridge between the mainland and the Island with the sea a sapphire blue on one side, and the sun dancing on the red and grey tiles, and sparkling on the windows of the houses sprawled out on the mainland. In the middle were the long silent ranks of rusting dead engines.

The area had the same chill quietness of the ancient battlefields of Bodiam and the Glencoe Pass, and was indeed the 'Valley of Death'. They were all there, the locomotives of Churchward, Collett and Hawksworth, Stanier, Ivatt, Riddles, Bulleid, Maunsell, and Urie, collective examples of the great men of steam, the last links from the father of them all, George Stephenson. It was the end, or was it? One glimmer of sunlight shone through it all, a few, and it was a few in those long silent ranks, bore the words 'Reserved'. The birth of the preservation societies was in being, with men prepared to see that steam would not die.

We were to see in the next few years the love for the steam locomotive come to life again, the rusting rails in a few derelict sheds would shine once more, the cobwebs would be swept away from the engineman's cabins, and the rust and neglect of the scrap-yard removed from boilers and replaced with new paintwork. The 'Open Day' at a locomotive shed was upon us and with it an appreciation of locomotives and the sheds that mothered them.

The general public had little idea of engine sheds except for a fleeting glimpse from a coach window. Most of them were tucked away down in a hole—Reading and Oxford were such examples—or they were away from sight as at Old Oak Common, but now there was an opportunity to visit some of the few remaining. Alas, the great cavern of Old Oak Common was no more as three of the 65 feet turntables had been ripped out, and most of the 200-odd engines were rusting at Barry. Reading and Oxford had been demolished, along with all the sub-sheds in the London Division, except for one, being my old shed at Didcot, which was to be saved to house a large number of locomotives from all over the country in preservation.

The first visit to my old shed was something of a shock. The great wooden doors were closed which was a sight I had never seen before. I don't think they ever had been closed from the day the shed was handed over by the contractors in 1932. I had the distinct feeling of being a stranger, but a walk round the north side and down the old empty number five road to see the familiar tin shed housing the stationary boiler with her 30-foot chimney, gave me a feeling of reassurance. Then I came across the empty pit of the turntable. It was an ugly scar, a gaping hole that once held the finest balanced table in the division.

Something else was also missing. There was another gap at the rear of my old shed, which I could not place for some minutes. The old country saying, 'Berkshire born and Berkshire bred, strong in the arm and weak in the 'ead' kept tumbling through my mind. It was a case of 'there it is—gone.' I knew I was strong in the arm, a Great Western shovel had seen to that, but weak in the head was another matter! What was missing? And then I realised, the coal dump was not there.

Our great fortress of a coal dump had been removed. This great square bastion built like Hadrian's Wall had disappeared with the locomotives it had fed. What type of man and machine had removed those blocks of coal, thousands of tons, with the base built up with huge lumps the size of a telephone box, twenty feet high and forty feet square, tapering gently off into an enormous blockhouse? All that remained of the food that fed the hungry mouths of the engines were two large patches of coal dust, with a few blades of grass struggling for life in an earthless world.

It was Barry all over again, until my next visit on an 'Open Day' by courtesy of the Great Western Society. I was home again; the shed was open, and donning an old pair of Great Western overalls I was able to pass off as a visiting member of the Society and clamber all over my beloved engines, creep about in the pits underneath them, and explore the shed to my heart's content.

I hope they will forgive me for this small transgression, but I was happy to be back. I was able to answer the hundreds of questions put by the visiting public, and in a small way repay my debt by taking some of the pressure from the genuine Society members.

The 'Open Day' is something of a carnival affair, with yards of rope and bunting protecting the running lines. The souvenir stalls, the publicity literature, the bright colours of the ladies' dresses, the exciting shrieking of the children, the whirl of many cine-cameras, people milling about, and of course in the centre of it all, the locomotives in steam with their paintwork beautifully restored, with brass and copper gleaming in the sunshine. Every movement produced the inevitable request shouted up to the lads on the footplate to make smoke enabling the perfect film to be taken. All this was mixed with the shrill blast of whistles, open steamcocks, and the crisp bark from the engine exhaust. It is a perfect day out made possible by a small band of devoted steam enthusiasts, but of course it does not portray the true locomotive shed of steam days. In the next chapter I hope to show the events and atmosphere of a shed, in the days of steam running.

Chapter Two

Didcot shed at the height of Great Western steam days made two vivid impressions on me while I was a Fireman there, both in complete contrast to each other. The first had to be seen on a hot summer day on a Sunday at about noon when one could walk out of the heat and bright sunshine into the dark coolness of Didcot station sub-way, with the station deserted and strangely quiet, and the booking office shutters down, both lifts at the bottom gaping open in the gloom. One's footsteps would echo as each steel-shod heel struck the cold paving to rebound from the far end. There was the soft drip, drip of water from some secret corner, and the damp musty underground odour that is a familiar part of sub-ways. Then the pattern of the echoes would change as the paving was left for the asphalt at the bottom of the steps. To climb up those steps was to begin a journey into another world, out of the damp coolness into the heat, across the sleeper-crossing with the tar and oil-soaked sleepers bubbling up into great blisters, mingled with the pungent tang of hot creosote so thick that one could taste it.

Then the walk down the cinder path between the coal stage and the carriage sidings, with the cinders crunching underfoot accompanied by the sharp whip-crack of the rails as they expanded in that simmering heat. The wagons of coal in the coal stage siding would reflect the heat, each one standing patiently waiting to be emptied, each axle box dripping molten grease to add to the other dirty stains of yesterday; then between the two cycle sheds to the engine shed crossing.

A glance up towards the coal stage would find a Churchward 43XX under the tip, with the coal piled up into a pyramid on her tender and her front frame covered with a heap of smokebox ash up to the footstep. Behind her would be a 28XX, her fire cleaned and the hot cinders adding to the heat. The long twelve-foot pricker and fire dripper's shovel would be propped up on the Fireman's side, reaching from the concrete path up into the cab.

The shed stands there like a large off-white barn, the tall square chimneys, smokeless, so characteristic of the Great Western shed. The 'Field' numbers 5, 6, 7 and 8, full of engines waiting for the early hours of the next day. The old *Comet* No. 3283 is blowing off gently from her safety valve, the escaping steam invisible in the heat of the sun. No. 1334, the old Midland and South Western engine, would be standing on number four road outside the shed, waiting to be prepared for the Didcot to Lambourn train later in the afternoon, and a bunch of shed sparrows would be clustered under the dripping leather bag of the water column.

Inside the shed resembles the stillness of a cathedral. Shafts of sunlight cut through the gloom, to sparkle back from polished brass and copper, and the engines in steam quietly bubble and gurgle. Then the peace is broken as a shovel rasps through coal, firebox doors are opened with a rattle as down the far end of the shed "Baggy" Fletcher, the steam raiser, starts lighting up an engine firebox.

He lines the box with small lumps of coal, leaving a space in the middle. The firelighters, one inch by one foot split timber, nailed together into an open box four spars high, are stuffed with cotton waste soaked in paraffin. "Baggy" places three on the shovel and lowers them carefully in the prepared space in the firebox, the fourth one he lights and tosses in. As the fire spreads to the others, he places choice lumps of coal on top, the dampers are opened, the firebox doors closed leaving an inch gap to increase the draught, and she is lit up. "Baggy" will return in two hours and add a bit more coal and she should by then be on the simmer, the water in the gauge glass beginning to move gently up and down. Four hours after lighting up she should be on the boil, with 40 to 80lbs pressure showing on the steam gauge, all ready for the Fireman to build up his fire for the road.

Harry King in the stores has finished his Sunday cleaning. The large pot-bellied stove shines with grate polish, the brass oil-taps on the tanks sparkle and the store has been squared up with headlamps in neat rows, and shovels stacked. Now he can relax with the News of the World except that I have arrived and soon my mate will be behind me, both of us wanting attention and service as we prepare the 'Forty-Three' waiting under the coal stage. She has been turned and brought round to number one road by the shed pilot driver, and placed nice and handy by the sand bin, so that two heavy buckets of sand need not be carried far.

I climb up onto her footplate to find every inch of the cab covered in coal dust and clinker so a wipe down of the coat hooks and cab side with clean cotton waste is necessary. Two sheets of newspaper are forced over the hooks, jacket hung up, tea-can and food-box placed up in the corner, and it is time to begin preparation.

The *Comet* stops blowing off as "Baggy" has dropped her dampers down a peg, one injector is singing away, and he sits on the rail near her rolling a cigarette and wiping the perspiration from his face. Other engines near *Comet* begin to smoke from their chimneys; rolling and curling languidly over the boilers to drift back along the others and then spreads out over the fields in a thin haze. "Baggy" is on his last round-up before the late turn man comes on to relieve him.

Ted, my mate, arrives, and we have a look round our engine together. She must have been on the road a long time before dropping into Didcot shed for service. The pile of smokebox ash is proof enough. It is a long time since she has seen the inside of Swindon works. Little things about her show her in urgent need of a major overhaul. The steam gauge pressure numbers are faded, the damper handles, steam cocks, and sand levers all have a lot of side play, the great reversing lever can be moved from side to side, the ratchet peg is worn and shiny and it is a safe bet that the axle boxes are in the same condition. It will be a rough ride.

We set about her, already the heat beginning to take effect, and the fire is spread thinly over the box. I build her up with as much coal as she will take, and close the firebox doors with relief. With 40 1bs showing on those faded numbers, half a turn on the blower will soon liven her up.

I hear a muffled swear-word from Ted underneath. With his sweaty, oily hands he has dropped the cork from an eccentric bar into the pit. I go under to him, check the ashpan and tread on the cork in the process, squashing it flat. Ted comes out of the motion, hands me the oil feeder and a new cork. With my longer reach I can complete the job for him.

Back on the footplate the pressure has reached 100 1bs. Ted gets me to move her forward an inch as the spokes of the driving wheels are fouling the axle box corks. Then I place her in mid gear, hand brake hard on, and cylinder cocks open. With Ted's arm stretched through those spokes we can't risk her moving even a quarter of an inch. By now, three-quarters of an hour have passed, the engine has been oiled all round, the injectors tested, sand boxes topped up, smokebox door tightened, ashes swept off, footsteps cleaned, clinker shovelled over the side, and the tender trimmed. The coal remaining on the worn floorboards is splashed round the firebox, so while Ted goes to the stores to top up the oil-cans and wet the tea in the tea-can, I ram my six-inch length of quarter-inch copper pipe up inside the 'pep' pipe, put on the right hand injector, stand well back on the tender, and wash off the footplate.

As that scalding water hits the boiler casing and live steam pipes, the heat rebounds in a solid wave, the coal dust and ash disappear, swirling away down through the damper guides. The joints in the floorboards reappear as the high pressure water roars into them, blasting out every last particle of dust. Ted stands back as I lift the running plate between engine and tender, and the last of the muck is washed down into the pit. Then I shut off the 'pep' pipe and injector, take the oil-cans and tea-cans from Ted, open up the large ejector, release the handbrake, push the big reverser into forward gear and give her a little steam with the regulator to take her up to the column for water.

We fill her up, then walk back to the enginemen's cabin for a wash; first the hands, then off with caps, overall jackets and shirts, and we enjoy the sheer delight of cold water dispersing sweat, and heat. The pleasure of washing away the last hour is exhilarating. We emerge completely restored, cool and comfortable again, ready to take this old lady out for another long hard day in her life.

Ted sets the regulator just off the valve so that she drifts quietly off the shed up to the signal. As we pass the coal stage, the first cup of tea is already down, and the second cup poured and ready as we stop. I read in the newspapers of people in factories and offices walking out because it is too hot to work. We thought we

were lucky if we could prepare an engine outside the shed, and really lucky that we did not have a big tank engine. They were not just hot on a summer day, they were sheer hell.

The second aspect of Didcot shed relates to a time in the shed's working life when most of the hard work applicable to the day ahead is carried out.

The day starts with the alarm clock going off at 2.15 a.m. A wash and shave, followed by a cup of tea, then on with overalls, jacket and mac, and out into the quiet dark streets and sometimes driving rain.

To walk out of a freezing sleet storm into the haven of the station subway is completely the opposite to the previous description. At 3.30 a.m. the station is alive with all the sounds of a busy railway. There is no echo of footsteps this time, but the whine of the lifts, and the rumble of platform trolleys. A vacuum-fitted freight roars overhead on the down main line, to be replaced by the sound of the Whitland milk on the up main line, a sound quite peculiar to that type of train.

In the subway the first sound of her is the high-pitched whistle, blasting away as she nears West box, then the oscillation of milk tanks builds up into one mighty continuous roar as the engine pounds overhead, followed by the screaming of the wheel flanges as the tanks buck and sway. The rail joints beat out a pattern so quickly that they almost merge into one sound, and then she is gone, the last vehicle rattling away into the darkness, all over in the time it takes to walk a few yards.

A coal train passes overhead on the up relief line, each rail joint capturing distinctly the solid weight of forty tons as the wagons pass from rail to rail. Then we are through the subway and up the steps.

A long line of coaches and parcel vans block the way over the crossing and the passenger pilot is waiting for the coal train to pass East Junction. We stand there in the driving sleet, the north-east wind slicing through clothes. Then the coaches start to slide forward and it is safe to cross. No sharp tang of hot creosote now, the years of oil and grease droppings now covered with freezing rain have turned the sleepers into a skating rink. We cross over and trudge down the cinder path, heads down, shoulders hunched up with no crunch of cinders underfoot, but a dirty black quagmire of muck to slosh through.

The first whiff of the shed comes with the black smoke driven up the path towards us and we begin to pray that the engine is inside the shed. The rain cuts into the face like needles, and we are cold, wet, and fed up with it all, even before we start.

The first impression of the shed at this time in the morning is one of stark raw ugliness. There is no glamour nor any possible conception of the beauty of the steam engine. The office windows are steamed up, the tall lights round the shed disappear and reappear through the smoke. Everywhere is organised chaos with drivers oiling engines by the light of a flare lamp, the wind whipping the flame until it roars like a blow-lamp. All are wearing dirty old macs kept stored away for mornings like this. Firemen swearing because of all the mornings in the year, the sand boxes have to be empty on this dirty day. Each water column has a 'Devil' alight under it; a tall, dustbin-shaped stove with the chimney reaching up to the arm of the column, belching out flame from the 'T' piece. The barrel of the stove is red hot, and a pile of ashes is under the spindly legs. Heat applied in an antiquated manner to keep the water columns from freezing proved proficient on good Welsh steam coal in Brunel's days so why change it? It also keeps the spare Fireman busy for he has the 'Devils' and the sand drier furnace to attend to, in between keeping pressure up on the stationary boiler. Then if he has a spare minute, the shift Foreman will find him an engine to prepare. There are always some Firemen who find it a bit of a struggle to get out of a warm bed on a dirty morning, and to come on duty an hour late to find your engine already prepared by the spare Fireman is very pleasant!

There is not one road without activity. The two Collett 'Twenty-Twos' are ready to couple up and go off shed for the early Winchester goods. The Didcot yard pilot engines are being prepared, the depot pilots are busy in the first stages, three engines are being made ready for Moreton Yard, and behind in the shed, the later departures are being stoked up by the steam raiser.

The engineman's cabin is full of men coming off duty, men coming on duty and men awaiting orders. The storeman has his hands full dealing out oil and cotton waste, so much so, that drivers line up at the counter to be served and the requisition pad grows smaller as each man signs for his requirements.

The fitter passes with large open-ended spanners and a heavy hammer to attend to a minor defect on an engine, the tools indicating that brake blocks have seized on, as his mate trails behind him looking distinctly unhappy, half submerged in a dirty tattered old raincoat, weighed down on one side with a tool-box so heavy that he walks with a pronounced limp.

The sleet lashes each man, hands chilled with the bitter cold and the half-smoked roll-up becomes sodden and is dropped into a pocket to join a dozen more indicating mute evidence of sudden call-outs. The warmth of the fitter's cabin is now a dim memory.

The offending engine is dealt with in a practised manner. The lock nut is slackened and with it the adjuster, and the Driver is asked to blow off the brakes. The rodding is then belted with the 'Brummigam' spanner, the adjuster given half a turn and the lock nut tightened. Brakes are applied for a test, a slight clearance and then a re-test. Tools are then picked up and a course set back to the warmth of the shed. The shed fitter and his mate are a special breed of men. Like the enginemen, both serve the steam engine, they love it and at times they hate it, but always they care for it. The fitters have a far larger repertoire of swear words than the enginemen, which they use each time a spanner slips and removes a piece of skin, or a brake block drops on the toe of a boot.

The enginemen have a great admiration for the enormous vocabulary enjoyed by fitters, but treat them with respect and kind words, because they know that only a greenhorn cleaner or young fireman would dare to say 'Did it hurt?', when a fitter is seen hopping round on one foot.

Chapter Three

Each Railway Company owned some fine locomotives but more important, they also had the finest collection of men in the country's labour force to man them, for no matter how well the steam locomotive was designed, it was only as efficient as the two men on the footplate. The designer could produce figures on paper of the total output of any given type of locomotive but, without the skill of the fireman swinging the shovel with all the artistry of his trade, keeping the engine on the boil so that the driver could exercise his skill with the regulator, cut-off and braking, all could be lost. However, with two men working together in such unison, output figures could be produced far beyond those of any designer. I hope I am not biased in any way when I say that the Great Western engine was one of the most handsome looking locomotives anywhere in the world, and could outrun, and outsteam any comparable locomotive class for class, all on a standard of design begun by Mr. Churchward in 1903. We were proud of our locomotives, and to illustrate the point the reader has only to compare a photograph of the U.S.A. Transportation 2-8-0 freight locomotive with any Great Western locomotive.

The U.S. engine, like many of the other companies' engines, fairly bristles with bits 'nailed' on. There is the Westinghouse pump projecting from the smokebox, exposed valve gear, oil pipes, steam pipes, sand pipes, and bits of plumbing twisting and snaking their way all over the boiler, but the Great Western engine stands clean and proud. The U.S. engine had a great deal of influence on future design for the British Rail standard because of the accessibility for oiling and maintenance, and this came with the 'Austerity' Class 2-8-0 of Mr. Riddles. But the Great Western engine properly prepared would run without any attention to the inside big ends, so there was no need to place it all on the outside. This point was proved on the L.N.E.R. A4 class. The very high speed runs with *Mallard* and *Quicksilver* were troubled with the inside big ends running hot, but this was overcome with the fitting of the Great Western big end, so the inaccessibility of the Great Western part did not matter. They were built like a Rolls Royce and indeed ran like one, and the driver of ample proportions who found that oiling the inside motion from the pit a bit of a problem would find there was always the skinny engine cleaner ready to supplement his 'fag money' by 6d to do the job under the guidance of the stout gentleman standing in the water below him, and at the same time learn something about locomotive lubrication.

As for running, this was a byword, be it a lowly old 28XX or a 'Castle'. I have run passenger trains, express vacuum fitted freight, and loose coupled petrol trains on the good old 'Twenty-Eight', with a smoothness that was just not possible with an 'Austerity' or a U.S. locomotive. The 'Twenty-Eight' would run, not perhaps with the fleetness of a 'Castle', but nevertheless, fast enough to keep time should the occasion demand it. On a petrol train, the skill of both driver and fireman could be taxed almost to the limit. We would pull away from Swindon with an up Avonmouth train made up of 40 tanks, all loose coupled, and by the time we passed Shrivenham we would be trotting them along at a fair old rate, through Challow, running like the wind. On passing Steventon, we would shut off and screw down the tender handbrake hard, in case Foxhall distant was on. Now the 'Twenty-Eight' had severe braking power, so to overcome the problem of knocking the guard over in his van, there was a slight delay between the application of the vacuum brake and the blocks biting. But once the vacuum was applied, an extra turn could be given on the hand-brake, and braking with these petrol tanks now became a work of art, for the surge of the tanks would begin, and when it came, it was like a giant hand pushing behind. The gentle braking would go on, a little at a time by the driver, the fireman watching and gauging with his mate the amount of tender brake he applied in assistance, easing it off, winding it on, until the surge had subsided to gently stop at the signal. The art of handling a locomotive was as much in stopping one as running one, because, had the distant signal been off, it was then a matter of gently tightening up all those loose couplings, by easing off the hand-brake, giving her a little steam with the regulator, until the very slight snatch was felt, and then open up and run again.

The U.S. locomotive on the same type of train was another matter altogether. The power and steam were there, but we would never run one like with a 'Twenty-Eight'. The method of lubrication was of the most primitive kind for such a very good heavy freight locomotive. The axle shaft ran on white metal bearings packed with oiled cotton waste, and any attempt to run would result in the tender boxes squealing like a pig. The noise was loud enough for a signalman to come to the window and pray that we would clear his section before the wheels dropped off. Thus it was a set pattern of driving to open the regulator, peg it on the ratchet, link her up, and let her make her own pace.

The performance of the British counterpart, the 'Austerity', was about half-way between the U.S. engine and the 28XX class, but with such a rocking, bucketing, clanking and shrieking as to give one the distinct feeling of insecurity. It was a simple locomotive with no frills, built, as its name implies, to meet a need for locomotives to handle freight movement with the minimum of shed time, but it was disliked by Western enginemen. We were used to better things, and for freight trains, the 28XX was the master.

One locomotive I have not yet touched on was the L.M.S. class 8F 2-8-0. This locomotive was to become the War Department choice to replace the ageing 30XX class, and the contract for their construction went to both the Southern Works at Eastleigh and to Swindon.

The Swindon-built engines were numbered 84XX and they looked like an updated 28XX, and no wonder, for they were designed by Mr. Stanier who, although now C.M.E. on the Midland, was an ex-Swindon man.

We felt at home on these engines, so we forgave the left-hand drive, outside valve gear, poppet safety valves, and the live steam injector handles which needed a clout with a coal pick to open, because they were a direct continuation of our beloved 28XX class. Besides this, they carried a small oval plate on the front framing which read 'Built Swindon Works'. They would run well, and to a Western man that was what steam was all about.

Perhaps before we go on to the different classes of locomotives and the work we carried out with them, it would be advantageous to see just what kind of men they were who ran the finest railway system in the world. From the Chief Mechanical Engineer to the shed labourer with his number 8 shovel, they were all united in one thing, being the Company they worked for which was in my case the Great Western Railway, or as we referred to it, 'God's Wonderful Railway'. The fierce pride one held in one's membership of that Company was the secret of the success of the Great Western. It was a family concern, son following father, generation after generation, and more prevalent in the locomotive department. It was the dream of most small boys to become an engine driver, but in my area it was a dream just to become a 'Great Western' man.

In the shed men were, as always, a cross section of the working community, good and bad, tall and short, cheerful and morose, but with one thing in common, the love of the steam locomotive, and pride in their job. The foreman and his deputies, the fitters, boilersmiths, and firedroppers, the drivers, firemen, cleaners, store-men, clerks and labourers, all the 'back-up' services that went into the running of a shed, made it a privilege to work in the company of gentlemen. One might wonder at the shed labourer and his number 8 shovel, but the word labourer is much under-estimated, for he was a highly skilled man. He would keep the pits clean, light up an engine, coal, drop fires, blow tubes, and carry out all the hundred and one jobs without which a steam locomotive would never leave the shed, and still at 3.00 a.m. on a dirty morning crack a joke with some poor unfortunate who has just arrived from a warm bed.

Chapter Four

The Great Western steam locomotive from the fireman's side of the cab is the very beginning of steam on the shed. The spare fireman's burden, the stationary boiler, so far removed from the glamour of the mighty 'Kings' and 'Castles', but nevertheless a steam engine, was as important in its way as the aforementioned. All sheds needed power for tube blowing, boiler washouts, pumping, etc., but only the Western could come up with a boiler house such as described in this chapter. It was a masterpiece of improvisation, and so simple. Looking back on it now I can see the wisdom of it all.

From time to time as the Collett 0-6-0 22XX class replaced the old Dean Goods engines, Swindon would find that they had a perfectly good boiler mounted on a worn-out frame, so the cab would be removed, and the boiler lifted off the frame and the frame scrapped. The boiler would then go into the boiler shop for some small modifications, in addition to an overhaul. The regulator would be removed, and replaced with a large steam valve, and then the coach steam heating valve would be blanked off, steam brake, vacuum gauges and fittings removed, together with the lubricator. Our stationary boiler was now ready to be lifted onto a wagon and transported to its last home.

At the shed, the boiler house would be completed except for a side and roof ready to receive the stationary boiler. The best example of this can still be seen at Didcot at the bottom of number 3 road next to the lifting shop. All that was needed was for a pit to be dug out, concreted, and a brick cradle to be built each end of the pit. When the boiler arrived, it was lifted on to the cradle, the pit now becoming the ashpan, the side of the boiler house bolted on, and a roof added. To the smokebox protruding outside was added a 30 foot chimney, supported with stay wires. But for all this, it was still unmistakably a Dean Goods engine. All that now remained was to couple up the main steam valve and lay on the town water supply to the injectors. She was now ready for the spare fireman's enjoyment, and if there was no spare fireman, one would be booked on her. To be booked on the stationary boiler was the time to start scouting round for a duty swop, go sick, have a grandmother pass away, be called for jury service or attempt to con some young sprog of a fireman into thinking that it was a wonderful experience to work on the "old lady", and that he would learn a lot about steam, and so he would, because that "old lady" could be just as demanding as a main line run with a rough old "Forty-Three".

Her fuel was coal of course, but in the loosest sense of the word. It consisted of pit sweepings, coke, ovoids, coal dust, old paper, overalls, mouldy food, oil-soaked cotton waste, foremen's bowler hats, and now and again it was said an odd engine cleaner or two. But her steaming depended a lot on the direction of the wind.

An old-hand fireman would use his loaf, and supplement her diet with some good Welsh steam coal purloined from the nearest engine, and on this 'borrowed' coal she would perform. On washout day an old-hand fireman would always be booked to fire her. Somewhere, there was some collusion between the boilersmith and the shed foreman, but there was always plenty of steam when it was most needed.

Firing her was as much a work of art as firing a mobile locomotive. The firebox was chest high, and with no exhausting from the chimney the little-and-often-all-round-the-box' rule did not apply. She thrived on a good thick bed of fire, with the blower half on, dampers and boiler house door wide open, a bracing north wind, and both hands put together in prayer, until washout started. Then to see the speed with which the water level dropped down the gauge glass was to make one forget all about the promised land and start using some basic words. It was I think the nearest to the old coal-burning ships you could get on dry land. On a busy morning no foreman would come near, neither would any of the cleaner lads. Perhaps they believed she fed on young cleaners, as it was possible in that dark inferno, because even the old shed cat found another home.

With the day's work over, you could run the water level down. The boiler pressure was 165 1bs but at this she was only on the 'titter', so we would give her a good pull through with a pricker until she began to roar through her safety valve and rock on her cradle. On went the injector, and the dirty work began. Her fire would be blacked in with all the slop one could find, then it was off with the blower, shut the dampers and firebox door, and then go outside and look at that 30-foot chimney. Thank goodness there was no Smoke Abatement Act in those days, or green belt areas, for on a nice sultry day with a low cloud base it was a sight to see.

The smoke would roll out of that tall chimney, slow, thick, oily, and so heavy that you could almost carry it, up past the coal stage until it spread out in one great all-encompassing blanket over the station. Then the fun would begin, and the telephone bells would ring and it was time to go to the toilet. But one last touch was needed. A good thick lump of wagon grease mixed with coal dust was smeared on the firebox handle.

The shift foreman would be sent in haste as a result of those telephone bells and the first thing he would do would be to turn on the blower and open the firebox doors. Now shift foremen are a good lot of chaps, usually ex-drivers promoted who wear nice suits and white collars, and find dirty jobs for spare firemen in between firing that stationary boiler. They do not get their hands dirty any more, but the call of duty is strong, the urgency of the occasion is pressing, and memory short. It was nice to see them looking round for a clean ball of cotton waste to wipe their hands but never a word was spoken, as they were true gentlemen. They had been caught, but rank and time was on their side. I caught one of my old mates, Ralph Painton who had been made up to foreman, with that trick, and next day found my food-box bolted to the supporting bracket in the roof of the shed, and had to bribe a fitter with 20 cigarettes to go up a 30 rung ladder to get it down.

The stationary boiler was indeed a good basic training for a fireman, for if he could fire her and obtain her full potential, he had no fears whatsoever of going to that other place down below when his days were over, for he had been there already.

The obvious step forward in steam power proper was, of course the 0-6-0 Pannier Tank engines, and in this the Great Western excelled. It was by far the largest collection of standard locomotives in the world. We were quite rightly proud of them, for they were utterly reliable, economical, and with the Stevenson slide valve motion, easy to maintain. Some were very old, re-builds from the old saddle tanks, but age did not matter. They would be found hammering away in every shunting yard on the entire system.

Every driver and every fireman was weaned on the little tank engine, and to lift a 60-wagon coal train out of a yard for reforming was the basic training for all the main line work to come. They had a sharp characteristic 'bark' when exhausting, except those fitted with the spark arrester, and they admitted a 'whoa' from the chimney, but in no way at the expense of power. With the firebox doors open the movement of air sucked into the firebox was very considerable, and cycle trouser clips were favoured by both driver and fireman, not to keep coal dust from flying up inside the legs, but for comfort, as the construction of the male is such, that a vacuum in certain quarters is not appreciated! The other hazard from this movement of air at high speed was a very serious one. The most mouth-watering succulent meal on the footplate was bacon fried in the shovel, and to receive a whiff of that beautiful tang drifting from the cab of a pannier tank on a frosty morning was to create a craving so strong as to completely obliterate all thoughts of other problems. It would start the nostrils twitching and the lips and tongue searching in anticipation, and this was the most dangerous moment. It was known that to open the large ejector on a big engine to create vacuum was a quick way to remove bacon from a shovel, but to open the regulator on a pannier tank engine when your mate had his bacon on the shovel in the firebox was to see if your reflexes were as good as you thought they were. That bacon would disappear up the chimney so fast that it took a moment of thought to realise it was no longer there. We knew all about Mach 1 and the sound barrier long before the jet engine was developed. This did not often happen, particularly if it was the driver's bacon, but when it did it was no good saying 'sorry mate' for even the most gentle of mates would find words he thought he had forgotten to curse you.

Chapter Five

Shunting a busy freight yard was not just a case of moving backwards and forwards with a string of wagons, it called for the closest co-operation with four men working together as a team. The under shunter who changed the hand points and braked the loose wagons, the head shunter who carried out the actual shunting, and the engine driver and fireman who provided the power. The fireman had a very important task in this operation as he had to judge his boiler pressure to perfection. He had to provide steam in sufficient quantity to provide the power, but not enough to blow off through the safety valve and obscure the driver's vision, as all shunting movements were carried out to the shunter's hand signals. In some yards the driver did not even see the shunter as he operated from the fireman's side, so all signals had to be relayed by the fireman to his driver. Daylight shunting with hand signals was a straightforward manoeuvre, as was night shunting to signals from the shunter's hand lamp, but shunting in fog was another story. This was carried out by the shunter blowing a whistle. It was no use clanging the shovel on the firebox ring, or allowing her to blow off, or using the injectors. She was made ready before any shunting started, and then both driver and fireman would hang out of the cab in the damp cold straining with both ears.

The whistle code was one blast to come ahead, two to go back, and three to stop. So you would go forward at a gentle pace, and on hearing three blasts, brake hard. Depending on the load to be shunted and the gradient, the driver would sand the rails all the way from the end of the yard to the train to be broken up, and then open her up to full gear and full regulator. With a 57XX class tank the blast from the chimney could be heard for miles, the echo rebounding from cutting and yard buildings, and the cinders coming down like a hail storm. But all this show of power was lost on nature around us. The shunter's cat would stretch in the sun, the rabbits would sit up on their back legs from the safety of the field and completely ignore it all.

On a hot summer's day when shunters wore white shirts or perhaps no shirts at all, it was time to have a little fun. We would fill up the boiler just that little bit too much, and if the water in the gauge glass was chalky white indicating a washout so much the better. When we opened her up she would prime, showering the yard with fine wet soot. A clean white shirt covered in very fine black spots from the smokebox of a 57XX class tank would be a real test for some of the washing powder advertisements. The first warm day that called for the removal of shirts for the first time since the previous summer, exposing all that pale pink skin, was also a challenge to any full-blooded fireman. A bit of good wet soot never did anyone any harm, and it was nothing that couldn't be removed with hot water, carbolic soap dipped in the sandbox, a drop of paraffin and a good stiff brush. There were always plenty of helpers to hold the victim down on the table in the mess room, and he finished up with a red chest just the same as if he'd had sunburn. It was good 'clean' fun to liven up the duty, and they always paid us back, sometimes by placing a fog detonator under the wheel or if we laid our cap down for a moment it would be placed under the wheel and neatly cut in half with the first movement.

Sometimes a shunter would be brave enough to come up onto the footplate and while the driver was engaging him in conversation the fireman would remove the gauge frame, then gently tap the glass with a spanner. The ensuing roar of escaping steam and boiling hot water would cause the shunter to depart in such a hurry that he never used the steps. They were a grand bunch of lads, who could give as good as they got, and it was a pleasure to work with a good head shunter and his mate.

Fly shunting was a good example of their skill, but before this was carried out both men on the footplate and on the ground had a little conference as to the exact requirements to facilitate this highly dangerous movement. There could be no slip-ups, as it was completely against the rule book. But often this was the only way to get round a shunting problem without a lot of work, so each man had to be sure and have complete confidence in his mates. The engine would couple up to a string of wagons and start off at a good speed with the shunter running flat out beside them. At an appropriate spot he would give the stop signal, the driver would bang on the steam brake, then open up again, and as the first application of the brakes brought the buffers on the wagons up together, the shunter would uncouple with his shunting pole. By this time the engine with the front wagons was 'going like the clappers' to clear the points ahead with the shunter still running. Then as soon as the last wagon attached to the engine had cleared those points, they would be set for the other line, allowing the second string to go rattling past on their own with the under shunter in attendance to brake them.

It was not often that it went wrong as conditions had to be perfect, but when it did there was the most unholy bang imaginable, and if it happened to be coal wagons, it produced the biggest cloud of dust ever seen.

On those very rare occasions, when a big 'squaring up' took place, it was a case of closing ranks against the inevitable enquiry from both traffic and loco departments. Such excuses were given as "The sun was in my eyes," "I tripped over my shunting pole", "The steam brake seized on" or, "My attention was diverted by the gauge glass breaking". An answer for every incident was always ready. Everyone knew it was a routine shunting movement that for once had gone wrong, and as long as too much damage was not done, only a right old blowing and bellowing would be administered to all concerned. Honour was satisfied by heads of both departments and we all got down to running a railway again.

All heavy shunting yards had young drivers or firemen passed for driving on the footplate. Men who had just put down the shovel after many years, and one would think that they were glad to be rid of it, but this was not the case. Without exception they all encouraged the young fireman to have a go at the regulator, and it was not long before he could handle the engine as skilfully as his mate. I think this was one of the reasons why the Great Western had such success with their main line trains, as the engine-men loved the locomotive, and each man knew the requirements of his mate. The shunting yard was the perfect apprenticeship training ground for driving and firing, as from the first day as a fireman you began to learn all about the steam locomotive. You fired it and drove it, and if a spindle gland began to blow you packed it, you oiled it, renewed the gauge glass, and found out why the fore gear eccentric bar was opposite to the back gear eccentric bar. Above all, apart from knowing what to do if the motion did break down, you found where the telephone was and sent for the fitter or another engine.

The amount of shunting operations worked by engines from Didcot shed was considerable. Moreton Yard required two engines, Didcot Yard four engines, and the Ordnance Depot with its 80-odd miles of track, eight engines. The Ordnance Depot working was a sedate occupation compared with the yards. Between each supply shed in this vast area was a level crossing without any protection such as gates or signals. It was the responsibility of the under shunter to walk ahead of all movements over these crossings, and our responsibility to blow the whistle. I think sometimes that more steam was used through the whistle than through the valves. A vast amount of stock was moved up to the top yard for marshalling into trains.

In the depot was the material for the entire British Army, and just about every item that could be used was there, some of it from the 1914-18 war, some from the days before as we would still pass by great mountains of horse-shoes stored between barbed wire and wheel-barrows, the latter stacked up in their thousands.

Most of the Drivers were the older chaps nearing retirement, or on light duties, and to me they were fascinating. They were the original firemen from the days of Dean and Churchward, and they could talk about the first 28XX class, the three French engines, and the birth of the 'Castles'. They were the men who had made it all possible for Mr. Churchward's ideas to mature. One of the shunters on the magazine pilot was Mr. Joe Perks, and he had a host of stories of the early days, as his father was the fireman to driver Goldsworthy who had No. 103 *President* as his regular engine. To hear these elderly gentlemen reminisce about the 'Atbara', 'Badmintons', 'Rivers', 'Armstrongs', 'Counties', and The

Great Bear made a young fireman realise just what the impact of the first of the 40XX class and the 28XX class must have been to these men.

The amount of chat about the 4-4-0 'Counties' was not very complimentary. I had heard my own father talk of their rough running, and this was confirmed by others. One of my Depot mates told me that they were impossible engines to run at any speed, and the tank version was as bad as its sister tender engine. They were all glad to see them withdrawn, yet there was a peculiar sense of regret in the passing of *The Great Bear*. My old Dad had fired her several times, and had said that she was very shy to steam, but even he had that feeling of pride in her. What it could have been if Mr. Churchward had been allowed to develop her further, but as the years passed, even he began to lose interest in her. My own regret is that I was born too late to have any recollection of her.

Depot shunting had its moments, interesting to a cleaner covering a firing duty, and to the junior fireman. The demand on the boiler and fire was light, so there was enough time to learn one's trade. It was in fact the 'nursery' of young firemen. The drivers were all kind men, and still young enough at heart to practise the leg-pulls and practical jokes that seem to be part and parcel of an engineman's life. It was not unusual to spray a red-tabbed staff officer with the coal watering pipe as he stood on a crossing waiting to cross, or open the cylinder drain cocks as we passed a detachment of A.T.S. girls, but I shall always remember dear old Ike Rolf and the way he boiled an egg. The shunter asked Ike to boil him an egg one morning, so I filled the shovel with water and Ike placed the egg in it. We boiled that egg in the firebox for 15 minutes until it was as hard as concrete. At the time I thought this was a joke, but Ike was a perfectionist in jokes, for as he said at the time this was only the first stage, and sure enough he was right. A few days later came the request to boil another egg but not quite so hard this time. Once more the shovel was filled with water and brought to the boil, but Ike just sat there with the egg in his hand. Fifteen minutes later he placed it in the water just long enough to make the shell hot, and then he took it into the shunters cabin and handed it over. On Ike's instructions, I had followed, as he had said that Stage Two was about to take place and would be worth seeing, and indeed it was. The poor shunter had waited fifteen minutes for his egg and, expecting it as solid as a few days previously, he hit it hard with a spoon. The joke was well and truly completed. That egg covered not only a very large area of ceiling but also the Great Western issue waistcoat. Ike explained to me later that I had learned a very important piece of philosophy in life — if a job is worth doing, then it's worth doing well.

Two other parts of shunting were away from the tank engine. One was a job we all enjoyed — the station pilot; the other was detested — the 'fly'.

The station pilot was provided to tail main line passenger trains either by adding or removing coaches, horse-boxes, or milk tanks, making up coach sets in the sidings and transporting those sets to the bay platforms, and acting as stand-by engine for any main line failures. If we had an old 'Duke' as pilot engine, the foreman always had a 'Hall' in steam on the shed just in case, but as a rule we did not have many failures at Didcot, for somehow the top link men would struggle on to Reading or Swindon. They would spot the old 'Duke' on the up or down trip, and to a 'Castle' man even if she was rough, another 20 miles was preferable than changing over engines at Didcot. Bert Edmonds, my uncle at Old Oak Common, had told me that he would rather jump over the river bridge at Goring than run into Paddington on the up Weston with the old *Comet* on the front. There were compensations on the station pilot however. We would stand in front of Didcot East Junction Box on the spur waiting to tail trains, and on a Saturday we had a first-class seat to watch Didcot Town football team in action. Any goals scored for the home team would be accompanied by a series of short blasts on the whistle, and as half the team were railwaymen this encouragement was as good as another goal. In the evenings, particularly in the summer, our education was further enlightened by the antics of some of the courting couples behind the bushes in the fields, but we were gentlemen enough not to blow the whistle and disturb them.

Another highlight on the morning turn was the slip working. Both the 8.00 a.m. Weston and the 4.55 a.m. Fishguard slipped at Didcot, parting from the main train between the up distant and home signals at Foxhall Junction. If all went well, the guard would stop the slip coach on the hand brake in the station, as the vacuum he held in the reservoir tank was for emergency only, but there were occasions when things went wrong. We would watch the main train go by with the slip coach keeping pace one coach length behind, so that we would have to go half-way up the main line to Moreton and drag it back. As this was within station limits no wrong line order was issued for the return, but the poor old guard would keep well out of sight for enginemen have a habit of making quite unnecessary remarks about the driving qualities of some members of the traffic department.

How the 'Fly' got its name I don't know. There were named goods trains such as the 'Coco' and 'Long Tom' but the 'Fly' was far removed from these runners. The 'Fly' was the goods equivalent of the stopping passenger train, and we would stop at all the stations and shunt their goods shed and yard. The arrival of the 'Fly' was also the high spot in the day at some of the country stations, with the senior porter taking charge of shunting, and the lad porter assisting. Our guard, if he was one of the old hands, would sit tight and let them get on with it, because it was no good interfering even with the best intentions. The 'Fly' had arrived, and with it a chance to play trains with a real steam engine, and play trains they did, enough to make a real shunter weep. We would go back and forth with half a dozen wagons, first on one road, then on another, until we passed the point of anger and frustration, and the job became laughable. The local coal merchant would have his wagons placed in a certain spot, as would the farmer, and so it would go on even if it was tipping down with rain, until we said "enough is enough", and packed up and left.

The local 'Flys' to Reading and Oxford were used by our own engine prepared on the shed, and usually we worked the round trip. The up 'Fly' from Swindon was worked by travelling as passengers to Swindon, then preparing the engine on Swindon shed. Some real old rubbish they would give us too. Any engines for sheds between Swindon and Old Oak that needed a washout, tubes cleaned, glands packed, and super-heaters blowing were booked to work home on the 'Fly', but very occasionally we would receive a brand-new engine just out of the Works, and then the arrival of the 'Fly' would take on a special significance. The porter would find a new uniform with such speed that one would think he was a quartermaster of stores, and when the Station Master appeared likewise out would come a camera. Then one dirty old fireman would take photographs of these illustrious gentlemen posed so proudly in front of the new engine. There were many promises of copies of these photos, but they never seemed to come out satisfactorily, the excuse being that just at the moment when the button was pressed the gauge glass was blown through or a dirty great thumb got in the way.

In my day the Wantage tramway was still working, with *Shannon*, now preserved at Didcot, fussing her way round Wantage yard overshadowed by the might of a Churchward 'Forty-Three'. Perhaps I have been a bit hard on these country stations as the arrival of the 'Fly' was something special in their working day, being a change from dealing with calves and piglets in transit, plus a wagonload of farm 'fertiliser', tilley lamps to prepare, and tickets to issue. They were railwaymen who had more than their fair share of work, with none of the glamour. I know that I would rather shovel coal than hump 20 tons of seed corn in two hundred-weight sacks on the goods deck.

One of these porters told me a yarn that I must include, because it shows the working on a country station. One day on the local stopper a large hamper arrived and on the label were the words 'Valuable cat, consigned to Lady X', who lived in the local manor house. Being a curious sort of chap, he opened the hamper to have a look, and the cat promptly shot off up the main line with the Bristolian not far behind. Drastic measures were called for, as outside the station stood a large Rolls Royce with a uniformed chauffeur. The station cat was quickly found and stuffed into the hamper to go for a ride. The station staff waited for a phone call during the next day or so because sometime during the night the station cat came home. The suspense was almost too great, but on the third day another hamper arrived, identical to the first one, again bearing one valuable cat, addressed to the Manor House. The Station Master said 'Philip, my lad, you let the first cat out of the bag, so you must deliver the second personally, and find out about that bloody first cat'.

Philip duly trudged up the hill with the hamper to the Manor, rang the bell and waited with a heavy heart. Her Ladyship answered the door, and expressed much pleasure in this personal service, so much so, that she gave our Philip 'ten bob' for his trouble. He enquired as to the health of cat number one and her reply lifted a great weight from his shoulders. Her Ladyship explained how James, her chauffeur, had taken the hamper into the kitchen, placed it on the table, and when he opened it dear pussy shot out through the open window and had not been seen since. Philip returned to the station and explained that they were all off the hook, keeping quiet about the 'ten bob'. He works with me now, and we often chuckle over that yarn. He was known as 'Nutty' Hazell and with that surname it was obvious, but our Phil knew how many beans made five alright.

As a Didcot fireman my last experience with the small tank engine came with the auto-car working on the Wallingford branch.

It was not often we were called upon to work the little 14XX class except when a holiday vacancy or sick turn came up, so a week or two at Wallingford was a pleasant change. Although engines were supplied from Reading shed, Wallingford, with its staff of two drivers and firemen and one shed man, was a sub-shed to Didcot, and so they were our lads.

My first week at Wallingford was on the late turn. I rolled into the station yard on my old A.J.S. motorcycle, giving her plenty of unnecessary stick on the throttle just to show that a main line fireman had arrived, but the station was bare. I was too early, because the 'Bunk', as she was known, was somewhere between Cholsey and Wallingford.

My mate arrived and I introduced myself to him. He knew my old dad well as they had both been firemen together, but he left me with no doubt whatsoever that I could never be as good as the old chap. I was just another main line fireman from Didcot who thought he knew it all. Well, we would see. Our little train ran in so I had a chance to look her over before we left on the first trip, and I liked what I saw. She was a delightful little engine, and with her big driving wheels and tall chimney perched on top of her black painted smokebox she looked like a little steam roller, but that was an illusion which I was to find out when we started to work her. She would run like a little deer, and so smooth that the rail joints rang out with the 'clickity click' one associated with a coach. She was immaculate, not a blemish or oil spot on her paintwork anywhere, and a credit to Freddie Dancer, the shed man. He was on regular nights, and his main duty was to coal her, clean the fire, and care for her as she would only return to Reading for washout, but Freddie carried his duties far beyond those laid down. How he loved that little engine, for every bit of brass sparkled, every bit of copper gleamed, every bit of paint shone, even the oil feeder and oil cans were burnished, and the regulator handle and reversing gear handles looked as if they were chrome plated. Freddie was a man quick to laugh and in my first week I gave him plenty to laugh about, although my mate did not think it a laughing matter at the time.

The first run into Cholsey was without incident. I had laid a good fire in her and topped up the boiler, and it was just a matter of enjoying the run. On the return trip my mate coupled up the regulator rod, told me to link her up as she began to run, but above all to see that he had plenty of vacuum for stopping at the other end. Then he made his way up to the front of the coach. I blew off her brakes and watched with fascination as the whistle blew, the regulator opened up and we moved off with just myself on the footplate. This was something new, and it seemed queer to be on my own with everything operating as it should without any physical movement on my part except linking up her valve gear. I enjoyed that first run as much as any run I can remember, but the afternoon was young, and I was to start a series of misadventures that lasted several days.

On arrival at Wallingford we had to carry out a bit of shunting, so I had to uncouple the coach. This was nothing new; the steam pipe, vacuum pipe, and coupling, but with the addition of the regulator rod, and it was carried out quickly and efficiently, after all I was a main line fireman.

We moved forward, there was a small 'cheep' from the whistle, and a sharp bang as the whistle chain between coach and engine parted. I had forgotten all about that whistle chain. My mate gave a sniff of disapproval, but I was not the first and would not be the last. When we finished the shunting and coupled back up to the coach he produced an 'S' hook to link the chain — I was learning. We carried out another trip, then returned to shunt once more, and as we moved away the second time again the whistle went 'cheep' and the bang followed. My mate was not amused, for his opinion of main line firemen was confirmed. Well, anyone can make a little mistake like that. On the third try later in the afternoon all went well. To some extent I had redeemed myself, that is until the last trip when we uncoupled for shed. Yes, the whistle went 'cheep' and the chain went off with a bang, this time breaking close to the coach and rattling up against the back of the bunker. I could see that my mate was controlling himself with considerable effort. It was the end of the day, perhaps tomorrow would be better, and anyway he had run out of 'S' hooks.

Dear old Freddie waited until he had gone before he started laughing. He was still at it when I started up my bike and crept quietly out of the station. Instead of blasting up the hill out of Wallingford with the big single cylinder of that old motorcycle bellowing away, rebounding from the houses, I took her away gently, 'linking' her up through the gears until she sang as sweetly as the little twin-cylinder 14XX simmering in the shed. Subconsciously I was driving her like a steam engine, allowing her to take her time before changing up a gear. It was a beautiful starlit night, the bike was running free, and I had much to dwell on. Indeed, even today, my son informs me that I handle the car as if it were propelled by steam.

I had to admit that this first day had been a disaster. Three whistle chains was, I suppose, something of a record, but I could draw some comfort from the last break. I had not forgotten it, for on that last trip it was dark and I just hadn't seen the blessed chain.

The next day started with some uncertainty. My mate greeted me with a growl, and laid in the firebox tray half a dozen 'S' hooks. But Freddie Dancer had gone one better. During the night he had made a large cardboard label and tied it on the screw coupling. It read one word on each side 'Whistle'. Good old Fred, what with those 'S' hooks and the label, I should not forget.

I started a drill as practised before take-off with an aircraft. Whistle chain, steam heating pipe, vacuum pipe, regulator coupling rod, screw coupling, and then we were untied. As my mate eased open the regulator gently, we both waited for the 'cheep' and bang, but all was well, this time, and he began to brighten up and converse again.

The second trip also went off without incident. I untied her from the coach and we carried on with the shunting. My mate gave me a toffee so relations appeared to be improving, but on the third trip I really hit the jack-pot.

I uncoupled with the familiarity of a genuine Wallingford fireman, and jumped back into the cab. We pulled forward a few yards, there was a 'twanging' from the rear, followed by a mighty thump on the back of the bunker. We stopped, climbed down and went round the back of the engine. Now in this technical world there are a great number of very clever men who can listen to the internal combustion engine and by sound, diagnose big ends rumbling, crankshafts grinding etc, but now I too had become an expert in the diagnosis of mechanical sounds, as applied to the steam locomotive, particularly to No. 1407. First the whistle chain breaking, and now I knew what a coach steam heating pipe sounded like when it was stretched and pulled off the coach; it made a 'twang' and a loud thump.

We both looked at the pipe, as it lay there on the sleepers, still connected to the engine steam pipe, with all the bends of the reinforcing wire stretched out straight, and a small dribble of water escaping from the broken end accompanied by a wisp of steam.

Even after all these years I can still remember that moment. It had gone so quiet, except for the gentle simmering of the engine and the distant grinding of a farm tractor far away, all was still, even the birds had gone, and my mate was breathing very heavily. To his credit and in respect for his friendship with my father he took only half an hour to calm down and begin to speak in English I could understand. Because of that friendship he did not refer to my upbringing or ancestry, but there were plenty of other objects to compare me with. He had the advantage of 40 years over me, and with it he too had acquired a very comprehensive command of the spoken word. I thought it wise while he was examining the pipes to remove the coal pick, bucket, and other throwable pieces of locomotive equipment.

Things were very strained for the remainder of the afternoon, but as we had a spare steam heating pipe in the shed, I was able to fit it to the coach. There would be no complaints from the passengers, but while I was engaged in this repair my mate was spending a long time in the station office. I could almost see the telephone wires glowing with the heat.

On the next trip to Cholsey to meet the up stopper I half expected to see a relief fireman step out, but to my surprise no one was there. On the way back into Wallingford on my own in the cab I brooded about the incident. I had been a first-rate clot, and the leg-pulling when I returned to Didcot was something I did not want to think about, but in situations like this the brain begins to function and place things in perspective, for somewhere in the dim past, long before my time on the Great Western, I had heard a story, and it began to filter through.

My attempts at conversation were greeted with curt replies, which was to be expected. With the innocence of youth I asked him who was the fireman who years ago forgot to couple up the coach, and left the passengers sitting there at Wallingford while the driver and fireman went blissfully off to Cholsey, light engine.

He looked at me for some moments without speaking. I thought I had gone too far, but then his eyes twinkled and he burst out laughing, and we began to be mates again. The last trip gave me a chance to redeem myself. As we left for Cholsey the gauge glass blew out, and I had a new one in before we stopped at Wallingford. My mate thought it was smart work, and it was, for everything went right. Then on the return trip as he shut off from the front of the coach, the regulator would not close. I watched it come down, and then go right up as he tried to slam it shut, but she was still taking steam, so I pulled out the pin and shut her off. He was pleased about that one. Perhaps main line firemen were not so bad after all. From then on, my time on the 'Bunk' was a happy one. I returned many times, and it was a period in my firing days that I shall not forget.

Of the two locomotives I fired on the branch I think both No. 1407 and No. 1447 were about equal. Mr. Collett had designed the perfect small branch line engine, for with boiler pressure only 165 1bs and 800 gallons of water carried when full-up, the weight was just over 40 tons, so it was a delightful little locomotive. The cab was something of a surprise, being roomy and comfortable, while the screw reverser gave just that little more space to swing the shovel than the lever type allowed, and indeed they would steam well. I should have liked a run on one on the main line just to see what they would do flat out, but the chance never came. However, I had learnt one thing from them. I now knew the stretching capabilities of steam heating pipes.

Chapter Six

On my return to Didcot shed I was given the job of spare night fireman, so any interview with the shed foreman regarding broken whistle chains and steam pipes was delayed long enough to lessen the sting somewhat. However, that week was to hold tragedy.

I had long held dear to my heart the beautiful 29XX 'Saint' class introduced by Mr. Churchward in 1902. Most of them were 'Courts' or 'Ladies' but the originals were 'Saints' and were referred to as such by enginemen. They were tall and elegant on their 6ft 8½in. driving wheels, and very deceptive in movement, with boiler pressure the standard 225lbs to supply 18½in. cylinders. They would start off slowly with the great side-rods coming up and over in an easy graceful manner, then after a dozen swings of the shovel you could look over the side and see those side-rods going round just that little bit faster. A little more attention to the fire and one would look up to see the trees and telegraph poles sliding past at speed, but as they got their teeth into the load they would start to run, or perhaps 'run' is not the right word. A 'Castle' with her four cylinders would run, but the 'Saints' would lope. To see one of these 'Ladies' on a goods train was sacrilege, and such was the occasion they nearly brought about the end of my days, for, as much as I loved them, they could kill.

In the early hours of one morning during that first week back, I was 'mated up' with Charlie Forbes because his fireman had overslept. We had orders to relieve a goods train in the down gully at Didcot North. I was looking forward to the run as I had worked with Charlie before. He was a nice chap, cheerful and a good engineman to fire for. He had been a fireman at Weymouth before being posted to Didcot as a driver, and knew all about rough trips on heavy gradients and how to treat an engine so that his fireman did not get a wet shirt. We arrived at the head of the train to find No. 2975 *Lord Palmer* and what a treat she looked. She was one of the early 'Twenty-Nines', with straight frames and the small Churchward cab, but it was her condition that took our breath away, for she was just out of Swindon sheds and in brand-new guise.

She still had the old lever reverser, but everything was newly painted, her wooden floorboards were unblemished having neither coal dust in the joints, nor oil stains. We could hardly believe our luck. The Reading crew were upset to see us, because for once they had a locomotive as perfect as one could ask for, and were fully expecting to go through to Banbury with her, and were not at all keen to hand her over to a Didcot crew.

They left her with regret, and after we had had a look around we blew up for the signal, and within minutes it dropped. As it did so, there was a shout from below in the dark. It was Charlie's regular mate, out of breath as he had run all the way from the shed. As he climbed up to that tall footplate it was my turn to bemoan my luck. I collected up my belongings, said goodbye to Charlie, and climbed down to return to the shed. Instead of a run on that beautiful locomotive I should now be back preparing another engine, or firing the stationary boiler.

As I walked back, *Lord Palmer* began to glide away, the wagons clunking past one at a time, slowly gathering speed, and the flanges squealing on the rails. I felt cheated and despondent, but that fireman had saved my life. Before I reached the shed he was dead, and poor Charlie so badly scalded that he died within the hour.

Charlie had been routed down the goods loop to Appleford crossing. As he got about halfway, the down main advanced starting signal with Appleford's distant signal underneath came off. Charlie, thinking he was on the main line, opened up *Lord Palmer* and ran into the throw-off points protecting the main line at Appleford.

Lord Palmer ended up in the field on her left-hand side, with the tender on top of the cab and half-a-dozen wagons on top of that, with Charlie and his mate underneath it all. I often think now, 'There but for the grace of God, go I'.

The next Sunday morning, *Lord Palmer* was dragged out, re-railed, brought back to the shed, and placed by the shed wall on number five road. She was not too badly damaged, but her left side was covered in mud, her cab bent and hand rails twisted. I climbed up on the footplate, her boiler was covered with coal dust, mud, half-burnt coal, and lagging dust. She was as cold and lifeless as the two lads she had killed. I left her with a shiver, never to see her again, and the charm of the Twenty-nine went with her.

The death of these two fine men was keenly felt not only at Didcot shed but at every Great Western shed and even at sheds of other companies, because as enginemen, a little of us all had died with them. We knew that when all the glamour of handling a steam engine is swept aside and the 'chips are down', firing a large locomotive with over a thousand tons moving behind can be a tough occupation. We were all brothers bonded together by steam.

My old dad was inconsolable as he was very close to Charlie, and as an engineman himself he could appreciate the circumstances that led to the accident. One Sunday afternoon we drew out together the area of Didcot North showing the existing signals. We crossed out and added others which we thought would improve the signalling because we could see this happening again. The drawing was submitted to the London Division suggestion scheme for consideration, but it was turned down, though we did receive a very nice letter of appreciation, informing us that improvement was forthcoming. In fact, a long sand drag was built at the end of Appleford loop later.

The old chap's assumption that this could happen again was to be proved right as a few years later another locomotive finished up in that field, this time a 43XX class Mogul, and several others were to be glad of that sand drag.

On the whole the Great Western signalling was excellent, and with A.T.C. our safety record was the best in the world. The wartime blackout was a help because signals could be seen, there being no other lights to cause confusion. After the war when things got back to normal, to run between Southall and Paddington on a dirty wet night with the steam and smoke beating down, drifting and swirling along the boiler, was a real headache, with street lights, traffic lights, neon lights, all greens and reds, and all in line with our signal lights.

We would run into Paddington, with eyes red and sore as a result of hanging halfway out of the cab searching for our path through that constellation of colour. From time to time we would shut off, giving her a whiff of vacuum, with that small nagging doubt, until one or the other would shout a confirmation of a suspect sighting to the other. One by one the yellows and greens of the colour light signals would slide by, the bell in the cab would ring out, the buzzer give a short 'whoop' to be cancelled quickly, and then we would glide into the bright fairy world of Paddington. It was as if one had entered another world, with this great cavern of a building, the harsh blare of a taxi horn mingling with the voice of the young lady on the station tannoy announcing our arrival. Her voice was always so metallic and distorted, the echo rebounding back in one's ears just that split second behind her speech. The passengers scurrying by without even a glance into the cab, and the nonchalant way the porters weaved in and out driving their 'tugs' with a long line of trolleys all added to the scene. We would sit for a few moments completely bemused by it all, for the transition from the utter concentration of the last twenty miles into normality was too much for the mind to accept.

Now and again a passenger would stop and spare a few minutes to thank us for arriving on time, or for a safe journey, and for every three that did so, two were sure to be ecclesiastical gentlemen, and it was not their calling that prompted them to stop, but a genuine interest in the steam locomotive. They could converse with some knowledge on the subject, and were delighted to be invited onto the footplate. It was a real pleasure to be in their company. It was such an unlikely combination with two dirty, weary enginemen, who ten minutes previously had been searching their soul and silently praying that the green light spotted through the murk was theirs and not a traffic light on a bridge, enthusing on the merits of a 'Hall' against a 'Black 5' with a very enthusiastic gentleman wearing his collar back to front. Having just referred to soul searching and prayer, I feel there was a connection, and these worthy gentlemen knew that four hands and eyes, two brains, and a great deal of faith had delivered them to the safety of the Paddington platform. I am sure that many a fine sermon delivered from the pulpit on a Sunday morning began life in the cab of a Great Western locomotive.

I think most firemen enjoyed the run into Paddington as I know I did. It was not only the end of the line, but also a chance to see the world go by, and as with all the big London stations, Paddington was something special after all the country stations.

The Paddington Station Master was special too. This gentleman was THE Station Master; the ultimate end of all the dreams of the country station lad porter, and a most imposing gentleman he was. Dressed immaculately in morning suit with top hat, he would patrol his station with such an air of stateliness about him he portrayed all that was the Great Western.

One morning Ralph Painton and I ran in with the 7.04 a.m. from Didcot. I untied the train, dropped a headlamp on the tender bracket ready to follow the coaches out and almost bumped into the Station Master as I returned to the cab. He walked past and stopped a coach length from us, quietly watching the activity around him. He was within what I might describe as a good throwing distance.

We had No. 5935 *Norton Hall* and for once she had a slight defect. Normally she was in perfect condition, but this morning her regulator gland was leaking, so we had placed in the tray over the firebox a lump of cotton waste to catch the drips until we got round to tightening up the gland. When squeezed out that lump of waste was just right in weight to come into contact with that top hat. Now Ralph and I had worked together for some time, enough to read each other's thoughts, and as I picked up the wet waste he looked at me, then at that top hat, and he grabbed my wrist. Temptation was strong, but this could not be the target. However, fate came to the rescue, because along the platform came a man without a care in the world. He had a paste bucket in one hand, a roll of posters tucked under his arm, and over his shoulder a billposter brush. As he passed the Station Master, Ralph put two fingers in his mouth and let out a piercing whistle. Round went the brush and off came the top hat. It was so neatly carried out, and so quickly over. Ralph climbed down onto the platform, picked up the hat and with all the dignity of a driver made the poor man apologise for his action. Then he handed the hat over to the grateful owner, and returned to the engine with such a forced expression on his face that I could see he was having a job to control himself from laughing. I still think I could have hit that hat, because with Ralph I had had plenty of practice, for his aim was deadly. He could hit a rabbit on the run, and also hit the pot at Snow Hill. If any ex-enginemen read this they will remember the pot, and take off their caps to a gentleman of unique distinction. This gentleman's garden backed on to the main line just outside Snow Hill station. At the bottom he had rigged up a net between two poles, and in front of the net, balanced on top of a post, was a beautiful chamber pot. We would prepare for that target miles away, placing to one side nice handy lumps of coal of just the right weight and size to have a sporting chance, and then we would let drive as we passed. That chap never bought any coal, and he must have thrown away his coal hammer years ago, because his bucket was filled each day with coal just the right size to fit the kitchen grate.

But to return to Paddington, the art of running in was not to make the fire too high. The last shovelful went in when passing Slough, and with it a prayer. Rules at Paddington and Ranelagh Bridge turntable were very strict. No smoke, and no blowing off at the safety valve. So the fire was allowed to run down with the boiler, and it was a chance to sit down and help your mate search for the signals.

We would open the firebox doors, drop the dampers, leaving the back one on the last peg, and pray for a run in. However all too often we would start coming up to yellow lights as we caught up the train in front, and then it was a case of just keeping her rolling in the hope that we would not be stopped. If that happened from Ealing Broadway onwards we would be in dead trouble, for with the fire run down and half a glass of water showing, the boiler pressure would drop back quickly as we ran her with ten or more coaches into Paddington. Sometimes it was touch and go with not enough pressure to blow the brakes off, and more than one crew had the embarrassment of being towed in from a dead stop.

On arrival at Paddington the chimney would be grey in colour on the inside, just like a car engine running on a weak mixture, then, as the coaches were pulled off, we would follow down the platform until the 'dummy' or ground signal was reversed, and drift down to Ranelagh Bridge to turn.

As soon as we had turned and filled up with water, I could set about making up the fire for the return journey, and with the boiler level down, there was plenty of room to keep topping her up with the injector. The fire would be built up slowly, the back damper wide open with the firebox doors, then she would burn through without too much smoke, and each time the pressure came up to the blowing off point, the injector would go on and knock her back a few pounds.

Backing on at Paddington gave a fireman a chance to build his fire right up, because the engine was outside the station, and if she did smoke a bit it was only until departure time. Once away, I used to let her 'go' to Old Oak Box, after which came a good pull through the fire with the pricker, while my mate opening the regulator wide, and with the reverser only back a few turns, gave her plenty of steam. The reverser was then wound back to 35% cut-off so that nearing Ealing Broadway, the fire was a white hot mass. She would blow off hard under the bridge, so it was on with the injector, and then she would hold the pressure without the needle moving off the red line. Now we could begin to fire her without worry of too much smoke, because smoke was the mark of poor firing. If the exhaust was tinged with smoke as each shovelful was placed in, then she was just right. The old rule applied; little and often in the right place at the right time.

The 'Hall' class were good engines, perhaps just that little bit heavy on coal when on a stopping passenger train with ten coaches or more, but once on the run you could wind them back to 25% cut-off, ease down the regulator, a little at a time, and then they would fly.

The 49XX and 59XX were particularly good, but although of the same class, the 69XX's were inclined to be a bit sluggish and required a bit more 'stick', although on goods trains they were excellent, a good reliable locomotive all round, and a pleasure to work on.

As with all Great Western engines the cab was standard, comfortable and roomy although Great Western engines could only be worked successfully standing up. It was, of course, possible for the driver to sit on the small wooden tip-up seat, once the valves and regulator were set. If he did have a regulator that was inclined to creep down, then the V-shaped wooden peg was placed between the guide rod and stop. This peg was contrary to regulations and kept out of sight, but it was a handy bit of equipment to have in the pocket. Even so, the driver had to stand up to stop as he could not reach the vacuum brake or ejector sitting down. On the 29XX class, he had a large reversing lever reaching back so far into the cab that he had to half lay across it to see through the eyeglass.

My old dad was a bit on the short side, so he either stood on the cylinder steam cock lever or his food box. Once when I was his fireman on No. 4056 *Princess Margaret*, I suggested that I give him a bunk up. The reply was a well-aimed stream of smoke drawn up from the bottom of an ancient briar pipe, which was equivalent to a lungful of Welsh steam coal smoke on the up main line halfway through Honeybourne tunnel. The next time I swung a shovelful of coal, a foot was stuck out so that I had some sweeping up to do! Such is life, R.H.I.P. (Rank has its privileges.)

The fireman was not much better off, for he could only sit down depending on several factors. These were a light load, downhill, or stopped. His steam gauge was either right up on top of the boiler casing behind the fountain head and obscured by the injector handles, or, with the later engines, it was placed with the steam heating gauge on a steel plate angled so that he had to get up to see it. In all cases the water level in the gauge glass was hidden by the shut-off valve handle and gauge lamp bracket. Therefore, a good fireman stood up. However, my old chap thought it was right and proper, because in his firing days there was no seat at all. The funny thing about it all was, that when he let me drive, the engine steamed better than it did when I fired, and the water in the glass never seemed to go down. He would sit back on that fireman's seat and grin at me like a Cheshire cat. Again, I think it was a case of R.H.I.P.

He did teach me one trick, however, to be used at periods where we could expect to stand at signals for a length of time during the night. The engine bucket, I now found, had uses other than those intended for it. The bucket was hung on the balance weight arm of the signal, and into it went a handful of ballast, then when the signal 'came-off', so did the bucket. I think signalmen thought they might catch us asleep, but enginemen were a crafty lot.

In later years when I was district relief signalman, I would sometimes at night have a train in the goods loop for an hour. I would open the end window, get 'line clear' from the box ahead, ease over the points, carefully slide in the locking bar, take up the slack on the signal wire and gently pull over the lever. Sure enough, clang would go a bucket.

As fireman to my own father, I found that no favours could be asked, and none were given, and the start of the duty began at home. The fact that firing was a dirty occupation was no excuse to start that way, and he could be as tough as any Sergeant Major. Boots had to be polished to Guardsman's standards, overalls clean, finger nails and hands as clean as any office worker, and collar and tie worn. His theory was that a clean engine crew led to efficiency, and we walked down the road shoulder to shoulder as Great Western enginemen to the shed. For all this, he had a sense of humour second to none, and his brother Bill at Reading was as bad. They would delight in relieving each other, when Bill would look down from the cab and make some caustic remark about trusting the engine to this Didcot crew, while the old chap would reply to the effect that once the Reading crew were off the footplate we could begin to make it a fit place for Didcot men to work on. Then a right old slanging match would begin, and this was very effective if there was some poor unfortunate driver learning the road. Then when the desired effect had been produced, and the driver stepped between them to stop a punch-up they would put their arms round each other and dance round the footplate. The art of leg pulling between these two appeared to carry to the point of madness to the uninitiated.

The engineman's journal, which was the log of duty, had to be handed in on completion of each duty. It covered all aspects of the locomotive working for the day, including reporting the weather conditions in a small square that read 'State of weather'. This small square was a challenge to most drivers, ranging from 'bloody hot' to 'flipping cold', but if records were taken from this information, we were never asked to clarify any of the entries. On a hot day father would enter 'Heavy snow' or on a very cold day 'hot', not for the purpose of confusing records, but just for the hell of it. He was the only engineman at Didcot who had the reputation of having his own arm-chair on the footplate, and this came from an incident at Westbury. The staff association there held a Christmas Draw, with the first prize being an armchair, and the old chap won it. The next problem was how to get it home, and this was a challenge indeed to any red-blooded driver, but he managed it by carting it home on the footplate from Westbury to the Newbury bridge just outside Didcot where it was lifted down and placed deep inside a bramble hedge.

After taking the engine to shed, father returned to the Newbury bridge and collected his arm-chair. Thank goodness it was before the times of panda car patrols, for with the local bobbie tucked up in bed, and at 2.00 a.m. in the morning, a Great Western driver walking up the middle of Didcot with an armchair on his back, would have had some explaining to do. The old chap could talk his way round any situation, but he had to admit that he might have been beat on that one.

One day we booked on and were sent to Foxhall Junction to relieve the 12.40 Reading to Aberdare, and found, not only the 'Aberdare' No. 2651 at the head of the train, but brother Bill also. The usual argument took place as to the enginemanship of Reading against Didcot men for the benefit of Bill's fireman, but then the day started to go wrong. We had made a can of tea at Didcot West Box and before drinking it a procedure had to be carried out. No can of tea was ever stirred, either with spoon or spare gauge glass. We would take the lid off, catch hold of the handle, hang out of the cab and swing it round and round with centrifugal force keeping the tea inside the can. But not today; the old chap was swinging the can when one end of the handle came off and brother Bill having climbed down after making a smirking remark had just reached the right distance, when a dollop of hot tea hit the back of his neck. To Bill it looked as if it had all been planned and brotherly love was no more. The regulator was opened a little more smartly than usual and we clattered over the Junction and on down the main line towards Swindon with some most uncomplimentary remarks being hurled after us.

The old 26XX 'Aberdare' engines were nothing to shout about. They were built in 1900, and at that time were considered the best in goods engines, but after 45 years of work they were past their prime. They were of the 2-6-0 wheel arrangement with inside cylinders, and a small cab and when I worked on them they were all fitted with the R.O.D. tenders taken from the 30XX class. The most objectionable part about them however was the steam reverser as it was almost impossible to keep them linked up. You could give a snatch on the lever and hope that the indicator came up to somewhere near the position required, but they would hold this for about half a mile and then begin to creep forward into full forward gear.

We shuffled along in this fashion, with the big old side-rods clanking from the slackness in the pins and bushes, and striving to keep the pressure up to the 200 1bs mark, with her tubes blocked and leaking and her brick arch on the point of collapse. Father pegged the regulator on the first valve, and let her take her time, for to keep moving at all was better than stopping for a 'blow up'.

As anticipated we were diverted off the main line at Wantage Road, and down the relief line to Challow. The next main down train passed us at Circourt intermediate signals with a great deal of whistle blowing and fist waving from the crew, as we had knocked the run out of them before the van cleared Wantage points. The usual comradeship between all Great Western footplatemen was forgotten as we returned the compliment. The toffee-nosed express men from Old Oak with their sparkling 'Castle' obviously thought the railway was for their exclusive use, but we both had a surprise as their engine drew level with ours. We then noticed that the whistle blowing and fist waving was coming from Uncle Bert Edmunds, my old dad's brother-in-law. Father reacted as quick as he possibly could before the 'Castle' was out of reach for as his brother had been given most of the can of tea back at Foxhall, Dad felt that his sister's husband might as well have the dregs. These were thrown across the small space separating us, and the wet tea leaves flew all over Bert's legs. His fireman had the injector on so we had the 'pep pipe' turned on us, but as he was in a hurry his aim was poor, while Bert was in the process of opening up his posh 'Castle' to make up lost time. Then the whistle blowing ceased, the fist waving turned into a two-finger salute, and then they were gone. We continued until we were turned into Marsden Yard, as Control had decided to break up the train there and give us a transfer load for Swindon before sending the engine to shed.

We uncoupled and pulled over to another road where our guard was waiting. He was a gruff old gentleman nearing retirement, and being an old gentleman who loved familiar things about him, he was wearing his old uniform cap, issued to him way back in 1920. It sat on his head like a large dinner plate and had done so through countless rains and snows, winds and suns which had turned it from black to a mixture of dirty grey and mouldy green. But sadly today this was the end of the road for Sam's well-worn cap.

I think it must have been his advancing years that made him scorn the shunting pole to couple us up to the train. As I saw him move in front of the wagon and hold the coupling up ready to hang on our hook, I informed Father. Dad stopped the engine about a foot short, then on the shout 'ease up' he gave her a little steam.

As I pointed out earlier, the 'Aberdares' were fitted with the R.O.D. tender, and had a very deep well at the rear end, at least two feet deep, having two drain holes going right through the tender to take away excess water when the tank was overfilled. Over a period of time these holes became blocked with coal dust, as indeed was the case with our old 'Aberdare' and instead there was now about two feet of dirty black water sloshing about on top of the tender.

When she touched that first wagon and Sam hung on the coupling, the dirty black water came over the top in one great deluge to drench Sam right through to his underclothes. He emerged completely swamped, spluttering and swearing. As gentlemen, we could only do one thing, which was to get Sam on the footplate and dry him out. So up he climbed, and we helped him to undress. When we removed his jacket, waistcoat, and trousers, we found that Sam did not go in for 'Y' fronts or jockey shorts. No, Sam did not go in for that new-fangled stuff, but wore some thick wool combinations of 1900 vintage. The most interesting part about these was the small flap at the rear, secured by two small buttons on each side, obviously for use when nature called. But this flap was soaked, and it must have first priority if Sam was to sit down.

He stood there with his back to the open firebox while we unbuttoned the flap, and with each of us taking one corner, held it out to dry. It did not take long, and as it began to steam, it slowly turned a golden brown, so we returned it to its proper place. Sam had an expression of extreme pleasure on his face as the warmth of that flap came into contact with his bottom. But then he made the mistake of sitting down on my seat, and as the golden brown wool and especially the buttons were still very hot, he gave a yelp and quickly stood up again.

While all this was going on, his cap was drying quite nicely. I had hung it on the injector handle so that it had all the heat of the fountain head to penetrate the inside. Unfortunately the combination of rapid heating on wet cloth over 25 years old is not an ideal one, and naturally it began to shrink. With the heat the stitching parted piece by piece so that the wire stiffener came through, the peak began to bubble and separate from the hat. There was only one solution, the hat was destined for the firebox, but first we removed the faded G.W.R. badge as a memento.

Sam never looked the same again, for part of him had disappeared with that old hat. We did notice however, that he always used a shunting pole to couple up after that.

I cannot remember if any of the 'Aberdares' survived to the end of steam, as they seemed to fade away, probably being cut up on reaching Swindon when overhaul was due. During their life they must have contributed a great deal to freight movement. I found them on the whole to be fairly good steamers, but each one needed their own special treatment in the method of firing, as one would like a 'haycock' fire where another would like a thin fire. Therefore, I would compromise, and pack the back corners of the firebox tight, building it up level with the firebox ring, and then slope it all towards the front end, gradually thinning to a foot deep under the brick arch. The exhaust did not have the crisp bark of the usual Western engine, but was more of a 'whoa', so the blast in the firebox did not cut up the fire. If the driver was content to set the regulator and let the loco take its time, plodding along at its own pace, this was possible, by splashing the coal round to keep the red needle somewhere near the red mark on the steam gauge. At 200lbs pressure, this was chiefly a case of watching the safety valve, and with the numbers on the gauge fading and the needles either bent or quivered this was difficult. I cannot remember one 'Aberdare' that was steady, and certainly not one of these locos steady enough to ride on in comfort as they would pitch and roll that much that one was often pleased to see a relief crew come aboard.

The 'Aberdares' and the R.O.D.'s were two classes of locomotives whose disappearance I certainly shed no tears over. Even a rough old 'Churchward' 43XX Mogul was preferred but I will describe these locos in more detail.

Chapter Seven

The Churchward 43XX class was born in 1911, and became one of the largest classes of mixed traffic locomotives on the Great Western. They were in fact, the first attempt by Mr. Churchward to standardise the Great Western locomotives. The wheels, side-rods, cylinders, and various other parts were common to other engines and in later years, when the 'Grange' class was designed to replace the 43XX class, parts from this class were used in building the 'Granges'. The 'Forty-Threes' were very fine engines. With the 2-6-0 wheel arrangement they were the first 'Moguls' to be built for the Great Western. Cylinders were 18½in coupled to 5ft 8in driving wheels, and with boiler pressure of 200lbs. this gave a tractive effort of 25,670lbs. This so called tractive effort was always way above our calculations as enginemen, our interest was only in the capabilities of the locomotive regarding pulling power, steam and running. Compared with other main line engines such as the 28XX class, 'Castles' and 'Kings' they were not a large locomotive and not much heavier than the 'Aberdare'. The small Churchward cab gave them almost a stubby appearance, and the two bracing bars between the smokebox saddle and front buffer beam made them appear top heavy at the front end.

Throughout their life they retained the small 3,500 gallon tender, and this enhanced the overall picture of the engine. Some survived to the end of steam, still giving sterling service. They were found all over the Great Western heading all types of main line and branch line trains. Long before the introduction of the 'Hall' class, the 'Forty-Threes' were hammering up and down the main lines with express passenger and goods trains, and proved to be the mainstay of locomotive working on the Great Western.

From the driver's point of view these were good strong locomotives, and as with all steam locomotion the maximum boiler pressure was essential. With the safety valve just beginning to lift they could be loaded to the limit and still plug away.

The firemen either loved or detested the 'Forty-Three', probably because it was a common used engine and as such sometimes suffered. However they were not often in tip-top condition as were the three allocated to Didcot. These were steam with a candle in the firebox.

As a young fireman I detested them, mainly because of lack of experience and partly because I did not understand them. I always had just enough steam, and water in the boiler, but never quite enough to relieve me of that feeling of insecurity. Often a distant at caution, a bit of a downhill run, or a signal stop saved me and gave me a chance to pull her round. It was a feeling all firemen had from time to time, on a dark night on the old

West Midland line, (known as the 'Worse and worry'), you would catch sight of the distant for Moreton-in-Marsh and have the feeling of relief, for in a few more miles you could stop at Campden for brakes to be pinned down before dropping through the Honeybourne tunnel.

No, engineman enjoyed that bit of road for it was a drag all the way from Oxford. The worst type of train was a load of empty cattle trucks in a high wind, for it felt as if you had 80 'number ones' on the back. Number ones, were 10 ton wagons filled with coal. The 28XX class would make light work of it, but the old 'Forty-Three' would plug away, regulator wide open, with the great reversing lever being dropped forward a peg at a time until she was down to the forty-five mark. As the flap was dropped with each shovelful, the blast in the firebox would whip trouser legs, and snatch the coal from the shovel as soon as it reached the ring. With good Welsh steam coal, we could give her something to bite on, but all too often, it was hard northern coal, ovoids, brickets, or a mixture of both. At one time, we even had coke, and with this type of fuel it was like throwing feathers in the firebox. The northern coal was not too bad. It was either Derbyshire Brights, which, of course, was house coal, or, great slabs of coal which had to be broken up with the coal pick, and required a great deal of effort. It had to be turned over and hit with the grain, then it would split down in slices like pieces of slate, and any attempt to hit it any other way would be the same as hitting rock. But once in the firebox, it would burn with an intense heat, giving off such a thick smoke that you could smell the tar in it. Thank goodness the Great Western shovel was a man's shovel, and not one of those bitty little things the other companies used. Those slabs of coal would slide all over the place, but with the Western shovel you could get enough to keep the fire up.

Regarding the tractive effort of this engine, the sheer all-out power, was a sight to see. Pulling out of Didcot East Junction up gully, or from the West curve and over to the down main at Foxhall Junction, each cylinder would take a charge of steam and would go over hard on that side, then over to the other side, and each blast from the chimney would be in unison with the movement of the cab. No cross-Channel steamer ever rolled so much in a heavy sea, but it was not a roll to give cause for alarm, just a solid punch from each piston.

They would keep this up as the lever was linked up, a little at a time until they began to get the load on the move, and then they would settle down to a steady pace. On passenger trains they would run at such a speed as to be deceptive to the unwary, and on stopping trains they would accelerate with the fleetness of the 61XX tank class.

My feelings were changed towards these engines by a driver learning the road. With my mate Ted Hurle we took over No. 5339 on a Reading to Gloucester goods at Didcot North, routed via Honeybourne. We had a fair run to Oxford, but I was not happy about her steaming, and with the long drag in front of us to Moreton it did not give one cause to jump for joy.

We were stopped at Oxford station North Box to pick up this driver, and when he climbed up onto the footplate it was with an expression of pleasure. He introduced himself and to our surprise it turned out that he was not only an ex-Carmarthen fireman, recently promoted to driver, but No. 5339 was a Carmarthen engine, and to him it was like greeting an old friend in the wilderness. Before we had reached Wolvercote Junction, he had his jacket off and was ready to start firing this old friend, and the way he set about it was an education to me. At the same time he converted me to being an admirer of the Churchward 43XX class. He lifted the long pricker out of the tender rack, pushed the fire all over the box until it was a flat bed, and then began to build her fire up. With the firebox flap down and the doors wide open, he packed her solid in the back corners and under the firehole ring, and then began to build her up in the middle, giving her the odd few pieces up the front end. All this time the cold air was being sucked into the firebox in great gulps.

As she bucked over the points at Wolvercote and headed towards Yarnton, the steam pressure dropped to 160lbs, and the water to half a glass. Ted pushed the lever forward one more notch, raising one eyebrow to me and looking a bit apprehensive. But our driver-fireman knew his business, and picking up the back damper to its full travel he jammed the gauge glass spanner under it. This had the effect of opening that damper the full distance. The front damper was lifted, not as I expected to the first notch, but just off the face, and he secured this with the lubricator spanner.

The next move was to oil the slides and coupling bars of the firebox doors. He then closed up the doors tight, leaving just the small air hole. She sucked air through that hole with a high pitched whistle, each whistle being accompanied with the slap of the firebox doors against the back plate as she punched her way towards Handborough. With the steam pressure steady at 160lbs he placed on the exhaust injector, and that too, began to sing in symphony with the exhaust. The faded needle on the pressure gauge began to creep up a little at a time, and at 180lbs, Ted was able to notch her back a peg, but our new mate suggested he give her full regulator. Ted pushed it up until the handle was up in the cab roof, and the old girl was now being handled as Mr. Churchward intended her. The lever came back another notch, and she was now on the point of blow-off. This expert Carmarthen man now began to fire her, opening the doors in one sweet motion for each shovelful, and sliding them up as he withdrew the shovel. He kept the back corners tight, giving her one in each front corner and one at the front end, while the rest was just inside the fire-hole ring. I looked inside, and it was a solid platform of fire just inside the box, stretching forward for at least three feet, with the flames whipping up and curling over the brick arch in angry tongues of fire, much the same as my fire would look. But beyond this, I could see the reason for his success. The fire was so intense that it was white hot and so bright that it hurt the eyes, like the heat in a steel works when a crucible is being tapped, or the incandescent mass one sees when the molten metal pours out. It was all there in that firebox. I half expected to see the fire bars dripping as they melted, but Swindon fireboxes do not melt, for this was the fire for which she was designed, and she was responding to it perfectly.

Passing Handborough she was lifting her safety valve with the injector still on, and a glass full of water showing. At Kingham the distant was on, and as Ted eased the regulator our driver dropped the front damper, opened the firebox doors, and lifted the flap in its place. The exhaust injector blew out, he turned, shutting if off and turning on the live steam injector, with boiler pressure just off the 'blowing off' point. It was a perfect example of firing skill. As we hit the A.T.C. ramp, off came the distant signal and we were away again, with the injector off, flap down, firebox doors shut, front damper lifted, and the spanner placed underneath it again.

Ted did not need to be reminded again, and as the regulator was lifted wide open, we blasted through Kingham as if the distant check had not appeared. She steamed as steady as a rock until Ted shut off for Campden, and we eased gently to a halt for the brakes to be pinned down.

While we were stationary the front damper had been closed, fire doors open, and the flap down. At first the intense heat had Ted shifting his position as his trouser legs began to scorch. Then the sting began to recede from the fire. The live steam injector had been on for some time, and when we dipped our nose into Honeybourne tunnel we still showed a glass full of water. We pulled away from Campden, with the engine working hard against the pinned down brakes and the brake on the 20ton guard's van. But the firebox flap was left down, and steam pressure dropped to 160lbs as we entered the tunnel and Ted shut off. Again it was a beautiful piece of expert firing. We drifted down that bank through the tunnel without one wisp of steam from the safety valve to obscure Ted's view, to come to rest in Honeybourne loop. The remaining part of the journey was uneventful. We moved back on to the triangle and set off on the gentle run to Gloucester, through some of the most beautiful countryside anywhere in the world. On through Cheltenham we travelled passing the race course, and rounding the corner into Gloucester. As we drifted past the L.M.S. shed, a fireman gave us a cheery wave from the footplate of a Stanier 'Jubilee'. Did he realise I wonder, that his engine was directly descended from the grimy old 'Forty-Three' clanking her way towards the station? I doubt it. His 'Jubilee' was in magnificent condition, gleaming with new paint and all ready to go on some express passenger train. But the Swindon look was there, and it was not difficult to see our 'Forty-Three' in her.

Our relief crew then arrived and we made our way to the station for a cup of tea. We were sorry to part company with our Carmarthen friend, for he was booking off duty and Ted and I were to make our way home as passengers. He had enjoyed himself working on an old Carmarthen engine, even though he had not been able to learn much of the road, as he had been firing her, but I had learnt a great deal and my old mate Ted had raised an eyebrow or two on the driving methods.

We discussed this at some length on the way home. As regards firing, there was no formal training given, one just picked it up, and the front damper treatment was new to me, although our friend had told me he only used it on the 43XX class when heavy working was called for. The 43XX class had none of the sophisticated damper arrangements as fitted to the 'Halls', 'Castles' and such like, as there was no front, front middle, back, and back middle dampers. There was just a straightforward up and down front and back damper, each lifted up and pegged in one of the two notches cut in the handle. They rattled and shook with the amount of play in the rodding, and were constantly falling down and closing, but I was looking forward to tomorrow, and a chance to try my hand. A front damper open would normally create the wrath of people on the shed, and was never done, so this was really something new to me. On the shed, particularly if inside the shed and over the pit, the shout would be heard, 'Shut that bloody front damper', because the draught and gases set up in the firebox would begin to work with a resonance that would start with a gentle thrumming, advancing and receding each time building up to a louder pitch until it reached such a pitch that the very building began to vibrate, therefore, until this time, the front damper opening method was very much out. Tomorrow would be a very interesting day!

On the driving method it was very much a matter of style as practised by each man. Mr. Churchward favoured the short cut-off and full regulator with his engines. Some men used this method chiefly on the main line expresses, but some drivers preferred a longer cut-off and drove on the regulator. Some, like my Ted, used a little of both, so the full regulator method was something new to him too.

Ted made it quite plain that if we had the same train tomorrow with a 43XX engine, I should be the driver as he wanted to try this new firing method out for himself. It was the first time for a long time that we both looked forward to a return to the 43XX.

The next day we awaited orders, both hoping for the Honeybourne job, but Control gave us a trip to Westbury via Reading West. We walked over to the up gully to relieve the Banbury men, and for once we had the pleasure of a brand new 'Austerity' class to work upon which was a relief after working on some of this class on previous occasions.

When the Banbury men had gone, Ted said that I could drive her to Westbury, but my answer was short and sweet, as I told him to 'shove off'.

I intended to enjoy firing this new locomotive masterpiece myself, but my first attempt to open the live steam injector valve ended with me losing a lump of knuckle. She was so stiff on the spindle that I had to slacken off the gland nut before I could move it, Ted laughed at the sight of blood, after all, he had offered. But my turn to laugh came when we cleared the gully and set off along the relief line towards Reading. She was so tight in the valves that Ted could not link her up. I had to give him a hand, for she was tight on the regulator, and Ted's arms began to ache long before we reached Reading. It was a change to have a new engine of this class, and she steamed without any effort. We swept around the corner at Reading West like a passenger train, with the road clear ahead, and after the fits and starts from Didcot it was a change to run smoothly. I helped Ted link her up, then he set the regulator and let her have her head.

Through Theale, Aldermaston and Thatcham, I sat on the seat rocking back and forth with her motion, and for once all the distants were off through Newbury. We clattered over the points at East Junction and through the station in a flash, with our safety valves lifting right under the footbridge. As I looked back I half expected to see them tumbling down. The Didcot men standing in the Bay platform with the Winchester passenger gave us the 'hit them up' sign. Ted took his teeth out and showed them a row of pink gums, while I gave them a naughty code on the whistle. Then we pounded our way up through Hungerford, twisting and turning up to Bedwyn, over the top of Savernake, and then with regulator almost shut, firebox doors open and injector on, down the glorious sweep through Lavington with feet up and a well-earned cup of tea in hand. It was one of those trips that make up for all the rough ones, when you have got tubes blocked and leaking, superheaters blowing, and dirty fires clinkered up with dirty coal.

At Westbury, we were relieved by Taunton men, and the eager way in which they climbed up onto the footplate showed that they too were not used to such fine machinery as a new 'Austerity'. We were sorry to leave her, as it had been a very nice run for a change.

We walked over to the shed and into the enginemen's cabin for a break, then after half an hour the shed foreman found us, and told in no uncertain terms that regulations state that we must report AT ONCE to the foreman when arriving at the shed. Ted pointed out that we could not find him, and in our experience, shed foremen were very busy men, and therefore the best course of action to take is to stop in one place. Ted with his eloquent tongue and my sweet smile mollified him to some extent, and for once he believed this Didcot crew, for it was obvious that we were not the bunch of skivers he was used to. We had our orders, being told that outside the shed we would find No. 5322 already prepared for the 10.30 a.m. Westbury to Banbury. We collected up our gear and walked out to find her. She looked a weary old work horse, her paint faded to a dirty grey, and from her safety valve cover to half-way round her boiler casing she was streaked with dry scale. Her smoke box was a patchwork of rust stains, and she was covered with the grime of many miles. We climbed up on her and took stock of our surroundings.

The Westbury men had made a good job of preparation, and although the fire was thin from standing several hours, she was clean. Her boiler front had been wiped off, clean paper placed behind the lubricator and gauge glasses, and the footplate swept clear. Ted now informed me that his chance to fire the 43XX class had come. I pointed out to him that with a clean fire, ashpan empty, and a fresh engine such as this one the odds were in his favour. This reply was a stock phrase being 'In as much as hither to forthwith', and he agreed with my suggestion that he was pulling rank wholeheartedly. My argument that he was an old gentleman who needed to conserve his strength was met with a 'Belt up' reply and I was told to help him get the fire to his liking. So we set to. While Ted levelled out the fire with the pricker, I looked round for an old fire bar, which was placed across the brackets of the tender tool-boxes. Then as Ted built up the fire to his liking, I shovelled the coal forwards into the 'hole', filling her up over the top of the tool-boxes. That old lady was taken off shed as ready as she would ever be, and I opened her cylinder drain cocks and gently moved her back over the points, and into the yard. (Lap and lead steam is all very well, but she had been standing several hours, and lap and lead water lead to no cylinder covers.)

We backed onto our train, the guard giving us the loading, and, as was usual it was an old-fashioned load. The yard foreman cleared some odd wagons, as a few more over the odds with each departure was one way of clearing the 'odds and sods'. We put up 'F' headlights, one headlamp under the chimney, and one in the middle of the buffer beam, as the regulations stated for a through goods, not that it was so important. The signalmen would cross us over or put us in the loop if we did not run up to expectations, but we should see. My old mate was so eager to be the fireman that I wondered if he would notice if I dropped her down a notch, or if I was late linking her up.

As we pulled through the station towards Heywood Road, Ted had her on the boil, and I took her away gently, taking up the slack on each coupling until a wave from the guard confirmed that he was in his van. Ted closed up the firebox doors, and we wedged the front damper open just the same as in No. 5339 the day before. I gave her almost full regulator and she started to rock over and back with each blast up the chimney. As she got her teeth into the load, I gave her the lot and then started to pull that great lever back a bit at a time. As the blast sharpened with the increase in speed, it was time to notch her up a bit more, until she was as far back as she would go, still maintaining speed and punch. Punch was the right word, as we made our way up towards Edington and Bratton. The exhaust injector was singing away with the water in the top nut, and boiler pressure steady. Looking back down the bank you could see where we had left the yard. She was belting away, with smoke going up like a volcano, and the ashes showering down on the wagons behind. The engineer's fear of the hammer blow on his rails could be felt as she punched her way forward. Ted had been firing her all the way out, and she responded by blowing off as we reached Lavington. His face was flushed from the fire, but he was happy. Old man indeed! I told him to stop smirking and bend his back.

We cleared Savernake in fine style, running well ahead of time for this type of train. I slammed down the regulator, then opened it on the jockey valve so that the valves and pistons would not run dry. The lever was eased into the 45° position, and down went the front damper and the firebox flap. In went the tea can and we swept majestically down the spiralling twisting curves towards Hungerford, through the beautiful Kennet valley. With a feather of steam whisking away from the safety valve, the blue smoke haze drifted back along the snaking wagons, Ted sat on his seat gulping down great slurps of scalding hot tea with the satisfaction of something truly earned.

The coal in the tender well was down, so with Ted keeping an eye on the signals I removed the fire bar from the tool box brackets and pulled the coal forward with the coal pick. As the side plates were exposed the shovel was slid in and more coal brought forward. We came up to Newbury with all distants off, and as I still had the shovel I held on to it, for Ted had done enough. It was my turn now. We slid through Newbury with hardly a murmur from the chimney, and all ready to pick up water on the troughs at Aldermaston. We were catching the up stopper, and this was enough to take the run out of us. The water scoop went down, but we were unable to fill the tank. However we still had plenty in to reach Goring.

We rounded the curve at Southcote Junction and over the bridge at Reading with the tender brake just rubbing, and all the wagons buffered up. At West Junction, the road was set for the down relief, so we let her run clear of the points, then set her at a steady amble towards Didcot and home. It was a gentle pace, chugging along on time, dropping the scoop at Goring and topping up the tank. Then began the clearing up for our relief. But it was all in vain. We sighted Didcot East Junction signals, not for the down loop but for the main line with all the distants off for Didcot North. Seven and a half hours on duty, and back at our home station only to find the road cleared for us to carry on. Well, one cannot stop on a main line and ask for relief, so we would have to go on to Oxford. Ted had a snooker match that evening, and I was in love, with the young lady who is now my wife and she would be waiting. Would she fancy a young fireman who was not on duty? Such thoughts are the spur to fast running. If we opened her out perhaps we could make Oxford in time to catch the up stopper back home. As we passed

Didcot North Box the signalman came to the window, and we shouted we needed relief at Oxford. He nodded his head, stuck up his thumb to indicate he understood, tapped his bell 'on line' to Appleford, then promptly forgot us. Culham was passed in a flash, the wagons behind jumping and swaying, scattering dust and paper. The porter sweeping the platform waved his fist at us as we came tearing down on to Radley. With the whistle chain pulled down we made the porters run over the crossing as we blasted through and the more we hammered that old girl the more she steamed. She hadn't had a run like this for years. But it was not our day, for as much as we enjoyed this running, love and snooker were much in our minds. It was with sinking hearts we sighted the distant off for Hinksey South, Hinksey North, and all the way through Oxford. We would have to see the job out.

It was a very dejected crew that clattered through Oxford station, and if the guard did not know the road through from Westbury there was not much he could do about it, but stoke up his little stove and hang on. We shut off to cross Wolvercote Junction, letting her run down a bit as there was no point in belting her now. Ted would have to fix another date for his snooker match, and love would have to wait, and thank goodness, she did.

The rest of the journey was a steady plod, through Kidlington, and up the bank to Tackley without much enthusiasm from us and then down the sweeping curving of the dip through Heyford. The tank was topped up once more at Aynho troughs and soon we pulled into the loop outside Banbury shed.

From Heyford I had let the fire run down, but it was just a matter of levelling it over with the pricker and splashing a bit round her box. When we stopped, I ran the pricker through the fire and could see the fire bars. It would be an easy one for the fire droppers to deal with, and in that respect the Great Western fireman was lucky as other companies expected the fireman to clean the fire. I uncoupled, and we ran up over the points to drop back on the shed. Off came the 'dummy', and we backed smartly in, clear of the main line. As we blew on the whistle to inform the signalman we were in clear, there came such a clatter from under the tender that we both knew we were off the road. Almost as soon as it started, it stopped again and we ran smoothly again. We moved No. 5322 on to the ash pit; she had served us well. I had changed my mind about the 43XX class. I could now see what Mr. Churchward had in mind when he built them so long ago. Mind you we did have our rough trips, leaking tubes and dirty fires did not help — but now, on the whole, I enjoyed working on them. The 93XX differed from the other Moguls as they were fitted with the Collett 'Castle' cab, and the dampers worked by guides and quadrant levers. Nevertheless, like the early 43XX class, they were very fine locomotives.

As we walked back to the station, we had no thoughts of reporting to any shed foreman. From Didcot to Westbury via Reading, and back via Oxford to Banbury was enough for one day's work. We had been on duty for eleven hours, most of it engine time, and not hanging about waiting for signals. It had been a busy day, but we had food for thought as we walked past the shed points. The chairs were broken for a dozen yards, and the sleepers were freshly splintered, farther in the shed road the check rail was scored where a wheel had run up it. There was no doubt about it, we had come off the road, and by a sheer fluke, had re-railed ourselves.

The next morning we were summoned to the foreman's office and asked to write a report on our coming off the road at Banbury shed. But we knew nothing about coming off the road. Did we leave the engine stranded off the road, or was she found on the ash pit? Professional pride was wounded. To think that we could do such a thing, the indignity of it. Authority must look elsewhere for the culprit, Ted had missed his snooker match, and poor old Bill Young the Foreman was snookered. He could shout all day, but our engine was left firmly on the road on Banbury ash pit. As for me, I was in love, and could not be held responsible for any coherent statement. We could have gone over the bridge and into the river and I would not have noticed. So we got away with it, but we all knew what had happened. As we were clearing those points, the signalman started to put them back a little early. We had been seen, but not exactly reprimanded. Just told to be a little more careful in future.

Chapter Eight

The Great Western engine to follow the 43XX class was, of course, the 'Grange'.

As a replacement for the ageing 43XX class, the design of the 'Grange' was a masterpiece. It embodied all the standard parts of the locomotive that it was succeeding, with the addition of the 'Hall' boiler and cylinders. It was in fact, a 'Hall' with smaller wheels and had the edge over the 'Hall' for all out power. At first glance it was difficult to see the difference between the two locomotives. However, the 'Hall' frame was straight, all the way from the smokebox to the front portion of the cab, but the 'Grange' frame dipped behind the cylinders before carrying on to the cab. To see that slight difference, brought a feeling of joy in my heart. We had nothing against the 'Hall' class, as they were a very good engine, capable of any task, but the 'Grange' was something special. They had a gentleness about them, a tolerance, and an air of tranquillity that would forgive any transgression on the part of a ham-fisted driver or inexperienced fireman. They were one of the most loved engines on the Great Western, being the Fireman's dream engine and the driver's home from home.

Climbing into the cab of a 'Grange' gave one the feeling that it was to be the perfect day. No matter the weather, the load, the poor coal, or any other factors. One knew that there would be plenty of steam, a comfortable ride, and a sit down. They were the free steamers, the fireman's friend, and if ever a hard word was spoken against them then I never heard it. Seventy-nine 'Granges' were built and I must have fired them all. Not once, can I remember a bad trip. When my generation of firemen laid hands on them, they were only a few years old, but as they aged, they still retained their passive nature and gentleness. But this gentleness could be deceptive, as when the time came to move the Grange' it could react with an aggression that belied any thoughts of tranquillity. Those small 5ft 8in wheels would start to attack with such power that more than one passenger guard has been left standing on the platform. Then she would up her heels and run, as if the gentle lady had turned into quicksilver.

I was fireman to my old Dad and later to Ted Hurle, and this meant that I was the driver if a 'Grange' was at the head of the train. Both of them had been made up to drivers before the introduction of this class, so they both looked forward to handling the shovel, and I did not mind, as no fireman in his right senses ever gives up the chance of driving. To grasp the warmth of the regulator handle, ease it open and feel her come to life with movement is a wonderful feeling. From the fireman's side you see it done a dozen times each day, but to move over to the right-hand side, particularly a 'Grange', and carry out the driving, gives one complete fulfilment.

The warmth of the cab is comfortable, the aroma of warm oil, steam, and burning steam coal mixed up with hot paint is almost sensuous. The way it embraces one, it is the maternal warmth of the female, bewitching, as the eternal enchantress that transforms, by heat, from the chill of death into a living source of power. From the humble pannier tank to the mighty 'King' no engineman would consider the steam locomotive as 'It', but always as 'She'.

As with the light aircraft pilot, so it is with the engineman. She is handled by feel, through the soles of the feet, and palms of the hands, and deep inside the feeling of her working. If she begins to labour, she is eased, if she sounds dry, she is lubricated, and if she wants to run, then she is free to run. The wood shaft of the ejector is pulled down, with steam roaring up through the chimney. The twin needles climb the gauge as the air is sucked out, holding at 25lbs then dropping to 23lbs as the ejector is closed and the small one opened. That too will be closed when speed builds up enough for the vacuum pump to start slapping away and the clip on the reverser is snapped down. The regulator is eased open, and she begins to move forward, gently at first to take up the slack on the wagon couplings, then the slight snatch is felt and the side lamps on the guard's van begin to flicker. The whole train is now on the move. As the side-rods go round, she gives one sharp beat from her chimney to each quarter turn of the wheel, gradually sharpening as the speed begins to increase. Then she is slowly wound back, allowing her to make the pace, and on each turn of the reverser, the beat softens, but still hard enough to catch the steam and smoke drifting into the cab, snatching it to pause and swirl, then sliding over the flap into the firebox resembling a fast flowing stream. The soles of the feet register each rail joint, the slight rumbling of the wheels; metal on metal. The deeper note of a culvert crossed, and the hollow booming of underbridges all contribute to the wonderful movement of the steam locomotive. This reaches deep inside one and lulls one into complete harmony with this lady.

It was on a dark night that Ted and I were in charge of No. 6865 *Dymock Grange* running the 4.15 p.m. Gloucester to Old Oak Common. She was the perfect lady, running with just a wisp of steam in her cylinders, and steaming so well with the flap down, warming the cab, Ted was firing her, splashing it round the box with a twist of his wrist completely lost in self-satisfaction. I had one foot on the sand lever, my right hand resting on the reverser clip just letting her run, and was enjoying every moment with this beautiful engine. The A.T.C. bell rang out shrilly, as the shoe ran over the ramp. We were at peace with the world.

We ran down through the deep chalk cutting at Pangbourne, with its gentle left-hand curve, feeling her heel over slightly with the camber, we had main line from Didcot, praying it would continue through Reading. I leaned out of the cab to catch the first twinkle of Pangbourne signals, but caught instead the angry glare of three red lights, being the tail lamps of a goods train as they jumped and swayed. For a moment, I was mesmerised and unable to believe what I saw. I shut the regulator, and stood up all in one quick movement. Ted glanced up from his firing, and the expression he saw on my face was enough for him to dive to the side and look out. He turned round and swung into the handbrake as I gave her some vacuum, but we were running too fast, we were sliding up to those red lights quicker than we thought, and the realisation of the facts swamped over us both. The utter relief that we were not going to pile into the rear of that train was so great that we both sat down, hearts pounding with the air being sucked into our lungs with great gulps. In fact the train was on the up relief line, and the clot of a guard had not removed the red shade on the off side, for several seconds giving us grave doubts. It had been a severe shock. For the first time ever I saw Ted really angry and as we passed that van we blew the whistle and shouted, but nothing stirred. The guard was either asleep or dead, and it would have been the latter if Ted had got hold of him.

Because of the incident, the run had been taken out of us, and the next distant was at caution. We were diverted over to the up relief, and with it the dread of a changeover. All enginemen detested the changeover arranged by Control, as they preferred to go through and work back. But this was not an easy operation, and at night, or during fog it was almost impossible. It was just a matter of stopping opposite the other locomotive and stepping over to the other footplate. Unless, of course the operation was from loop to loop, when it would mean a walk over to the exchange point.

For the guard, it was more difficult still, as in the first place he was so far at the rear that communication was out of the question giving him little knowledge of the changeover, and secondly, both trains had to pull up and try to position both brake vans opposite each other to enable the change of guards to be affected. In all, it was a long, drawn out operation, and nine times out of ten one would find that the engine one had just left, had a clean fire with coal brought forward, all in anticipation for a run, and the exchange engine was completely the opposite, with a dirty fire, no coal forward, and all the signals off.

Control could sit in a nice warm office miles away and work it all out. On the road on a dirty night these changeovers were not appreciated by the crews. However, there were exceptions and we could only see one side of it, that being our own. With Ted and his snooker match, and me in love, if getting home could be managed by a changeover, we would move heaven and earth to persuade Control it was a matter of life and death.

We had one good ally in Reading Control, and that was dear old Bert Povey. If he was on late turn, somehow, he would arrange that I could meet my young lady at a respectable hour, and that Ted would meet his snooker date. The changeover was then looked forward to with some eagerness, but there were many firemen and drivers in the same situation as we were, all wanting to meet loved ones or with other things to look forward to.

All went well on this trip, however, and once over on the up relief we ambled through Reading, with the aroma of baking biscuits thick in the air. There was sign of rain on the way, as we passed through Sonning cutting, empty of photographers at this late hour, and on through sleeping Twyford to rumble over the expanse of Maidenhead bridge, into Slough, with its jumble of factories all giving out the distinctive smells of their products. As we drew closer to the 'Smoke', so our progress was slowed, and we began to receive distant checks. The gentle running of *Dymock Grange* was unfortunately a bit too free for the lad in front, so we eased her down a little, just enough to keep her from being stopped by signals. As we drew into Acton yard, and alongside the slowcoach, poor chap, we noticed he had an old 'Aberdare' which was in a bad way. The blower was hard on, and the fireman was ramming the pricker through her in an effort to raise enough steam to reach Old Oak shed. But there was no need, as we were going on to shed also. So we uncoupled and passed over the points to back on to the worn out old lady and gave her a tow to shed.

As we left *Dymock Grange* on the ash road, we both knew we should meet her again on another train, in some other place, each time we worked her remembering those bad moments back at Pangbourne. A chat with Bert Povey in the Control office would give us the information we both required. All we wanted was the name of that guard and time was on our side, as we had plenty of patience, and there would be another time and another place.

The slowcoach had in a way done us a good turn as by the time we had left *Dymock Grange* at Old Oak our time was up, and for once we could walk away with a clear conscience without reporting to the shed foreman. It was a rare pleasure to leave a 'Foreign' shed without the guilt of sneaking away. So to hold one's head high and stride out was savoured as a gourmet savours a rare dish. We hitched a lift in the coaches of the 5.30 a.m. from Paddington, and settled down to rest our eyes travelling back home to Didcot. And we did only rest our eyes as we had learnt a lesson the hard way a few weeks previous. After climbing into coaches in Old Oak carriage sidings, they turned out to be the wrong ones, and after going to sleep we woke to hear a very pronounced Welsh voice announcing we were in Newport, telling passengers to change for the Western Valleys. This of course meant that we were on the wrong train. It was easy to do this as a country crew with the straw sticking out of their hair should not ask the Cockney boys, 'Please mister, are these the coaches for Didcot?'. It was still easier to return from Newport than Plymouth, if you know what I mean.

A glance down the list of 'Granges' will show that these beautiful locomotives had equally beautiful names. Names like *Arlington Grange, Bucklebury Grange, Burghclere Grange, Morehampton Grange*, roll off the tongue with a beauty fitting the grace of the lady they adorn. The gentleman who had the envious task of deciding the names of the 68XX class must surely have had the background of the Welsh Valleys, as only the eloquence of a Welsh politician or Chapel minister could have thought of comparing beautiful buildings to beautiful locomotives.

Their smaller sister locomotive the 78XX 'Manor' class, was however another kettle of fish altogether. At first glance, one could mistake a 'Manor' for a 'Grange' until one saw the numberplate. No doubt, the 78XX was a godsend to the lads on the Cambrian, after years of working the 'Dukes', but to the main line men they were classed as a de-tuned 'Grange'. Of course they were designed to cover the routes banned to the larger and heavier locomotives, and were a replacement of the ageing engines which had given a good account of themselves in early years. They steamed well enough and gave a comfortable ride, but to the crews in the London Division they appeared so sluggish. They had no 'poke' and with their full load on behind they were worked to the limit. The 'Grange' could be worked hard with always a little bit in reserve, but not the 'Manor'. I fired them all, and by the kindness of my mate, also drove most of them. From working each side of the footplate one had the feeling of not having enough power. The exception I can recall was No. 7808 *Cookham Manor*, now well cared for in my old shed at Didcot by the Great Western Society. She was a really good 'Manor' and Ted Hurle and myself belted her down to Southampton one day on a Troop special, and we had a tight schedule to catch a boat. On this trip, we scared the pants off a Typhoon pilot. It was at the latter end of the war when our R.A.F. lads were shooting up German troop trains in France. We had to stop in the middle road at Newbury to take on water and Ted swung the water column round and left me to fill her while he nipped round with the oil can. When we had both finished and returned to the footplate we found this young pilot officer waiting for us. He produced a footplate pass signed by Mr. Milne our General Manager which gave him permission to travel on the footplate between Newbury and Southampton and return. This situation was meat and drink to my Ted. This pilot was a nice young chap, not much older than I, and as we gave *Cookham Manor* some stick out of Newbury he explained that his job in the R.A.F. was to fly a Typhoon over France and dive down with great speed and velocity, drilling the boiler of the locomotives full of holes. On pulling back up out of this high-speed dive he expected to see the locomotive gushing out steam in all directions. If this had not occurred he would then fly up the train and give them a couple in the cab just to make sure. He went on to explain that all the drivers over there wore berets and gloves, and he was so interested in the effect he had on a steam locomotive that he applied for a footplate pass to enable him to fully appreciate it from the other end.

As I said, he was a nice young man, well brought up, Marlborough School and all that, but as he was talking to me, Ted removed his teeth and placed on his head a scruffy old beret he kept for oiling underneath the engine. As the pilot turned to Ted to suggest that he called him Heathcliffe, just to set the trip on a good footing, I pulled on a heavy pair of leather gloves. If we were to belt *Cookham Manor* over the Winchester branch I would be catching single-line tokens at a fair rate of knots, and Heathcliffe's face showed some doubt as to whether he should have taken a footplate trip after all. He may have thought that his education had finished at Marlborough, but he was sadly mistaken, as his education into the operation of the steam locomotive was just to begin. Ted and I were very close to each other, so much so, that a nod and a wink were enough to convey that we were both of the same thought. This nice young man was eager to improve his experience of life – so who were we to disappoint him?

Ted only eased the regulator a shade as we shot off the main line at Enbourne Junction, and *Cookham Manor* gave a kick and a lurch, waggling her behind just enough to make Heathcliffe grab at the gauge glass frame for support. I advised him to sit on my seat and hold tight, as we were in a hurry, and to remove his cap or it would end up on the head of some grateful tractor driver in the fields below. *Cookham Manor* was now steaming well, and it was possible to drop the flap for long periods which on a warm sultry day helped the situation. Unfortunately R.A.F. blue shirt collars turn black with good honest sweat and coal dust, and Heathcliffe began to sweat. As we swooped through Highclere he looked at the bridge at the bottom of the bank, and it appeared as small as the eye of a needle. He then asked me if it was possible for this big engine to go through that little hole, and we told him we didn't know but we should soon find out. So he shut his eyes and when he opened them again we were through Burghclere and heading down the other side into Litchfield, rattling through the station with the flap down and *Cookham Manor* blowing her head off. Ted gave her a little steam from Whitchurch to Sutton Scotney and then opened her up for the short bank to the top of Worthy Down. As he did so, she slipped with a roar, giving Heathcliffe a nasty turn. In Typhoon terms, he thought we had slipped into coarse pitch, but she gave a shudder and began to bite, pounding up the bank and sailing over the top in fine style. It was now downhill all the way but she gave a bad lurch over Winnall Gas sidings, and we were into Winchester Tunnel, which, to my surprise, excited our passenger and he began to cheer up. Perhaps we had laid it on a bit thick, so Ted replaced his teeth and exchanged the old beret for his cap. The next move began to reaffirm his doubts as Ted came over to my side and I took over the driving. He looked at me with such an apprehensive expression that I could see the wheels turning over inside his head.

I let *Cookham Manor* drift her way gently down to Eastleigh where we were stopped for signals in the station. Heathcliffe shook hands, thanked us and took off up the platform, saying that he could hitch a lift back to Greenham Common in a Dakota. We were sorry to see him go, as his pass covered the return trip and we were sure to be sent home light engine.

A week later we had a copy of a letter he had sent to the Locomotive Superintendent thanking him for making the trip possible with the added rider that in future three rockets would find their way into the cab on the first run in. Somehow I don't think any preservation society has an ex-R.A.F. Pilot Officer named Heathcliffe in their ranks.

We did our expected return light engine run after leaving our train in Millbrook docks, with orders to take her to Reading shed. This was the second time that day we picked up a passenger. As we slowed down to stop at signals at Southampton Central an Army lad gave us the hitch-hike signal, and when Ted nodded his head, he jumped aboard.

He was making for Doncaster, and seeing a Great Western engine he guessed we were heading north, so he was delighted to learn that we could take him as far as Reading. Any chance of giving him a 'vintage' Ted and Harold trip was quickly dispelled, because his dad was an engine driver at Doncaster shed and he had spent many hours on the footplate with him.

We offered him our sincere condolences that his dad had unfortunately joined the wrong railway, was stationed at the wrong shed and driving the wrong engines. He somehow got the impression that the only railway that had engines worthy to work was the Great Western, so to cheer him up we stuck a cup of tea in his hand and gave him a cigarette.

Leaving Southampton we ran main line through to Winchester Junction where we left the Southern to run over the new loop line back on to the branch again at Worthy Down. We were back in Western territory, and Ted made a gesture to gladden the heart of any lad on his way home to join his poor old dad on the L.N.E.R. He asked him if he would like to drive a Great Western engine. He was off of my seat in a flash, and flushed with pleasure he drove her to Theale where Ted took over before any prying eyes caught sight of him. He had to admit that *Cookham Manor* was a very nice engine, but out of loyalty to his dad she was not quite up to the L.N.E.R. standard. We dropped him off at Reading West station with instructions as to how to get to Reading General. Ted had written down a connection for Paddington, so with a bit of luck he would be home before nightfall.

He went on his way, a very happy young soldier, but there was a sequel to this story a week later. Ted and I booked on to find a letter addressed to both of us c/o Didcot Locomotive sheds, and the words Great Western Railway in very large block letters. It was from our soldier's dad, who thanked us very much for the kindness we had given his son, and the condolences over him being an L.N.E.R. driver. He pointed out that he was in the top link at Doncaster driving Sir Nigel Gresley's A4's up to King's Cross and back, and that if we would like to leave our little *Cookham Manor* at home, he would show us a real steam locomotive. I sometimes wonder what he must have thought when in later years the A4's hot inside big-ends were cured by fitting a Great Western big-end.

Yes, the lads at Didcot have on their hands one very good locomotive in *Cookham Manor*. When I saw her last in July 1973 at an Open Day she was at the bottom of number one road, her frames jacked up, her boiler, cab, and fittings inside the lifting shop, all in a state of heavy overhaul. She deserves the attention, and will repay for years to come the work being put into her.

Chapter Nine

The fact that the Swindon design team were past masters at improvisation and conversion was well known. There had been conversions from the old broad gauge engines to standard gauge, dual purpose engines were converted quickly, and the old 'Duke of Cornwall' class married to the 'Bulldogs' creating 'a mongrel' of a locomotive referred to as the 'Dukedog' class. There were also saddle tanks converted to pannier tanks, the old R.O.D. engines of Mr. Robinson fitted with Great Western boilers, and after the 1926 absorption of all the Welsh independent railways, conversion treatment of these, at the Swindon shops.

In each case conversion was a complete success, with locomotives of all shapes and designs going into one end of Swindon works to emerge a few weeks at the other end as standard Great Western engines.

This policy of improvisation was to have a profound effect on the future of other companies in later years. At Swindon, there were many men who were to be influenced by the standards set by Mr. Churchward and his successor, Mr. Collett, and by such men as Stanier, Maunsell, and that great man of vision Mr. Bulleid. Mr. Churchward would have loved the advanced design of the Merchant Navy class *'Channel Packet'*. A quick view of later Midland and Southern locomotives produced by Mr. Stanier and Mr. Maunsell after their appointment as Chief Mechanical Engineers of their respective companies all show the outline of Swindon policy. It was the vintage years of locomotive building, and at Swindon a conception took place that was to have far reaching results in the success of Great Western locomotive power.

In 1925, demands required a 'mixed traffic and excursion type' locomotive; something that had the power to handle all types of trains, to go over most of the routes now covered by the 'Saints' and 'Stars', and at the same time, could be used as a heavy freight locomotive. In fact, a brand-new design was needed.

Past experience of improvisation and conversion now began to pay dividends but something far beyond the early conversions was required. Swindon genius came to the forefront with an idea that would save a colossal amount of shareholders' money in the introduction of a new design of locomotive. At the same time, it should prove, at little expense that the idea would meet the requirements of the demands for the increased traffic.

Charles B. Collett, from the known facts, took what would be in this modern day and age be an analysis. He withdrew from service No 2925 *Saint Martin*, fitted her with one of his 'Castle' type cabs, lifted her off her 6ft 8½in wheels and placed her back down on 6ft wheels. As he sent her out into service, he must have had some doubts, but it was a move in the best traditions of his predecessor George Jackson Churchward, using standard parts of a 'Saint' to become a mongrel of a locomotive that became a class in its own right. The 'Hall' class locomotive was born to start at 49XX and was to become one of the most successful locomotives in the world. So much so that Mr. Stanier created the 'Black 5' from this basic design.

As the 'Halls' came into service the question was not what they could do, but if there was any duty which they could not cope with. One after another, they steamed out of Swindon Works in such a procession of standard uniformity that Henry Ford would have been glad to be associated with them. They continued unchanged until Mr. Hawksworth modified the frames with the introduction of the 69XX series in 1940.

To the enginemen who had to work them, they were just about perfection in a mixed traffic locomotive. They had the grace of the 'Grange', and almost the power of the 28XX class. To open one out was to unleash power that was almost unbelievable. The exhaust would give out that crisp bark so familiar to the Great Western engine with the addition of a 'crack' that there was no doubt this was a 'Hall' being worked hard.

On the stopping passenger trains, if the load was up to ten coaches, the fireman had some work to do, as they would scoff coal as fast as it could be fed into the firebox. But on a runner, they would settle down and run as economically as the rest of the 'Castles', 'Stars', and 'Saints'. If there was a failure on one of these locomotives or the need to run the train in two or more parts, then a 'Hall' would be given the duty. Such was the respect for them, that the crew would get stuck in and run and keep good time without difficulty.

The close relationship between the 'Hall' class and the 'Grange' was evident, but where the 'Grange' was forgiving to the inexperienced fireman the 'Hall' was a demanding engine. It was no good just throwing the coal in, hoping she would steam. The fireman had to be on top right from the start. The familiar 'Haycock' Great Western fire was built right up to the firebox ring as used on the big four-cylinder engines, sloping up towards the brick arch in a distinct ridge, and dropping away sharply towards the front end. With such a fire, the 'Hall' would perform perfectly.

This type of fire, used so much on the Great Western locomotives, was the result of the firebox design. The firebox was designed around the supply of good Welsh steam coal. Where other companies could use a flat, thin fire, for burning the hard northern coal, the Great Western firebox required a very thick fire. Once this fire was built up correctly, firing became one sweet motion, with the fire built up in the ridge, and with both back corners packed. The shovel could be slid in over the burning mass, with the blast taking the coal over the top, where it would slide down under the brick arch. Now and again, the front corners would require a couple of shovelfuls and a twist of the wrist as the shovel went in, would place it exactly in the right place. There was no throwing it in; the platform of fire combined with the long Western shovel, produced steam in abundance. When the back end burnt through, the shovel was rammed down inside the ring, easing the whole mass of fire forward and then it was packed up tight again. It had one added advantage. When the back end was burnt through nicely, the shovel would be slid in, taking a small portion of fire with it and leaving behind a glowing flat platform, just the right size to accommodate a tea can. At this point, the regulator was firmly closed, just a few seconds out of the running time. The can of water would boil so fast that there was just time to reach the coal pick to lift it out by the handle.

Firing a 'Hall', like all main line engines, was practiced perfection, it was almost mechanical repetition, and as natural as breathing. The sweetness in which the flap was dropped in time to meet the swing of the shovel was only the result of experience, and as with all repetitive movements it had its dangers. Once the swing of the shovel had begun its journey to the firebox nothing could stop it, except if your mate was in a playful mood and stuck his foot out, or leaned over and closed the flap. When the latter happened a steel shovel met a steel flap and the shock wave up the arm was really something, in addition to having a shovelful of coal all over the footplate. But sometimes it was the unexpected that happened and then usually a disaster to the participant. This was the case on two occasions, during my footplate days and on both occasions when I was driving.

The first time was when I was firing to Ted Hurle. We were running the 6.15 p.m. Southall to Severn Tunnel Junction freight with No. 4991 *Cobham Hall* and having a good run. Ted had indicated to me at Foxhall that I would be driving on the down trip, so by the time we passed Steventon I had the train well and truly on the trot. Ted was swinging the shovel with ease, so much so, that I was toying with the idea of sticking my foot out especially as was making such easy work of sliding that shovel in and out. Then unexpectedly Ted sneezed. At that point he had also started to swing the shovel but the explosion caused his teeth to shoot out where they landed on the coal in the shovel grinning at us. What followed, was as if in slow motion. Ted saw them, and I saw them, but nothing could stop the swing of that shovel, as they slid in that holocaust still grinning with the escape from bondage. Ted withdrew the shovel slowly, still bemused with shock, getting down on his hands and knees and peering into the fire as if to will them to return. Then he started to swear, using words he had picked up in France in 1914, Welsh words he had learnt, and good old-fashioned English words he remembered from the days when he was a farm boy.

I stuck my head outside the cab, oblivious to the drenching rain, as I did not have the courage to face him. I laughed until I could laugh no more, and each time I looked at him, I started again. Long after those teeth had melted, Ted was on his knees deflecting the fire with the shovel to see if they were still there, and while this was going on *Cobham Hall* blew her head off. It was as if she loved to be fired with teeth, but it is said that something in life is learnt every day, and Ted had learnt that day never again to fire a locomotive with his teeth in. After that experience they were always tucked away in his pocket.

The second incident was with my father, and firing to him, was one way only, as with Ted Hurle. It was no surprise when we climbed up on No. 5930 *Hannington Hall* in the up gully at Didcot East Junction that he took over the fireman's side. We were working the 11.00 p.m. Bordsley to Reading freight, calling in at Moreton Yard to make up the load. *Hannington Hall* was in a bad way, as she had been on the road a long time, and her tender held just enough coal to see us through to Reading. As I blasted her out of the gully father removed his jacket, and reaching for the long pricker, gave her a good pull through. It was a hard pull out of that loop as the curve was tight and each wagon wheel was dragged, rather than rolled, to pull the train out. It was a movement that called for full forward gear and plenty on the regulator, but not too much to make her slip. The pricker, together with the blasting, had a good effect on the fire, livening it up, and she began to look good on the steam gauge. Father consulted his watch to note our departure time, and this was to be for the last time.

All drivers carried a heavy pocket watch in their waistcoat pocket, not only secured with a watch chain, but also with a rubber gauge glass ring round the winder. This rubber ring stopped the watch from sliding out of the pocket when bending down. But father's number one watch was in for repair, and he was using his second string watch, which was slimmer in size and had no watch chain or gauge glass ring. Passing the rear of East Junction Box the old chap decided to show his skill with the shovel. Indeed he had told me to watch every movement he made if I wanted to see a real expert in action, and on the very first swing of the shovel out slid his pocket watch and into the firebox. Thank goodness it was a cheap watch. He stood there looking at me, shovel in hand, waiting for me to laugh, but he had brought me up, and he knew I would not laugh at my dear old dad's misfortune. I just put my arm on his shoulder and asked him if that was the way the expert fired a locomotive or was it not just possible that coal would be better.

There was no reply to this thirst for knowledge. He very deliberately placed the shovel back in the tender, and removed my cap to follow his watch into the firebox. Then, and only then, did he make any remark and that was to keep my mouth shut. I think he was upset, but worse was to come. We picked up our full load at Moreton and headed for Reading. *Hannington Hall* steamed as she had never done before, as did *Cobham Hall* on her diet of teeth. It was one of the little peculiarities that made a steam engine a living thing, and so *Hannington Hall* digested her pocket watch to the advantage of her boiler. We left the load at Reading West yard and took her to shed, using the last scrap of dust in the tender to get there. Leaving her on the ash road, we collected up our belongings and made our way to the enginemen's cabin for a cup of tea before reporting to the foreman. To say that the good Lord moves in mysterious ways is something of an underestimation, for sitting in the cabin was the old chap's brother Bill. The usual exchange of friendly insults were passed between the two brothers and when the opportunity arose, I had a quiet word in the ear of Uncle Bill who knew how to extract the full potential from his newly acquired knowledge. All the way up father had been looking for signal box and station clocks, as a driver is at a complete loss without his watch. So the time was ripe for Bill to strike. He took his watch out of his pocket, looked a bit puzzled, shook it and held it up to his ear, asking his brother if he had the right time. The old chap looked sad, because he realised his son had blown the gaff, but he was never at a loss as to how to deal with a situation. He had the time, alright. It was time that brother Bill applied for a new cap as Father emptied his tea into it, making it time to depart from the cabin in a hurry. But all's well that ends well as I lent Father my watch which I had omitted to tell him I had with me. It pays to keep an ace up the sleeve at times!

During my firing days most of the 'Halls' passed through my hands except No. 4911 *Bowden Hall*. She was damaged so badly in 1941 in a German bombing raid that she had to be cut up. Neither did I fire any of the 79XX class, as they were built after my time on the footplate, and in the true sense were B.R. locomotives and not Great Western, but no doubt were as good as the early 'Halls'.

The 49XX and 59XX were the originals, and I think most footplate men will agree that they were the best. When the 69XX came into service in 1940 there seemed to be a break in the continuity. The engine looked the same, the dimensions were the same, but somewhere in the production there was a change. The 69XX class was the conception of Mr. Hawksworth, and true to Swindon tradition it was a good locomotive. There had been some changes made from the original 49XX class, including new superheaters, main frames, and a different method of mounting the cylinders. The enginemen who had to work them found the changes very evident. Although there was no shortage of steam, the working of the engine was very noticeable, with the sharp whiperack of the 49XX and 59XX missing. The crisp bark typical of the Great Western was there, but that little something extra was missing.

We had three 'Halls' at Didcot — namely No. 5935 *Norton Hall*, No. 6923 *Croxteth Hall* and No. 6952 *Kimberley Hall* —giving us a real chance to notice the difference. All three would steam freely but when it came to running, *Norton Hall* would run the wheels off the other two. When it came to acceleration *Norton Hall* would bite into the load with ease, whereas the other two had to be punched. When it came to shutting off, *Norton Hall* could be shut off much earlier than the other two and would require a good stiff one on the vacuum for a station stop, whereas the 69XX's could be run up much farther before the brake was applied.

One would think that coal and water consumption would be heavier on the 69XX's but I never noticed it. The engine to me appeared to have no 'feel' about her. The 69XX's seemed to be without character, and I thought, at first that perhaps it was my personal opinion, but as time passed, the other enginemen came to the same conclusion and I knew it had to be the locomotive.

It might sound as if I am 'knocking' the 69XX's, but this is not so. They were fine locomotives, and like all the other engines, they performed far beyond the limits on loads allocated to their class. The truth is that I preferred the 49XX's and 59XX 'Halls'. This difference in class of engine was illustrated in a one-week period I had as fireman to driver Warr.

'Tack', as he was affectionately known, was a prime example of the senior Great Western engineman; stern, heavily built, waxed moustached, and immaculately clean. He could handle a locomotive with the finesse of the expert. The fact that I had known him all my life, went to school with his twin sons, worked with his elder son, all three being firemen, and knew that the fourth son was soon to follow the family tradition in true Great Western style made no difference in my approach to him. I would add that even his wife was a driver's daughter. From my school days, through my cleaning days, to firing days, he was still very much Mr. Warr, Sir, and so I addressed him in this manner on that first day. Any repetition of that form of address was quickly dispelled, as I was informed in no uncertain terms, that I was not just his fireman but his mate. For this outwardly stern man to give me leave to call him mate was one moment not to forget. There was a sly grin under that Sergeant Major moustache, a distinct twinkle in his eyes, and I knew that working with 'Tack' was going to be a wonderful experience. Our first duty was working the 3.45 p.m. Didcot to Paddington, and returning with the 7.50 p.m.

She was a beautiful engine and the pride of the Didcot stud, but we could only expect to have her for a couple of days at the most as she was on the list for a boiler. Preparing her was a treat, as she was kept so clean, and raising the pressure was a simple job by just spreading the fire over the box, building it up gently with the blower on a quarter of a turn. She would then come round on the clock with no effort. We backed on to our train and coupled up to ten coaches and one parcel van, being the best part of 400 tons.

Having worked this train before, I knew that a 'Hall' could make a large hole in the tender. On a stopper with a load of this size, I realized this engine could scoff coal in an alarming manner, and as Dick Warr took her away I got stuck in by giving her plenty to bite on. She barked her way out of the station and over to the up main line so quickly that we were past East

Junction box before I had placed the second shovelful in. Dick was winding her back and snapping down the clip before we reached Moreton bridge. I gave her a bit more passing Aston Tirrold signals, only to see Dick shut off after which *Norton Hall* ran with the wind into Cholsey. On looking in the firebox I found that if I was not careful I would black in the fire and without doubt my mate was the reason for this. He was driving the engine so that she was burning the minimum of coal. I should also have expected it as I knew I was working with an expert, and for all the sharp whip-crack echoing and rebounding between chimney and cuttings, *Norton Hall* might sound as if she was being thrashed but the valve cut-off was so far back that another turn on the screw would put her into mid-gear. I had expected to be firing her almost non-stop, and with good reason as I had worked this train many times with the same engine and with many good drivers, my time being spent piling the coal in. But Dick had been a driver for a long time, and coming from the days when a bonus was paid on coal economy he could work an engine with a candle in the firebox. We did burn coal, of course, and with that dead weight to lift out of every station even a Great Western engine had to be fed, but with Dick's driving I did not have to shovel any more than was absolutely necessary.

It was a perfect trip, marred only by a small incident at Paddington. We ran in on time and almost before we had stopped, a small man with a very big shovel jumped up on to the footplate, scrambled back into the tender, and with much haste and energy began to shovel coal forward. Dick gave a sly grin and began to make up his train log, while I uncoupled and placed a headlamp on the tender lamp bracket. When I returned to the footplate a sizeable amount of coal had been brought forward. As this state of affairs was completely new to me, I enquired from our small friend why, after all these years, had the management decided to employ men to fill the tender hole on local trains. He opened his mouth to reveal a row of black stumps. 'And why not', he said 'you're the bleeding first part of the bleeding Fishguard, aren't you'. There was no need to reply, as the truth began to sink in with Dick slowly shaking his head. No, indeed we were not the first part of the bleeding Fishguard, for she had just run in next door pulled by a 'Castle' with a large hole where the coal should be. The word 'Bleeding' was comparatively mild to the words he then used. And he seemed such a nice little man; far too small for that great shovel he used, but he realised his mistake, and had to admit it. What upset him was, that he, a Cockney, had been taken in by a straw-sucking muck-spreading, moon-raking yokel. But such insults were easy to bear. As we moved back along the platform following the coaches and as I had a couple of tons of coal brought forward, I called over to the 'Castle' saying that we could not stop to give a hand, as it was time to get the cows in for milking. It was the only time I have ever seen a man actually jump up and down in a temper, and he was so beside himself with rage that he could not control his emotions. But the railway is the one place where you can learn a little more about the job each day, and this particular chap, had learnt that he should open his bleeding great mouth and ask in future.

The next four days saw a change of engine for us. Tuesday and Wednesday, we had No. 6923 *Croxteth Hall,* Thursday and Friday, No. 6952 *Kimberley Hall* and then on Saturday we were back to *Norton Hall* once again. It was on the four days without her that the difference in class was so noticeable. Although the 69XX type did not burn any more coal, or use any more water than did *Norton Hall* it was the running and the overall operation where one could sense the change. The 69XX's seemed to lack the whip-crack in the exhaust and also lacked the fire of *Norton Hall*. It was as if they had to be driven and punched along, whereas *Norton Hall* would glide, and where they would just run, *Norton Hall* would fly. This was no illusion; this was pure fact. We also found this difference between the 28XX and 38XX class. Where the 28XX would bite into the load, the 38XX class although identical in every way except for the cab, had to be punched. Somewhere, there was that little something missing, and yet in spite of this state of affairs, they were still fine locomotives.

The 40XX 'Star' class being the forerunner of the 'Castle' were loved by all enginemen, but as they aged, they became rather a rough ride. After a thorough overhaul at Swindon they would emerge as good as new, and equal the best of the beloved 'Castles'.

It would require a book alone to capture the merits of each class of engine I have had the privilege of firing, and at times, by the kindness of my mates also had the chance to drive. However, I can shed no tears in the passing of the 'Aberdare' and R.O.D. class, but to be fair, they were worn out, and past their best long before I laid hands on them. I find it best to remember the few happy times spent on them. There was, however, one very bad trip on a 30XX that stands out in my mind which is a story I will relate later.

That week I spent as fireman to Dick Warr was one of several very pleasurable occasions I worked with him. There was one time, however, by sheer coincidence that the wheel turned a full circle, when on a particular occasion I was firing to Dick, his son Gerald was firing to my Dad. I had grown up with Gerald and his twin brother Bill, having gone to school with them, worked in the same cleaning gang with them, and shared in the same escapades with them. Now we were sharing each other's fathers on the footplate. It never occurred to either of us to change duties, as my old chap was as much loved and respected by the Warr boys as I loved and respected their father. To work with two expert drivers was satisfaction enough for anyone. It was Dick who first showed me the different way in which two railways looked after their respective footplate crews. As we ran over the Southern metals between Winchester and

Southampton, we came into close contact with the Southern lads, and a great bunch they were. We were supplied with cotton waste for wiping our hands and cleaning down on the Great Western while the Southern men were issued with hand cloths. A great deal of swopping took place when the opportunity arose, as we both preferred each other's issue. However, the one thing I could not understand was the Southern system of promotion. I could swap waste with a Southern fireman who was old enough to be my father. This was due to the fact that on the Great Western, you moved up the scale to driver as vacancies arose and a Southern fireman could remain a fireman all his life. I used to feel sorry for the dock pilot fireman, as those little engines were worked on the hand brake; and to see a 25-year-old driver shunting with a 50-year-old fireman winding that hand brake round and round made me feel very fortunate that I was an employee of 'God's Wonderful Railway'. I should think those hand brakes were the best oiled brakes on any railway in the world. But when I think back, some of those men did have one shoulder developed larger than the other. I remember sitting next to a Southern fireman in the canteen at Eastleigh one day. His name was Vince Hawkins, and he was a boxer of such repute he could fill the Albert Hall. I pulled his leg about those hand brakes, and suggested that he must do his training on the dock engines. He just laughed and asked me to feel his biceps which were like solid rocks. If it was not the hand brakes that developed those muscles, it must have been the canteen tea. Footplate men enjoyed a good strong cup, but the ladies in Eastleigh canteen made tea that would make the tea can leak at the seams after a few pints of that brew had been poured into it, as the solder began to dissolve. Therefore it was wise to place dentures in the pocket for the same reason. Natural teeth such as mine, in those days would take on the beautiful light mahogany colour one associates with expensive furniture. No wonder it was called 'The Strong Country' in that area — it was nothing to do with the beer I can assure you.

Chapter Ten

The last few chapters have been devoted to the tank engine and the passenger engine, but now I should like to tell you about the heavy freight locomotive. It would be true to say that the 43XX, 'Granges', and 'Halls' were mixed traffic engines. However the 28XX class were primarily freight and it was rare, except perhaps on a really busy summer Saturday that they were seen on a passenger train. The 30XX R.O.D. class or Mr Riddles' 'Austerity', never worked on passenger duty being solely intended for freight - thank goodness!

In some ways, I have to admit I have rather knocked the 30XX R.O.D. class, but the truth is that they were the most detested locomotives on the Great Western. The fitting of Swindon parts did improve them to some extent, but they never were and never could become a Western engine. However, some credit must be paid to them as the basic design of the old Great Central Robinson engine was to prove that it was possible to achieve years of hard work for the least possible financial outlay. It was often called by enginemen, the £100 engine. If that figure was true then it must surely have been the cheapest engine in the world.

They would also go on for ever, for even if the boiler pressure dropped, there was no problem of the vacuum brake leaking on, as there was none. A simple steam brake and tender hand brake, was all there was and even that was not needed at times because if the regulator was closed they just stopped. Even allowing for a favourable gradient they were hard pushed to go downhill; as in effect it was a two speed engine. It could plod forward, plod backward, or stop, but regardless of direction it would pull.

Worn out, leaking steam, tubes blocked, poor coal, or all these conditions placed together, it made no difference. Like the oxen, it would pull, and the word 'it' is all that can cover this lumbering steam energy converter, for in the wildest of imaginations it could never be referred to as 'she'. It was just an ugly uncomfortable old work-horse.

To see one at the head of the train was the start of a stream of unprintable words between the driver and fireman. To find one booked to be prepared and taken out of the shed was the excuse to look at every inch of the engine in the hope of finding a defect serious enough to refuse to take it over. When Mr. Robinson built these engines, he built them to last a thousand years, and in this age of property development they would have been a boon to the demolition experts. All that would be needed was a short length of rail leading up to the building to be laid flat, and then to steam a 30XX and head her straight for it, so saving hours of labour and explosives. But, as I have said, they would pull, and even pull when the steam gauge began to drop.

This pulling power with the steam pressure dropping proved to be a godsend on one occasion which I shall never forget.

Ted Hurle and I booked on late one afternoon on a hot humid Saturday, and the shift foreman, Bill Snow, was waiting for us. He hardly gave us time to collect our bits and pieces from the locker room before he was telling us to get a move on. The sister engine to our *Norton Hall* was waiting on number 3 road all ready to go back to her home shed at Reading, where she was urgently wanted for an evening passenger train. It was 5.30 p.m. and No. 5934 *Kneller Hall* was booked out 6.30 p.m. from Reading, so we needed to hustle her home at once.

Ted had a quick look round her, checking the trimmings in the slide bars, and topping up the oil cups, while I piled the coal up over the tool boxes on the tender. She had been stood for a couple of hours, and as a result her fire had grown thin. Most of the coal brought forward was in large lumps, so on the quick dash up to Reading I could build her up all ready for the local man to take over. We took her up to the shed signal, and before Ted had stopped, I climbed down on the bottom step and ran ahead to phone East Junction ground frame. The lads in the box must have been warned by Bill Snow of the urgency, for as we were turned out of the shed and up the main line, the distant signals dropped before we had cleared the junction. Ted opened her up and I began to build up the fire. With no load behind her *Kneller Hall* began to fly. All I can remember of Cholsey was the roar as we passed through, and at Goring the fire was beginning to look respectable, with all the large lumps in the firebox burning through into the 'haycock' fire. I began to pull forward the smaller pieces with the coal pick after which we both picked up the fall plate between the engine and tender tilting it back on the hinges.

Ted gently eased down the scoop over the water troughs as at the speed we were going the scoop would only have to skim the surface to top up the tank.

We filled her up over the first few hundred yards with water gushing out over the vents and pouring down the gap where the fall plate had been. Ted looked at me with a grin, for it was a standing joke between us that when he operated the scoop, the fall plate was always lifted, having learned our lesson after once having a soaking. Ted was an excellent driver but he just could not top up a tender on the troughs. We crossed over on to the up relief at Pangbourne and went on into Reading station almost before I had time to sweep up the footplate. We backed on to the coaches of the train in the up bay platform, and after coupling up I was back on the engine only 25 minutes after leaving the shed at Didcot.

We sat down to enjoy a cigarette while we waited for the Reading men to relieve us, but our break was short-lived for out of all the men at Reading, who should come up the platform towards us but my father's brother Bill. It was as if we all haunted each other, and as he caught sight of me, I could see the little cog wheels in his head going round. He passed the cab with his mate without any attempt to relieve us and with a studied air began to examine the front of the smokebox.

She was plastered with the squashed remains of every type of fly between Didcot and Reading. From her buffers to the copper band round her chimney she was a mass of legs, wings, bits of bodies and smears of blood, all gently frying from the heat.

Passengers on the platform began to look round as Bill and his fireman began to mock the Didcot men on the state of their lovely Reading engine. Had they both spoken in normal tones it would have been easy to bear, but Bill was not one to pass up a chance like this. 'Never mind, dear little engine', he said 'you are back home with your Reading men who will love you and look after you. We will soon have you out of the hands of those wicked Didcot men'. And so it went on, and on, and on.

Thank goodness Ted knew of this leg-pulling between us as he had been with me long enough to know Bill, and how to retaliate. 'She was a rotten engine, she had a flat on the off-side driving wheel, her frame was out of line, and it was at great risk that we brought her out of the shed'. We left them walking up the platform to disdainful glares from the public, both of us enjoyed the encounter and the show we had put on, certain sure in the knowledge that at least 50 people thought that *Kneller Hall* was the personal property of one Bill Gasson. After a quiet cup of tea in the refreshment room we were ready to contact the Reading foreman by telephone as there was no point in walking down to the shed only to be sent back to the station again. Orders were quickly given to proceed to the down relief at Reading West and relieve a special from Brentford to Wednesbury via Stratford. That run through from Reading to Honeybourne was to turn out to be a memorable encounter but even more memorable was the return with a R.O.D. 30XX class engine.

Our train at Reading West was an engineering special, with 25 flats loaded with new sleepers. On that hot evening as we walked up the train towards the engine the tang of the creosote-pickled sleepers was so strong there was not a fly in sight. We debated about the wisdom of lighting up a cigarette or waiting until we reached the engine as I am sure that one match being struck would have resulted in the whole lot exploding. But we were lucky, as we were going to be in front of this little lot and the poor old guard was stuck with it. He would have to keep his windows and door shut. Ted had told him to hang on tight and to screw down the brake leaving Campden, as we intended to run through without stopping for brakes to be pinned down. He had protested at the idea of running through, as he wanted relief at Oxford, but Ted only grinned. If the signals were off, we would be round the corner at Wolvercote before he noticed.

He did not protest too strongly, as he was still a little wary of us both and he had reason to be. As a piano player he was in the semi-professional class, but at the same time he was suffering from a slight inferiority complex, and being a shy little man made it possible to take him in. A couple of months previous in the Banbury canteen Ted had conned him into playing some old sentimental love songs on the beautiful baby grand they had there whilst I notified the large lady behind the counter that he was playing them just for her. Ted and I then crept quietly out. We heard after that when he had finished, she clasped him to her ample bosom with a certain amount of passion, and he only escaped by going to the toilet and out of the window.

We relieved the Southall crew from whom we were taking over at 7.00 p.m. The engine was No 6868 *Penrhos Grange*, and as soon as they were off the footplate Ted went over to the fireman's side and told me I could drive her as far as Kingham and with a light load and a good engine we were both looking forward to a nice run. The sun was beginning to sink through the haze as I opened the large ejector to blow off the brakes. It was still very close and had all the signs of a thunderstorm brewing. Ted removed his overall jacket, took off his tie, and opened the top buttons of his shirt to allow a bit of coolness to the three hairs on his chest. As I eased her away he began to fire her. There was no trace in that heat of any exhaust steam from the chimney, only a puff of dark smoke to confirm each shovel of coal reaching the fire. At Scours Lane she was beginning to pick up her heels, and with the regulator a quarter open, she was linked up to 30% cut off. She was running so quietly that each rail joint on the engine, tender, and wagons could be heard as we passed over them. Ted hung over the side to find some relief in the breeze and he suggested that I would be more comfortable if I removed my tie. But it was not customary for a Great Western driver to be seen without a tie. Anyway, at that time Ted had the advantage as I had no hairs to show off on my chest.

We spanked along on the down relief in fine style, Ted allowing me to top up the water on the troughs at Goring without losing half of it down the vent pipes. Continuing round the avoiding loop at Didcot East Junction with all the distant signals off, I crossed over to the fireman's side and as we passed our shed we saw Bill Snow on number 5 road making up his loco stock book. We gave him a blast on the whistle to show him that his request of two hours earlier to get a move on had been met. We then rattled over North Junction points and headed towards Oxford.

As we thundered over the bridge at Nuneham, the river steamer was passing underneath. She cleared the bridge just in time for me to look down through the open hatchway of her boiler room. I had a momentary glimpse of polished brass, and a very round red face looking up at me. We pounded on, down into Radley, sweeping through and raising the dust which swirled along the platform behind us. At Hinksey the first distant signal on must have raised hopes for our guard. I shut off and let her drift, giving her just a little steam as each home signal dropped off one by one through Oxford. Then we were away again, shutting off only between Wolvercote sidings and the junction, to take the curve at regulation speed. Once clear of the points I could open her up again, set the regulator, and the cut-off, and let her make her own pace. Ted was enjoying himself as *Penrhos Grange* was running and steaming in the manner of a true 'Grange' class engine. It was one of those days when it seemed a sacrilege to expect to receive payment for doing such an easy job, but the problems were to come. It was just as well we extracted the pleasure from this beautiful locomotive when we did.

Between Charlbury and Ascott, Ted decided that he would try his hand over the troughs, so I stood on the seat and made no attempt to lift up the running plate. We were running at a good pace, so the water gauge began to climb up a little rapidly, but Ted was confident that he had everything under control. For once he was going to pick up water without soaking us both, and as the gauge moved towards the last few inches he began to wind the scoop back up. It was too late. Unbeknown to Ted the tender water gauge was showing a false reading, still indicating 200 gallons to go, when the tank was actually full. Perhaps I should have told him when I realised this when passing over Goring troughs, but it was worth keeping quiet to see the speed in which he jumped back and scrambled to stand on his seat as that water cascaded down over the coal and all over the footplate. I remarked that perhaps an ex-Llanelly tank engine fireman was not used to a proper main line engine which resulted in the hand brush being used with much vigour to brush all the water and slurry over to my side. By the time we reached Kingham and changed over sides, Ted had cleared up all the muck.

Despite our earlier comments to the Guard, we stopped at Campden in accordance with the 'General Instructions for Working Inclines', and also because of a notice at the side of the line reading 'ALL DOWN GOODS AND MINERAL TRAINS MUST STOP DEAD HERE'. Besides, the signalman was watching, and he was known to have a 'thing' about enginemen who did not stop. Our guard was looking up the train in case we had changed our minds about the brakes being pinned down, but I waved him back and as we eased away we could feel the drag as he wound his hand brake on. Ted had to punch her a bit to drag her into the tunnel and down the bank. As she dipped her nose he shut off and as I began to wind on the tender hand brake we entered the tunnel exchanging the last of the summer dusk for the black musty gloom. The acrid fumes from the chimney now began to drift into the cab, stinging our eyes. I eased open the blower to suck it into the firebox, the only sounds now, the muffled rumble of the wheels, the slap of the vacuum pump, and the grinding of brake blocks on the wheels. The vacuum pump slapping away gave us an indication of our speed, for it never changed its pace. Ted had the load well in hand and in no time we were out of the tunnel and dropping down into Honeybourne as the night closed in over the countryside. After the tunnel the heat of the day was gone, the air was clean, and the lights of Honeybourne were twinkling around us.

I climbed back on the tender as we stopped, and began to shovel the coal forward as Ted went round *Penrhos Grange* with the oil feeder. We had run non-stop from Reading and enjoyed every minute of it, we were also both now ready for relief and a cup of tea. I made the tea while Ted made enquiries about relief from Control. When he returned to the engine it was to say that our relief was on its way from Birmingham on the up stopper. This gave us a comfortable half an hour before they arrived to have our food and clear up, before getting work home if required.

The stopper ran in with our 'Brummie' relief on board. They were a good bunch of lads, joking and calling us 'my ducks'. They also said there was a right old cow of a loco coming up behind, and we should be relieving her before long. Control confirmed when we reported to them that a Wolverhampton to Westbury freight was on its way and that we would be required to work it home. Our hopes were dashed to the ground when we saw the engine taking water ready for the long drag back up through the tunnel to Campden. She was an old 'Aberdare' using up the last few months left to her. However, we breathed a sigh of relief when we found that this was not our train and we watched her pull away into the darkness, belching out a great pillar of black smoke from the hard northern coal she was burning, both of us thankful that we were not on her.

As she cleared the section our train came into view, and we nearly wept when we saw her, for it was an old R.O.D. No. 3030, and in a far more advanced state of dilapidation than the 'Aberdare'. The fireman I relieved said she was in a shocking state, and though her fire was clean enough and she would steam if the blower was kept on, you had to keep on top of her all the time. As for riding, he said it was just not possible to sit down, as every bolt holding her together was loose. There was no exchange of pleasantries, as they were only too thankful to get away from her themselves.

On that humid night that old R.O.D. was almost too much to bear for the slightest movement produced intense heat, which came back from her boiler casing in waves. But the job had to be done and the sooner we got on with it the better. Ted opened and shut the regulator, tightening up the couplings between the wagons until we felt the final snatch. I then waved the gauge lamp back and forth until the guard repeated the signal from his van. We now had the train all on the move, and I began to fill up the firebox, which was just as well that I did.

As we pulled away from the lights of Honeybourne out into the countryside the moon began to peep out from behind the thunder clouds, bathing the whole area in soft light. It was truly beautiful but as we climbed the bank we were aware that we were climbing into a black cloud. This turned out to be an understatement as the first sniff indicated that it was no low cloud but something much worse. In that still air heavy with moisture it was instead thick black oily smoke that was being trapped by the cutting and the atmosphere and it came from the old 'Aberdare' that was preceding us.

There was no warning that we were nearing the tunnel until the 'whoa' of steam from her chimney hit the first brick inside. It came with an abruptness that caught us both unawares and for one split second there was a moment of panic. It was as if we had been blotted out of existence, as every familiar part of our surroundings had disappeared. The glow from the gauge lamp was gone and I could not see Ted. The sudden blackness was so thick for a moment that I was afraid to move, and a choking feeling came over me. A complete lack of breathable air and loss of sight made me think it was the end of my life. Ted groped and found the firebox handle, and the shaft of light from the fire was enough to establish sanity. The exhaust smoke was being sucked into the cab and through that shaft of light all I could see of Ted was his knees and down to his feet. He shouted in my ear to turn on the coal watering pipe, and I dragged it forward and turned it on. Throwing my handkerchief into the shovel to join Ted's, mixed up with coal dust and wet through, we tied them over our noses and mouths. We then both lay down on the running plate with our heads over the side.

The air at ground level was at least breathable. From low down the light of the fire could be seen reflecting through the open rear damper and showed up in stark reality each individual piece of dirty oil-stained ballast, and each droplet of water on the bricks of the tunnel wall. The light would sharpen with each beat from her chimney as the air was sucked up through the damper and into the firebox, pouring through the spokes of the rear driving wheels. The great heavy side-rod would come round giving a muffled clang on the coupling pin as it reached the bottom, then it would go up and over, lost in the murk until it came round again. We lay there, still with wet handkerchiefs over our noses and mouths, unable to stand up in that poisonous air. With one ear half turned, we gauged the sounds of normal running against a possible slip.

This came without warning and with no initial hint of a change in the beat from her chimney. Instead the exhaust hit the tunnel roof a few inches above to blast back down to us in one gigantic wave of lost power. For a moment as we laid side by side the implication of the slip did not register. We saw the side-rod come round out of the blackness, and then she began her almighty slip. There was a momentary glimpse of the side-rod spinning round so fast that there was a blur of motion, lit up by the fiery stream of sparks as they came showering towards us from beneath those racing wheels. We both jumped to our feet, with Ted flying for the regulator as I dived straight for the sand lever, both of us moving together to the essential parts of her footplate fittings to stop her mad race to disaster.

Ted slammed down the regulator, then opened her up a little while I worked the sand lever back and forth. The roaring ceased and she gave a lurch and began to respond as her wheels found traction on the sanded rails. We had at last lost the pounding of a few yards back but were reduced to a walking pace. Each beat from her chimney was now distinct with a pause between each one, which was itself rather frightening, as we knew that one more slip would stall her in that filthy atmosphere.

To keep this old tub on the move would now require all the tricks we knew if we were to take her out of this black hole. If she could take a little more steam without slipping again we might just make it, but it would have to be soon. Already our eyes were running with the sting of the exhaust gases whilst even through the wet handkerchiefs the taste of sulphur was beginning to restrict our breathing. I gently worked the sand lever forward until the sand was just a trickle under the wheels, and then searched in the coal for a small hard piece of slate. Ted eased the regulator open a fraction and wedged the slate between the guide and regulator. She faltered a couple of times, both of us having a moment of doubt, as she almost slipped again, but inch by inch she dragged herself and her load up the bank.

That tunnel was only 887 yards in length, but it seemed as if it would go on for ever, as yard by yard she shuffled her way out, until at last we were out into the moonlight and fresh air. Now I could see she was down to 100 lbs of steam pressure, and I rushed to put on the injector when I saw the level of water in the gauge glass. As we passed the signal box at Campden, the signalman was at the window. Ted shouted to him that we would pull up to the starting signal and stop. We were both in a bad way, but it was worse for our guard because if we stopped at the actual signal box he would have been back inside that hell hole. Even if we cleared the tunnel, the amount of smoke drifting out was almost as thick as that inside.

We stopped and began to repair the fire and build up the steam pressure, and when we removed the wet cloths from our faces, we were a sight to see. We were both covered in soot, except where the cloth had been whilst our old R.O.D. was never fit to be seen in daylight. In the moonlight, she was grotesque, as the whole of her boiler and cab was covered by an inch thickness of soot. The handrails along the boiler sides appeared double in thickness from the soot, and the eye glasses on the front plate of the cab were thickly coated with it. It was as if we had been through a black snow storm. Ted walked back to the box to make a can of tea, and to see if our guard was alright. He found him already in the box with the signalman, clean, fresh and unmarked from that terrible ordeal. He had known nothing of the slip, as at the time his van had still been outside the tunnel, and it was only the sudden slowing down that had given him cause for concern. He had visions of us stalling and of him having to protect the train as per regulations.

By the time Ted returned with that very welcome cup of tea I had swilled off the soot in the cab, filled the boiler, raised the pressure until she was beginning to lift her safety valve, and had a wash in the bucket. So while Ted washed, I took her quietly away, handing her back to Ted as we passed through Kingham. Really, 'passing through', was hardly the way to describe the shambling, pitching, and thumping of this old ox. Then to cap it all we ran into the father and mother of thunderstorms that had been threatening for hours. It began with a sudden onrush of wind that whipped the soot from the boiler casing to cover us in minutes so making the wash at Campden a sheer waste of time. The moon disappeared as if it had been switched off, and suddenly down came the rain like a waterfall. We passed through Shipton to the crashing of thunder, so loud it even drowned the rattling of our old engine. The lightning lit up the countryside all around and the rain hammered down on the cab with the ferocity of hail stones. As soon as we were through Handborough we were out into the moonlight again, with our old R.O.D. as clean as if she had just come out of Swindon shops.

We rattled our way over the junction at Wolvercote and clanked our way up through Oxford. I could see the reflection of the station lights in the boiler, for the rain had removed every bit of soot and grime. I pulled some coal forward, made up her fire for the last time, and cleaned off the footplate. Through Culham, we both had a second wash in the bucket, and as we pulled up at the signal in the up gully at Didcot East junction our relief was waiting for us. It was 3.00 a.m. in the morning, and already beginning to get light. We climbed down from her utterly worn out for she had given us both a bad time. A 28XX would have waltzed that load up through the tunnel without any trouble, but we had to have No. 3030 'Dirty Gertie'. But she was clean now and as we walked away from her I looked back and saw her standing there with a wisp of steam escaping from her flower pot safety valve. This great hulking brute of a locomotive showed no trace of the encounter at Honeybourne tunnel about her.

At the start of this incident I wrote that the 30XX class could only be called 'it' and not 'she', but No. 3030 was known as 'Dirty Gertie', and she had lived up to her name to the end. But in that early summer sunrise she took on a new look; she was clean. So in future she was called 'Gertrude' by Ted and myself.

While Ted and I crept to our beds before the heat of the new day made sleep unbearable No. 3030 'Dirty Gertie' would shuffle, shamble, and clank her way up every relief line, goods loop, and cross-over on her way to Westbury, arriving there just about the time we both came back on duty in the evening.

There was a good reason for this unhurried progress of course. Every signalman knew the R.O.D. and its flat out speed. The message would go from box to box, and each signalman in charge of a loop would change his points to allow her to pass through, for each one knew from past experience that she would need a margin between the fast moving trains of at least half an hour to an hour, depending on the length of the sections between the next loop or cross-over. There was no doubt about it, the 30XX's might have been slow, but they would keep going, and with a capital outlay of £100, they had certainly paid their way.

Chapter Eleven

The next week we were booked to work the 9.20 pm stopping passenger train to Swindon. It was a duty that had some amount of spice about it because although running a stopping passenger train held no problems, the engine power which was provided for this run did. We could expect anything that had wheels, vacuum brakes, or the other odds and ends that made up a locomotive.

Booking-on time was at 7.45 pm, which was quite a long time ahead of the booked departure.

This was because the engine power could be anything from a pannier tank to a 'Castle', which we had to prepare beforehand. The management were obviously concerned about the welfare of passengers who wanted transportation from Didcot to any of the stations on the way to Swindon, but, at the same time, found it a convenient method of arranging the movement of a locomotive to the repair shops and so make it still earn revenue on its last trip. There was also a booked relief waiting when it ran into Swindon, so that Swindon Control had at their disposal a fresh Didcot crew to work back. Modern Time and Motion study experts could have learnt a lot from Great Western locomotive operators, for they could extract the full amount out of you for a mere four quid a week.

On Monday we were given No. 4038 *Queen Berengaria*, and as expected she was in a bad way, and her mileage must have been well over the top. There was no time between stations to allow her to run, for as soon as Ted had her linked up, it was time to shut off for a station. As it happened this was just as well, because her tubes were blocked, her superheaters were leaking, and she was so rough to ride on that I fired her and filled up her boiler while we were in the stations.

Tuesday was not so bad, as we had our own No. 6106 tank, with very definite orders from my old mate Ralph Painton, now the shift Foreman, to bring her back light engine, as she was needed for the 4.30 am Thatcham in the morning. So we escaped from the clutches of Swindon Control that night.

Wednesday brought us an old friend in the shape of No. 3441 *Blackbird*, one of the 'Bulldog' class, and looking back on it now, it was a sad parting at Swindon. She was heading for the cutter's torch, and we never saw her again.

On Thursday, it was the turn of a 'Dukedog' No. 3211, due to go into Swindon for her number to be changed and when we saw her a few weeks later all done up in new paint she had been renumbered No. 9011, her old number going to a new Collett 22XX class.

Friday was the last evening we worked the 9.20 pm, for it was a Swindon return duty on Saturday. Our shift foreman at Didcot must have been hard pushed for locomotives that evening as we had booked to us our own No. 5935 *Norton Hall*. Poor old Ralph Painton hovered round us all the time we were getting her ready, for he knew only too well what would happen to her if we gave her up at Swindon. He implored, he pleaded, and he threatened to have us both booked on the stationary boiler for a month if we did not return with her. So Ted swore that one way or another we would return with *Norton Hall* in the morning, but this was wishful thinking. We ran her into Swindon station to find our relief waiting, and, acting on instructions, Ted refused to hand her over. The Swindon lads departed, only to return with the Swindon Foreman. It was with much relish he informed us both, that once we had passed Steventon, we came into the Bristol Division and as such, London Division could cry all they liked. It was then that I found out that the State dividing lines protecting the escaping criminal from the local Sheriff in America was applicable also on the Great Western railway, for we had passed the State line, and any further lip and we would be in dead trouble. We were in trouble already anyway, not only with Ralph Painton but also with Bill Young, the Shed Foreman, when he got hold of us.

We climbed down from *Norton Hall* knowing it would be a long time before we saw her back in her home shed at Didcot again, and like good boys we reported to Control, not that we had much choice. The Swindon foreman did not have two six shooters to back up his claim, but he was on the footplate with two hefty great enginemen to throw us off if required. He also wore a bowler hat, and with that bowler hat went RANK.

The gentlemen in the Control office were very kind to us. They told us to have a cup of tea and ring again in an hour. Ted and I realised that the Swindon foreman must have had a few words on the telephone soon after we had reported as I just had time to pour the water in the tea can when orders came to relieve the 10.05 pm Bristol to Banbury standing on the up middle road. It was obvious that they wanted to get shot of us as it was all arranged in such a hurry.

Each evening earlier in the week we'd had time to enjoy a decent break before taking over the 7.30 pm Avonmouth Docks to Old Oak Common. We had become accustomed to the round working, down with the stopper, back up to Acton Yard, take the engine on shed at Old Oak, and then catch the 5.30 am coaches up to Paddington and home. This last evening, the carpet had been pulled from under us, and we were heading back towards Didcot, only half an hour after arriving at Swindon, with this train for Banbury.

It was no good moaning. We relieved the Bristol men on No. 5979 *Cruckton Hall* and were away as soon as they had climbed down. The engine made up for the change of destination as she was in beautiful condition, and with the light load and the slight fall in the gradient she simply few along. Firing her was just a matter of keeping a good fire up, and Ted had her linked back as far as she would go, with the regulator just open. It was one of those trips when I could sit down and enjoy the sleeping countryside. A few minutes before midnight we slid round the corner at Foxhall and headed towards Banbury. That light load should have warned me that the night's work could not possibly pass with me just sitting down and enjoying one of the rare runs to Banbury. We had not only been smartly kicked out of Swindon and the Bristol Division, but had also been conned into thinking that we were set for a run.

Nothing had been said about calling into Hinksey Yard to make up a full load, but when the distant signal for Kennington was sighted at caution no amount of whistle blowing would change the situation. Into the loop we went, creeping round the back road into the Yard to stop at the ground frame.

It was time for a cup of tea, so the usual exchange was made, two buckets of coal for one can of hot water, and in that respect the Hinksey ground frame men were reasonable. Signalmen usually demanded half a ton for the same facility!

When we left the yard, *Cruckton Hall* had to be punched. She was loaded up to the limit, and it needed sheer brute strength to drag that train out onto the main line at Hinksey North, and up over the hump through Oxford station. Ted handed her over to me to have a go, and she began to pick up a little as we passed Oxford shed. On the fall towards Wolvercote, I was able to wind her back to 35% cut off with half regulator, and we rattled over Wolvercote Junction and began the long drag towards Kidlington and Tackley Bank. I glanced back as we passed the advanced starting signal to see the lights on the brake van dance about as it too cleared the junction, and I knew our guard was in for a rough ride seeing that a few junction crossovers had made his van jump about like that. Kidlington cross-over, under the road bridge, was notorious for shaking up the liver, but we were beginning to run, as these 'Halls' could run, once they had got hold of a load. It was possible to ease her down a little before we passed through Kidlington station, and as the van cleared the bridge I opened her up, and she sailed past the cement works and up the bank over the top of Tackley, running like a vacuum fitted freight. We roared through Heyford, with the engine leaning over with the camber, and the wagons snaking and dancing their way behind us. This type of running was not good for the grease axle boxes, and as we passed through Fritwell, several were squealing their heads off, but there was no smoke or drips of flaming grease lighting up the sleepers. We dropped our speed as we passed Aynho box, and Ted took over the regulator again, as it was standard practice over the water troughs, but as I have said before, my Ted could not top up the tank without drowning us both.

At Kings Sutton we were diverted into the loop, pulling up outside the shed, there we were uncoupled, leaving the train for the pilot engine.

We then took *Cruckton Hall* into Banbury shed, having given us a very pleasant trip from Swindon.

There was no need to report to the shed Foreman, as we were over our hours and on overtime, but still had an hour to wait before we could catch a train home. I expect Control could have found us one to work back, or might even have allowed us to travel home as passengers in the guard's van. They were known, at times, to do queer things like that, but we were at odds with those faceless men behind their banks of telephones, and in the true tradition of honest God-fearing enginemen we skipped the formalities of the bowler hatted Foreman and Controllers, and nipped smartly into the canteen for a cooked breakfast.

As we ordered our breakfast, of bacon done to a crisp, and eggs sunny side up, a large statuesque lady came out of the kitchen. Not only was she a handsome lady, but she could remember a little incident with those enginemen and a piano-playing goods guard, and funnily enough we were the spit of those two engine-men. She had not run into the likes of my Ted before who, although Welsh only by adoption, could speak the language like a native. He ordered our breakfast in Welsh so that her thoughts of retribution were swept aside while she sorted this one out. I had to intervene as an interpreter which I did in the broadest of Berkshire accents. Poor lady, the seeds of doubt were sown, but she could only go as far to say that we were the doubles of someone she knew. I led her astray by saying that I had a twin brother who sometimes came into this canteen.

She cooked our breakfast to perfection, and when Ted took the plates back to the counter he complimented her on the skill of her cooking, but in the most charming of English accents. I was already at the door with both of our jackets and bags so that Ted would have a free run for safety, and in the intervening seconds while she considered whether to throw a plate or the dish cloth in her hand at him, he made it. The words she threw at us made us realise that the next time we came into Banbury canteen when she was on duty we should require our birth certificates to prove a point. That little incident and a good breakfast under our belt had dispelled all thoughts of Ralph Painton's pleas to bring home *Norton Hall*, which we had forgotten by now anyway. We booked off duty and made our way home—tomorrow was another day.

The weekend passed without thoughts of interviews by men with bowler hats. Monday morning came and we belted the Winchester goods over the branch, came home with the stopper, and brought on to shed, No. 2222 ready for the afternoon Winchester train. Walking down from the ash road towards the shed to book off we met Ralph and Bill Young. Bill had his bowler tipped forward over his eyes which was always a bad sign, and he beckoned with his forefinger for us to follow him. We had the distinct feeling that we were for it.

The interview was short and sweet, and *Norton Hall* had gone. It would have been bad enough if she had only been in the London Division, but Bristol Division now had her and it would be months before she came home again. The two other 'Halls' were in trouble too. No. 6923 *Croxteth Hall* was in the lifting shop, and No. 6952 *Kimberley Hall* was in for a boiler washout and tube cleaning, in addition to having a new brick arch built in her firebox. We realised that we would not be very popular with the Didcot passenger link men when they found that they had to work with any old engine. We explained, in vain, to Bill that a bowler hat man at Swindon held as much authority as he did, but Bill was not interested and we had to stand there and let him get it out of his system. But the Lord smiles on the righteous, for before the week was out we were to retrieve *Norton Hall* for Bill by the most outrageous piece of blackmail. We were enginemen defending our home shed, which today would be called hijacking but in Great Western days would be called using one's loaf.

As the spare crew that week, we had the odds and sods that came along, so it was no surprise on Thursday to be given the job of returning an engine to Reading shed that Didcot had borrowed for the weekend. She was one of the three surviving Midland and South Western 2-4-0s, No. 1336. At Didcot, we already had No. 1334, while Reading had Nos. 1335 and 1336, and all of these engines were used for the Lambourn branch. No. 1334 had a broken spring, so Bill Young had borrowed No. 1336 from Reading for the Sunday passenger to run to Lambourn. They were sweet little engines although a bit cramped on the footplate, but were free steaming and fully capable of working the Lambourn branch and engineering trains on Sunday occupations of the line. It was a pleasant job to return her home to Reading and which was to give us the opportunity of recovering *Norton Hall.*

We prepared her and then ran her light to Reading, leaving her on the shed ready for the afternoon men to take her out. As we were under shed orders and not Control, we reported to the shed Foreman who had another nice little job waiting for us. We were to prepare, turn and run No. 4036 *Queen Elizabeth* back to her home shed at Swindon.

As we walked over to her, Ted and I began to lay plans, as we both knew she was the pride of Swindon. Apart from firebox ash on her footplate and steps, she was immaculate—a Lady from end to end. We soon had her ready and turned, and with a feeling of excitement we took her off shed and headed towards home. Down the main line we swept, wondering if we could get away with a cheeky bit of blackmail. All the distant signals were off through Didcot, but Ted shut off and blew up on the whistle for shed. The signals went back, the points came over, and into Didcot shed we slipped. I ran ahead of her changing the hand points so that we came to a rest on number 1 road outside Bill Young's office.

Bill had had an extension built on to his old original office, enabling him to turn round in his chair and see up through the shed sidings. This particular morning Bill turned round to see what was the cause of the light fading through his window, and seeing the red buffer beam with No. 4036 painted on it, followed by the bulk of a great locomotive standing on 6ft. 8½in. wheels, was enough to make him move hurriedly.

He came out of the office door to find Ted and myself grinning down at him from a great height, and he clambered up on the footplate and asked what we thought we were playing at. We both had the greatest respect for Bill, so we sat him down on the seat and explained our proposed plan. Both Ted and I agreed that Bill would have made a fine horse trader, as he was artful enough. Bill tipped his bowler over one eye realising, knowing the pair of us, that there was more to come. If Bill was as good at trading as we thought he could be, he would let us off the hook by taking a chance with a certain Swindon bowler hatted gentleman and at the same time regain *Norton Hall*. It was easy enough, as one telephone call offering to swop *Norton Hall* for *Queen Elizabeth* gave Bill the trump card. He took a very long deep breath, and then let the air out with a whistle. All the little cog wheels under that bowler hat began to churn around the pros and cons as he sifted through the implications of taking such an action. We began to wonder if we had misjudged our Foreman for if this went wrong he would be in the manure deeper than we were, Ted's remarks during his deliberation turned the scales, 'Horses for horses'—three little words, which were enough for Bill to make a move. He climbed down with a determined look on his face and disappeared into his office.

Ten minutes later we were back at the shed, signal ready to run, *Queen Elizabeth* light to Swindon, with the knowledge that *Norton Hall* would be waiting for us, I had learnt that the old saying that there is more than one way to skin a cat, was true.

We spanked her along down the main line to Swindon in half an hour, making up a little of the time lost on Didcot shed, and it was good to be alive. She rode like a coach, with the reverser back almost in mid-gear and the regulator just open enough to admit steam to her valves. No wonder Swindon wanted her back, for she could have been lost in the London Division for months. We left her on the shed all ready to be taken out again, and went to the shed office where we were requested to report to the Foreman. We had been seen by him as we came into shed and he 'wanted words' with us.

It was obvious to us both who this would be. It had to be the same gentleman who had taken *Norton Hall* from us the Friday before. Ted and I held a little conference outside his office as we had to have some plan of action to take the wind out of him before he started on us. We arrived at a strategy that would defeat him in a 'pincer movement' so we knocked the door and bowled in catching him unawares. Ted opened straight away from 'Good afternoon, sir, I've got my birth certificate' and then I said 'My parents are married, sir', and in one bold stroke we had countered two of the descriptions he would use on us. He burst out laughing and told us that Bill Young had advised him that we talk our way out of trouble, but he admired the way in which we were loyal to our shed. He then told us never to pull one on him like that again. I thought that perhaps Ted was pushing our luck a bit too far when he replied that he thought that using one's initiative was the way to exchanging the footplate for a bowler hat, but the reply was a good one. The bowler, he said, was earned by leaning on Drivers and Firemen, particularly those from another Division, and we had better collect *Norton Hall* before he gave a demonstration of this leaning technique.

He had made his point, and we had made ours. Honour to both Divisions was satisfied, and we climbed up on our beloved *Norton Hall* and took her home. Bill Young was pleased over that little incident, although he did admit it made him sweat a bit, and he made us promise we would never push him into a corner like that again. He knew we would do anything for him and he would do the same for us. After all, we were the pair who could re-rail No. 5322 at Banbury without any help, so pinching a 'Forty' was all in the day's work.

The next week brought a bonus to both of us, for we were booked to work the 3.35 pm Didcot to Winchester passenger train. This was a through train from Oxford to Southampton, and the Oxford men would work it up to Didcot, leaving Oxford at 2.58 pm, always with a 61XX tank. When they had uncoupled in number 5 platform they would go into Didcot Depot to work the Workmen's back through to Banbury while we took their train over the Didcot to Winchester branch. Our normal working was to change over with the Winchester men at Burghclere on to the goods and return home, but this week good fortune was with us as both Winchester men were unavailable. The Fireman was on holiday and the Driver was sick, so we could work right through, returning home as passengers via Basingstoke and Reading.

It is always a nice feeling to enginemen to know that they could ride home 'on the cushions' and with this particular train it was an enjoyable duty. We always prepared our own engine for this trip, and we could rely on a Collett 22XX class, which at Didcot, were always in beautiful condition. Boiler pressure was the standard 200lbs for a small engine, cylinders were 17 1/2 in diameter by 24in stroke, all coupled up to six 5ft 2in wheels, and with a load of three 35 ton coaches and perhaps the odd horse-box the weight of around 130 tons was just enough to hold them down. We had the two best little engines that week, alternating each day between No. 2222 and No. 2221. They thrived on the classic haycock fire, chattering away through the exhaust as only the 22XX class could. With no back working Ted decided that every other day I could drive, so I had No. 2222 on my driving days. Although I enjoyed every engine Ted allowed me to handle, the 22XX class was one of my favourites.

On this train I could take her out of the station, over the points at East junction, and once on the branch I would give her half regulator and begin to wind her back to 30% cut off, snap down the clip, and sit down to watch her little wheels fly round as she scampered up the banks. It was a class of locomotive that needed to be worked hard and the harder they were worked the better they responded. They loved to have something to pull, and they would ride like an American rodeo bronco once they got moving. Firing was completely out of the question, as was sitting down, and both Driver and Fireman had to hold on tight as they bucked, bounced, twisted and kicked. They were the ideal locomotive for hard branch line working, and a credit to their designer Mr. Collett.

The week progressed well, with both of us enjoying every minute. We would run into Winchester Chesil at 5.30 pm where the Southern men would be waiting with a 'T9' to take the train on to Southampton. We would then uncouple and slip into the little shed, turn the engine ready for the early shift coming on in the morning, and clean the fire which was a simple enough job after only a few hours of engine working. While Ted oiled her, I would shovel the coal forward, filling up the front end of the tender. We would then fill up her boiler, damp down what was left of her fire, and have her bedded down for the night by 6.30 pm. We were now ready to wash and walk up through the City to Winchester Southern. It was worked out to a fine art as we walked out of the station yard just as the pubs opened, which was one hour and a half before our train left a mile away. The average engineman was not a hard drinking man, far from it; but to be free from all responsibility with the work behind you, and with just over an hour to wait for transport home, it was a precious break from the normal pattern of our working life and we savoured every second of it.

The first pint never touched the teeth, the second was enjoyed with a lazy contentment, and then we would wander up through the city, gazing at the contents in the shop windows, until we arrived near the Southern station, always, of course, leaving ourselves enough time for one more leisurely pint. Now we know why the Winchester men were so contented, and we debated in a light-hearted manner about the chances of a transfer from Didcot. Ted suddenly remembered the previous week, for if this was the just rewards for pinching a 'Forty', what would be the reward for pinching a 'King'?

There were three possibilities. We would definitely meet the General Manager. There was no doubt about that at all, and probably be stuck somewhere in the middle of Swindon Works shunting out of the workshops, far, far, from the main line. Or even more likely, we would be split up, and, apart from this happening through normal promotion into another link, this certainty would not be worth the risk. It was a tantalising thought, and each time we spotted a 'King' tucked away behind a shed we knew that it was possible to sneak her away.

The Sunday passenger working over the Didcot to Newbury branch was only one train each way, and to Lambourn instead of Winchester. It was a little 'perk' job in the passenger link, and in the summer, one to enjoy. But when I fired on this duty it was the only time I fired a locomotive wearing an overcoat. There was no turn table at Lambourn so it had to be tender first in one direction.

As I have mentioned before, the Lambourn branch was the prerogative of the Reading men, except on Sundays, with the little Midland and South Western Engine No. 1334 allocated to Didcot for this Sunday duty. The Dean goods engine was also allowed on the branch, and we worked many racehorse specials from Lambourn with them.

This particular Sunday I was firing to Jack Wilkins. We booked on, prepared No. 1334 and left Didcot at 3.30 pm with three coaches and the engine heading towards Newbury. It was a good trip over the branch, and although the little engine was steaming well and giving no trouble, the weather was against us. We had started off in a cold mist, but the nearer we came to Newbury the thicker it got, until it became so bad that we had to creep into the platform. Engine first gave us some protection from the cold, but when the time came to return and leave Lambourn, it would be tender first all the way home which was not a happy thought. We left Newbury at 4.40 pm already beginning to find the night closing in on us. We proceeded up the sharp 1 in 93 bank to Speen and eventually groped our way to Lambourn. I found there, that a Fireman's duty now included pumping. So we filled our little tank and then had to replace this water in the storage tank so that the Reading men would have some in the morning. It was an operation I should have enjoyed had the weather been better.

This pumping operation was so simple. A long, one inch pipe was connected to the tank, and working on an elbow joint it was swung round level with the whistle. The drill was then to take off the whistle, connect up the pipe with the union nut provided, and then tie down the whistle chain. The steam would then start a little pump working. However there was one thing about all this which I could never work out. With the whistle connected up to that pipe, my boiler water was going down. So I had to start firing her and using the injectors as the amount of water I pumped up, just about equalled the amount I had drawn from the tank. To one, such as I, brought up on sound Great Western engineering there was the touch of the Irish about this. Had I climbed up the iron ladder to the top of the tank I am sure the last rung would have had a notice board bolted to it with the word 'Stop' painted on it.

With the pumping completed, we made a can of tea. At 6.30 pm as we started off towards Newbury the fog began to freeze, forming a layer of frost on the coal. Running tender first, we had no protection from the weather, and the fog swept over the end of the tender into the cab in the form of chilling ice. In the light of the firebox it was as if we were about to be engulfed in an avalanche. I began to shiver whilst Jack had jammed himself against the boiler, but before we had reached East Garston his face was grey and pinched. There was only one choice left to us in this frosty place. Either we could run with the firebox doors closed tight, and so be able to see to some extent where we were, or we could run with the flap up, get some warmth but be blinded with the back glare from the light reflecting from that bank of fog.

We both came to the same conclusion which was to put the flap up and damn the fog. We were the only train on the branch, and if we ran through a station we would simply set back. As soon as we spotted the glimmer of the Tilley lamp at East Garston, Jack pulled down on the little single-handled regulator, gave her a good stiff shot on the vacuum brake and we shuddered to a halt. I began to fill up her firebox with as much as it would hold, and then put on my overcoat and curled up against the boiler, ramming my shoulders between the gauge frame and cab. We crept from station to station, each one emerging as a vague shadow in the hissing light from a solitary Tilley lamp, until we left Speen and felt our way down the bank into Newbury.

Approaching Newbury there was one signal from the branch, which allowed movement either into the bay platform or the main line platform and which was perched out over the branch, projecting from the brick retaining wall of the banking. We crept forward so slowly that we could count the bricks in the light of the fire, but no signal came into sight. There was only one way to find it. Jack stopped and I lit the flare lamp, climbed down, and walked forward, only to lose No. 1334 as soon as I had passed the tender. The fog was so thick I could just about see my feet. At first I thought I had walked under it, until my feet hit the wooden ramp over the wire. Then I found the ladder bolted to the wall, which was ridiculous, as I was standing under the blessed thing and still could not see if it was on or off. So I walked back to Jack and asked him to give me five minutes and then blow the whistle. I stumbled back to the ladder and very gingerly climbed up to the extension platform by holding the flare lamp out as far as I could. I could just see the outline of the signal, but not the indicator. Jack gave a long pull on the whistle chain and the response was immediate. There was a twang as the wire moved and a squealing, groaning, rasping noise as rods and bars crusted in frost moved through guides, and that signal dropped down in one almighty clang, shaking the whole platform. I found my way down the ladder step by step and climbed back onto the footplate. We both looked up as we passed under the signal, and from the shaft of light from the firebox just caught sight of the indicator, which routed us to the up main platform.

It was a pleasure to stop in Newbury platform, indeed it was as if we had re-entered our own world. There were people, station noises, and the feeling that we had come in out of the void of nothing. We dropped the flap and crouched down in front of the fire with the warmth seeping into the very core of our chilled bodies. I could see that my hands were cracked and bleeding where the skin had split, the hot water drips from the injectors in that cold did not mix kindly in these Arctic conditions. We could both have drunk a scalding hot cup of tea, but we were already late and it was time to leave and head back out into the fog and make for home.

Jack pushed over the regulator, and No. 1334 gave a little slip, and then found her heels. He took her out of the station and down towards the junction at walking pace, but as soon as we had cleared the platform the fog closed in on us. Jack held on to the regulator and hand rail, and I to the gauge frame and tender hand brake, waiting for the tender to lurch as she turned on to the Didcot branch. It came before we expected it, with the flanges squealing as the wheels bit into the curve, and then we were on the branch. Jack gave her some more steam and pulled back on her little reversing lever, and we climbed steadily out of Newbury until her wheels rumbled over the Bath road and into a clear starlit night. We could hardly believe it was possible, as looking back into Newbury we could see that the whole town was covered in an enormous blanket of fog. There was no gradual thinning out, the Bath road ran in to a solid wall of thick freezing murk, while outside this canopy of total blankness the houses backing up to the branch stood out in sharp reality. We caught the sight of warmth and home as through the lighted bedroom windows now level with the footplate we saw a mother bend over a child's cot, and a few houses further on a man stood in front of his dressing table mirror adjusting his tie. The last few feet of a church steeple stood out in the middle of the town, and then we were into the cutting and trees leaving this all behind.

On such a night, Burke and Hare must have worked in the loneliness of the graveyard. Charles Dickens would have loved it, and even now, after all these years, I still shiver at the thought of that awful journey home. Even without the fog, the air pouring over the tender into the cab struck deep into the very core of life, and we were so cold that it was an effort to move. In such conditions the brain became sluggish, and I had to concentrate on making the move to open the water feed for the injectors, and literally force myself to pick up the shovel. We ran into Didcot at the end of our limit, and I had to light the flare lamp and hold it under the coupling, vacuum pipe and steam pipe, before I could uncouple No. 1334 from the train as she was frozen to those coaches by a bar of ice!

We thankfully put her away on the ash road and made our way into the warmth of the engineman's cabin. We were finished, and we could both go home. The stove was glowing red hot, and the kettle was boiling, and neither Jack or myself could move until we had recovered. In our misery, we had not spoken to one another since leaving Newbury, for each one of us had been wrapped up in our own private world of suffering, but now with a hot drink inside us we could joke and laugh again. As the warmth returned to our bodies

The Didcot of Harold's youth. The station entrance has today altered out of all recognition. At the time the view was taken the railway was the largest employer in the town. It was at Didcot (loco) that Harold commenced his railway career in World War Two. *Commercial postcard*

Didcot loco shed had been rebuilt by the GWR in 1932. It survives today as the home of the Great Western Society. This is looking towards the front of the shed with the water tower and coaling stage on the left. During World War Two a covered ash-shed was provided over the two lines immediately to the left which was to prevent the glow from fires being seen by an enemy aircraft. *BR*

Viewed from the west side with the two lines on the left leading towards the turntable. The large building at the rear was the repair/lift shop. That immediately at the front of the shed was the sand drier. *BR*

The shed interior; the offices stores and mess rooms were on the left-hand wall. *BR*

Coaling stage and water tank. Both survive today although sadly the locomotive does not. *BR*

One of Harold's first introductions to firing was on the stationary boiler. Didcot had one such – this unreported location had two. The boiler was used to provide steam for wash-out purposes. *Crécy Photo Archive*

Inside the lift shop at Didcot, the domain of the Foreman Fitter. *J.R. Fairman*

Firing turn alongside 8F No. 8400 (one of the type built at Swindon) and seen in less than ideal external condition at Moreton goods loop in 1944. *Author's collection*

Harold on the footplate of a 22xx at Compton (DNS line) in 1944. The cabside window has been plated over due to wartime conditions. Harold would sing the praises of these 0-6-0 engines, describing them as 'baby Castles'. *Author's collection*

SR 'Remembrance' class No. 2327 *Trevithick*, on which Harold worked in World War Two and which led to praise from a loco inspector. *Author's collection*

Duke class 4-4-0 No. 3280 leaving Southampton Town (Terminus) on its 56-mile journey back to Didcot with more than twenty stops on the way. *C.R.L. Coles*

American 2-8-0, a type on which Harold fired several times. The whistle reminded him of the American prairies, the cab seats were well upholstered and the crews had fun with the pop-type safety valves. *Maurice Earley*

Harold admits he preferred GW engines but acknowledged some of the LMS 2-8-0s had been built at Swindon in World War Two. He comments they were fine engines; apart from the brass live steam handles for the injectors – guaranteed to leave a blister on the palm of the hand. *Crécy Photo Archive*

LMS 2-8-0 stopped for water at Reading. Several 'foreign' engines worked on the GW in World War Two including, as Harold describes, some terrible little Midland 0-6-0 tender engines. *Maurice Earley*

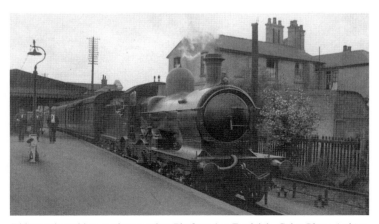

Didcot train waiting at what was then Platform 1 at Eastleigh. *Crécy Photo Archive*

No. 2282 was the one member of the 22xx type that Harold disliked, not because of the engine but because it was paired with an old R.O.D. tender! *C.R.L. Coles*

No. 3267 *Cornishman* at Winchester Chesil. *Crécy Photo Archive*

Dean Goods No. 2516 about to enter the tunnel at Winchester with a northbound goods train. Harold disliked the brass hard wheels fitted to these engines but '… as she was an old lady she was forgiven'. The view was taken before the DNS line was upgraded in 1942–43. *Lens of Sutton collection*

The new World War Two locomen's hostel at Didcot; this is where Betty worked. *BR*

Winchester Chesil station. Harold and his mate once briefly considered asking for a transfer here. Harold's long-time mate Ted was also friends with one of Winchester drivers, Tommy Keough.

Whitchurch after World War Two but still retaining the alternate black/white blackout stripes on the lamps. It was at Whitchurch where Harold's mate was the victim of a practical joke, believing eggs could be obtained from a smallholding adjacent to the railway but instead ended up being chased by a large guard dog! *Crécy Photo Archive*

Coaling at Didcot – this view taken in the very last days of steam. The method involved had not changed over decades. Harold also spent some time working on the coal stage. *J.R. Fairman*

One of the little ex MSWJ 2-4-0 engines which was used for the Sunday afternoon Lambourn service. It is seen here outside Didcot shed. *P. Earl*

County No. 1000 *County of Middlesex* on Down milk empties at Didcot. Harold used to say the sound of a milk train passing was totally different to anything else – probably on account of the six-wheel stock. *I.J. Hodson*

The fireman is hard at work on Hall No. 5945 *Leckhampton Hall* as it climbs near Chipping Campden. *M.J. Esau*

Another route with which Harold was very familiar was the Berks & Hants line from Reading to Westbury. Here a travel-stained 53xx 2-6-0 approaches Southcote Junction with a westbound goods. The crew faced an ever-increasing climb for much of the way to Savernake summit – but then they could relax all the way to Westbury. *Crécy Photo Archive*

A Lambourn branch train leaving Welford Park for Great Shefford and Lambourn. *Maurice Earley*

2-4-0 No. 1336 at work on the Lambourn branch. Upon arrival at Lambourn on the Sunday train, the Didcot crew would be required to pump water, a task that could use almost as much water as was pumped! *Crécy Photo Archive*

Not one of Harold's favourites, a 'Westernised' R.O.D., sometimes referred to as 'Dirty Gertie'. This one is at Ivor Heath heading towards Reading in 1944. *Crécy Photo Archive*

No .3454 *Skylark* serving out its last days on a pick-up goods at Maidenhead. *Crécy Photo Archive*

Another 'Bulldog', this one the unnamed No. 3419, on a down goods approaching Didcot with the signals off for the station avoiding line. *Crécy Photo Archive*

Slightly easier going for No. 5979 *Cruckton Hall* near Milton just west of Didcot. Harold preferred the original type to the later modified engines of the class, the latter he referred to as having to be 'punched' more to achieve the same results. *M. Mensing*

A 'Hall' with a small tender – No. 4912 *Berrington Hall* on the west curve at Didcot with a Wolverhampton to Margate train. *J.F. Russell Smith*

Running-in turn for No. 6026 *King John* working a Swindon to Didcot local. Harold reports they would often work a stopping service in the opposite direction with an engine destined for Swindon works, sometimes returning with another engine fresh from overhaul. *T.E. Williams*

Station pilot duty could sometimes mean the pilot engine being commandeered should a failure occur on a main-line train. Such was the case here when on 25 September 1964 No. 4959 *Purley Hall* was used to replace a diesel failure. The replacement is seen at Swindon. *Crécy Photo Archive*

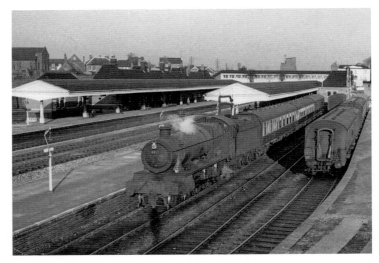

Another 'Hall', this time No. 4917 *Crosswood Hall* at a station Harold knew very well – Newbury. The engine is standing in the Down bay with a stopping train to Westbury, the same bay where Harold would sometimes set back into if there was a lay-over on a Didcot to Winchester/Southampton service. On the far left is the Lambourn bay. *Bryan S. Jennings*

From the same location but looking the other way – westwards. The 'Mogul' has likely come up from Westbury, whilst a train is signalled to leave the Down main platform. Newbury remains open today although the signal box, signals and bay platform/sidings are long gone. *Bryan H. Kimber*

No. 6961 *Stedham Hall* at rest after arrival at Paddington. Didcot crews had an afternoon semi-fast turn to Paddington using one of their allocated 'Hall' class engines. It was at Paddington that Harold experienced the incident with the flare lamp, bosom and gin bottle. *Anthony A. Vickers*

This time a 'Castle' at Paddington, No. 4091 *Dudley Castle*. Although Didcot had no allocated duties involving members of the class, when on a relief turn crews might find themselves working on almost any type of engine. This included members of the 'Castle', 'Star' and 'Saint' types. *Crécy Photo Archive*

The interior of Old Oak Common depot – here there were four turntables under cover. *C.R.L. Coles*

A 22xx at Newbury on a Didcot-bound train. On the opposite side of the platform is the stock for what is a Reading local. *Crécy Photo Archive*

Atmosphere at Winchester. Harold and his mate would sometimes leave their train here and take a leisurely walk through the city to the Southern station to return to Didcot via Basingstoke and Reading. When working engineers' trains during World War Two improvements on the DNS line, this might instead involve a bus journey over the Berkshire and Hampshire downs, which on one occasion involved the incident of the ferret. *Henry Meyer*

Down Swindon local leaving Steventon. *D. Fereday-Glenn*

Trains crossing at Worthy Down, Winchester branch. *Crécy Photo Archive*

Wallingford terminus (after the engine shed had been taken out of use). Harold spent a few days as the fireman on the branch service to Cholsey, where initially he did not do too well with the whistle …

Accident at Appleford Crossing. Harold was extremely fortunate not to be involved in a similar incident resulting in fatalities. *Author's collection*

No. 2221 on the Newbury to Didcot service. *J.F. Russell-Smith*

No. 5943 *Elmdon Hall* outside the running shed at Swindon. Harold and his mate were involved in some subterfuge involving the foremen at Didcot and at Swindon concerning a Didcot 'Hall' class and a Swindon 'Star'.

Late afternoon train between Newbury and Didcot recorded near to Hampstead Norris. *D.J. Beavor*

One of Harold's last footplate trips was on the restored *City of Truro* when it was based at Didcot and working a regular turn to Southampton. The engine is seen here on the Down run paused at Eastleigh.

… and on the reverse working at Burghclere. *Hugh Davies*

Didcot Foxhall Junction signal box. *BR*

Foxhall junction signal box interior. *Author's collection*

Signalman's view from Didcot West signal box towards the station.
Author's collection

Harold's first signal box – Milton. *Author's collection*

Top link men: driver Albert Potter and fireman Bert Peedell on No. 5057 *St Fagans Castle. Author's collection*

The man who started it all, Uncle Bert Edmonds and his fireman Vic Smith. *Author's collection*

LAST TRAIN FROM PLYMOUTH

Driver A. J. Edmonds

After 44 years on the railways, an engine-driver made his last run from Plymouth to London today. He is Driver A. J. Edmonds, who comes from Tonbridge, Kent, and has been driving trains between Plymouth and London for the past five years.

An engine-driver on the Great Western and the Western Region of the British Railways for 32 years, now, at the age of 65, Mr. Edmonds is retiring.

He told the "Herald" that throughout his 44 years on the railways he has never had a day's illness. He has driven all the crack trains on the Western Region, including the Cornish Riviera.

Bert in characteristic pose recorded in his final days as a driver.
Author's collection

Milton signal box interior. *Author's collection*

At the end of its career, No. 5055 Earl of Eldon in a sorry state at Reading in 1964. The engine was withdrawn and scrapped soon after.

No. 70026 *Polar Star* having come to grief in soft ground at Milton in late 1955. The main line is on the embankment above. Recovery involved tying rails to the wheels, setting the engine upright and then pulling it back on to a specially laid siding from Milton depot. The latter was undertaken by No. 3212.
Author's collection

The line between Didcot, Newbury and Winchester did not last much longer either. Infrastructure had already been curtailed in some places such as here at Kings Worthy, recorded on the last day of passenger services south of Newbury, 5 March 1960. Passenger working between Didcot and Newbury ceased in 1962 and the whole line south was closed completely in August 1964. *Derek Cross*

Demolition at Upton & Blewbury. Near to here was where Harold lost the brake whistle on a runaway towards Didcot. *Author's collection*

we became almost intoxicated with the sheer luxury of this room with its two tea-stained wooden tables, wooden benches and a row of lockers backing onto a dirty white-washed wall. In the centre of it all was the roaring red-hot stove, and at that moment we would not have swopped it for the Savoy Hotel.

It was a journey as a Fireman that I shall never forget, and was one of the bad times. But as always, there were good times, and my next trip to Lambourn was a good one, and another that I shall always remember because of a pair of brown boots. It was spring time, and still with a nip in the air. Ted Hurle, my regular driver, and myself found we had a plum job on our hands, for we had to prepare No. 2532, one of the Dean Goods engines at Didcot, and run her light to Lambourn to work a horse-box train as far as Banbury. It was Doncaster sales time, so traffic in racehorses was heavy on the branch. Ted was very happy as he loved the 'gee gees' and he had a little black book containing all the information from tips, touts, cross-eyed ladies, and the chap who drove the milk cart. He was the last of the great gamblers, taking as much as two hours working out cross doubles, trebles, and each-way bets, to speculate three bob with the bookies. He could never understand my lack of interest in it all but my interest in fillies was in the two-legged variety, as I was in love and saving hard for the future. The bookie owned a Rolls, and Ted owned a bike, so that was enough for me.

We left the shed long before time and belted over the Didcot branch like a cat with its tail on fire, and then on to Lambourn before the horses arrived. We backed on to a dozen horse-boxes and waited. Ted had a look of anticipation on his face, and as soon as the first of the string came into the station yard he was off to meet them. The punter was loose and out for information. No more cross-eyed ladies for Ted, as the stable lads and trainers were the real thing.

Now we come to the brown boots. Ted was known for those boots, as he always wore brown, and polished them to a degree only an ex-army man could achieve. He had spent hours on them with a bone, spit, polish, and a velvet buffer, and the gloss was so high that it blinded one to look at them. No dust ever had chance to settle, for it just slid off, and to see Ted walk over obstacles in the shed was to see all the daintiness of a ballerina performing the Dance of the Sugar Plum Fairy. The way he tip-toed over a lot of large brown piles left by previous horses made me laugh out loud, but Ted had it all worked out. Lambourn to Doncaster was a long way to send horses to lose races, and as each one of these were prospective winners, he wanted their names. So out came the little black book.

Loading temperamental racehorses was a work of art. The stable lads could lead them as far as the ramp but then they would come to a dead stop. Ted knew from his army days that the way to move a mule was to light a little fire under it. However, one could hardly light a fire under £2,000 worth of racehorse. They would stand there prancing about, with twin jets of steam escaping from flared nostrils, eyes wild with fear, until much pushing from the rear and pulling on the front end had them one at a time into the selected horse-boxes.

Ted stood back smartly during the antics of one horse which was spoiling his boots. He stood there on one foot, with the other cocked up behind him trying to scrape it off with a bit of wood, but worse was to come. One beautiful brown yearling would not move, and Ted, with good intentions, went round the front end to help calm it down. I think the sparks from steel-shod hoofs steered him away from the back end, and I could just see the top of his cap over the back of the horse as he stood there stroking it. Suddenly, there was a noise very much like the sound of a locomotive picking up water over the troughs, and gallons of water started cascading from a great height onto a hard surface with Ted beating a hasty retreat in a cloud of steam.

When he eventually did emerge, I was standing on the platform hanging onto the handrail of No. 2532. I had no more laughing left in me, and he sloshed towards me with his little black book still clutched tightly in his hand. From the knees downwards, he was soaked, and his brown boots were stripped of all polish for ever. As we still had plenty of time before our booked departure, his overalls and trousers were taken off and draped over the injector handles to dry out. His boots were placed in front of the open firebox doors, and his socks washed in a bucket of hot water. He sat on my seat and looked back up the train, with his shirt tail tucked under him to keep out the draught. Still that horse stood there, defying all attempts to make him go up the ramp into the horse-box. But revenge was sweet for Ted when it did come. A broken-down old car came into the yard and stopped, and out of it jumped the head lad. 'Lad' was not the correct way to describe this gentleman, for he was a wizened little gnome of a man, dressed in cloth cap, thick woollen sweater and riding boots. He had a quick look round the yard and spotted the equipment he needed to move horses which was a single tall strand of stinging nettle which he plucked out of the ground and walked over to the reluctant horse. The treatment that followed was swift, sure and effective, for as he lifted the horse's tail and stroked him gently with the nettle, the animal moved up the ramp into the horse-box so quickly that he was in there with the door closed behind him before he had time to think why his tail had been lifted.

Ted's clothes were dry by the time we left for Newbury, but not his boots. He had to drive in his socks, standing on a newspaper, while I tied his laces together and hung the boots from the gauge frame. When he did eventually manage to get them on, he offered to do the firing, but for once I preferred to keep my side of the footplate. You see, the wind was blowing in from the south west, so I was breathing fresh air, but even so, each time I bent down with the shovel I could detect a distinct smell of horses.

We stopped at Compton to pick up a further six horse-boxes full of horses from the Ilsley and Blewbury stables. I did, in fact, drive here to pick up the boxes and back them on to our train while Ted again chatted up the stable lads. The little black book came out once more, and I did notice one name in there with a thick black line under it meaning that this one owed Ted a new pair of boots. The train was now complete for Doncaster, and we pulled away from Compton and ran non-stop into Banbury, where an L.N.E.R. Thompson B1 was waiting to take over. I uncoupled, backed into the shed, turned our little Dean Goods, enjoyed a can of tea, and then ran her light engine back to Didcot.

The Dean Goods engine was a wonderful little locomotive, the sole survivor from the days of the 'Atbaras', 'Badmintons', 'Rivers' and 'Flowers'. They were the engines of my father's youth, yet still going strong and capable of working any job except the hard hitting runners. The word 'Goods' was somewhat misleading. Although in the 1900 period they were used as a goods engine, most of the firing I had done on them, was when running passenger trains. The very fine Collett 22XX class was introduced to replace them, but it never quite succeeded in sending them all back to Swindon for breaking up. Thank goodness one still survives in Swindon Museum where she stands, with pride, next to *City of Truro* and *Lode Star*. Perhaps it is wishful thinking to expect her to be taken out again one day and steamed.

The good times in locomotive working like the story just related went a long way to make up for places like Honeybourne tunnel, the rough old R.O.D. engines and the dirty nights. But there was tragedy as well as comedy as you will see.

Chapter Twelve

One day black comedy came to my uncle, Driver Bert Edmonds. Bert was a top link man at Old Oak shed, and his day's work entailed belting down to Plymouth and back or running the 'Bristolian' up and down at 100 mph. One of the jobs he covered was the 2.15 am newspaper train from Paddington to the West of England via Bristol, returning with the 7.45 a.m. Weston-super-Mare. It was a hard day's work for both him and his fireman. The engine was prepared for them, so they would leave Old Oak shed as soon as they could, and back on to the train. Vic Smith, his mate, would dash off to the canteen for a can of tea, as it was the only chance they had to get one. One Tuesday morning Vic was followed up the platform by a police inspector and constable. Vic climbed up on the footplate of No. 5066 *Sir Felix Pole* and told Bert to hide as the 'Fuzz' were coming to take him away. Bert's reaction to this was that they were more likely to come after young Firemen who spend their evenings up in the West End whooping it up. But much to Bert's surprise, it was him the Police were after with some questions they wanted answered.

They knew that Bert had been on the same train the day before, and that he had been relieved by Driver R. Hart when he ran into Paddington. He was asked to explain how Driver Hart had found a lady's leg in the water scoop when the engine was over the pit in Old Oak shed.

This took the wind out of Bert. Little minnows found their way into the tank via the river and the water troughs, but a lady's leg was another matter. Bert then asked where the remainder of the poor lady was, and the answer let him off the hook. She was found scattered all over the up and down main lines at Goring at 8.23 am on the previous day. Bert produced his log book, proving that at 8.23 am that day he was standing in Chippenham station, and was not booked away until 8.26 am. The Inspector then questioned Bert's entry of '½-82 Didcot' and Bert explained that he slipped two coaches at Didcot, at 9.04 am which in fact, were scheduled to be slipped at 9.03½am at 82 mph. The Inspector was impressed as 30 seconds late was not much, but Bert Edmonds prides himself on running to time and that half a minute to him was as bad as half an hour. Anyway Bert had an alibi, so he was in the clear. Bert quickly stuffed more tobacco into his pipe thinking that the morning had started with comedy with the arrival of two policemen, and then tragedy with the news that they had brought concerning the lady. He had to find out how *Sir Felix Pole* had picked up the lady's leg.

When they ran back into Paddington later that morning with the up Weston, Driver Hart had the rest of the story. (*Sir Felix Pole* had done a quick run down to Bristol and back after Bert had handed her over, and it was on this trip that she [perhaps that should really be 'he'] had run down the lady at Goring. I know from experience that it is very upsetting to walk round to the front of the engine intending simply to remove a headlamp only to find the A.T.C. ramp covered in bits of skin, bone and hair. The human body is not built to be hit with a 600-ton hammer travelling at 80 mph. It was just a part of footplate life, but how do you stop children placing coins on the rails, and overenthusiastic engine spotters lying a foot away from the rails with a camera poised for that award winning shot? Footplate work was not all glamour and excitement, but it had its moments.

There were some jobs that had problems other than just running between stations, such as when Bert was in the Oxford link they had an issue that was a nuisance to all enginemen. This was a particular passenger train that was booked to stop at certain stations on certain days, but not on every day, which was so easy to forget.

Bert was running this train from Oxford to Paddington but which was booked to stop at Ealing Broadway just on Wednesdays and Fridays, being non-stop on the other days. All went well until Friday when Bert's mate changed with another Fireman, who suffered from a bad stammer. In the normal turn of events, if the Fireman thought that his mate had forgotten about a stop he would remind him, as this was all part of working together. Bert was engrossed in keeping time and belting away towards home, but on approaching Acton West, his Fireman could see that Bert had forgotten all about stopping at Ealing Broadway. There was no sign of him shutting off, so he went over to remind him, but the harder he tried to tell him, the worse his stammer became. Bert hammered through Ealing and into Paddington, but it was too late. Angry passengers clamoured round the cab demanding an explanation, and it was only then, that he was able to understand that 'st-st-s.t:st' was an indication to stop. Bert was a bit upset, as he prided himself on fast running and keeping to time, but he couldn't blame his mate. He did however think, perhaps, that if he had begun to speak as they passed through Reading there would have been a sporting chance that the booked stop at Ealing Broadway could have taken place.

When father and I got to hear of this, the usual leg pulling took place, but it back-fired on us both a few weeks later. We were booked together for a Sunday special and we left our warm beds, washed, had a pot of tea, and walked down to the shed for a 3.30 am start. As we called through the timekeeper's window to be booked on duty, we wondered why he started laughing. We looked at each other a little puzzled. There were no shirt tails hanging out or anything like that and we thought that the man must be round the bend. We went over to the glass cabinet to find the number of the engine that was booked to us to prepare for this special, it was No. 4905 *Barton Hall*. The duty list said 'Driver Gasson and Fireman Gasson,' On Duty 3.30 pm. Off shed 4.30 pm.'

No wonder the timekeeper was laughing as we were 12 hours too early, and crawling out of bed at 2.30 am on a Sunday morning just to walk down to the shed and back was no joke. The timekeeper was sworn to secrecy, and we could trust him to keep his mouth shut. I can assure you that we returned to bed a lot quicker than we got out. When we reported for duty in the afternoon at the proper time, all was well, and no mention was made by the day shift man. However, we had not allowed for the Great Western underground communication system which had been operating between sheds. Before two days had passed, Bill Gasson in Reading shed knew of that Sunday morning incident, and Bert Edmonds at Old Oak shed had also heard the whisper. We received a letter from both of them on the Wednesday morning, containing just two words. On opening the envelope, a single sheet of paper fell out containing the words, 'We know'.

The directors were very proud that the Great Western was a family railway, but they only knew the half of it, except one director. This was Reggie Hanks. I can call him Reggie now, but if I were to meet him again he would be very much Mr. Hanks, Sir. He was loved by all the enginemen who came into contact with him as Reggie was not by any means the usual director who arrived at Paddington complete with brief case and rolled umbrella. The normal way to see Reggie arrive to run the railway was to watch him climb down from the footplate, dressed in a pair of old overalls and wiping his hands on the cotton waste. In later years, after the end of the steam locomotive and the destruction of so many signal boxes, I parted company with British Rail, Western Region, and joined the security staff of the Old Morris Motors Company. To my delight I found Mr Hanks on the Board of Directors, and in those days, this company was very much like the Great Western, being a family concern. Looking round now at the number of ex-Great Western men employed there, gives a good reason for the success of the company, for Billy Morris found that our background and training produced men who cared.

I have often been asked which was my favourite engine as a footplate man. I must exclude the 'Twenty-Nines', the 'Stars', 'Castles' and 'Kings', as they were specialist locomotives designed for a specific type of express passenger train. However, I did fire them many times, but not in the normal course of duty. Didcot enginemen laid hands on every type of Great Western engine, and it is these engines and the men that worked them that this book is all about.

I think most ex-enginemen would agree that the 68XX 'Grange' class would be at the top of the list, for their free steaming and versatility, with the 'Hall' class close behind. For branch line workings and other duties that required power without weight, the Collett 22XX class were supreme, but the all rounder was without doubt the 43XX class. However, there was one engine in a class of its own when it came to heavy freight working, and this was the favourite goods engine throughout the system. The good old 28XX class, the brain child of Mr. Churchward.

To men brought up on the 'Dean Goods' and 'Aberdares', the 28XX must have seemed the perfect goods engine, which it was.

The first to see the light of day was No. 2800, built in 1903 and the last, No. 3866 built in 1942. I think I must have fired every one of them. They all had the little 3,500-gallon tender, as fitted to the 43XX class, and I think it enhanced the appearance of them. The large tender would not have looked right tied onto the long low profile of the 'Twenty-Eight'. With a boiler pressure of 225 1bs, cylinders of 18½ins by 30ins, coupled to eight driving wheels they produced a tractive effort of 35,3801bs. They were very fine engines compared to other freight locomotive, and this meant that we had a locomotive on the Great Western in 1903 that could pull 100 wagons each loaded with 10 tons of coal all the way from Aberdare to Old Oak Common. Other companies were still messing about with two engines coupled together to move 60 wagons. The 28XX class was also an engine that would run if required, and the tight timings of the vacuum-fitted freight trains could still be kept with this class of locomotive on the front. They were wonderful free-steaming engines, and they gave a ride as would be expected from a machine weighing around 120 tons with the tender. The method of driving depended on the type of weight of the train. A trainload of petrol tanks would require heavy working to get them on the move, but once they began to roll, the regulator could be gently tapped down and the big reversing lever pulled back into the last notch. The 28XX would really run, with the big heavy side-rod spinning round in a blur as the little wheels flashed round.

To start them with a heavy train called for much skill, as the power was enough to part couplings on the wagons if care was not taken. It was the standard start applicable to all freight movement with loose-coupled wagons, but extra care was needed. All my mates, including my father, began the movement in the same way. The ejector was opened to blow off the brakes, and the reversing lever placed in full forward gear. Then the regulator was opened, just enough to begin the first forward movement and then closed again, only to be opened once more. This went on for some time to tighten up all the couplings, and the engine could be 30 yards or more ahead before the guard's van began to move. When the guard's van eventually did move, the final snatch was felt on the engine. If the load was a heavy one, such as 'Long Tom', which was the name given to the 100-wagon coal train, the 28XX would sit down on her springs with that final snatch. This was the time to make her work, and the method favoured by her designer was then brought into use. The regulator would be lifted right up until it was wide open, and then that tractive effort figure would be blown sky high. She would be given a little sand under her wheels to kill any chance of a slip and by the time the train had travelled half a mile the lever would begin to be pulled back. After the first mile had passed the train would be on the roll.

The Fireman put as much into this as the Driver as every ounce of steam the boiler could produce had to be provided. The fire had to be thick and plentiful, and it had to be kept up. A hole in any part of the fire would reduce the boiler pressure so quickly and to such an extent, that it would take several miles of hard work to replace the damage done. I found that it was worth the effort of pulling the pricker through and making the fire up to my liking before giving my mate the nod that I was ready.

Unless it was a main line stop for relief purposes, no Driver worth his salt would blow up for the signals before his Fireman was satisfied with conditions in the firebox and boiler. This was part of the team effort and close working, and it was a happy state of affairs. A good engine crew were two men very close to each other, each knowing the precise requirements of the other. The steam engine had to be worked, and its success depended on two men each of the same mind. There were occasions, of course, where personality clashes were unavoidable, but they were rare, so perhaps I was lucky during my days as a Great Western fireman. I fired to every Driver at Didcot, and found every one a gentleman, for never at any time did they attempt to move before first asking me if I was ready. Nowadays, the second man, as the fireman is now called, sits in the cab of the diesel and of course has different duties to perform. But I am sure that he cannot reach that special intimacy with his mate that the steam locomotive demanded.

With the 28XX well on the move, the skill of two men working together also came when it was time to stop. Unless an emergency stop was required, which could injure the guard, the stopping was a planned manoeuvre, and was carried out with great care. The regulator would be closed down, the lever eased down into the 45% cut off, and the tender hand brake screwed down a little at a time, bringing all the buffers of the wagons up together. The driver could now begin to use the vacuum brake, retarding the movement until the stop was made. It was a very highly skilled part of locomotive handling to plan a stop with 1000 tons on the move at exactly the right spot to swing the water column round. It had to be right the first time as there was no going back if an over-run was made.

I have made a point of choosing two favourite engines. The 'Grange' and the 28XX class, but to be fair, I should say that they all were my favourite engines except the 'Aberdares' and the R.O.D. 30XX class. I know I am not alone in this view. The part that hurts is when they went it would not have been so bad if they had all gone to Swindon for breaking up. At least they would have returned to the Works that built them, but to leave them rusting in private sidings to fall to the torch of men who may not have had any conception of the heritage they were destroying, is to me a very sad affair.

The passing of the steam locomotive has been mourned by many, and not only by the enthusiast but also by my old mates who remained behind to man the diesels. They agree that it is nice to go to work in a clean uniform and return clean, but they admit that they do miss very much the warmth and 'feel' of steam. There are many names on the list of men who volunteer to drive and fire the steam engine on Open Days, and to once again hold the regulator and swing the shovel on the main line steam runs. It is with regret that I am unable to place my name on that list but I am sure that I could maintain the boiler at the gentle speeds they are now restricted to, but this must be my punishment for leaving the service.

I can look back on my life with no regrets. I was once a Great Western Fireman, and had the good fortune to fire almost every type of locomotive the Great Western operated, and also drive most of them. Either side of the footplate it was a pleasure to work them. There were many rough trips with the blower hard on, tubes blocked and leaking, superheaters blowing, dirty fires and poor coal, but the job was completed by two men nursing and coaxing the poor old ladies along. All I have now is the memories of those wonderful days, so my journeys must be nostalgic journeys through the pages of the written word. I hope, in these pages, the reader can smell the smoke and warm oil, can feel the bucketing and swaying, and can hear the sharp crisp bark of a Great Western locomotive at work. If, in these pages, I have re-captured the unforgettable aroma of steam then it has all been worthwhile.

In twenty years of railway working, the amount of material which I could put into a book would require a volume of great size. 'Firing Days' was the first book of my reminiscences as a Great Western Fireman, and in this second book, I have tried to bring back more memories of footplate working. In these forward-looking days when man can be placed on the moon, it is very pleasant to remember the days when a boy's ambition was to be an Engine Driver. Alas, progress made sure that I could not be a Driver, so I will settle for the very happy days I spent on the shovel.

NOSTALGIC DAYS

Introduction

When I sat down and compiled my first book 'Firing Days' it was to fulfil an ambition of many years standing. The three years of hard work had been worthwhile when the letters began to arrive from readers who had enjoyed it, and with those letters came requests for a further reading.

From these requests the second book 'Footplate Days' was born, and as I packed my typewriter away, I thought that perhaps readers would have had enough of my reminiscences of Great Western footplate work, but the very welcome letters kept arriving, not only from all parts of the United Kingdom but also from as far away as America and New Zealand, and these letters always asked the same question: when will *book three* be ready?

Book three grew in the same way as *Footplate Days* with little pieces of information coming together, and conversations with other ex-footplate men that began "Do you remember?"

"Did I remember?" How could I ever forget?

Writing this book brought it all back, particularly those conversations with my dear old Uncle, Bert Edmonds, one of the long retired "Top Link" drivers from Old Oak Common Shed.

The final problem came with choosing a title. It would be nice to keep the "Days" series, and as I was reading my introduction to *Footplate Days* I found it: 'Nostalgia' — an apt description of what this book is all about.

Again my dear wife Betty took kindly to my disappearing act into my den, and but for her valuable proof reading, unbiased criticism, and the endless cups of coffee, I would have given up, because I found that a typewriter can be much more demanding than a "Castle".

Harold Gasson
1980

Chapter One

What could it have been like those few short years ago when the Great Western steam locomotive was as much a part of the landscape as the elm tree, when, for example, on 25 March 1948 an engine history sheet was filled in at Swindon for a 4-6-0 named *Wightwick Hall* priced at £9,648 (including the tender)? That particular story ended on 17 July 1964 after this locomotive had run only 640,645 miles, and the history sheet finished with the words 'sold to Woodham's Bros. Barry'.

There was a time when the strange world of the footplate could be viewed at any main line station. The thick powerful lines of a 'King' or the sleek beauty of the 'Castles' was sure to draw a crowd of small boys, admiring males, and if the fireman looked a bit of a lad, the ladies too! Even the fussing brash little pannier tank snorting up and down in the goods yard could draw such attention. The only locomotive left out of this admiration was the humble freight locomotive, the 'cart horse' and the men that worked them.

What was this unnoticed world of freight movement where no speed records were made and no performances produced worth writing about in the railway press? It was nothing but punching away up adverse gradients day in, day out, or pitching and swaying down banks with the handbrake screwed down hard. Here locomotive working was far removed from the glamour of the expresses, and yet those men running the expresses would have still been perfectly at home on the big lumbering 'twenty-eights' and 'forty-threes'. They had come this way themselves; for there was still excitement and satisfaction in making a good run with a heavy freight train, and it began at home, in dressing into overalls, pulling on boots, that last warm embrace, then setting off to work.

One August afternoon I plodded down the dusty cinder path towards Didcot locomotive shed with a distinct feeling of injustice. It was hot, very hot, on this afternoon, my jacket was over my shoulder, hooked through the loop with my finger and my 'Grimsby' box swinging from my right hand. Already I could feel the beads of perspiration forming under the leather band of my cap.

There was no joy in my heart as I walked into the cathedral coolness of the shed to meet my driver, Ted Hurle. We had begun the week on the early turn, looking forward to the weekend with anticipation. I should have now been strolling along the river bank between Reading and Tilehurst with my lovely young lady, and Ted would have been quietly cycling over the Berkshire Downs towards a certain village, where, when the pub was open he could pour pints down very thirsty stable lads in exchange for "fortune-making information". But the best laid plans go astray, progressive overtime during the week, and the returning to each duty after twelve hours' rest had brought us both to this late start.

I 'booked on' and found Ted waiting for me in the enginemen's rest room. I was bemoaning our bad luck, thinking of my young lady stuck in the hostel with all those lecherous young off-duty firemen in residence, but Ted with the experience of the older man, had the answer to my gloom. As he explained, doing all that overtime had increased the savings account, consequently the wedding was that much nearer, and he would be that much more better off by not pouring pints down the bottomless throats of stable lads who gave tips about fast 'gee-gees' that were not so fast when he came to place his hard earned money on them.

Perhaps this 4.30p.m. relief turn was not so bad after all. We had no locomotive to prepare, perhaps we would relieve a goods heading for Swindon, then a quiet pint in the Staff Association Club before heading for home and an early finish. I began to brighten up, after all there was always Sunday not even used up yet.

We walked back up the path together, over the crossing, past the yawning well of the subway steps, and along the Up Yard to the Control Office. Bob Beck the controller, was standing in the doorway, his jacket off, his tie loosened, mopping his brow with his handkerchief. The little wooden building that served as Control Office and enginemen's rest room was like an oven.

The Up Yard pilot engine No. 5735 stood simmering nearby, its cab empty, for both driver and fireman were sitting on an old sleeper in the shade of a coal wagon on the next road. Further down the yard the ring of couplings could be heard as the Centre Pilot eased up a long string of wagons for the shunter to join up.

Bob informed me that the 10.30a.m. Banbury to Westbury had left Oxford and he required us to relieve the Banbury men. Not so bad, a gentle 'doddle' on the Up relief to Reading, and with a bit of luck an early finish after all. Ted and I made our way back up the yard, over the shed exit road, over the Down Loop and both Oxford main lines to the Up 'Gully'. We sat on the grass bank waiting for our train to arrive, and before long a column of dirty smoke and steam could be seen behind the trees towards North Junction. We both looked back. Could I hear the harsh roar of a blower above the distant exhaust from that chimney?

The 10.30a.m. Banbury came slowly into view, at its head a tired travel-worn old 'forty-three' workhorse, rocking from side to side, steam leaking from her cylinder pressure valves, a volcano of black smoke erupting from her chimney as she clawed her way painfully round the curve towards us, her long train curving away behind her, the wheels squealing in protest as the flanges bit into the bullhead rail.

No. 4377 came to a rest with her tender opposite the water column. She looked huge, the high level of ballast had placed her footplate twelve feet above us. She was dirty with years of neglect, her spokes caked with grime, her framing was so thick with dirt that her wheels had worn a rim in a half circle of hardened sludge, and she smelt of old age. Ted swung the water column round as the Banbury fireman scrambled over the coal to lift up the tender flap. As I moved forward to climb up on to her footplate, the injector gave a cough and a grunt, spitting out half a gallon of scalding hot water on to the sleepers, splashing one of my boots. I stepped back smartly, right into a two inch deep puddle of slurry, and it in turn shot up inside my trouser leg and ran down into my boot.

A welcome indeed. Ted gave a rich chuckle. It was a situation he could appreciate and he began to open the water feed valve on the column. He was so entertained by my misfortune he forgot that the Up 'Gully' water column was a local 'old sore'. The square on the valve handle was worn to a half circle, and as he wound round that valve it came off the spindle and clouted him on the knee-cap. The old saying "he who laughs last" was true after all! I side-stepped the spitting injector overflow pipe and climbed up, tapping the feed valve on the tender as I passed. The injector picked up cleanly, leaving just a dribble to trickle onto the ballast. The ritual of relieving was over quickly. Ted exchanged and received the necessary information on the state of the train and the engine, whilst the fireman assured me that she was steaming freely, and although she rode a bit rough she was a 'good un'. However it was with almost indecent haste that they climbed down and walked off.

The tank began to overflow, so I climbed down, shut off the water, then went back up the tender steps and threw off the bag, while Ted went round oiling the slide-bars and glands. I shovelled forward some coal, enough to see us to Reading, so that when Ted returned to the cab we were ready to go. Ted yanked on the whistle chain to blow up a 'crow' and the chain snapped in his hand. I should not have laughed, because he used my cap to lift the whistle rod. The points slid over, and the signal dropped with a thump to route us on to the Up relief line.

The ejector was opened blowing off the brakes, then Ted applied the vacuum to allow me to ease the tender hand brake, he then blew off the brakes again and lifted the regulator as I fully unwound the hand brake. We began to move as the couplings tightened up one at a time until the whole of the train was on the move. As she took up the weight Ted gave her full regulator, opening and closing, waiting for the slightest sign of a slip. It was then this poor old lady began to talk to us. As each cylinder took a charge of steam she lurched over and began to groan, as her valves came back she gave a piercing squeal, her big reversing lever began to jump in the ratchet, and the red needle on her faded steam pressure gauge quivered with every blow as her great side rod came slowly up and over.

Ted increased her oil by giving the sight feed lubricator half a turn as we pulled painfully out of the 'Gully' and on to the Up relief. The signalmen at Didcot East Junction quickly ran to slide shut their windows before we filled that long greenhouse with smoke and ash. As the guard's van cleared the points Ted was able to pull back the reverser a few notches and ease down her regulator. No. 4377 began to cease her violent protesting and by the time we were passing Moreton Yard the regulator was tapped down a bit more and she began to settle down to her own pace.

I began firing her now, repairing the holes torn from her firebox, nursing her back to health as we ambled along letting the old lady take her time. At this pace she was almost comfortable to ride on although she knocked in her axle boxes, her cab rattled and shook, her reverser threatened to jump out of the ratchet, and she had begun to lose steam pressure. I had not been mistaken, I had heard a blower back at Didcot. It was time to give her some help, so with half a turn of blower to keep her burning well, I piled some coal into her. After another half turn on the fireman's friend "the blower", she had come round to the blowing off mark within a mile, so the live steam injector was put on to top up her boiler. She should have accepted this without any trouble. After all, I had been told that she was a 'good-un' but a glance up at that faded steam pressure gauge told me that she did not like cold water spraying into her boiler one little bit. Whew! I had lost forty pounds of pressure between Moreton and Aston Tirrold.

It was time to take some drastic action. I lifted the pricker out of the tender rack and Ted stood back on the running plate as I swung it round. It slid into the firebox and I began to stir her up, ramming that pricker right down to the front end, pulling it back through the fire, the barb ripping great furrows of red hot coal, the smaller pieces dancing up and down with the blast. The heat came back into the cab in a searing wave. I withdrew the red hot pricker and returned it to the rack, then lifted the front damper just off its face. Now we would see what she was made of.

I began to fire her, packing the back corners of the firebox, building up on that thick bed of fire. Ted pulled her back another notch on the reverser and the blast softened, she was taking less steam in her valves and pistons. I said a silent prayer to Allah, and, bless her, she began to respond. The steam pressure needle began to climb and the cab settled down now to a quiet grinding. We had found that happy spot applicable to all steam locomotives, the spot where she would run and steam to the best advantage.

As we ran up towards Cholsey I turned on the exhaust injector and hot water began to spray into her boiler. We were winning, she liked this treatment. Ted and I grinned at each other, after all it was only to Reading, or so Bob Beck had said and another poor blighter would have to pound her up to the top of Savernake. We swept under the bridge, sitting on our tip-up seats, swaying with the movement of the cab into an ocean of golden corn fields which stretched for miles either side of us.

Our old "forty-three" was settling down, holding her own now. She had ceased her groaning and squealing as the extra lubrication reached her valves and pistons. I began to fire her with regularity, flap down, a swing of the shovel, then flap up. Each shovelful produced a puff of black smoke from her chimney to roll back over the cab and be swept over the fields, leaving behind the distinctive pungent aroma of the burning of good Welsh Marine coal.

The exhaust injector was singing away keeping the water level dancing up and down just below the top nut in the gauge glass. I was neither gaining nor losing on that water level, everything was just right now. We swept through South Stoke with a cheery wave to the lady coming out of the back door of the Pub below, with a pile of washing in her arms. We then ran through the chalk cutting towards Goring, round the slight curve, clattering through the station picking up speed nicely now for the run over the water troughs. They came into view, four narrow ribbons of water shimmering in the sunshine, curving gently round between the rails towards Purley. I eased down the water scoop, just skimming the water topping up the tank. We then headed towards Pangbourne, round the tree covered chalk cliffs that curved into Pangbourne station, past the red tiled Mock Tudor houses peeping between the trees, then out into the flat meadow land that ran alongside the river.

Cabin cruisers cut through the placid water, raising a bow wave which spread across the river and started the moored boats bobbing in a frenzy of curtsey movements. The skippers with grim determination gripped the steering wheels, their white caps tilted Navy style as they navigated their craft on through the complex of shipping, with their ladies in scanty bikinis laid out on the cabin roofs. They neither glanced up nor altered course. We were an intrusion, a reminder of a working world far, far away, to be forgotten.

I began to clear up ready to stop at Reading, but as Scours Lane signals came into view we saw that we were to continue running on the Up relief, not as we had expected into the Goods Loop. A horrible doubt began to form, and became a reality. We had been "conned", we were the ones going through. The poor blighters pounding up to Savernake would not be Reading men, it would be us!

Between Scours Lane and Reading West Junction the lookout boy gave us a friendly wave. The lookout boy was a familiar sight to enginemen. From his lofty position in the top of a tree he could see up the lane to the Oxford road, and all over the scrubland. He was the sentinel, the early warning system, protecting the fifty or so males squatting around a blanket at an illicit game of Pitch and Toss. It was worth our blast on the whistle and frantic gestures towards the road which were answered with the classic two fingered sign; "cry Wolf" had been played out, but it was worth it just to see one or two round the blanket jump up all ready to run. Did the local "coppers" ever catch that game, I wonder?

Ted shut the regulator and put his left foot up on the bar at the front of the reverser, knocked up the clip with the palm of his hand and eased that big lever forward. We drifted over the running lines and as soon as we felt the rise of the bank he gave her a little steam, increasing as the weight began to pull. We mounted this curving rise towards Reading West. Below us in the triangle, Reading locomotive shed lay under a pall of drifting smoke from the chimneys of the rows of 'Castles', 'Halls', 'twenty-eights', and the sisters of our old girl. Two small boys watched us with interest in the lane below, their spotter's books all ready. They turned away, as we did not have a great curving nameplate on our top frame, we were of no importance to them.

We rambled over the Oxford Road bridge, through the sleepered platform of Reading West station baking in the sun and under the overhang of trees. Trees, deep green and heavy with leaf. Chestnut trees with broad leaves and sycamore shimmering in the slight breeze, welcome shadow indeed. In a few more months they would shed those leaves to fall over the rails, giving the 'Kings' and 'Castles' some moments of anguish before the sand was spread to give the speeding wheels welcomed grip. Soon we were passing Southcote Junction and heading West towards the sun.

As we ran alongside the Bath road busy with traffic, I began to fire her again. This time with serious deliberation as this was not the gentle amble up the relief line to Reading. This road to the West I knew well, enough to know that apart from the odd mile or so of "flat" railway at Aldermaston and Newbury, it was a solid grind for the next 32 miles, culminating in the heavy pull from Bedwyn to the summit at Savernake.

Ted dropped the lever forward one notch and gave her half regulator, then he stood back on the running plate to catch the slight breeze. I began to sweat as I shovelled in the coal, the drips from my forehead staining the floorboards in single drops. I removed my overall jacket and hung up my cap. My shirt was already wet through and sticking to my back and by the time we reached Savernake those floorboards would have a six inch wet band between the firebox and tender.

Through Theale I hung over the side to cool off, and watched the Tiger Moths on their "circuit and bump" training programme. In the hot air they came floating over the hedges, the engines cut back, then with a sharp burst on the throttle they would bounce over the grass landing strip. I returned to the shovel. The exhaust injector had been on from Reading West so it was time to "top up" over Aldermaston troughs. I lowered the scoop further down this time and the blade bit deep into the water, spraying the excess out through the tender wheels. I felt like shouting "come on, come on, fill up, fill up", as the float crept slowly up the gauge. We were running out of trough and needed every drop of water. At last we were full and with a bit of luck we could keep going through Newbury instead of stopping for water.

Round the slight curve we came, through the empty sleeper platforms of Newbury Racecourse station, the scene of the loss of so much of Ted's money. We passed the lattice steelwork of the foot bridges with all distant signals off through Newbury middle road. The safety valve began to lift as we came pounding through the station. We blew a 'crow' on the whistle to our mates on the return Winchester passenger standing in the Bay, then our exhaust hit the road bridge at Newbury West with a "Whoof".

Our side rods were knocking with a thump as that great knuckle end came up and over. The wagons and box vans rattling along behind caused a swirling cloud of straw, old labels and other bits of railway debris and dust to rise and obliterate the quiet calm of a country station.

We were approaching Enborne Junction now, with the twin rails of our beloved Winchester Branch curving away to the left. What price now for the peace and quiet of the rolling Hampshire Downs on this lovely summer evening. Our old 'forty-three' gave a kick and a lurch as she passed over the junction points, as if to remind us we were heading West not South. As we passed under the signal box window the faint tinkle of the block bell came over the noise of our engine.

'Ting-ting', 'Train on line' to Hampstead Crossing. On up the bank gently rising, the bark from the chimney growing deeper as the train started to drag. We passed through the lush green meadows of the Kennet Valley, full of sleek cows munching contentedly away, tails swishing lazily from side to side as they gazed at us so passively. I was firing now without a break, the coal going into that raging furnace was digested almost at once, and slowly the boiler level began to creep up.

A quick sharp rise up through Hungerford followed and as we passed over the tops of the houses, we could look down into the back gardens and on to the rows of runner beans and potatoes, or perhaps the quiet haven of a pub lawn with the pint pots standing on the rustic tables, and envy the lucky lads drinking. One even held up his glass in a salute, rubbing it in. He was probably an off-duty footplate man. We returned that gesture with a rude code on the whistle, and we were right, he understood.

We began to feel the climb in earnest now, but the old lady was holding up well enough. My boiler water level was well up so I could afford to concentrate on maintaining a full head of steam for the ferocious last few miles beyond Grafton. As we passed through Bedwyn I fired her for the last time, and the firebox was full, so once over the top of Savernake she would roll all the way down to Westbury with just a few shovelfuls to keep on the boil.

Once through Bedwyn, Ted had to drop the lever down again and give her full regulator. I shut off the exhaust injector, but even then she began to drop in steam pressure. Perhaps it was because I had put the shovel down and the sweat stains on the floorboards were beginning to dry.

As Grafton came into view she was flat out with the lever right down, regulator full open, and as her speed dropped off she began to rock, first over on one side, then over to the other side. Each cylinder was taking as much steam as it would hold, back and fore, right down to the springs, the exhaust exploding with a roar out of her chimney. It was a wicked way to treat this poor old lady, to thrash her for mile after grinding mile, but it was the only way, for had she slipped we would have stalled, so she had to be thrashed as she had never been before. Looking back over the events years later, I can still feel for that old 'forty-three'.

No. 4377 had been built at Swindon in 1911 with superheaters, vacuum brakes, two 18½ inch cylinders and a Churchward boiler to supply them, and was termed as a mixed traffic engine. Here she was doing the work of a 'twenty-eight' and it must have been an awful sight as we clawed our way past the junctions at Grafton and under the old MSWJ line yard by yard.

As I levelled the fire over with the pricker, it was a white hot incandescent mass dancing in time with the blast. Again as I withdrew the pricker Ted stood clear. It was white from the tip to half way up its length where it dulled to a cherry red whilst tiny specks of coal dust ignited as they touched. In that searing heat they instantly burned out to cascade in a shower of stars which were extinguished before they reached the worn, stained floorboards.

The cab was shaking to bits and there was a half inch gap between it and the boiler, the safety valve bonnet was rattling, the frame was jumping, and above it all that great reversing lever was jumping so badly that Ted rammed the coal pick in the quadrant. I closed the firebox doors and at once they began to slam up against the firebox, the air shrieking as it passed through. The exhaust was one gigantic column of power climbing forty feet into the blue summer sky to be caught by the breeze and sent rolling and tumbling down into the valley behind us. The cinders rolled and swirled along the van roofs, rattling on the curved roofs down into the gutterings then falling down to join the burnt out cinders of other years and other struggles between man and machine.

All at once it was over, we were through Savernake station and as her nose dipped down, so did the water in the boiler. I put on the live steam injector and the water began to bob back in sight. We had won, the despair of the last few miles was behind us. We had made it because we were a close team working together, and without that we would have failed. It was recovery time now and I hung over the side of the cab to feel the cool breeze on my brow wash over me to channel down the front of my shirt which by now was moulded to my back like a second skin, I was whacked. I watched Burbage siding slide by, as Ted closed the regulator then lifted it a shade giving her just enough steam to lubricate her valves and pistons. I heard the firebox doors being opened and Ted gestured me to sit down as he placed the tea can on the shovel, for there is nothing like a scalding hot cup of tea after a good sweat. I looked ahead to see Pewsey come up towards us, and as the sinking sun caught us, that old locomotive became a thing of beauty, she was poetry in motion as the pistons slid back and forth, the rod glistening between the slide bars, I slurped that cup of tea and had started on the second before Ted could wet his lips with the first. There was a hint of the word 'guts' from somewhere over his side and the reply of 'nuts' from my corner as we sailed over the little hump just short of Woodborough. We then drifted down to Patney, the wagons coasting along behind.

As we swept round the slight curve I looked back beyond the vans and wagons, rattling and swaying as they danced along to see the first flickering light in the bullseye as our guard lit his side lights. With the sun sinking, the shadows of the engine and train ran with us in a soft outline, sliding over the meadows and corn fields, slipping over hedges and ditches in complete harmony, almost a mirror reflection of the original, the feather of steam from the safety valve, a wisp of steam escaped from the whistle; the injector waste pipe dribbled water; my movement between engine and tender as I reached for the tea can; all these were reproduced in silhouette. It was a peaceful time, the shadows began to lengthen and our old engine began to change shape. She became fatter, her chimney taller, and in my imagination she began to take on the shape of a Broad Gauge Gooch locomotive of one hundred years earlier.

All enginemen had favourite spots to enjoy on any route, particularly during the summer months and we were now coming up to one of them, the long swoop down the bank to Lavington. Mile after mile of twisting and curving rail with nothing to do but sit on the tip-up seat and enjoy the run. The old 'forty-three' was also enjoying it. She ran free without knocking, groaning or protesting, with just the swish of her wheels going round, and the heavy "click-click" as she passed over the rail joints accompanied by the slapping of her vacuum pump.

There were other places to be enjoyed for me anyway. There was the swoop down from Tackley bank heading towards Banbury where the line twisted and curved as we hammered through Heyford station with the severe camber tilting us over and the cylinder skimming the platform edge. Another favourite was the Up road at Wolvercote running alongside the canal. One could see the polished brass on the gaily painted narrow-boats chugging their way softly through the still water. If you were lucky you might see the lightning flash of the kingfisher, crimson and blue as he plunged in and out of the water near the lock, a minnow wriggling in his long beak, so swift there was hardly a ripple in the water.

Then there was the dull deep rumbling when passing over Nuneham bridge, looking down on the willows which shaded the river, bending gracefully to touch the water. One might see a moorhen with her chicks, paddling away from the bank, her bow wave spreading out over the placid flow of the river, her chicks bobbing up and down in her wake. Sometimes we would see the dragonflies skipping, swooping and skidding over the surface, to vanish, as a flash of silver snatches them from sight, leaving only a widening pool of ripples.

It is only now with nostalgia for the days of the steam loco motive and the deep-seated urge to write about those happy days that I can begin to appreciate what the Great Western was all about. I was part of a family. I had, in common with so many steam firemen before me, followed father's footsteps on to the footplate. I was a G.W. man and, looking back over the years, I can still feel the pride I had and still hold in that knowledge. I had been in no way instrumental in placing the 'Great' into the Western, but had in my small way helped to keep it there. The men who had made the Western 'Great' were gone, but I can remember the Didcot members. They were the men who had fired on the Broad Gauge, the young firemen of the 1880 period. Men like Joe Beckenham and George Bowering, Arthur Hitchcock and Jack Wiley, Jackie Wilkins and Harry Cudmore, men who had fired to the Broad Gauge drivers, and those drivers had in turn fired to the first Great Western drivers. They were the lads who could remember the Gooch locomotives.

They had taken them out of the old wooden shed at Didcot, to be followed by the 'Armstrongs'. The old gentlemen I remembered had followed with the 'Deans' and 'Churchwards'. They had fired to drivers who wore a bowler hat and sported heavy black beards. Their uniform was a black serge jacket, thick corduroy trousers, and the inevitable dangling watch chain, threaded through the waistcoat buttons to anchor down in the pocket. A watch, and what a watch it was. I still have one; the casing made out of gunmetal of such proportions as to defy all the elements including the pull out regulator and reversing lever of the 'Iron Dukes'.

It was the day of gleaming brass, burnished copper, tallowed paintwork and open cabs. Joe and his mates not only cleaned those gigantic eight foot driving wheels but also the spokes, and, behind the spokes. The inside cylinder covers were scoured with brick dust until they shone equal to a chrome finish. Smokebox rings, brackets, dart handles, handrails and buffers all received the same treatment. Then they climbed up on to the smokebox foot step, on to the grab rail, until they could stand on top of the boiler barrel and clasp that tall chimney with the embrace of an ardent lover as they polished the copper band. Even the whistles protruding from the weather board sparkled in the sunshine.

No wonder those big handsome broad gauge locomotives stand square and proud in the old photographs, and the enginemen too stand square and proud. These big strong silent men fitted the locomotives like a glove. There was only one thing in these photographs missing and that was not even a smile, not even a trace of a twinkle in the eyes, not a hint of humour. But the reason was there. They were not only in the process of making the Western Great, but they were doing it with no uniform issue, for a working shift of 12 hours, for three shillings and sixpence. Yet they were at that time the elite in the ranks of the working man. Harry Cudmore told me that William Dean had a sense of humour alright. As these lads were so busy building up the Great Western he thought that they might like a change in the working conditions, so he cut the "tanner" off the three bob and gave them another two hours to work, and that is why, I think, photographs show them without a smile. The sheds somehow got together, not an easy task with the long hours and shift duties, and decided to send a deputation to see Mr. Dean at Swindon. It is recorded, 'A meek and humble memorial was presented to the GWR Directors late in 1879 asking them to receive a deputation from the men' and from this they obtained a meeting. The minutes read as follows, 'It is still more sad to reflect that the deputation came, some of them nervously, as if they were going to trial by Assize, and they left empty'. All that they had asked for was a 10 hour day and that it be recognised that 150 miles for the passenger men and 120 miles for the goods men, constitute a day's work.

They carried on, there was not much else they could do. Driver Thomas Shuter was fined 7/6d for running an axle box hot. Such was their pride in the job that driver Jack Almond ran the Bristol express from Paddington to Didcot, 53 miles from start to stop in 47 minutes. But there were complaints, one driver spoke of being on Pilot duties for 40 hours, another for periods of 20 and 24 hours and as such his faculties were impaired and his energy abated. A locomotive inspector was appointed to look into these complaints and his findings were made known. He had found cases of drivers being on duty for 36 hours but reported that 'when in a siding they had the opportunity of going to sleep on their engines'. There is no record of what would have been the outcome if he had caught them asleep on their engines, but sleep they must have had and their energy replaced, because as Joe used to say to my old dad, they somehow found the time and energy to make sure that there were plenty of young recruits to replace them when retirement came round.

They were craftsmen, proud of their calling. If William Dean was not amused of their idea of a day's work, they were proud of the locomotives he gave them to work on, proud enough to carry on the tradition of enginemanship which enabled the design and development of the Swindon built locomotive to reach perfection. Joe and his mates were in a unique situation although they did not know it at the time, because their working life on the footplate spread from the last of the Gooch engines right through to the 'Castles' and 'Kings'. It was as if Orville Wright flew at Kitty Hawk and carried on to pilot a Jumbo Jet.

This transition from broad gauge to standard gauge and on to the big locomotive was mercifully a gentle one. The classes of locomotive to pass through their hands made it the golden years of Swindon power and there can never again be a period of time quite like it. In handling this vast build up and changeover of locomotive power, they put the 'Great' into the Great Western for all time and this wealth of locomotive working was handed over to my father's generation.

As this generation served their long hard apprenticeship of firing, the knowledge soaked in a little bit at a time. This knowledge coupled with the arrival of the 'Saints', 'Stars', 'Castles' and 'Kings' began to pay dividends and Great Western locomotive power was on the march. That vast reservoir of knowledge was then passed on to my generation, and we seized on it with eagerness and used it, but as it was to turn out for such a short time. The arrival of the diesels, at least for me, brought the end of the line.

It must have been a wonderful time in those early days of 1880 apart of course from the pay and working conditions. Joe saw many miles of track laid as the system expanded, whilst I, at the other end of the scale, saw so many miles lifted. Those men were in on the building of the Didcot to Newbury branch, opened on 12 April 1882 and the extension through to Winchester on 1 May 1885. They began working the branch with the little Armstrong 0-6-0 tanks, the open cabbed 2-4-0 Metropolitan tanks and the 3230 class 2-4-0 tender engines.

I awoke with a start! After that day dreaming of the past, we had slipped through Lavington and Ted began to give her a little steam as the signal lamps of Edington and Bratton loomed up. I gave her a little coal, enough to see us into the yard and on the shed. We clattered over the points of Heywood Road Junction, the curving Westbury cut-off racing away into the darkness and then crept through the station and into the yard. The shunter slid his shunting pole between the tender and first wagon, there was a loud metallic ringing sound as the coupling swung down and we were parted from our train. Five minutes later we were leaving our dear old 'forty-three' on the ash road.

I looked back at her as we walked away and felt compassion for her. She was old, dirty and rough, she had known better days, to some she was just a lump of scrap, but we had hammered the living daylights out of her and she had not let us down. A little bit of me remained on her, perhaps I would never see her again but I would always remember her. Now, years later as I write and think about her, I can see her, a tired old lady desperately in need of the rest she so richly deserved.

We had a bite to eat in the enginemen's cabin then reported to the foreman. His eyes lit up as did all foremen's eyes when an unexpected crew turned up. It was the sort of look members of the inquisition must have given their victims; a "what can I sort out for this lot" look. But I am being unkind, he did sort us out a job, to relieve some Weymouth men and take a light engine back to Swindon via Trowbridge.

We took off running light with a Hall, No. 4960 *Pyle Hall* scheduled for Swindon Works and a complete rebuild. We left her on Swindon shed just after midnight and as we had now been seven and a half hours messing about with engines, it was time to have a good meal and go home. There was nothing due on the 'Up' until the 1.40 a.m. Swindon parcels, so we set off for the canteen where I sat on my own, tucking into a plate of bacon, eggs and fried bread swimming in half an inch of thick grease, topped off with a rich dark brown cup of three hour old tea. Poor old Ted couldn't face it. He sat at the other end of the canteen crunching a curled up scrap of dry toast and burping each time he looked my way. I mopped up the grease with a slice of bread. Ted turned away, perhaps the digestive systems of older people deteriorate over the years, or, so I suggested to him. His reply was most uncomplimentary.

We caught the Parcels as far as Foxhall Junction where the Swindon driver slowed down to allow us to scramble off, then we walked over to the shed and booked off at 2.30 a.m.

Walking up Haydon Road towards home I began to reflect on our pay and conditions compared with the old fellows of 1880. Working from the new Didcot shed over the Newbury branch I used to think sometimes that I was hard done by, belting a 'twenty-eight' with a full load or that old 'forty-three' we had left back at Westbury. After all it had been a fair day's work or perhaps by contemporary standards I was justified in thinking so. The standard of 1880 and their 3/6d a day for 120 miles was a lot of mileage for a small engine. To Westbury via Reading or from Didcot to Southampton and back, with a full load each way and a firebox three times the size of the old locomotives was a fair comparison. As for wages and hours, well, we just had completed an average week as follows.

Monday   We ran from Didcot to Swindon with No. 2803, returning through Reading with No. 2876, then back to Didcot with No. 3121 a little 0-6-0 LMS engine, having covered 86 miles on a duty of 12½ hours.

Tuesday   To Southampton and returned with No. 6864 *Dymock Grange*, covering the 116 miles in 14 hours.

Wednesday Our duty was to Old Oak Common with No. 2926 *Saint Nicholas* returning with No. 4703, covering the 103 miles in 11½ hours.

Thursday   North to Banbury with No. 3837, back to Swindon with No. 4909 *Blakesley Hall* then back up to Didcot on No. 8404, one of the class 8Fs built at Swindon for the LMS. A distance of 124 miles and a 12 hour duty.

Friday   This of course was with that old 'forty-three' to Westbury and by the time we arrived home another 116 miles and 10 hours had passed. Therefore eleven locomotives had passed through our hands, covering about 545 miles over a period of duty of 60 hours during that week.

My pay for that week came to £4.1s.2d or roughly a bob an hour. Looking at that old pay slip I see that I did have some stoppages, nine shillings and 6d. in all made up of: 4/11d National Health Insurance, 2/6d Life Assurance, ld Staff Association, ld Railway Convalescent Homes, and 1/11d Mutual Aid Society. Income Tax? I must have paid some although there is no record on the slip, but I can't see any government allowing a young single man to have all that money to throw about.

The next week I worked on the Stationary boiler. A duty of 48 hours with no overtime and no night rate. My pay after the stoppages came to £2.9s.8d. It was the week my cigarettes gave way to the 'roll-up', and yet now I would gladly pay them to be able to swing a shovel again.

Chapter Two

Is it a good thing to look back? I think perhaps it is; a little nostalgia gives pleasure to those of us who can remember, and provides information to younger folk. Looking back is a habit of each generation and I am no exception. When I was a boy the senior drivers would talk for hours to a willing listener; Joe Beckenham would talk of working on the Dean 7ft. 8in. 4-2-2s with affection, of running from Paddington to Didcot in 49 minutes with No. 3065 *Duke of Connaught* and from Paddington to Oxford with No. 3252 *Duke of Cornwall* in 62 minutes. I've done it the other way with a 'Castle' and we have gone like hell in the night to reach Paddington in the hour from Oxford.

It was that part of the main line that Joe loved. He would talk of shutting off through Acton and just letting her run, with no outside connecting rod to flash round, no loose coupling pins and slack bearings to clank and knock, no bucketing and swaying on the footplate, just that great single driving wheel spinning round with the effortless grace of a gyroscope. My uncle Bert Edmonds started firing on the 'Dukes' at Oxford, where they had such a job in climbing up the bank from the shed to the station. The shed pilot would be on stand-by to give them a shove. At 6.05 p.m. every evening the shed and station staff would be out, waiting for the 'up' Worcester and 'down' Paddington to pass, the big 'Singles' gliding along and passing halfway through the station like a zephyr of wind.

Joe would speak with revulsion when referring to the convertibles and one in particular, a 4-4-0 tender engine No. 3527. She was for some time his regular engine beginning life as a broad gauge tank, rebuilt from an 0-4-2 into an 04-4 standard tank, then with typical Swindon skill of rebuilding she ended up as No. 3527. To look at she was not unlike a 'Bulldog', working out her life on the Didcot to Winchester branch, but although she steamed freely enough she rode badly so Joe hated her. She was a convertible and that was enough. He would compare her with the 'Singles', knocking the former and enthusing over the latter, but I can see now a lot of his chat was "tongue in cheek" for he knew only too well that a lot of the 'Singles' left Swindon as 2-2-2 broad gauge engines.

I was far too young at the time to take in all that Joe could tell me. The very fact that I was on the footplate with him was enough to keep me completely absorbed in all around me, but when I look at photographs of the 'Singles', I can appreciate the love Joe had for them. That great polished dome, the brass band on the splasher arching over the big wheel in a strip of gold, and in the centre of that imposing wheel the axle box burnished up to glitter in the sunshine, they were indeed a handsome sight.

I can just remember what a polished dome looked like, it must have been when I was very young. I know I had been taken down to the old wooden shed at Didcot where my old dad had met Joe, his regular driver and they had taken me onto the footplate of their engine No. 3454 *Skylark*. On the next road stood No. 3272 *Amyas* with a brightly polished dome. Joe held me up and I remember our reflections were as distorted as if looking into a trick fairground mirror. There are incidents which stand out in a small boy's memory with such sharpness that it lasts over a lifetime. I can remember this one with such clarity that it could have been a few days ago. The image of a fat, comically distorted boy held in the arms of an equally grotesque little man, and in the background, *Skylark*'s cab and tender curving away on either side, reflected in that sparkling brass dome.

Another incident was to see these fine old gentlemen on their way down Station Hill towards the shed. They did not go to work as other men, they 'proceeded' to go "On Duty" — they were Great Western enginemen, they were the master craftsmen of a steam age on their way to practise their skill on the footplate of the Great Western's beautiful green engines. It was of no consequence if it was in the early hours, or the engine waiting their attention was an old 'Armstrong'. The pattern was the same, they were on a par with the village policeman, respectable, sober God-fearing men. They strode down the hill, boots polished, overalls starched, jacket brushed, cap peak shining and set square, the crossed watch chain threaded through a waistcoat button hole, the small medallion and watch key hanging from a small piece of chain, swinging gently with the ponderous gait of their walk.

Even noticing a small boy was something, but a greeting was acknowledged by a grave nod of the head, and yet I was to find them to be the most kindly of men. One, driver Jack Wiley, petrified me. He was such a large man, and I was such a small boy. When I did overcome my fear of him it was to relieve him of sixpence, and to find there was nothing about him that suggested that he ate small boys for dinner. I had gone down to the old wooden shed with father, for it was Thursday, and pay day, and when he was home on that day it was an accepted part of life to go with him, as indeed did the sons of other enginemen. It was, in a way, the first step the Great Western made to ensure the continuity of future enginemen for I cannot remember any restrictions placed in the way of the sons of the footplate men.

We arrived at the shed just as Jack stopped with a little saddle tank engine, who had dropped on shed to collect his pay. I looked up at this giant of a man and squeezed closer to father.

The method of payment was peculiar to Great Western sheds, and lasted into my working days. We would first go to the timekeeper's counter, not unlike a station booking office, where father would collect his pay check. This was an oval brass disc, that had 'Great Western Loco' stamped round the face, with the number of the disc in the middle, in father's case number 50. I can remember that although these brass checks were only used once a week they were all polished up. I was to find in later years that a cleaner's duties did not stop at boilers, wheels and big dollops of cotton waste. Father handed his check over to the pay clerk, and in return he received a small round tin box, also with the number 50 stamped on it. Inside this box was his pay, the notes folded over, leaving a little room in the middle for the odd silver and copper coins. It was a long way off from the pay packet. Those tins had been in use for years - the days when a pound note kept its value. Father would extract the notes and silver, with the odd coppers becoming my pocket money.

With their usual efficiency the Great Western provided a large wooden box for the collection of the empty tin boxes. This was about the size of a tea chest, made from heavy timber. Its back was hinged to allow the removal of the tins, but the top was not open or flat, it was angled down in a sharp 'V' with a slot in the middle, just wide enough to allow the empty tins to pass through. Enginemen would drop their tins down so that they would roll down and into the box. Small boys now had to earn the coppers they had just received, it was a ritual practised by every father. I was given the empty tin, placed back a few yards, and expected to toss that tin into the box. It was not so easy, with the angled top causing the tins to bounce out again. On this particular Thursday I could not get father's tin into the box, and tears of despair clouded my eyes as I wanted to go and hide. Then along came Jack Wiley. He bent down, gave me his empty tin, and held up a sixpence, without a word being spoken.

Despair turned to desperation as I threw that tin high into the air and it dropped cleanly through the slot and into the box with a clatter. Jack was delighted, and he handed over the sixpence.

Holding my hand he walked with me over to his engine, informing father that he could collect me at the station. We stopped at the bottom step, Jack preceding me up on to the footplate. He paused on each step until he reached the top, then he eased his prominent front portion over the handrails and followed it in. By this time I had climbed up two steps, while Jack had turned round and a rich 'Brummie' accent so unfamiliar to my ears came out of the sky to say, "You'all coom up 'ere with me, my dook". Then two enormous great hands came down under my arms to pluck me off the steps, up and over the handrails, and deposit me on the fireman's seat. I can remember my legs dangling from that seat, my finger nails digging tightly into the wood underneath me, and seeing a large hole containing a fiery furnace. Then there was a movement of levers and we began to move. The furnace began to suck in air, almost pulling me from my perch into that hole. Jack must have seen my concern, because he lifted a chain and a flap came up shutting off that fire. On arriving at the station, his hands came under my arms, and again I sailed up and over, to be placed on to the platform and the safety of father's warm hand.

That sixpence had been earned but it was some years before I was to earn another from the Loco staff. Again I had gone to the shed on a Thursday, but by this time the new shed. I suppose as an eight year old I was beginning to feel my feet, strong enough to take up the challenge from Fred Holt that I could not turn his engine, or earn sixpence for doing so — well, we would see.

The locomotive was No. 3807 *County Kilkenny* standing on Number 2 road. I climbed up onto her high footplate and rode down to the turntable with Fred, where he balanced her to perfection. She was so 'spot-on' that as we walked back towards the end of the turntable our weight caused it to tilt. Fred gave me a start as I began to push, then stood back, and I felt the weight of the locomotive. Then I was away, pushing with a great deal of effort. It was a surprise, a good strong gust of wind would have turned her. I looked back at Fred with a grin on my face, that sixpence was as good as in my pocket. Fred stood there with one hand on his hip, the other holding his cap while he scratched his head. He was what is known as nonplussed, but there was an explanation. Neither of us knew the cause at the time, and as Fred now began to follow me round he could not see what was going on at the other end. What had happened, of course, was that someone was on at the other end, pushing, and with the bulk of *County Kilkenny* on the turntable, plus the bridging girders, they were always out of sight.

There had been some artful collusion between my old dad and Arthur Hitchcock, as much to help me as to confuse Fred. Whilst Fred and I had been busy backing the locomotive off Number 2 road, they had gone through the shed and out at the bottom end, to wait behind the Lifting Shop. As Fred and I climbed off the footplate they had run down our blind side to the other end of the turntable, ready to push.

It was years before Fred found out. I was firing to him one day, and he brought up the subject of how I turned that engine on my own. I told him how it had been done and he gave me a grin and said I had not seen the last of *County Kilkenny*. It was the only 'County' that I can remember as they had all been scrapped long before I joined the Great Western, and they had gone with the grateful thanks of the enginemen. As rough riders they had earned a reputation, although my old chap had said that they would steam and pull well enough. Yet as this class of locomotive was being broken up at Swindon, the Southern were building an identical engine in the 'School's' class which was to prove to be one of the finest 44-0s in the world. It was a beautiful locomotive and a credit to Mr. Maunsell and his design team. With all the interchange trials to come, I now regret that there was no interchange of enginemen, as I would have loved to have had a go on a 'School's'.

Fred was as good as his word, I had not seen the last of *County Kilkenny*. He took me home with him when we had finished our duty, and there in his front room over the mantelshelf arched that great nameplate from *County Kilkenny*. It held pride of place, the focal point of the whole room. The sun shone through the window and bathed it in a soft golden glow, the richness of the deep green paintwork and the thin red outlining accentuating the heavy brass letters. Dead she might be, but part of her lived on to find a good home. That nameplate was Fred's pride and joy and he lavished as much care on it as he did his garden, and his garden was a showpiece.

Fred is gone too now, and the nameplate with him. But 32 years later, from a source far removed from railways, I was given a Great Western engineman's pocket book, and imagine my delight on opening it to find on the inside cover the words 'Fred Holt — Didcot Loco'. So over the years he had reached out and touched me, and it was fitting that the book had found a good home, if only I could trace that nameplate to go with it!

In my boyhood days, Didcot had just about every kind of Great Western engine to be seen. The 'Dean Goods', 'Atbaras', 'Flowers', 'Badmintons', 'Dukes', 'Counties' and 'Bulldogs', some of which survived for me to work on and now I look back with affection. I can recall No. 3269 *Dartmoor,* No. 3267 *Cornishman*, No. 3290 *Severn*, No. 3291 *Thames*, and a whole swarm of 'Dean Goods' soon to be replaced by the wonderful little Collett 22XX class. Indeed No. 2259 and No. 2254 had already arrived, and what joy they gave to a fireman after years of working the old locomotives. An engine fresh from Swindon shops after a complete overhaul was a treat indeed, but to have a brand new design was something special. My old dad said that it was a pleasure to go to work knowing that one of the new 'twenty-two's' was booked for the duty. It could be argued that I was to some extent, biased towards Great Western locomotives, but in those happy days of fine steam locos, as a Great Western fireman I placed myself in the same class as the owner of a Rolls.

There was an alternative of sorts, of course, and I was fortunate to be firing at a time when the Great Western had a few foreign' engines on the stock book. There were the Stanier 8Fs, with big gold LMS letters painted on the tender, the eighty-fours, we called them. As all the 84XX class had the small plate on the front frame stamped 'Built Swindon', we treated them as Great Western engines but fitted with left hand drive. There were USA Transportation Corps 2-8-0s of Major J.W. Marsh — hulking great locomotives with the footplate comfort of a Pullman coach. The Southern engines from Mr. Urie's stable, and the beautiful Southern 'Remembrance' class.

All were very fine engines, but, as good as they were, it was a warm comfortable feeling to climb back on to the familiar Great Western footplate.

Mr. Churchward could be likened to a race-horse breeder, for when he introduced the first of what later became the 'Saint' class, No. 100 *William Dean* in 1902, he began the first of a long line of thoroughbreds. With the expertise of Swindon in re-designing and re-building, the resulting crossbreeds produced another line of thoroughbreds, each class of locomotive becoming a success in its own right. The 'Hall' class which in turn produced the 'Grange' and the 'Manor' classes was a perfect example. Mr. Churchward was, in my opinion, the one man since George Stephenson to achieve such a far reaching impact on the design of the 'big' main line locomotive. It was indeed fortunate that he was succeeded by Mr. C.B. Collett, who carried on the Churchward tradition to such good effect.

It has been reported that when a Footplate Inspector was asked to name his favourite locomotive, he said that given a stud of Churchward 47XX and Collett 'Granges', he could cover all the requirements of the Traffic Department. This statement brought some dismay to the gathering, who expected him to enthuse on the merits of the 'Castles' and the 'Kings', but he was right. The big 47XX class and the 'Grange' could have dealt with almost all that came their way. But with respect, from a fireman's point of view, I would add just one more engine to his choice, the Collett 22XX class. These could cover the branch line workings that would have ruled out the 47XXs, and at the same time, were available to shunt out goods yards that would have caused the 'Grange' a little embarrassment, still being able to cope with light main line duties. This fine little locomotive was introduced in 1930 as a 'light mixed traffic' engine intended to replace the veteran 'Dean Goods'. But this was not to be the case. The 'Dean Goods' although almost fifty years young were indestructible and some lasted well into British Railways days. What the 22XX class did was to complement the 'Dean Goods', then consolidate and establish itself as a distinctive class in its own right.

The 22XX was a compact little locomotive. In this day and age it would be called a 'Mini' but the 22XX was not a mass produced means of transport, it was a baby 'Castle' with the front bogie missing. The A.T.C. ramp was naked to the eye, as if to give the impression that it was there to stop the high smokebox, perched up on the saddle, from tipping forward. This was an optical illusion, for fitted with the 'Castle' cab, and the small 3000 gallon tender, it was an attractive little engine, and loved by the drivers and firemen. A few were paired with the 4000 gallon ex-R.OD. tender, and this marriage turned a little beauty into an ugly duckling. One of our engines at Didcot No. 2282 was fitted with a tender of this type, and although she steamed as freely as her sisters, she ran like a coal tub. In fact, when she was running tender first, one could, with good reason, think it was a weed killer train approaching.

For a small engine the cab was a delight, large and spacious, except that instead of the combination of four quadrant dampers, they had the simple up and down front and rear dampers secured by slotting them onto a cross peg, and the vacuum ejector was fitted with the standard steam-brake attachment. There was no exhaust injector, in its place there was a small cone live steam injector on the left hand side, which was ample to cope with the demands on the boiler.

As with all small Great Western engines, 45 minutes was allowed for preparation, although in common with most firemen I liked an hour, so I would arrive on duty early to give me this extra time. Providing there was enough fire left in the box to spread over the firebars, the fire could be built up gently, using the back damper wide open and the blower on just enough to draw air into the firebox. The boiler would generate steam so quickly one could stand and watch the pressure gauge and see the needle move up the scale, but this was no time to hang about, the sandboxes and the smokebox had to be checked, making sure the former was full and working, and the latter was empty and tight. It was best to check that the front damper was closed before leaving the footplate, as when the driver was up behind the big ends oiling the motion he would have his back pressed up tight against the front of the firebox. I would think that those sand boxes were as simple as one could get in locomotive design. Providing the sand was dry the gravity feed would place the sand just where it was wanted, even in a gale. Not that the 22XX was in the habit of picking up its feet, but when it did it was like a small volcano erupting up the chimney.

We used our allocation of 22XXs mostly on the Didcot-Newbury-Winchester and Southampton Branch on duties that were tailor made for them, covering both passenger and goods working. To see the 4.30 a.m. Didcot to Winchester goods pulling away from the yard with two Collett 22XX's at the head, was a sight and sound to send the recording enthusiasts of today into rapture. The 'bark' of 'twenty-two's' in full song was a sound never to be forgotten.

We would chuff gently out of the yard with just a hint of the crisp bark associated with this class of engine. On the footplate one could feel her straining to get away as we crossed over the 'Up' and 'Down' relief lines, through the crossover, and then over the 'Up' and 'Down' Main lines, with the wagons snaking and wagging behind us. Then we were onto the Branch, with the six mile climb of 1 in 106 to Churn in front of us, and the fun would begin.

The 28XX class, the 'Halls' and 'Granges', the Stanier 8Fs and the big 'Yanks' would pound up this bank with the action of a beam engine, the big side rods going round with a slow lazy movement, but the little Colletts would attack with the aggressiveness of a terrier dog. They would be placed in full fore gear and full regulator for about half a mile, both chimneys setting up such a racket as to wake up the whole town. Indeed, when duties placed me in bed at this hour, it was possible to trace the progress of the morning Winchester goods, right through to the top of the Berkshire Downs. On reaching the first bridge, both regulators would be eased down, the reverser wound back to the 35% cut off, and both regulators opened to the second valve until the top of the bank was reached.

At this point, the slow feed left hand injector was put on and firing began, and was continued until we reached the top. The back corners of the firebox were packed tight. The shovel dug into the mass of fire to fill any air holes, then under the firebox doors, then built it all up into the Great Western standard 'Haycock'. The blast on the fire would ensure that as fast as the back end was filled it would work its way down. If the flap was used it would be snatched out of the hand as soon as it was halfway up to be slammed up against the ring. The exhaust steam and smoke would curl round the cab roof to pause, between each blast, then to go pouring over the top of the flap into the firebox. When the fire box doors were used they would slam up against the ring, the air sucked through the small hole in a high pitched whistle keeping time with the bark from the chimney. We knew the principles of the ram jet long before Frank Whittle applied it to aircraft.

Once through Upton and into the forty feet deep chalk cuttings, the blast would hit the walls and echo back, adding to the shattered silence of this quiet peaceful place. The night was over, and with the passing of the morning goods the day's work had begun. On a summer morning the rabbits would run ahead, leaping, twisting and scrambling frantically up the sheer cliffs in a blind panic to escape from the bombardment. In the winter, we would plough through heavy snow drifts, the sand lever working over-time to prevent the slip that would end our progress. The barking chimneys would cause the inch thick telephone wires to dance in tune, shedding their icy casing in long fragments, to be chewed up, pulverised and cast out from under the wheels to fill the cutting with a fog of atomised ice. And yet, the little 'Collett' could cope with it all, for on the passenger workings they became a different locomotive, they would fly along dancing and bouncing, as frisky as a young colt freed from the restriction of a harness.

Conversely the 'Dean Goods' on a three or four coach train would roll up the banks, the little push-over regulator set half way across the guide, the reversing lever set almost in mid-gear, the blast on the fire so soft one could place the shovel right in the fire-box to spread the coal round. The Collett 22XX however, would scamper up, the chimney barking away with the rapidity of a machine gun, a wisp of steam from the safety valve whipping back over the coaches. Now and again there would be a sharp twitch under the cab where the rear drivers found a bad patch in the road, to remind us that we had a baby 'Castle' weighing 80 tons as against the 126 tons of her big sister. The 22XX needed three or four coaches tied on behind them — the 105 to 140 tons was just enough to hold them down and give them something to bite on because without those coaches they would have flown.

We never ran a Collett 'Twenty-two' at speed when light engine running was required. It was far easier to set the regulator just off the jockey valve, and wind the reverser back to 18% cut off, then they would scamper along, giving a little kick on the rear drivers at each facing and trailing points, just to remind us that it was safe to sit down, until the next set of points. In fact, it was only when running light, one was able to use the tip-up seat.

The little Collett was described as a light mixed traffic engine but mixed traffic is far too embracing. They were excellent branch goods engines, superb branch passenger engines and very handy when it came to shunting. I was lucky to come to know these little locomotives as a boy, along with many other types such as No. 3448 *Kingfisher* and the two little M.S.W. J. 2-4-0 engines Nos. 1334 and 1335 which were still in service at Didcot when I became an official fireman.

Even when the 'new' shed at Didcot was opened in 1932, there was quite a big staff for a small shed, but nothing compared to Old Oak Common of course. With a locomotive stock of 40, Didcot shed needed 53 drivers and 53 firemen. The shed staff was similar in numbers, and included office staff and foremen, boilersmiths, fitters, mates, shed labourers, firedroppers, in fact all the highly skilled people required to run a locomotive shed. When one also took account what we then called the Traffic side, Didcot was truly a railway community.

The alternative to railway work of course, was farming, where it was the delightful delicate aroma of the cowshed, combined with plodding through deep muck to collect cows for milking, or following a team of horses ploughing out the earth for next year's corn. It was no surprise, therefore, to find that most of the local lads came from miles around to exchange the cow shed for a good lungful of burning steam coal. The Frewin brothers came from Wallingford for each duty, and Bill Prior would walk from Chilton village, every bit of six miles, work his duty, and walk home. Such was the calling of the steam locomotive. They were a collection of men that the railway system will never see again. It was much more than just another job, it was a way of life. The 'forty-year man' was commonplace, and the Western was in the golden years of becoming 'Great'.

The pride of the locomotive department was fostered with loving care by the Company itself. As I have written, one began as a very small boy going to the shed on a pay day, and the odd rides at the shed down to the turntable and back. The next step was to arrange that these lads had a chance to handle a shovel. The time to catch them was at about 13 years of age, and although there were never any explicit instructions to locomotive foremen to allow lads onto the engines, there must have been a gentleman's agreement for foremen to look the other way when this occurred.

On most Saturday afternoons I would be with father on the footplate, shunting in the yards with a little pannier tank engine. One Saturday I came into contact with No. 3272 *Amyas* again. Father was covering the Passenger Pilot duties, tailing trains to add or remove box vans, horse boxes, extra coaches, and shunting coaches from the sidings into the bay platforms. An afternoon spent on the footplate of the Passenger Pilot was one of the 'plum perks' enjoyed by drivers' sons. It was a chance to exchange the 'tankie' for a tender engine, and stage three of the Great Western's visions of the future began to ferment.

For the recipient it was an opportunity not to be missed and training in the art of swinging a shovel began in earnest. On a tender engine there was room, with no scratching and poking about to drop the coal just inside the firebox as with a small tank engine. This was the chance to swing and twist, sliding the shovel over the firebox ring. One became involved and interested, and the succession and acceptance into the close family relationship with the Great Western Locomotive Department was one step nearer. In a couple of years another generation was on their way to Swindon for the examination.

There were no advertisements in the papers for railwaymen, as there was no need. Continuity was assured as it was a successful system, proved beyond doubt over the years, and used by each railway company.

The time and location for my Passenger Pilot turn was all arranged beforehand. In my case it was through Cow Lane bridge, up the path used by the East Junction signalmen, and when the running lines were clear, a signal from father would have me scrambling over the signal wires and rodding, and up on to the footplate. There was never an angry shout from the signal box, as they all knew me to be 'young Harold' going to spend the afternoon with his Dad, and anyway, they had their own sons in the box with them as the Traffic side also knew the value of continuity.

I walked down the road with a feeling of excitement, wearing my old footplate clothes. Father had learnt that mothers do not appreciate their sons coming home from these Saturday jaunts, their school clothes covered in coal and oil stains. I was going on the Passenger Pilot engine with the sure knowledge that it would be a 'big' engine for a change. With luck it could be a 'Hall' or at least a 'forty-three', but as I neared the station an old 'Duke' was pulling out of Number 1 bay platform. She went right up on to the Newbury branch with a string of coaches, then once clear of the points, she propelled them over the main and relief lines into the sidings. I hoped that she was not the Passenger Pilot, but she was. It was poor old *Amyas* waiting for me to join her.

I can remember it was a hot afternoon, and with it another incident to store away in the memory, for I discovered that mother made two brands of lemonade, one for the boy, and one for the old chap. She used to boil up a gallon of water, add lemonade crystals and let it stand until it was cool. It was then diluted to taste. My measure was half an inch in the bottom of a tumbler topped up with cold water, but the stuff she provided for father was a man's drink. As I climbed up on to *Amyas* he reached behind the tool box produced from a bucket of water a two pint bottle of mother's lemonade and handed it over to me. This was not like the wishy-washy gas filled products one can buy today, but neither was it anything like I had at home. It was cold, and the colour was a beautiful deep yellow. This lemonade had body, and like an old Port it had to be rolled around the mouth, and gently allowed to slide down the throat, leaving behind a thin skin on the teeth and a slight furring on the tongue, to be savoured for an hour afterwards. So it was I joined *Amyas* ready to enjoy the afternoon and learn how to fire a steam engine.

Amyas was nearing the end of her life and would not survive the year. She was run down, even at the low shunting speeds she knocked and clanked, and to draw ten coaches up out of the sidings produced more steam from the front end than reached her cylinders. The polished dome so glorious in the sunshine of her prime years, was now covered in several coats of paint, dirt streaked and greying, but even knowing she was to make her last journey in steam soon, was no excuse for footplate standards to fall where she was spotless.

Her cab and boiler casing shone, countless rubbings with oiled cotton waste by numerous firemen had removed or thinned the green paint through to the deeper green of earlier years, the whole merging into a soft patchwork of colour. Her copper injector pipes were burnished into a warm light brown sheen, small hollows in the copper showing up clearly the evidence of many knocks she had received. The brass tank of her sight feed lubricator shone clean and smooth, the roughness of the casting polished away over the years of her long life. Even the brass strip on the screw reverser had been polished so many times the valve cut off marks were barely discernible. The regulator handle was smooth and warm in the hand, unhappily soon to rust away as the dampness and chill crept through her as she awaited the end at the place of her birth.

It was a wonderful afternoon. I was allowed to fire her, shaping the fire round the box, the back corners packed tight, the coal burning with a long curving flame, rolling under the brick arch then whipping up and over to lick against the tube plate as the draught from the open damper and fire box hole caught it. As the needle of the pressure gauge moved towards the blowing off mark I was shown how to work the live steam injector, and how this operation caused the water in the gauge glass to rise as the boiler filled. It was all so easy, I was at that stage of tender years not to know that the Passenger Pilot was one of the few undemanding duties for a fireman.

I was allowed to drive her back, light engine, into the spur, and to pull on the whistle chain with three short blasts when we were inside, clear of the main line points. I was then given a fistful of that multi-coloured cotton waste for my own use. I had arrived, and as I sat on the fireman's seat the 'Saints', 'Stars', and brand new 'Castles' would come striding out of the station, the enginemen looking down from their elevated footplates on to this poor worn out old lady but not with disdain, as they too had spent their fair share of time on her sisters. It was the special look of superiority of all main line crews pulling out of a station with a big four cylinder engine. They were the aristocrats of the main line, the big glamour boys, the 'hard hitters' working on the 'runners'. We were very much the small fry — we were seen, then promptly forgotten.

It was a feeling I would become very familiar with in later years, as we swept by on the main line, past some poor unfortunate colleague shunting out any of the goods yards of the small stations with the local 'pick-up'. No matter that perhaps yesterday we were engaged on the same duty. Today you saw them and that was all. A wave from their footplate might be acknowledged by a nod of one's head, or if in a charitable mood, we might reply by lifting a hand. That was an indication that all was well, the engine steaming freely, the coal first class and that we were at peace with the world. With a parting blast on the whistle we would be gone. If opposite was the case then there was a game to be played out, a deliberate piece of play acting, deception, cunning, call it what you might, but practised by all enginemen in the same situation when passing our mates on the 'pick-up'.

We could be in dire straits, running on the main line five minutes in front of a named express with 150 lb of steam on the pressure gauge, the water level bobbing in the bottom nut and the blower screwed as far as it would go. But honour would not allow our circumstances to be seen by our mates. If we had been seen in difficulties we would have been the subject of much ribald mess room talk. So the pricker would be placed back in the rack, the blower shut off and we would be sitting down so unconcerned for those vital few minutes as we passed to much whistle blowing. As soon as we were out of earshot, on would go the blower again and we would get stuck in, praying that the next distant signal would be at caution so that we could recover a little. A mile of running without the regulator open was a saviour, many, many times. The day was to come when I knew what main line superiority was all about.

Main line superiority actually started a long way from the main line. It began in the dark confines of the shed as a member of the cleaning gang. To become a fully blown member of a cleaning gang meant acceptance, and as in all industries where adventurous young men work in gangs, full membership meant that an initiation ceremony had to be carried out. It was short, not so sweet and not a bit like a wedding. In its way it was a very serious and memorable part of life, for it was one of the first steps towards manhood, sorting out the men from the boys. Some young lads would leave when their time drew near. It was too much to face because there was no help at hand, as firemen, drivers, foremen and shed staff kept well out of the way. The 'boy' was about to become a man, and when it was all over he would be addressed as an equal by all.

It began when walking into the cleaners' mess room on the Monday night at the start of the first night shift. When I look at that door next to the gents toilet at Didcot shed now, I still remember that first night. I walked in and as I did so the 15 watt bulb was switched out, and two smoking flickering flare lamps were lit, and the familiar mess room became at once the sacrificial chamber. I was lifted up by many hands, carried over and laid face up on the table after which many hands held me down. I was about to be anointed. A slightly similar ceremony to one that took place centuries ago, in fact it is mentioned in the Good Book, but not in the way this anointment was to take place. To start the senior cleaner climbed on to the shoulders of another cleaner who stood on a bench, and from a great height and with a leer on his face, with much concentration and deliberation he began to pour a pint of heavy lubricator oil all over one's most private possessions.

That oil came slurping out in a thick channel to narrow down with a pencil slimness as it spread. It would have been a help if they had warmed the oil. When it was all over their gentlemanly instincts came to the forefront. It was time for the cleansing ceremony; they all trooped out leaving the cleaning materials consisting of a bar of carbolic soap, a good stiff scrubbing brush, a quarter of a pint of paraffin, a handful of dry sand and a bucket of hot water, and, if you could clean the oil off with that, you could surely clean a locomotive. I can say from experience I did not attempt to ride my bike for a fortnight!

As a full blown cleaner one now took a step towards better things. I was no longer addressed as 'Boy', it became 'hey you' but although the anointment with oil was over there were two more tests to pass. One was to remove the foreman's bowler hat, the other to remove the chargehand cleaner from his cabin, without being caught.

With this in mind plans had to be made. As we were already on nights, target number one had to be the chargehand cleaner. Three methods had been tried with some success by previous lads. One could tie his cabin door to the door of the boilersmiths, then kick both doors and run, or one could lay cotton waste along the gap at the bottom of his door, set it smouldering and shout 'fire' after wedging it, or one could bung up his chimney with wet cotton waste and smoke him out.

There had to be another way and it was me who found it.

The stove in the chargehand cleaner's office was the standard type fitted in all the cabins. A cast iron pot-bellied incinerator designed to burn good Welsh steam coal. The chimney was also cast iron with an elbow bend where it entered the top of the stove. This elbow was cast with a slot to take a damper, being a flat bit of iron that slid in and out as required to regulate the draught. By one o'clock in the morning that stove should be drawing well enough for the chargehand to push the damper in. He had allocated all the work, and had checked that we were all on the job, so, from his point of view it was reasonable for him to think he was safe to bed down for a couple of hours. Now if one was to take two fog detonators, straighten out the lead straps, make a bend at the end of the straps and tie on a long thread from the cotton waste, it should be possible to lower them carefully down the chimney and on to the top of the damper where a fog detonator would cook to perfection.

I climbed up the ladder and along the catwalk of the roof, counting the chimneys until I came to the right one before I carefully lowered the detonators. According to my calculations, explosives should go up, so he would be grateful to have his chimney cleaned, but it never works out that way, some of the blast can go down as well. I climbed down from the roof and crept back to No. 6106 which was the engine I was cleaning and waited with the others for the bang. When it did come we were all disappointed, as there was no loud explosion, but just a dull thud as if someone had slammed a heavy door.

We waited, and his door opened to allow a large cloud of grey dust to come billowing out. It seemed to move towards a pannier tank, where it stopped, although there was some movement in the middle.

When the dust had settled a bit, it was just possible to see a figure coughing its lungs up onto the frame of the tank engine. It was Ernie Didcock our chargehand. He began to recover and get his breath back, and then I heard words I had never come across before, so all in all we had the impression that he was a little upset.

He got over it in time, but there were threats of us being sent home, and worst of all 'The Sack', but it blew over, as no real harm had come to him. The boilersmiths took him in, and Swindon stores van delivered a nice new stove three weeks later complete with a new damper. A month to the day, Reading sent two nice gentlemen to replace the window, repair the brickwork round the frame and put in new glass. It was a stunt designed never to be repeated as a cowl was fitted to that chimney and to my surprise and delight it is still there.

The second target, the foreman's bowler hat, had to be a day shift operation as the Boss did not work on nights. This duty was delegated to the shift foremen who only wore trilby hats and could be discounted. Also the shift foremen were drivers doing supervisory work who might go back to the footplate on occasions, and we could be sent to fire to them. There was no reason to stoke up trouble for the future. The Boss foreman was another matter. He was a much envied man who had the odd Saturday and every Sunday off.

As with the removal of the chargehand, there was a time honoured method of removing a bowler hat whilst it was being worn. A ball of wet cotton waste could be counted as a prime mover but it had several disadvantages, as one could miss and be caught. Therefore a new approach using basic scientific methods was called for, using two drawing pins from the notice board and a good strong length of thread from the cotton waste.

Bill Young our foreman was a man of habit, and his habit of inspecting his shed at dead on 9.00 a.m. was to be his undoing.

I was tightening up the dart handle on the smoke box of No. 3448 *Kingfisher* when he came out of his office. Bending down on the framing I was able to line up the height of the bowler with the door post. As soon as he was out of sight we went into action, the drawing pins were pressed into the woodwork, and the thread stretched tight across the doorway. We then awaited his return.

It was a long wait. We should have had sense to inspect the pit on Number 1 road opposite his office and call it off for another day, but young men do not possess any sense; they are thick, their heads are filled with solid bone, they are idle, good-for-nothing imbeciles with a total disregard for authority. Well, that's what he said on his return! We had forgotten to inspect the pit for water depth.

As he walked through that doorway the thread whipped his bowler off, it bounced once, and landed in the pit, so quickly that it was bobbing brim up in the sludge before he realised that it had been removed.

He stood there with his hands on his hips looking down into the pit. There was just enough sludge in the water to prevent a proper ripple. The displacement of the bowler was just enough to create a slight swell, but it proved the point, that bowler hats do float, and can be removed from heads by using science.

The recovery of the hat was another matter, the only scientific instrument at hand being a coal pick. A (kindly) fireman came to the rescue, hooking the spike end of the coal pick inside the rim, but by doing so caused the brim to tilt so that a little sludge slopped in. As the hat was lifted out the red silk lining became a porridge grey. The last engine on Number 1 road had received a boiler washout, so everything now had an explanation. As Bill took repossession his comments were unrepeatable. It was years afterwards I noticed that Bill had developed a habit when entering his office of always waving his arms about in front of him before entering. He did this even in the winter when all the wasps were gone and visiting enginemen put it down to Bill becoming slightly eccentric as he aged, but we knew different!

Cleaning locomotives did not end with their outsides. The tightening up of the dart handle of *Kingfisher* I described had been the end product of part of the inside cleaning, for I had been engaged in blowing tubes. The instrument provided for this operation was the steam lance, which was simple and effective, being a long piece of tubing tapered at one end to form a high pressure nozzle. The other end was clipped to a one inch flexible length of pipe, which in turn was coupled up with a union nut to the take-off valve from the main steam pipe of the stationary boiler. Alternatively it could be connected to the take-off valve of another engine that was in steam.

Every Great Western locomotive was equipped with this valve on the smoke box. To control the steam lance a valve was fitted, and worked with a small lever. The procedure was to start at the bottom line of tubes, poke the nozzle end into a tube, pull the lever and blast the tube through, thus clearing it out.

This should have been a straight forward operation, but one learned fast. It was advisable to wear cycle clips, tie string around the wrists to secure the sleeves, button up the overall jacket and pin it tight with a safety pin around the throat, jam the cap on, tie a handkerchief over the nose and mouth then crawl into the smoke box. The lance could now be used, and one hoped that the tube was clear, but if it was blocked then all the precautions taken were worthwhile. The back pressure would blast back high pressure steam to pepper one with cinders at high velocity.

When the dust had settled the old fashioned tube rod had to be used. This was a half inch steel rod, long enough to ram down the tube right through to the firebox. Once the tube had been rammed through, the lance could be used again, and so it went on, across the tube plate, a row at a time until all the tubes were clear.

The next stage of cleaning came at the other end, in the firebox, and that was an experience. Nine times out of ten the Driver booking defects had reported 'corks on tubeplate' so into the firebox we would go when it had been emptied, but with eighty odd pounds of steam pressure still in the boiler, it could be very hot.

The equipment provided was very simple, a sack, a handbrush, flare lamp, a short tube rod, a hammer, and most important of all, a coal pick. All the tools were laid out on the floorboards, the flare lamp was lit, the sack laid over the hot fire hole ring then you laid on your stomach, and slid feet first into the firebox. Next the tools were laid out on the brick arch, with the exception of the coal pick. This was insurance, for it was jammed in between the firebox doors to keep them open. It was not unknown for another cleaner to sneak up onto the footplate and close the doors with a parting remark of 'Let's see you get out of that, whack'.

Work could now begin. The clinker corks were clouted with the hammer, then the short tube rod used to clear up inside the tube. After each row had been dealt with it was time to stick your head out of the firebox for some cool air, and at the same time to half straighten the back, for it was impossible to stand up in a firebox. The whole operation had to be carried out in a crouching position.

Once the whole of the tube plate was clear it was brushed down, but by this time the brick arch was piled up with clinker and ash. Once again one found that the Great Western had provided the means for clearing the rubbish, for one brick had been left out in each far corner of the arch, so that all the muck could be brushed through onto the fire bars and into the ash pan.

On a summer day a hot firebox was not the place to hang about in, but in the winter it was a very desirable place. The cleaning would be completed, the sack pulled in and laid on the fire bars, then you could tuck yourself up in the back corner and have a quiet smoke. Now and again you would tap a stay with the hammer in case the chargehand was lurking about, for he knew from bitter experience that when cleaners go quiet something is wrong. The funny part about it all was that nobody wondered why winter fireboxes took longer to clean than summer ones, unless the foremen too could remember back to the days when they cleaned fireboxes.

Because of the labour shortage we sometimes had to act as fitter's mate. I had one month of that and it was enough. Two weeks were spent packing spindle glands on Pannier Tanks and 'Dean Goods' engines. It was not so bad sitting on the motion with the boiler casing pressing into the back of the neck, or using an enlarged cork-screw to pull out the old packing. The tricky bit came with packing in the new graphite twists, ramming them in with a thin blunt chisel, placing the gland back on the bolts, finding the thread for the nuts and lock nuts, then dropping one into the pit, and on recovering the nut, knocking the spanner back down while you were wriggling your way back up into the motion. It was during this period I learnt that the English language can be used in many brutal ways to express feelings, but worse was to come. After two weeks I was moved into the lifting shop to further my education.

Whenever I now go into the lifting shop at Didcot locomotive shed on their 'open days', I still remember that period of two weeks, and Churchward Mogul, No. 5379. She was in for attention to valves and pistons, and I was given the job of decarbonising the pistons, spending a week on each piston. I had carried out this job on my old A.J.S. motorcycle, and the instructions were clear in the hand book to use a soft scraper such as a flattened piece of solder, but on no account to use a screwdriver. It was a surprise to find that a steam engine collected carbon, and had such dirty great pistons, but it was a bigger surprise to be handed a whacking great lump hammer and a cold chisel large enough to complement this persuader.

The instructions were straightforward. You placed the chisel at an angle with the left hand against the piston head, and then belted that chisel with the right hand using the lump hammer to come into contact with the chisel head. This very sophisticated operation to remove carbon could be entrusted to any cleaner. At the first belt I expected to see carbon flying all over the place, but glancing up at the smirk on the fitter's face was an indication that it did not work out that way. I just made a small mark on the carbon, and the next blow produced a small chip of carbon flying off, just large enough to show the metal of the piston underneath. It was, I think, the most soul destroying job I have ever encountered. Hour after hour, small chips scattering onto the floor, and at the end of the day another four inch patch uncovered, and there was always the thought that the other piston was still waiting for my attention.

After cleaning both pistons my right shoulder ached from wielding that lump hammer, whilst my left hand was sore and bruised from the few times I had missed. So there and then I made a vow, that never again would a cleaner use that chisel. Now, after 30 years, it lies in my tool box, a reminder of the days when I learned many new words!

The prime objective of joining the Great Western locomotive department was to become an engine driver. It was even possible to become a foreman, but qualifications were required for that position. It was hinted, alleged, and darkly suggested that a certain number of stop blocks had to be knocked down before one could be considered for a foreman's job. Basic economics said it was cheaper to make a man up to foreman where he would not be able to drive locomotives and therefore knock down stop blocks. But, of course, this was all part of shed 'ribbing'. Before one could become a foreman or a driver, one had to become a fireman, and his main occupation was to work with a shovel. So far, except for filling the foreman's coal buckets, we had not been near a shovel. There was no training as such in the art of firing, as the Great Western had another method in introducing one to the shovel, in slow easy stages. One first had to prove that one could use a shovel, and in a busy locomotive shed there were so many types and shapes of shovels.

The first shovel to be placed in one's hands was a Number 8. This, on its own, was just another shovel. It had a shaft and a 'T' handle, nothing strange about that, it was just like dad's garden spade. It was at the other end where things began to go wrong. At that end any similarity to a garden spade ended, for this was a king size shovel. It had a great square blade big enough to lift half a hundredweight. It was a diabolical instrument, placed gently into your hand with a pat on the shoulder from the chargehand, and then he turned you in the general direction of the coal stage. At last, the unison between man, shovel and coal was to take place.

It was an exquisite moment to walk on to the coal stage, and to toss a coin as to who was to take the steel wagon against the wooden one. A ten tonner loomed high in the half light, so why toss to see which wagon to empty? They surely both held the same amount of coal, but alas, I still had a lot to learn. I drew the wooden one, knocked up the clips, and two tubs were filled as the coal came tumbling out. This was easy, nothing to it, until I slid the shovel in along the wagon bed, and I found the reason for tossing for the choice of wagon.

Wooden wagons were used for things other than the transportation of coal. The floor boards were uneven, and six inch nails had been inserted to secure items in transit with the last two inches of nail bent over in the process. As I slid that No. 8 shovel in as hard as I could the blade went under one of these nails. The shock wave went up the shaft, up my arm, and out at the elbow joint. I stood there stunned, and then the pain came. It was not a gentle pain, but a roaring rasping pain which left me trembling, gasping for breath, and, as in the lifting shop, added to my vocabulary.

When the last shovelful of coal was thrown out of that wagon I sighed with relief. The No. 8 shovel was now polished with not a trace of black paint to be seen on its once virgin blade. There were enough bent six inch nails in the floor boards to stock a shop. I borrowed a sledge hammer and belted those nails over and into the wood until they were flush, and felt a lot better for it.

After a period on the coal stage it was time to move on and be introduced to another type of shovel. If we were to become firemen we had to know how to throw coal into the firebox, but, we also had to know how to throw it out. Each engine carried such a shovel in case this had to be done out on the road, so we were led to the fire droppers' pit. Each engine as it came in had to be serviced, the fire had to be cleaned, or if the engine was in for a boiler washout the fire had to be thrown out completely. For this a special shovel was designed. It had a two foot square blade tied on to a twelve foot handle, all steel from end to end. It weighed enough to make one cough on the first attempt to lift it. To complement this tool was a steel bar, used to break up the clinker, and to complement the bar was a steel pricker, used to hook up the clinker so that the shovel could be used. With all this twelve foot long steelwork about, all that was needed was a cleaner eager to learn.

The Great Western had it all worked out. They allowed one hour to prepare the fire on a big engine, and three quarters of an hour for a small engine, so it stood to reason that the allowance for emptying the firebox was the same. But this did not always work out as planned, as an engine could be on the road for a long time, an empty tender would show that, and it could have burnt a load of poor coal. Engines would drop on to the ash road with the clinker up level with the fire hole ring, or, they could come off a train at short notice and arrive on the shed with a box full of fire, but either way they had to be cleaned out.

The only way to tackle this sort of job was to shovel all the fire to one side of the box, throw out the clinker, shovel the fire back over on the cleaned side, then throw out the clinker from the other side. It sounds simple enough, but lifting that twelve foot long shovel was no joke. It was red hot, so a heavy leather glove plus a pad of wet cotton waste had to be used by the left hand as the shovel was withdrawn from the firebox. With a tender engine it could be managed without much trouble, but on a tank engine it had its moments, enough to learn a few more words.

Once the firebox was clean, there remained only two more jobs to be carried out before the engine was moved forward to the coal stage. The ash pan and the smoke box had to be cleared, and it is a debatable point as to the merits of one to the other, because a lot depended on the wind. With the ash pan, both dampers were opened wide, and you climbed down into the pit with the ash rake. If the tender end was chosen then nine times out of ten the water scoop came into contact with the head. If the engine end was chosen the ramp could be missed by ducking lower only to clout the head on an axle.

Whichever end one started there was always somewhere from which a drop of water would drip with uncanny accuracy on to the back of the neck.

With the rake in the hand it was now a question of pushing the ash to and fro until the ash pan was empty. With each push and pull the ash would cascade out of the pan, drifting up through the motion, up through the spokes of the driving wheels, and covering everything with a grey film of dust, including the poor lad responsible for this operation. The selection as to whether to start the tender end or engine end was arrived at by careful study of the wind direction. Obviously going in with the wind should have meant that the ash would be carried away, but again careful design in the building of the locomotive altered all calculations. The wind would drive under the engine, channelled through the pit to arrive at the ash pan as a gale, then it would eddy up round the boiler, whip round the smokebox, and come howling back down the pit to fill the air with dust. So at either end there was no escape. It was a matter of push and rake, head down, teeth gritted, until the job was finished and the dirty grey figure could climb out of the pit.

The last job was the smokebox. Again, depending on the state of the fire on the engine when she came in, and the amount of ash in the pan, one could guess on the amount in the smokebox. With a 'home' engine it would not be much, perhaps a foot deep, but with an engine that had been on the road for some time it could be up level with the locking bar, half way up the smokebox. One approached the smokebox door with a certain amount of caution, but for this operation there was no No. 8 shovel. By far the best tool was the fireman's shovel, so by devious steps we had almost reached our goal.

Hand over hand we would proceed along the top framing to the smokebox. Knocking up the locking handle and unscrewing it a couple of turns, giving the dart handle a quarter of a turn and pull. The smokebox door would then swing sweetly open to allow half a hundred weight of black cinders to slide out and cover one's boots. This was first shovelled off the front framing, then one could begin to shovel it out of the smokebox onto the ground, and, as with the ash pan, the wind would whip round the smokebox door, and try to blow it all back in again! But endeavour must prevail. The smokebox door would be swung round and closed, enabling her to go forward for coaling.

All this effort had produced a clean firebox, smokebox and ash-pan, with an engine all ready to be prepared for the road once again, but it had left behind a pit full of ash, a pile of clinker, and a heap of cinders. Whilst one was in the pit shovelling out the ash, the forward planning of the Great Western came into being. Without the aid of computers, measured day work, slide rules or gentlemen in white coats consulting stop watches, somehow the wagons one had emptied on the coal stage had made their way down the bank, and arranged themselves in a long line on the ash road siding, all ready to be filled with the cinders, ash and clinker. Once again the No. 8 shovel was picked up and used as it was designed to be, and so, one was introduced to the shovel and its variants.

It was good basic training and at the same time using that training to advantage, for when the time came to use the fireman's shovel, it was an old friend. It had a handle attached to a long narrow blade and with it one could twist the wrist, flick, turn, slide, and place the coal just where it was required — it was a beautiful tool. In addition one could wash the hands in it, and bacon and eggs fried in it were far superior to those cooked in any frying pan on the market. That fireman's shovel was just one of the small parts that went into making the Western 'Great'.

On a recent visit to the Torbay Steam Railway I was met with a very pleasant surprise on entering the reception hall of Queens Park Station at Paignton. For there, hanging in a place of honour on the wall was a fireman's shovel, which drew me with affection.

The posters and the book shop were forgotten, for here was the instrument responsible for all the successes of the great record breaking runs. Yet the people gathering round No. 4566, the beautiful little tank engine that had just arrived, ignored the shovel on the wall.

I had, over the years, used the shovels of all the other companies but they were heavy and narrow and quite devoid of any character. To the ordinary person it might seem stupid to talk of a shovel in such a way, but then, steam enthusiasts are supposed to be a race apart. The Great Western shovel was a fitting companion to a Great Western locomotive, balanced to perfection, it completed the unison between fireman and firebox. The only thing I could never understand, along with every other fireman, was how that firebox grew in size once a fire was in it.

I knew from cleaning days that it was not possible to stand up inside a firebox, and yet once that fire had been built up and the locomotive was being used to pull 500 odd tons that firebox assumed gigantic proportions. It became a raging furnace, its demands for fuel only met by a brother to that shovel hanging on that wall at Paignton. Without a doubt it was a fitting gesture, and the mark of 'someone who cared', to hang it there.

A book on Great Western engine working would also not be complete without a few pages devoted to a band of ladies who were to be found all over the system where crossroads meet. In their way they helped to make the Western 'Great' for they provided the 'Double Home' lodge.

In my day as a fireman the 'change-over en route' put an end to lodging between shifts, but I knew of these ladies. There was one in Old Didcot, Mrs. Kate Bennett, who provided such a service for men from Severn Tunnel Junction shed, Wolverhampton and Westbury. I would look at these strange men dressed in enginemen's uniform, and wonder with a small boy's mind, how could there be other men wearing the same clothes as my dad? To me in those days the Great Western began and ended at

Didcot. Looking back now, what on earth could they also do in such a small place except go for a walk, or go to the pub?

Father, I knew, went to a far off town called 'Brumigum', where there was a place called the Bull Ring. He would bring back large brown paper bags filled with all kinds of biscuits, and sweets of every colour not to be found in the village shops. This 'Brumigum' was a wonderful place. I knew too that he stopped with a lady called Annie and it was only years later that I found that Birmingham was not a fairyland, and from what he told me about Annie and the 'Double Home' lodge, it was not a high class hotel either.

All the Didcot men lodged with Annie, in a little terrace house tucked away in the maze of streets, later to be swept away, with the old Bull Ring, in a holocaust of fire and destruction as aerial warfare rained high explosives and incendiary bombs into those little back yards. I never met Annie, but from what I heard of her she was a kindly soul, cooking meals and providing beds in what must have been very difficult circumstances with a 24 hour turnover of enginemen. This turnover created problems for it was common practice to arrive in the early hours, light a candle, then after a wash, creep up to bed to find that another was just leaving it. The bed, of course, did not have time to cool and if the needs of nature called, a groping hand under the bed would locate the required receptacle, and, in the gloom the reward for this discovery was often a wet thumb. Neither father nor his mate ever did explain how they emptied that pot, except that it was advisable to hide one's boots!

Meals were taken in the kitchen, a table being pushed up to a window overlooking a small back yard, but this window always had the bottom half slightly open for the benefit of the cat.

Annie in this respect was typical of her generation. Home was not complete without a cat, but where other ladies enjoyed the company of an ordinary cat, Annie owned a tiger, a whacking great ginger tom, whose sole delight was to jump through the window and land on the table. He then would walk down the middle with great confidence, secure in the knowledge that with Annie there he would come to no harm.

He would pick his way delicately through the plates, sniffing at some morsel of delicious sausage, his tail straight up, while all around him were a lot of rough, uncouth enginemen, knives and forks poised, with one eye on his progress and one eye on Annie. He had the luck of the Devil, as plans to stop this parade were laid and thwarted, for Annie was always there. When his end did come it was just as swift, without the aid of planning, a combination of luck and circumstances, plus quick thinking by two men.

Quick thinking to deal with an emergency was part and parcel of footplate life. Ginger was up against the experts, and as expected, those experts acted instinctively.

Ginger as usual came through the window, landed on the table, and began his parade to the other end. He was not to know that on this day, the Insurance man was due to call. The brass knocker was lifted to 'rat-a-tat' on the front door, the echo rebounding up the passage in a hollow boom. Annie got up from her chair and padded up the hallway to answer the call, and with her movement the experts went into action.

Ginger had begun his journey back up the table, his tail still upright and weaving from side to side, but as Annie's slippers were heard, slapping their way up the passage towards the dining room, the escape route was quickly cut off and the window closed. A Birkenhead fireman who was just about to spread some mustard on his sausage, changed the direction of the knife and very gently wiped it on the exposed backside of Ginger. Only a fireman used to the delicate setting of an exhaust injector could have used such finesse. So gentle was the touch of the knife that Ginger took two more steps forward before coming to a sudden stop. Then he extended his claws and stood on tiptoe, his back arched up and his fur stood out like stiff golden wire. There was a long low whistle as the air expended from his lungs. He came back on his hindquarters as his muscles stood out, then with one almighty leap he was gone, straight through the closed window.

Ginger never came back, perhaps he headed for the canal. Anyway, Annie was not without a cat for long. The same fireman brought her a little black kitten on his next trip, and that kitten knew its place. It never came near a table or a mustard pot.

Chapter Three

Footplate work was a life rich in incidents, no working day was the same, that was the beauty of it. As a boy I was enthralled by the stories of engines and drivers that my dad encountered. One in particular concerned driver Arthur Timms. He and his wife were a wonderful couple, they were more like an Uncle and Aunt to me.

Their bitch had given me the little dog that was my constant companion, so when he trotted off home to see his mum each day it was natural that I should follow him. Besides, Mrs. Timms kept a secret store of sweets, and she was glad of the company of a small boy when Arthur and dad were away.

On one occasion they had gone off to 'Brum' in the early hours, and for some reason the return working was cancelled, so they were sent home as passengers. Even in my day as a fireman this was a rare treat. To be able to relax on the 'cushions', feel the slight snatch of the train, and see the smoke drifting over the fields, and know that for once another fireman was hard at work providing the power to let one laze back half asleep. There was one drawback to this short lived Utopia, the travelling public, the fare paying passengers.

Enginemen travelling home on the 'cushions' are a clannish lot. They would be the first to admit that the public had every right to a seat in a compartment, but any interference with the privacy of 'overalls, steam talk and railway work' meant that the fare payer was to some extent an interloper, to be removed with all possible speed. In the competitive world the steps taken would be classed as tactics, but in fairness, it was only used against city gents. Ladies, children and vicars were all made welcome.

Arthur arrived back home with father, and related, to his wife's outraged indignation, how he had removed a compartment full of city gents in a most expert manner. I can remember the story almost word for word, not only for its simplicity, but because it was such a laugh to hear.

They had left the train in the yard at Birmingham and taken the engine on light to Wolverhampton, where they were instructed to return home. As the next Up train started from this point they were able to secure a compartment to themselves long before departure time. As departure time drew near, more and more people squeezed in, and Arthur found that his ample proportions were subject to some restriction.

As this was a local train it was all non-corridor stock, so, whoever got in was stuck there until the next station was reached. There were some disdainful sniffs and glances of disapproval from these office types at having to share a compartment with two dirty old enginemen, so Arthur began to implement a plan of removal.

As he said later, he had fired the old 'Dean Singles' and 'Armstrongs' up and down this stretch of line years before some of these lads had been born, and now, in his mature years, he was entitled to spread himself out a bit and enjoy the ride. It was to be a two stage operation, to remove a few at the next stop, and the remainder before they reached Birmingham, using two weapons, one for each stage.

Arthur was well built and sported a large composure. With the greasy old cloth cap he wore, his image did not complement the white collars and bowler hats around him. Under his shirt he had been blessed by nature, with a chest full of hair, so when he carefully, and with deliberation, began to undo his shirt buttons and exposed all that masculinity, there was a slight easing of the pressure, and when he placed his hand in that luxurious growth and began to dig deep there was a distinct shuffle-up. He was still scratching away, a look of exquisite pleasure on his face as the train ran into Wednesbury station. Four passengers made a quick exit, but six remained huddled up in one corner, so stage two would have to be used.

In common with most footplate men, Arthur, besides being an expert driver was an expert at growing flowers or vegetables. In common with these experts, he specialised, and his speciality was onions. The onions he grew were not ordinary onions for pickling or cooking, but magnificent onions, as big as cricket balls and as solid, with a bite that made a Bombay curry taste like custard. So when Arthur stood up, and lifted his wicker basket down from the luggage rack, and took out one of these onions there was a slight stirring at the other end of the compartment.

To show that he was a gentleman and familiar with the finer points of etiquette, Arthur laid a napkin on his lap, searched around in his pockets, and produced a knife, a knife honed down to the sharpness of a scalpel. The operation then took place, with all the artistry of a showman and the skill of a surgeon. The knife slid in and removed layer upon layer of dry skin, until the onion lay naked and glistening on his lap.

As a rabbit watches a stoat so did the remaining passengers watch this performance. Papers were laid on knees and forgotten, and eyes peered over the tops of spectacles. One passenger had an unlit cigarette between his lips, and a burnt out match between forefinger and thumb. Then Arthur delivered the coup de grace, biting into that onion, he began to scrunch. It was merciful at this point that the train was running into West Bromwich. The exodus began before the coaches had stopped, indeed, the actual stopping slammed the door shut behind them. Arthur leaned over, picked up an abandoned newspaper and settled back to enjoy a good read while he finished his 'fruit'.

As an example of a wicked bit of skulduggery it was a classic, designed to completely demoralise the opposition, and in their way most enginemen could equal it. This removal of passengers was also practised during my firing days. One of my drivers, dear old Bill Champ, went into battle with a most evil smelling pipe, that gurgled and made little popping sounds when he sucked on it, the smoke emerging from his mouth as a yellow-grey fog, while that curling up from the bowl was blue tinged and smelt of old drains.

Ted Hurle, my regular mate for so many years, could develop a twitch to discourage any interloper, being able to move his left shoulder, eye and nostril all in one movement. My old dad could produce the most body shaking, wracking cough imaginable, but, as I have written before, we were not entirely devoid of good manners. Room, conversation, and entertainment were always provided for ladies, children and vicars. In later years however, Management provided a reserved compartment next to the engine for its train crews. It was very considerate of them, but it was, at the same time, a two-edged sword, an insurance to cover any eventuality that might happen on the footplate ahead of us.

We loco-men at Didcot were lucky in one respect. Our duties were not confined to the main line, and the branch, in our case the Didcot, Newbury, Winchester and Southampton line, was typical of most branches. It was so divorced from the main line as to become a separate railway, and we knew all the station staff, their families, the plate-layers and signalmen, the farmers and coal merchants. We watched with interest the growth of wheat and cattle and the progress of ploughing and hedge trimming. We knew the branch as well as our own back yard, even the passengers became friends, for we took the children to school, father to work, and mother into Newbury on market day.

The tenders of 'Dukes', 'Dean Goods', Collett 22XX's and 'Bulldogs' were built not only to store coal and water for the firebox and boiler, but to transport bean rods, pea sticks, sacks of potatoes, and young fruit trees. On Mondays, which as every male knows is wash day, and a good day to be at work, station masters' ladies would appear from station houses with two empty buckets. They stood opposite the footplate as we ran into the station. They knew from long experience that the injector would be on, and from that little curly pipe came boiling hot soft water. If by chance the coal bucket also stood there empty, then it too was quickly filled.

One gentleman we took good care of was the brother of the beloved Dick Shepherd of St. Martin in the Field, for he had sustained the most awful injury to his neck. He was tightly strapped up, for the slightest jerk could endanger his life, and yet, in spite of this drawback he was the most cheerful of men. We would collect him at Newbury and take him through to Whitchurch, making each station stop in between on the hand brake and just a whiff of vacuum, stopping and starting so gently so that there was no possible chance of the coupling snatching.

Out in the sections, miles from civilisation, the platelayers would hold up an empty bucket, or go through a charade of warming hands in front of a fire. If there was time, a large lump of coal would be quickly thrown over the side, enough to keep them happy for a few hours, for they knew that on the return run we would remember them. The running plate would be stacked up with half a dozen large lumps, and they would be waiting, spread out over a quarter of a mile of the section, as the coal came tumbling over the side, one piece at a time, like large bombs leaving an aircraft. But it was not a one way traffic. The next day as we ran into the station, a ganger would be waiting with a couple of rabbits ready for skinning, and sometimes a couple of cock pheasants. Once, only once, we ran down a young deer between Woodhay and Highclere. We left a message with the signalman as to the exact location of a free dinner and the next day we collected a hind quarter as we ran in.

We would help load a stubborn calf into the guard's van; a poor little bewildered animal, his head, tail and legs sticking out of a sack. Sometimes if the back end was clean, it was easier to pick him up and carry him in, bawling his head off and covering us with slobber as only a calf can. We would give an excited school boy a ride between stations, to see in that boy a mirror image of oneself only a few short years before.

Only once can I remember baulking at helping to unload livestock from a guard's van. We ran into Compton and found our two minutes station time extended. I had seen the porter go into the van, but the minutes ticked away with no sign of him or the guard coming out, so I climbed off the footplate and walked back up the platform. When I reached the van and looked in I found both the guard and the porter pinned up at the end of the assortment of milk churns, trunks, crates of live chickens and other miscellaneous items of branch line revenue, by one very angry, large, billy goat. He had somehow managed to jump the link of what had been a short chain over the hook, so that the short chain became a long one, sufficient to cut off any chance of escape through the door.

Billy stood there, head down, pawing the van floor, breathing fire and thunder, his curved horns aimed at a point, level with our guard's navel. They were very frightened railway employees and there was nothing in the Rule Book to cover this situation. I told them to stop where they were while I went and enlisted help. It was a silly thing to say, as they were not going anywhere, but it was all I could think to offer for comfort. I ran back to Ted Hurle and explained the situation to him.

As always he had an answer to this problem, but then, as a fireman, he had worked the Welsh Valleys, where the transportation of Welsh mountain rams was commonplace. A bit of local knowledge was called for, far removed from the ideas that went into writing a Rule Book. He told me to go back to the van and tell both men to hang on as he was going to knock the billy goat off his feet. When the opportunity arose they were to run clear.

I passed this information on, wondering just what Ted intended to do. However, he had the tool to perform with, our engine, the little 'Collett' No. 2222, renowned for her quick acceleration. Ted blew off the brakes and opened her up. Her chimney blasted her up the platform the length of one coach, then Ted slapped on the anchors and almost stood her on her nose. That poor old billy goat went up to the other end of his chain with a thump, and at the same time the porter and our guard dived out of the door. At Newbury, it took four porters, two with shunting poles, to unload that goat. He bucked and kicked his way all up the platform, scattering waiting passengers in all directions, until he reached the exit. Here he became as docile as a lamb, for the station foreman had thrown the water out of the fire bucket over him. Here was one more railwayman who had met this situation before.

There was one occasion when we collected an unusual passenger at Churn Halt. This little platform was unstaffed and miles from anywhere. It was perched on top of the Berkshire Downs between Upton and Compton. If we had any passengers to drop there, the Guard would inform us, either at Didcot or Newbury. So far as passengers to pick up were concerned, we would slow down and stop if it was necessary, but it was not often that we did have a passenger to collect. These rare occasions were only in the summer when the odd rambler or a marksman from the rifle range required transport, but on this particular day, running to Newbury as light engine, we spotted a small white bundle on the platform. We stopped to investigate, and there curled up into a ball was one very lonely lamb.

At first we thought it was dead and had been abandoned as the Downs were usually covered with sheep. But not today, as they had all moved on leaving this one hungry and frightened lamb. There was only one thing to do. I picked him up, cuddled him in my arms, and took him back on to the footplate. We dropped him off at Compton into the loving arms of the station master's wife, where he settled down to become the family pet.

Churn Halt had another attraction at certain times of the year. In the fields nearby were to be found the most delicious button mushrooms, and during the mushroom season, light engines and the local goods would move about between sections, a little more smartly than usual, so that a quick stop could be made. Even before the engine or train had come to a stand, either the driver or fireman was shinning down the steps from the footplate to hop over the fence, cap in hand, to get picking. There was no need to look round as you stood where you landed, and picked them around you, five minutes being long enough to fill a cap to the brim. Sometimes we must have been just a little longer than five minutes, but never did the signalmen at Upton or Compton carry out Regulation 11, 'Train unusually long time in the section', as set out in the General Appendix to the Rule Book, perhaps because we shared our good fortune with them.

The branch, either side of Newbury, was like our own back yard. We knew it upside down and inside out, because most of the Didcot drivers had fired over it for so many years, and as my Ted had been up and down the Welsh valleys for so long, this switchback road held no terrors for him.

We ran everything that could be thrown at us without any incidents, although there were a few near squeaks.

Whitchurch was one of the worst places on the down road. After leaving Burghclere there was a little climb for about half a mile, then a little piece of flat about the length of a goods train, followed by the drop down to the other side of Whitchurch, like falling over a cliff.

We had a set pattern on this section of the branch, born from long experience. As soon as the engine dipped her nose down that bank, we would screw the tender handbrake down, and join all the buffers of the wagons up together. Sweeping down through Litchfield, we should have them in hand, enough perhaps to give the engine a little steam. There followed a very short section of rising gradient, but once over this, it was a matter of screwing another half a turn on the handbrake each time the driver gave her a burst of vacuum, and that way, we could drop down to Whitchurch with the train well under control. The protection for the Up road, was just outside the signal box in the form of a pair of throw off points that could land a down train in the road below. It was a fearsome place, and many a time we were ready to bail out, particularly in thick fog, but somehow we always managed to stop in time. It was with much regret that we lost all this lovely section of the branch to the Southern Region on 2 April 1950. The rolling Hampshire Downs would be sadly missed, as Enborne Junction onwards now became the territory of the Eastleigh lads. It was a fair swop in a way as we had been running into Eastleigh and Southampton for years, but we felt some concern for them as we knew just what that part of the branch was like. It was no place for the unwary, and it was not long before the first nasty incident occurred.

On 23 September 1954, a B.R. 'Mogul' No. 76017, was working the 7.0 a.m. from Banbury to Eastleigh freight, and its driver lost control of the train on the bank down into Whitchurch. I can only imagine the awful moments on that footplate when its crew realised that the train was out of control. I've had it happen once, and the feeling of utter helplessness is a thing I would not wish on anyone. The crew got away with their lives by leaving her, jumping, as she ran through the catch points and buried her nose halfway down the bank before rolling over, leaving the remains of six wagons spread all over the place.

The steam crane came from Eastleigh to the rescue with the breakdown gang: Bill Bishop was the driver of the crane, and when it came to dealing with this sort of incident he was the top man to have on the job. It was not an easy lift, they never were. No. 76017 had to be brought half way over, and propped up, to stop her sinking, before Bill could lift her right out and place her back onto the rails.

Bill had a repeat performance six years later in a carbon copy of the first derailment, and one that gave as much trouble as the first. But this time Bill knew the snags. She was lifted out but it was to be the last. The Eastleigh lads had learned the hard way.

During the winter months, of course, the branch could be a hell hole. As long as we kept running we were the sole means of communication between the villages that were strung out across the Downs to Newbury and Winchester. In the early days of the branch, there had been a period when trains had been snowed in for days but a lesson had been learned from this. In bad weather the shift foreman would send a light engine over to keep the cuttings clear of drifts, and it could be a hairy journey at times. The wind would drive the snow up into those forty foot deep cuttings, carving and shaping the ice into a beautiful sculpture, all up the face of the chalk cliff where it hung in a glistening sugar overhang. Then as we passed the blast from the chimney would bring great sections of ice down where it would be crushed, powdered, and flung out from beneath the wheels, filling the cutting with a swirling fog of ice dust.

Clawing our way up with a heavy train, we must have looked like some forbidding prehistoric monster with our front buffer beam, vacuum pipe and cylinders covered with caked snow, whilst above the round black smoke box, our chimney erupted a vast column of escaping smoke and steam. Above it all, raged the white wall of a blizzard sweeping over the top of the cutting, and without warning the sanctuary of the iced cliffs would suddenly drop away and we would be out into the weather, and the bleak desolation of the Berkshire Downs. The snow drove into the cab, to spit and hiss as it touched the firebox flap. The lovely green fields and gentle rolling Downs were transformed into an English Siberia. It was as if nothing lived in this wasteland except this black monster with its line of snow covered wagons snaking across the tundra, leaving a trail of smut and ash to mark its passing.

In July 1974, ten years after the closure of the branch, and twenty years after I had last worked over it, I took a day off from factory life and returned, making a start at Upton station. Here I intended to stand on the road bridge to take some photographs, but as I drove my car towards the station I could see that my carefully laid plans were to fall through. The new road on which I was driving had been formed by blowing up the station bridge and allowing it to fall into the cutting.

I turned off what once had been a quiet country road, into the station yard, parked, and sat there quietly looking round. The station house, in outline, was much the same as I had remembered it. To the right was the small cattle pen and goods yard. The goods shed was still perched on its small island platform, while across the remains of the yard, the coal merchants platforms were beginning to crumble, standing in isolation beside an empty trackbed.

As I left the car, and walked towards the station house to find out if it was permissible to explore my dear old branch, it was with delight and surprise that I found the occupant was one of my old mates from my days of cleaning and firing, Mick Slade, still on the footplate as a diesel driver. Mick, like myself, had blasted through this very station, shovelling his way up from Didcot, and up the banks I was soon to walk. Any talk of steam was quickly dispelled by Mick with the swiftness of a douche of cold water. He was now firmly a diesel man, glad that steam had gone for ever, and considered that anyone who hankered after the return of steam was quite mad.

I took stock of his surroundings. The platforms were empty, forlorn and grass covered, the edging slabs beginning to lift. On the Up side, clinging precariously to the rotting wooden fence, and struggling to survive, was a solitary rambler rose, the last red splash of beauty that used to stretch the entire length of the platform. The empty trackbed and embankment stretched away towards Didcot, twisting and curving through the fields, like the bony spine of some long dead monster. I turned south, and began to trudge up the 1 in 106 climb to the summit, leaving the roof of that sad station slipping from view.

Past the first small cutting, the old railway flattened out into an undergrowth of thistles and young saplings. The tangled remains of the old Starter and Outer Home signal wires, running through pulleys wrenched out of foundation blocks, threaded their way forward to disappear in a wilderness of new growth. Two young heifers gazed at me, impassively, through a gap in the hedge, not knowing that their grandmothers would have fled from the sound of open cylinder drain cocks from a 'twenty-eight', pounding up this bank.

At the start of the next cutting, I came across the body shell and stripped remains of an old Morris Minor car crouching amongst the nettles. A reminder of this 'throw away' world. I was then into the bank, deep chalk cliffs on either side, the remains of the platelayers huts standing drunkenly in a recess of the cutting, the concrete bins still full of small chippings, no longer required to be packed underneath the few odd sleepers rotting in the grass.

The memories came flooding back as I turned the next curve and came to the first overbridge, with its brickwork still showing the black stain of smoke from the countless chimneys that had punched their way through. The soot now was beginning to peel, revealing the brickwork to the sun and the rain for the first time in sixty years. It was all so peaceful and quiet now. The clink of the platelayer's shovel had given way to the whispering wind in the undergrowth. The sharp crisp 'bark' of a Collett 'twenty-two', scampering eagerly along, was now replaced with the noise of chalk fragments, as a rabbit scrambled frantically up the cliff face. The heavy rumble of the big American 'Baldwin', Class 8F 'Staniers', and Churchward 'twenty-eights', clawing their way, yard by yard, up this incline, was now reflected by the distant groaning of a tractor working in the fields high above.

I came across a barrier of rails, bolted into uprights sunk deep into the old trackbed. I climbed over and round the next curve, plodding on, breathing heavily with the climb. Then, just as I remembered, stood the three-arch bridge, tall, striding, over the 40 feet high cutting, towering over me, the centre arch framing the blue sky and billowing white clouds. I brushed my way through the undergrowth and sat down under the bridge, my back up against the brickwork.

I closed my eyes and drifted back, to the days when this bridge had meant the halfway mark going up, and 'nearly home' on the way down. I could see it, sliding into view through the eyeglass as we pounded our way up, a tall, gaunt, three legged bridge, that seemed to be looking down at us contemptuously from its lofty height. The arches were far too high to be a target for our blasting exhaust, and on the return journey it would assume the proportions of a model, as we swung round the curve and down into the bank, three thin legs spanning a deep gorge. We would then swoop down, rushing through with the wind, as if escaping from its clutches.

I opened my eyes to see a baby rabbit sitting on the other side of the bank, ears up, and nose twitching as he pondered over this stranger. As I moved to stand up, he turned and bounded away, tumbling over something in the tall grass. I crossed over and found the reason for his tumble as he scampered up the bank. Lying in the tall grass, was a firebar. How long had it lain there, and from which engine had it come? I left it there in peace.

I turned away a little sad, and made my way on up the bank, and as I rounded the curve, an hour out from Upton, I found the way blocked. This time the cutting was not filled with a deep drift of snow but with bales of straw, right up, level with the ridge. Four tarpaulins stretched across to form a roof. An ingenious farmer had found the perfect way to store his winter feed.

As I was determined to reach the top of the bank, I climbed over and carried on, through the last bridge, and to the top of the Downs. The last few hundred yards caused me some concern, as it had become a dumping ground or storage place, for farmyard manure, and as such, was in the process of maturing. Finding a flat piece of wood, I skirted the worst of the manure with great difficulty, using the wood to form a platform, and to clean my boots afterwards. From there, it was clear going to Churn.

As I left the bank behind, the trackbed stretched out ahead, the only sign of its path being the remains of the fencing on either side. The grass had grown tall, bending over where I passed through, and at last I came to the site of Churn Halt, with the goods shed of Compton just showing in the distance. There my nostalgic ramble had to end as there was no time to go further. I turned and saw my tracks in the grass leading from the top of the bank; I must have been the first mortal to pass this way for a long time.

It really came home to me, my dear old branch was dead, sleeping peacefully along the barrows on the nearby ridgeway and the old Roman encampments. In 1882 the first steam shovel had ripped this gigantic trench out of the Berkshire Downs, exposing the white chalk in an ugly scar across the countryside. Wagonloads of spoil had backed down behind the shovel to be tipped at Upton following down into Didcot so by building up the embankment.

Thousands of people had been conveyed along this old railway along with countless thousands of tons of material. Generations of locomotives from the little Metro tanks to the big 2-8-0 freights had been a pageant of development pounding up this bank together with generations of enginemen, myself amongst them.

The older generation have long passed on together with the steam locomotive, they had built it and worked it, now they were dead and the branch with them, but together they had fitted into the vast jigsaw pattern of the Great Western Railway.

I made my way back down the bank towards Upton. I knew that under the grass, rippling so gracefully in the gentle breeze, the trackbed was still there, wending its empty way right through to Newbury, and onwards from Enborne Junction, it continued across the Hampshire Downs into Winchester. Its scars were covered and softened with grass and chickweed, thistles and nettles. My branch had returned to the peacefulness of nature.

A skylark rose under my feet and climbed up into the blue summer sky, its shrill whistling growing fainter as it gained height. Then the agony of it all hit me, here were the remains of a perfectly good railway, a direct link between the Midland factories and the docks at Southampton. Yet for almost its entire length, the road ran alongside, choked up with continental lorries, snarling their way up inclines. Forty lorries equalled the loads we pounded up the same incline with one steam locomotive.

It was a sad walk back down that bank. My movements would flush out a pair of wood pigeons bursting out from a thicket, with frantic flapping of wings, leaving a trail of small feathers to float down into the grass, whilst pheasants squawked with indignation, as they scurried out of my way, the sudden noise as startling to me as it was to them. More rabbits scampered along in front of me, dodging from side to side in their haste to escape from a lonely sad man, who could remember another generation of rabbits who ran with the wind, ahead of a steam locomotive charging at them through this deep cutting.

I sat in my car at Upton station, and changed out of my heavy boots. The enormity of my nostalgic visit was too much to take in and retain perspective. I had even forgotten to use my camera. Then the thought struck me that I could return, it would still be there, and this time I would be prepared.

Nostalgia is a state of mind, of regret and reproach, sadness and disillusion, and it can slice deep into one with intensity. It is a personal emotional feeling that can be dismissed as a weakness, to be tossed aside by those who do not experience such feelings. It is said that one should never look back, never return, but from nostalgia can come memories, and from those memories, and the foresight of a few who used their cameras, the branch, and elsewhere too, it can all live again. Once more the 'Castles' can march proudly out of Paddington, and slide swiftly under the lee of Dawlish cliffs, and the big 'twenty-eights' can again pound their way up the very bank I had just descended.

There are men like myself who can remember, and men like my dear old Uncle, Bert Edmonds of Old Oak Common, now in the winter of his life, and who I must now turn to, and perhaps rekindle the memories of the 'Limited', 'Bristolian', the 'Red Dragon' and the 'Cheltenham Flyer'.

Chapter Four

A good example of what Bert Edmonds was like on the footplate can best be described from his and others' recollections of a particular run related to me. He was working one of the Up Swansea expresses with No. 5027 *Farleigh Castle*, an Old Oak Common engine and one that he was familiar with, and as it turned out it was a good job he knew her.

She was in a bad way, leaking steam where she should be tight and riding badly on her boxes, but steamwise she would hold her own with a good fireman. And that was part of the trouble. Through circumstances since forgotten, Bert had with him a spare fireman, a lad who was eager enough to please but who just did not have any experience with big passenger engines or fast running. He could only do his best.

Bert nursed *Farleigh Castle* as much as he could without losing time, but when he ran into Cardiff, the blower was on to keep the pressure up and he had half a glass of water showing in the gauge. They could manage to Newport but it was the voice on the station tannoy that confirmed his fears; "Newport, next stop, then fast to Paddington". Now Bert was not a praying man, well, not on the footplate anyway. It is true the Lord looks after His own, but in this case he needed some help, and it came with the arrival of an old workmate, driver Fred Nash.

Fred was in the process of learning the road between Paddington and South Wales, both ways, and he was now on his last trip back to the 'Smoke' before signing the book and taking his place in the Link. He was a very welcome addition for the long run home, and Bert explained the position to him knowing full well that his fellow driver would get stuck in, should the need arise.

The short run to Newport was made without any trouble, but that was just a lull before the coming storm. They had hardly come to a stand at the end of the platform before another member of Old Oak Common shed climbed aboard, in the form of Locomotive Inspector George Price. He was an old friend to both Bert and Fred, as they had gone through the mill from cleaner to driver together. Bert thought that he had joined them for the ride home and to check out the young fireman who, with good reason, looked scared stiff. He was working under the eyes of two senior drivers and now an inspector, but his fears were groundless. George Price had not come to see him at work. It was the two 'Royals' they were tacking on to the 'back end' that George was concerned about.

Bert was dumbfounded, as any Royal train working was unheard of without the driver and fireman being specially picked, and with a locomotive in first class order. Somewhere there had been a slip up, but the two Royal coaches were there, and the Great Western had to get them home.

George wanted Bert to have a 'banker' as far as Badminton, but as he explained, he had just his full load and no way would he suffer the indignity of having a tow, even if the engine was rough and fired by a young lad. Bert had plans up his sleeve, cemented by the arrival of Fred Nash back at Newport. Poor old George Price was not happy about this situation at all but little did he know what was in store for later.

It was Bert's habit, when with his regular fireman, to do at least 60 miles of firing each day. It was a two-fold arrangement and one that endeared him to all of his firemen mates: it gave the fireman a rest, and a taste of driving a big passenger engine whilst Bert also kept his hand in with the shovel, and as he explained to me, it kept him fit. For a man in his sixties that was a bit of an understatement, as Bert was as fit as any of his firemen.

He asked very politely if George would stand up in the fireman's corner out of the way, to enable Fred to learn the road by driving. Fred was pleased about this. Then Bert showed the compassion he was known for, dropping down the tip-up seat and told his young fireman to sit down and watch.

With the signal 'Right away' from the Newport stationmaster, watched by four platform inspectors, three station foremen, numerous porters and the ladies who cleaned out the female powder rooms, Fred took *Farleigh Castle* out of the station and over the river bridge. As they passed Maindee East Junction, Bert put on the exhaust injector, pulled the pricker out of the rack and began to stir up the fire. They were passing Llanwern before he was satisfied that he had a good enough bed to build upon. They were now committed for better or for worse, non-stop to Paddington, for with Royals on the back there would be no distant signal checks to help recovery should they run into trouble.

He began to fire her with all the experience that went back to the days of the 'Eight foot Singles'. First of all working on the back corners of the firebox, ramming it in with the shovel then building up under the firebox doors. He then put four good shovelfuls down to each front corner, six down the front end, six more straight down the middle, and now the hump of the 'haycock' fire began to take shape. This exercise continued, front, middle, back, until she stuck her nose down the incline into the Severn Tunnel.

Fred eased the regulator, tapping it down to the jockey valve. The water came down to half a glass, so Bert shut off the exhaust injector and gave her the live steam one to keep her from blowing off. They swooped down into the blackness, swallowing to ease the air pressure. The dank musty smell mingled with smoke, so familiar inside the Severn Tunnel, drifted back into the cab. Bert was having a breather, there was no point in firing now, as she was far too rough to ride on and she would only settle down when she was pulling.

The double white lights flashed by indicating they were at the bottom of the tunnel. She then began to lift her nose, Bert stuck his thumb up, Fred nodded and opened her out and as the weight of the train caught her she settled down, beating strongly, the blast bouncing off the tunnel roof as she bit into the climb out. The firing began now with serious deliberation, up over the 'haycock' hump, front corners and down the middle. The brick arch was white hot with the gases whipping up over and through the tubes, the rich steam and smoke mixture filling the cab and being sucked back into the firebox. Each time the flap was dropped, the cab, the tender and first coach, were lit up sharply with a fierce golden flash, which reflected and was then thrown back from the dripping tunnel walls, and just as sharply shut off as the flap was raised.

They burst strongly out of the tunnel with the water level well up in the glass, and the steam pressure steady at 200 lb. Bert was able to shut down the blower, then open it up to a quarter of a turn, the chimney roaring away as they held the speed on the short section past Pilning. They then began the long climb up to Patchway, through the short tunnel, hammering away, with the blast threatening to tear the bricks out of the roof.

The dust began to fly as Bert came to some 'duff coal'. Within minutes they were all black and in his eagerness to please, the young fireman flew off the seat and began tearing into the coal with the coal pick, pulling it forward, breaking it, and passing it through his straddled legs so that Bert could shovel it in.

At Coalpit Heath the speed began to drop, then held at a steady lower pace as Fred dropped the lever down. At Chipping Sodbury they were dropping two minutes, but had enough speed to top up the water on the troughs. Then on through the long Sodbury tunnel until Badminton came into sight. Three minutes down now, but that awful drag up from the Severn was miles behind them.

As they came up to the station, Bert handed over the shovel to his laddie and told him to keep the fire just as it was. Two shovelfuls in each front corner, two more up the front, and six down the middle. He was to keep the back corners packed tight, making sixteen shovelfuls in all into that firebox. He could then hang out of the cab for a breather, long enough to count up to twelve, ready to start a round of the firebox again, feeding her as much as she would take. There was no danger of 'blacking in' that fire with fourteen thirty-five tonners on the back.

Fred gave up the regulator and stood behind Bert and watched. He had heard stories about Bert Edmonds and hard running, so there was now a chance to see this in practice. He knew that there were three minutes to make up, but, what he didn't know, and neither did George Price, was that Bert intended to make up another six minutes once he was back to normal running time. This was why he had built up such a fire and had emphasised to his fireman the importance of keeping it that way.

To Fred's surprise, Bert left the engine set as she was. She was running well and there was plenty of time to start her racing later on. Through Hullavington they had gained a minute, and although the climb up to Wootton Bassett and the restriction round the curve knocked some of the pace out of her, they made up another minute passing Rushey Platt. Bert eased down through Swindon but still retained the two minutes. Passing Highworth Box he opened her up again and began winding the lever back a notch at a time, feeling for her to respond, which she did. At Marston crossing that lost minute was found, and they were on time. George Price checked his watch and gave the 'thumbs up' to Bert. The young fireman began 'to enjoy himself, the fire was perfect, he had plenty of water in the boiler, and the pressure gauge was hovering at blowing off point. *Farleigh Castle* now began to fly as she had been designed to, racing across the Wiltshire Plain with the bit between her teeth.

They shot through Shrivenham like a flash, the cylinder pressure valve slapping like a machine gun with the first of Bert's six minutes in his pocket. His fireman packed in coal as he had been shown, and Fred in the well of the tender pulled the coal forward. As they roared through Uffington, Fred signalled to the lad to sit down, while he had a go at firing her. He was completely caught up in the excitement of what was going on.

Another minute was gained through Challow and the third passing Steventon. George, up in the corner, was pleased. They were passing out of the Bristol Division into the London Division, and his report on the running of a 'Royal' would be a feather in the cap for Old Oak Common.

It was only when George realised that the usual four minutes between Steventon and Foxhall Junction had been cut to three that he began to know that something was up. They were running only just short of the 'Bristolian' timing, and shouted across the cab to Bert just as he pulled the whistle cord, as they approached Didcot. They hammered through the station, leaving porters clutching at their caps, drowning the station announcer on the tannoy, and setting the platform signs swinging and dancing as the displaced air rushed back in, with a cloud of dust.

Five minutes up as they passed Cholsey, George thought it about time to make a comment. He staggered across the bucking footplate and placing his mouth against Bert's ear, he shouted, above the racket, that he knew that one member of the 'Royals' would enjoy 100 m.p.h. running with a steam engine, but that the 'Royal' that counted might not be so pleased. Bert grinned and eased the regulator down just to please him, for he knew that the odd minute he wanted would come. It did so as they swept through Goring and Streatley, as he could now afford to let her run as she was. He sat on the seat, swaying with the movement of the engine, and sucking away at his old pipe, knowing full well that George Price was muttering away up in the corner, wondering how they were going to lose six minutes with the road clear right into Paddington. When this run was over there would be some hard words on that footplate.

On up through the green sweep of Sonning Cutting they went and over Maidenhead bridge. Quickly sliding through Taplow and Burnham, they met the sweet sickly smells from the lineside factories of Slough, West Drayton, Hayes and Harlington. The fireman could sit down now, his work was over. A long pull was given on the whistle chain as they tore through the bridge and burst on the station at Southall. Bert was then rewarded with the sight he had been waiting for back at Newport, Hanwell distant signal at caution.

George stared with disbelief at that yellow light rushing towards them, as Bert shut off, and began giving *Farleigh Castle* short sharp bursts of the vacuum brake. The cab filled with the acrid aroma of hot brake blocks. As the blocks bit in, the speed dropped off sharply and as they came up to the viaducts, the reason for it all became clear. A big round sign at the lineside reading '15'.

They rumbled over, then Bert picked her up again making her bark her way through Hanwell, settling her down with a few winds on the lever. They marched on through Ealing Broadway and Acton, past Old Oak Common, then drifted under the bridge at Westbourne Park and rolled into Paddington, sedately coming to a stop with a final shot on the vacuum brake two yards away from those big shining stop blocks. The clock on the station wall gave a jerk with the hand bang on time.

For some moments that cab was completely quiet, broken only by the singing of the injector. George, Fred and the fireman were all stunned, but Bert sat there on his seat grinning like a Cheshire cat.

George came over and placed a hand on Bert's shoulder. Then he thanked him, admitting that he had completely forgotten all about that speed check at Hanwell, and without that high speed running, planned and worked for so many miles behind them, they would have been late with a 'Royal'.

A call from the platform from a well-modulated voice made them turn round and look down, and there looking up into the cab was a tall gentleman dressed in the uniform of an Admiral of the Fleet. A bevy of less gold braid stood hovering with uncertainty behind him. He enquired as to which one of the four was the driver. Bert stood up and admitted that he was, and a clean white hand shot out from under a white cuff, and all that gold ringed uniformed sleeve, and firmly grasped Bert's grimy hand. He was congratulated for such a fine run and arriving 'on time'. It was then that Bert showed what compassion was all about, with a gesture typical of him. He brought his young fireman forward and said that this was the chap to be congratulated because, without his enthusiasm and hard work with the shovel, there would not have been enough steam to make such a fine run.

That laddie went home bursting with pride. His introduction to the 'Castle' class had not been a happy one to start with, coming as he did from the sedate pace and demands of a local working. That bucketing, swaying cab with its roaring fire and high speed running had been almost too much for him, but with Bert's tuition he had now had a taste of the 'runners' with one of the great men in Old Oak Common's Top Link, the gentle, understanding man, Bert Edmonds. The future held no terrors for that young fireman.

Royal Train working was of course nothing new to Bert. He shared this duty for many years with his old friend, driver Albert Potter. They had shared the same starting date together and would eventually share the same presentation dinner given by their Old Oak Common colleagues in their honour, when it became time for them both to retire. But Royal Train working, or the experience necessary for this, had started years before when they became firemen, in Bert's case, at Oxford.

A large number of the Old Oak Top Link men came from the country sheds, far removed from the sound of Bow Bells. They were more at home with the snort of a cow or the rough cough of a sheep, breaking the silence of the 2.00 a.m. walk to the shed. But surprising as it may seem, those country lads through a large number of different circumstances, found their true vocation in running the famous express trains on the premier routes of the Great Western.

Bert was no exception, as from the gentle branch trains to Fairford, Woodstock and Abingdon, he progressed on to the 'Singles', running to Worcester and Paddington. On these 'Singles' he worked with drivers such as Bill Soden, a big tough man who was as much at home in the ring, boxing the young University gentlemen, as he was on the footplate. Another was 'Cockney' Alf, his surname now forgotten, who differed from Bert, coming the other way to settle down in Oxford. When the 'Cities' took over from the 'Singles', Bert was firing to Frank Gleed, running trains at a speed he would become used to in later years.

A move now came, not to Old Oak, but to Cardiff Canton. Bert therefore moved his family and settled down in a little house on the outskirts of Cardiff at Ely. By good fortune his seniority brought him as a fireman on the 'runners', and it was during this period his vast knowledge of the road was built up. He already knew the road between Worcester, Hereford, Birmingham and Wolverhampton to Paddington, and as far west as Swindon. He was now firing to Swansea, Carmarthen and Fishguard to the west, Hereford and Shrewsbury to the north, and Bristol, Weston, and Taunton to the south. With the added bonus of the 'Castles' coming into service to complement the 'twenty-nines' and 'forties', it was a very exciting time, although at the time he would not have termed the run to Fishguard and back as such.

He was sent to Swindon in 1930 for the driver's examination, and on passing, found that he was to fill a vacancy at Canton shed. He "crossed the footplate" and took over the regulator with some degree of thankfulness, but it was short lived. The excitement of the main line gave way to the Dock and Yard Pilots. The only relief from shunting up and down was a move up into the Valley link where Bert found that the "screw" or "pole lever" was there to go forward and back. The linking up of the valve gear was unheard of, simply because the gradients up into the Valleys did not allow it.

Railway footplate work in the Valleys was far removed from the main line, so far removed it was in a different world. Leaving Cardiff it was a case of blasting a way up to Tonypandy with the coal empties, shunting them to one side at the pit head, then starting the awful journey back down. This was a well-planned operation from the start, and it had to be if the train was going to join the main line at Llantrisant, all in one piece. It was so easy to blow the code on the whistle for the signalman to set the points into the mile long sand trap, and hope to stop a run-away. The job of parting the train into many small portions to drag it out again for reforming was a long tedious operation, and the subject of an enquiry, so the planning to stop at Llantrisant began miles back at Tonypandy.

It started with the first move, moving the train out of the colliery yard at walking pace, never allowing the speed to build up. There would be two shunters, one on each side of the train, pinning down the wagon brakes using a brake stick to engage the handle, then with the weight of their body, they would bear down hard and engage the pin in the ratchet. This would go on all down the train, the engine working flat out against the weight of the train and the retarding effect of the brakes, until the driver was satisfied by the 'feel', that he had enough brakes down to hold them. A code sent on the whistle would then signal to the shunters, and from then on, they were on their own.

This was not a train movement for the timid driver, so Bert was glad of the foresight of the Cardiff shed foreman. For the first few days, he would allocate an experienced Valley fireman with a driver from the 'flat', just as the foreman at Old Oak would take care of an ex-Valley driver on the 'runners'. It was an arrangement not covered in any rule book, just a common sense understanding of railway working.

Bert took his time on that first trip, but even he was not prepared for the monumental weight that pushed him down the Valley. They rattled down through the little stations, blotting out everything behind the first wagon with a cloud of coal dust. Apart from the initial start, the regulator had been closed all the way, but he had made it safely thanks to his fireman's knowledge of working the handbrake. Bert had been lucky, it was a dry day, and Wales is renowned for rain. If the wheels had picked up on the locomotive there would have been a disaster. The Welsh engines were in tip-top condition with their sand boxes, and they worked. The ballast all the way down was covered with sand, so the occasions on which the trap was used were few and far between.

In later years, when Bert passed a coal train plugging away up to Badminton on the main line, he would remember that to get there, someone had brought it down the valley, and he would mentally take his hat off in recognition of a duty as exacting as running a fast train.

Passenger working was again a different world. There were no short sharp bursts between stations with enough mileage to link up the valve gear and enjoy a little run, and no water troughs to top up the tank, so it was the practice never to pass a water column. There was one trip that was almost a merry-go-round, leaving Cardiff and up to Caerphilly, round the corner to Pontllanfraith, on to Crumlin High Level, across the high spindly bridge spanning the Western Valley Line, and into Pontypool, returning to Newport. With Valley stations in some instances within sight of one another, and restrictions as low as 5 m.p.h. due to colliery subsidence, the little gallop to Cardiff was welcomed. After hammering the tank engines for an hour and a half, they had been working with the regulator open just long enough to shut it again. With margins so tight, Bert used to wonder how they ever kept time.

When the time came for Bert to move up into the next Link, it brought welcome relief, for it was back to the main line for most of the time. The jobs involved working freight trains to Neath and Swansea, 'vacuum' trains through to Fishguard, and local passengers into Bristol. The vast network of the Valleys was now under his hat along with all the main line knowledge, and yet he never gave it a thought. The shed foreman did when he checked the road book, as apart from the West of England, the routes that Bert had signed for read like a dictionary.

Bert was one of those rare gentlemen who never knew when to say 'no'. To have a driver on the strength with that route availability was the answer to a foreman's prayer. This particularly was the case with the summer excursions, for the Welsh have a longing to visit London, and with most of Canton's Top Link men committed to the regular service, Bert was pressed into main line running at last.

It was a period that was to prove valuable in later years, but this main line running with excursions and extra parts of the booked trains was done not with the benefit of the prime stud of Canton's locomotive power. For they, like their drivers, were already booked out as part of the Top Link working. Bert had to make do with the 'forties' and 'twenty-nines', but this was not as bad as it would at first seem. At this time in the early thirties, locomotives were kept in tip-top condition and burning the best steam coal available. After all, the Marine colliery was only a few miles away in the Western valley.

He took to the four cylindered 'forties' as a duck takes to water, preferring them to the 'Saints'. Although they were a very strong engine and would run, they were inclined to roll a bit at speed, but perhaps it was the speed he expected from them. When I was firing I never had the chance to find out, and to my regret I never had the chance to fire to Bert, but I heard all about him and his fast running.

In due course after a good spell at Canton, Bert set sail for Old Oak Common. Settling the family down in Saxton Road at Acton, Bert began to add route knowledge to the already phenomenal store he had in his head. He worked all round London's suburbia, running the local passengers and goods. He remembers with affection one of the little pannier tanks used on these jobs, because it had the names and nick-names of all the 262 drivers scratched in the paintwork of the cab. The names he can remember are well worth mentioning because of the humour of the unknown sign-writer. Charlie Shave was 'Barber', Bob Goddard was 'The Vicar', Bert himself was 'Smiler', but the classic must go to Charlie Noller, known as 'Rice pudding Charlie'.

Humour was part and parcel of sheds and enginemen. There was a period when the foreman decided to have a purge on departure times from Old Oak, insisting that all engines leaving the shed must be timed and the name of the driver given to the signalman. It was a failure from the start, as every engine leaving after 6.00 a.m. was driven by driver Charlie Hutchings, so that when 8.00 a.m. came round and fifty-odd engines had left the shed the inevitable happened — as all the previous drivers knew it would — the real Charlie Hutchings came along. It was only after a telephone call to the shed and an irate foreman had come to identify Charlie, that the exasperated signalman allowed him to leave the shed, with the promise from the foreman that name taking had come to an end.

Bert moved on up through the links, running goods and passengers. With the war now upon us he had the worries shared by most drivers. Long hours spent on trains, his children away in the Services, and his dear wife Annie alone in the house during all the bombing. But thank goodness they all came through unscathed although there were some close shaves, and when it was over Bert found himself working the vacuum fitted trains down to the West Country. The working again kept him away from home because all these jobs involved an overnight stay, 'double home' as it was termed, but he enjoyed the runs.

The 11.40 p.m. from Paddington Goods was a particular favourite. They left Paddington, called in at Old Oak yard, then ran non-stop to Tiverton Junction, where they put off a dozen box vans for the Duchess of Cornwall Creamery. The next stop was Newton Abbot where they booked off.

The locomotives used on these workings were always one of the big 'forty-seven' class, and Bert enjoyed running them as they should be run. He said that they 'wouldn't half roll' down the other side of Savernake, and they would scoff the coal, but his firemen didn't mind. Bert never thrashed an engine unless it was necessary, and he always took a turn on the shovel.

Bert came into the Top Link just about the time that the wartime speed restrictions were being lifted and at last he got his hands on the 'Kings'. It was with this locomotive that some passengers who made regular runs behind them began to take notice and start timing, for the combination of Bert Edmonds and a 'King' was a formidable one. When I pressed him as to which 'King' was his favourite he was quick to remember. No. 6014 *King Henry VII* was a marvellous engine, No. 6026 *King John* was in a class of its own, but pride of place went to No. 6000 *King George V*. Bert made no bones about it, his footplate at Paddington was a 'Mecca' for small boys when he had the 'George'. He was fortunate in having the finest firemen at Old Oak, for as he said, he couldn't have made those fine runs without them. They were so good that 20 years afterwards he could recall some of their names with affection. There was Dick Bedford, Vic Smith, Tom Ward, Tom Pitt, Danny Tobin, and, when he could pinch him off his old mate driver Albert Potter, he would enjoy the company of Jack Peedell.

It was while he was with Danny Tobin that Bert started a leg-pull that went a bit further than he had intended. It did no harm but it caused some serious heart searching by quite a few senior drivers, not only at Old Oak Common, but all over the Great Western Railway.

For a long time a rumour had been floating about the sheds that drivers would have to pass an examination on the operating rules again. This was an examination taken only by the firemen going to Swindon to pass out as drivers, which meant that they could be called upon to carry out driving duties while still being employed as firemen. They would undergo a further examination to pass out as fully qualified drivers, and that would be the end of it throughout their careers. The very idea that senior drivers would have to pass again after so many years was unthinkable. The only time that they went to Swindon after this was to pass a medical on reaching the age of sixty and then on each subsequent year until they retired at sixty-five.

This medical examination was brought in during 1951, and it so happened that Bert became the first man to go. He went to work that day in his best suit, booking on in the shed just the same as if it were a duty. It was in fact classed as such. He collected his pass and caught the empty coaches up to Paddington. There he had a cup of tea in the canteen where he received a lot of leg pulling from the youngsters about the 'old folk' and good wishes from them all. But each man was with him, for it was not unknown for senior drivers to come off the footplate through ill health. Bert had no worries over that score, as far as he knew, but doctors are likened to vets, they are a queer lot and he did have that row of bullet holes up his leg, a legacy from World War One.

Bert caught the train and settled down for the ride to Swindon. Now and again he pulled out his watch to check the running times until he remembered that this was a bad habit, only practised by the retired section sitting on park benches, all the way from London to Plymouth. When he arrived at Swindon he walked down the road to the Park Road headquarters, musing over the thought that the twenty odd years since he had last come this way seemed only a few years ago.

Bert sailed through that medical as he was to do each year until he retired. He caught the train home in high spirits, and it was while he was in this mood the seeds were sown. 'Old folk' indeed — he would give them something to think about, and that was an understatement.

Walking down to the shed, he met a driver who quite naturally asked him how he had got on at Swindon. Bert replied that he had passed the medical without any trouble, but that the operating rules had made him scratch his head. Having dropped this bit of information into the hands of a bloke he knew would make the most of it, he quietly booked off and slid home.

Bert's next duty was on a Sunday morning two days after the Swindon visit. He walked into Old Oak shed with Danny Tobin all ready to prepare No. 5066 *Sir Felix Pole* for an excursion to Gloucester. Old Oak shed even on a Sunday was a busy place, but the first thing they noticed was the lack of activity and one driver was obviously waiting for them. He was Bert Collins, the chap who ran the Mutual Improvement Classes on operating rules and locomotive failures, (for the benefit of firemen aspiring to pass the examinations for promotion to driver) and he knew Bert for the leg-puller that he was.

He asked the same question that the other driver had asked two days previously, how Bert got on at Swindon? Bert replied, leaving out the bit about being the first to be taken on the rules. Bert Collins was not satisfied and pressed a bit harder and wheedled out of Bert that perhaps he had mentioned to someone a little snippet about rule examinations. That explained the quiet shed, for Bert Collins had completely sold out of every kind of rule book and engine book that he had in stock. He said that if driver Bert Edmonds was to look inside the engineman's cabin, he would find at least thirty drivers and senior firemen, all sitting in a row with their heads in their hands, poring over the rule books laid on the table in front of them.

Bert decided to move with discretion. He got Danny to go to the locker and obtain his preparation overalls, but told him not to breathe a word that he was in the shed. He changed on the footplate while Danny went to the stores for the oil, then Bert slipped underneath *Sir Felix Pole* and oiled the inside motion. Danny worked hard to raise enough steam to move her, then they crept outside and found a quieter spot where Bert could finish his oiling. For once Bert did not go to the cabin for a wash, he cleaned up in a bucket on the footplate, then as soon as they were ready they slipped out of Old Oak shed and up to Paddington.

Bert breathed a big sigh of relief. It would be getting dark when they returned so he could dodge the odd driver, and the next day he was on the

'Limited' so he would leave from Paddington and not be back until late Tuesday afternoon. By then it would have all blown over. They ran *Sir Felix Pole* and her train full of W.I. ladies to Gloucester enjoying the super run with a light load. On arrival they shunted the coaches into the sidings and dropped onto the shed, their work completed until the return run in the afternoon.

Danny had run the fire down so he dropped the dampers, filled up the boiler so that she would stand for a few hours without any attention, then they went to the cabin for a wash and a cup of tea. Here they expected a quiet chat with the Gloucester lads, but those lads had no time for a chat, they were all busy studying the rule book. Bert beat a hasty retreat to *Sir Felix Pole* whilst Danny made the tea, and there he stopped for his break. He then spent the rest of the afternoon sitting on a park bench well away from drivers who might ask awkward questions.

The oiling of *Sir Felix Pole* ready for the return was made with the same stealth as at Old Oak. Danny curled up with laughter at Bert creeping round with an oil feeder in his hand, lowering his head at the sight of any person dressed in overalls. He had no sympathy for Bert. One of his leg-pulls had backfired. Once on the road and heading for home, Bert brightened up and began to sing, as the immediate danger was over. Danny was driving and Bert was enjoying himself on the shovel. He had it all worked out, as they were dropping on to the ash road at Old Oak, Danny could put *Sir Felix Pole* to bed, and he would creep off and catch the Underground to Acton, and that was how he got away with it.

Monday came round and they both set off for the West with the 'Limited', hauled by No. 6026 *King John* with the usual full load. They made a fine sight in the sunshine as they swept round the curve at Reading Main Line West Junction, canting over against the curve, but running smoothly so as not to tip the soup into the laps of the diners in the restaurant car. Bert had a good reputation with the waiters, they could serve soup without any trouble when he was driving. He waved to his brother-in-law Bill Gasson who was down in the yard of Reading shed, waiting for him to go by. He expected a cheery wave in reply but instead caught sight of a clenched fist waving at him. Bert felt a little sad. What had he done to upset old Bill? Danny was leaning over his shoulder, one hand on the water scoop handle, grinning like a cat. He knew Reading had heard about rule examinations. Bert sniffed and stuffed his old pipe full, the further he left Old Oak behind the further he left the trouble.

Easing down at Newbury for a speed restriction, he rolled through at 20 m.p.h. looking out for me and my old dad on the Winchester passenger standing in the bay. We were waiting for him, and both of us held a rule book high in our hands, and the naughty code known to all enginemen was blown on the whistle. Bert replied with the two finger salute while Danny had both his hands round Bert's throat as if to strangle him. Danny still had that wide grin on his face, it was a situation he was enjoying immensely. The number one Top Link Driver at Old Oak was a fugitive, but Bert was not one to give up. The whistle code was returned, then he opened up *King John* marching her up towards Enborne Junction with the bit between her teeth. Surely, he thought, he would be safe from the Great Western jungle drums in Plymouth.

They ran into Plymouth North Road on time as usual with Bert. In his eyes a speed restriction way back at Newbury was no excuse to run in late. When they arrived in the shed they again noticed the lack of drivers and firemen. In the cabin they found the now familiar sight of enginemen deep in study, rule books in front of each one.

Danny decided to risk a question. Why were rule books now the centre of such interest? The reply he received rocked poor old Bert back on his heels. Surely they'd heard, some unfortunate driver had been the first to go to Swindon under the new arrangements. He had passed the medical all right but he had failed on the rules, so they had taken him off the footplate and put a broom in his hand and now the poor old chap was pushing that broom up and down in the pits.

All of this came out with such conviction it must have been true and the local Union representative was going to bring it up at the meeting on Sunday morning. Bert made the usual noises in agreement, in fact he almost believed it himself. When he looked round for Danny's support he found him missing. Danny was outside, had he remained, he would have given the game away by laughing. Bert began to worry a bit now, a simple remark to one man back at Old Oak had swept right through the Great Western locomotive world, and he could not stop it, but neither could he admit to starting it.

Danny had the answer, for once he was in a position to be able to advise Bert how to go on. His advice was to keep quiet and act naturally, and hope and pray that Bert Collins would keep his mouth shut. Bill Gasson at Reading would keep his mouth shut, and Harold Gasson senior and Harold Gasson junior at Didcot would also, but Danny, Bert could rely on, as he was his mate. But as Danny explained, it was a big burden to carry, and he would consider it over a few jars always providing that Bert paid.

As rumours begin so they end, and this one was no exception. Within a few weeks another driver was sent to Swindon and he found that the medical was the only examination he had to pass. Bert was once again able to walk into the shed with his head held high as befits a Top Link driver. This yarn has remained a secret until now, 28 years later.

As each year went by, Bert continued to pass his medical. He loved every minute on the 'runners', sweeping along the sea wall at Dawlish, waving to the kids on the path and pressing himself up in the cab during the winter when the sea came crashing over the engine. There was the hard run to Wolverhampton with its tight timings which was part and parcel of the route, and hammering up through Saunderton Tunnel or sweeping down through Bicester with the pressure valves spanking away, and miles and miles of straight fast running down to Gerrards Cross. He loved that bit of railway because 'they wouldn't half "tank" along' by which he meant, that they were going as fast as he dare let them.

But one day it had to come to an end, and with it a record that would be hard to beat. Bert had completed 44 years on the footplate without once being away sick or late on duty. His last day at work was 26 May 1956.

His last trip was with the Down 'Limited', returning the next day with the 10.0 a.m. from Penzance. Such was his standing at Old Oak that when he arrived to book on for the last time, the foreman offered him a choice of four 'Castles' from which to choose. They were lined up ready, the night shift cleaners had polished them all up, and the young day shift lads were waiting for him to choose before they gave that locomotive the final shine. He could choose from No. 5040 *Stokesay Castle*, No. 5066 *Sir Felix Pole*, No. 5069 *Isambard Kingdom Brunel*, and No. 5055 *Earl of Eldon*.

Bert walked round them carefully, taking his time so as not to disappoint either the foreman, or any of the lads who had been so considerate. His fireman, Vic Smith, followed him. He had his own ideas as to which was the best 'Castle' as it was a long way to Plymouth and back. Bert told me that the choice was a very difficult decision to make. He had worked *Stokesay Castle* the week before and she was a good engine but she was becoming a rough rider. *Sir Felix Pole* was not so free steaming although she rode like a coach. *Isambard Kingdom Brunel* was the strongest 'Castle' he had handled and she was like an old friend, but *Earl of Eldon* was just about the best 'Castle' in the whole fleet at Old Oak. So Bert chose her much to the relief of Vic, who also preferred her.

Good news travels fast in railway circles, as well as bad news, but Bert was quite unprepared for the reception that was waiting for him at Paddington. The Station Master was there as indeed he would be on the return trip, and lined up on the platform waiting to shake his hand was the complete restaurant car staff.

Those Old Oak drivers using the canteen were on the footplate, and a horde of small boys were waiting to obtain the signature of one of the Royal Train drivers while there was still time. At last the shrill sound of whistles sounded down the platform and Bert opened the large ejector to boost the small one. There was a scramble to leave the footplate, and as the last lad climbed down, Bert gave a blast on the whistle, opened up the regulator, and for the very last time took the 'Limited' out of Paddington.

Earl of Eldon barked her way past Westbourne Park. From Paddington Departure box to Old Oak Common East and West boxes, the signalmen were waving from the windows. In Old Oak yard the shunting engines were pulling down both brake and train whistles. The foreman and Shed foreman had brought every member of the shed staff with them. Drivers, firemen, cleaners, boilersmiths, fitters, mates, firedroppers, and the lads from the coal stage, all lined up to see Bert take the 'Limited' out.

I think it was at that time that Bert realised that he was someone special. He had never before thought about it, but now he began to wish there were a few more years left. He linked the 'Earl' up, stuffed his old pipe full and settled down, slipping through Southall almost before he noticed. Then he remembered, the big diesels were coming in, and although Bert knew they would be clean to work on, he wanted nothing to do with them. The next generation, like his fireman Vic, could take care of them.

Bert eased down for the run round the curve at Reading. From old habit he looked down into the yard of Reading shed to see if Bill Gasson was about. He was there all right, and so was every member of the Reading staff that Bill could collect together. To a person outside railway circles it must have seemed as if the Royal Train was going through.

The jungle drums were still working as he ran through Newbury and again at every signal box window the lads were waving. Bert began to wish he was making his last run on the 'Bristolian' as he had to look out at every box in case he missed someone, so he talked Vic into taking over the driving while he had his fling on the shovel.

Earl of Eldon ran like a sewing machine. She must have known it was Bert's last Down trip. They ran into Plymouth dead on time, as it had been one of those perfect runs so well remembered.

The foreman was there to greet Bert and said that he had another 'Castle' for him to take back the next morning if Bert would like to. So he went with Vic to have a look at her. She was No. 5025 *Chirk Castle* and she was immaculate as only a 'Castle' can look when groomed to perfection.

Bert was deeply moved with this offer but he said as gently as he could that he would like to take *Earl of Eldon* home with him. She was taken over to the ash road where her fire was cleaned and her tender filled. While Bert and Vic were away for the night they coaled her with first grade coal, the tender was trimmed, the coal all broken up into nice size lumps for Vic to use, and the night turn cleaners shone her up, just as their opposite numbers at Old Oak had done the night before. When Bert and Vic came on duty that next morning she was all ready to take off the shed, and would have done credit to a 'Royal' train.

Their departure was a repetition of the day before. Every man and boy on the shed lined up to shake Bert's hand and wish him well, and when he backed on to his coaches in the station, the Press were there to record the moment. Had Bert known what was in store for him at Paddington, he would have swopped for a night duty to end his driving days. The Press at Plymouth was just a foretaste of what was waiting for him. Vic had an idea as he had been primed, but he was too good a mate to tell him, his dear old mate Bert was entitled to a good send off.

Bert took the 'Earl' out of Plymouth sighing with relief. It had been nice to receive the good wishes from his old mates, but he was a quiet, shy man, not used to having photos taken by the Press and having so many questions fired at him. He was pleased though that he had been promised copies of the papers, his dear Annie would be so thrilled.

The run home over the switchback road of the West Country was just as sweet as the run down had been. As the familiar countryside wound past Bert got to musing. They reached a section where they had run a tender box hot, and there was the spot where the wind had whipped his cap off. There was the place where *King George V* had nearly jumped the rails when a rail had broken. Bert began to feel a bit morbid, as it was the last trip, and never again would he feel the warmth of the regulator in his hand, and the strong heart beats of a 'Castle' or a 'King' pounding out through those four cylinders. He tapped Vic on the shoulder and beckoned him over to the right hand side, it was time he had his last fling on the shovel.

For an hour, Bert fired *Earl of Eldon* enjoying himself as a sixty five year old should never have been capable of doing. Bert might have reached retiring age in the eyes of the Railway, but in fact, he was fitter than a lot of forty year olds. Regular firing and using a spade in an enormous allotment had kept him that way.

That last run seemed almost too quick to be true as they swept off the curve at Reading West Main and up through the middle road. Twyford, Maidenhead, Taplow, Burnham and Slough slipped by. West Drayton, Southall and Ealing Broadway came rushing up towards them at such a speed, that Bert knew the moment was almost upon him, when he would have to shut that regulator. He took her through Acton still taking steam, then between Old Oak box and Westbourne Park the moment had to come or he would go right through Paddington and end up in Praed Street. Down it went, up with the clip, and the reverser was wound down. Bert was far too busy now to think of anything else, he had to reduce her speed. He made short sharp bursts on the vacuum brake, letting the pump restore the reservoir then more brake soon brought the speed down, filling the cab once more with the acrid smell of the hot brake blocks.

They ran past Ranelagh Bridge with its line of engines waiting to creep up to Paddington. Under the bridge, and rounding the curve and the criss-cross of crossovers with the wheels' flanges squealing in protest, they were soon gliding into the great cavern of Paddington with its honking taxi horns and the voice booming on the tannoy.

The vacuum brake went on, killing the last few turns of the wheels. Bert checked his pocket watch against the station clock and noticed, with satisfaction, that he had arrived half a minute before time. He looked back at the passengers spilling out, then turned towards the 'Lawn' to see a sight he had seen so many times before. British Movietone News people were gathered there with cameras and sound recording equipment together with BBC television. The sound engineers were running to keep up with the interviewer and cameramen, while a whole gaggle of newspapermen struggled to get past them.

Bert remarked to Vic that there must be a famous film star on board. This was a common sight at Paddington and Bert had seen them all, but as he turned towards Vic it was to see him sliding out of the cab and round the corner to stand on the framing. He was replaced by his old mate Albert Potter wearing a wide grin on his face, closely followed by the station master complete with his top hat. Following them came the Old Oak foremen and two loco running inspectors, Frank Wheeler and Charlie Darrel-Smith.

Albert Potter had run in on his last trip with the Up 'Swansea' some time before, and as he shook Bert's hand, it suddenly dawned on Bert that all this fuss was not for some glamorous young starlet, but for Albert Potter and himself. It was a reporter's delight, the two Great Western Royal Train drivers retiring, and both on the footplate together.

The situation on the footplate of *Earl of Eldon* had become impossible. Bert could not remember how it happened, but somehow he found himself on the platform with Vic on one side, and Albert Potter and his fireman Jack Peedell on the other. He was thrown to the wolves, as he later said, but the reporters were far from being the tough, hard men they were cracked up to be. They could see that both Albert and Bert were quiet, shy men, far more at home hustling the 'Bristolian' along at one hundred miles an hour, than facing them. So they treated them with consideration, and although both men were bemused with the flash bulbs going off and the microphones wagging back and forth between them, the skill of the reporting brought out everything that was required.

They found themselves in the coaches of the 'Limited' that Bert had brought up from the West Country, riding back to Old Oak. Bert hadn't been relieved and he worried about it, until Charlie Darrel-Smith assured him that he had arranged for a crew to take over. They had climbed quietly up on to the 'Earl' from the fireman's side while Bert and Vic were on the platform, so Bert settled down for the short ride back to Old Oak Common Shed.

It was some time before he could get away, there were so many 'goodbyes' to be said, and in any case, he would be back in the shed within a few days to clear out his locker. At last he was allowed to go, but there was just one more thing to do. He walked back up towards the ash road with his arm around Vic's shoulders, back to where he would find *Earl of Eldon*.

She stood there, quiet now, simmering gently, her boiler pressure down to a hundred pounds, at rest. In the setting sun the gloss of her deep Brunswick green paintwork showed the thin film of dust and flattened flies from her four hour run. A gentle trickle of water dribbled out of the injector waste pipe, splashing quietly on to the charred sleepers. Bert climbed up on to the footplate, crossed over to his seat of two hours ago, and sat down.

He was not normally a sentimental man where steam locomotives were concerned, but he had a fine feeling for a beautiful machine. He could sense its moods and match those feelings so as to obtain the very best in performance. It was a feeling shared by most of the Top Link drivers all over the Western, but there was no time for sentiment in the normal turmoil of running an express train. This visit back to the footplate was quite out of character for Bert, it was just something he had to do. He lit up his pipe and sat there quietly in the twilight for half an hour, puffing away as he listened to the gentle sounds of the 'Earl' settling down, thinking back over the years to when he began on an eight foot 'Single' at Oxford.

Vic sat on the other seat without speaking, for he felt that to disturb Bert now would have been sacrilege. He knew, too, that on the footplate of No. 5004 *Llanstephan Castle* standing behind them, Albert Potter was also sat there in the gloom. Two silent men buried deep in the memories of the past, each in his way making his peace with that part of his life that was over.

At last Bert got up, slid open the firebox doors and knocked out his pipe. He touched Vic on the shoulder, then he was gone.

I have never shown Bert any photographs of the massacre at Barry scrap yard. He knew it happened and it saddened him, but he felt much better when I told him that *Earl of Eldon* was not rusting away in a seaside scrap yard, covered in bird droppings and the playthings of countless children from the nearby holiday camp. She had gone home to Swindon where she was built, and had been dismantled on the 19 October 1964.

It pleased him to think that No. 6000 *King George V* had been saved, and that I had fired her, and that so many others had been saved from the cutter's torch. When I told him that No. 5051 *Earl Bathurst* was at Didcot and well on the way to main line running again, his reaction was one of unbounding enthusiasm. I can only hope that one day I can bring him to Didcot and once again place him on the footplate of a 'Castle'.

SIGNALLING DAYS

Introduction

With three books behind me I can now say with some authority that I enjoy writing, enjoy it enough to produce this fourth book, but only because of the many letters I receive from readers who write to me and ask 'When is the fourth book due out?'. Without those readers it would just not be worthwhile, so I say 'Thank you' for the encouragement that you have given me over the years, it *is* worthwhile to remember and to record those golden days of steam and signalmen, because that is what this book is all about.

'Firing Days', 'Footplate Days' and 'Nostalgic Days' are steam from beginning to end, but this book is a collection of reminiscences from my many years in the signal box together with some odd trips that I 'pinched' on the footplate.

Again I must thank my dear wife Betty for the unstinted help that she has given me with her valuable proof-reading, and the hours she has spent on her own while I bashed away on my old steam typewriter, and I thank my publisher, who has such faith in me, because without him there would be no 'Signalling Days'.

Harold Gasson,
1981

Chapter One
The Parting

The pale December sunshine struggled bravely to inject some warmth and life into the dried and shrivelled dead heads of the late summer roses, covered now with a sugar coating of hoar frost.

It was just before two in the afternoon on a Monday as I made my way down the road towards the loco shed, feeling plump and contented with one of mother's large dinners under my belt, her suet pudding lying just under my belt buckle, heavy and solid enough to last a growing lad until the time came to snatch a hurried sandwich at Ranelagh Bridge later on, for I was on my way to prepare 5935 *Norton Hall* to work the 3.45 p.m. to Paddington. I was early by half an hour, as my booking-on time was 2.30p.m. but with that dinner inside me I wanted a gentle preparation with time for that suet pudding to settle.

Noticing the hoar frost clinging to the lawns and privet hedges I realised gratefully that the cab would be a warm haven, for it had all the makings of a bitter cold evening. By the time we headed out of Didcot Station the sun would be spreading a crimson blanket over the horizon and the chill air would be beginning to bite, the oil thickening, the injectors on the point of hesitation as the water-feeds began to freeze, and the hands, alternating between heat and cold, would begin to split as the warm water softened the skin. Some firemen wore gloves to prevent this, and so did I when I had to lean out and catch single line tokens at speed, but for firing, it had to be bare hands, ever since the time when I lost the shovel in the firebox due to wearing gloves. After that, I put up with split thumbs and cracked knuckles, although the decision to handle buttons was something to ponder over and put off for as long as possible.

I walked into the Booking-On Hall and called out to Joe Hermon the Time Clerk that I was here for the 3.45 p.m. to Paddington, and he gave me the usual 'thumbs up', then he asked me to hold on for a moment. There was a shuffling round of various papers, then he produced a brown envelope and handed it to me; typed on the front was 'H. H. Gasson. Fireman. Registered No. 27297'.

Letters for firemen were almost unheard of; we sometimes received notes, usually to report to the Foreman, for a change of duty, but letters could be a posting to far-away places, and out of the question for a young fireman in love! Well, there was only one way to find out, I had better do it now before my hands became covered in coal dust. I began to sweat as I opened that envelope and started to read, then all at once things began to fall into place, and I recalled plans I had almost forgotten about.

This letter was to inform me that as from January 1st, my request for transfer from the Locomotive Department into the Traffic Department was to take effect, and that I was to report to the Reading School of Signalling for training at 8.0a.m.: a ticket was attached. There was a P.S. in the form of a warning, which stated that after the last turn of duty with the Locomotive Department all clothing and equipment from the said department must be returned to the stores, any items missing would be valued and that amount deducted from my wages. Some of my equipment was handed back of course, except for two gauge glasses (handy for stirring paint) and one new set of overalls and cap (which might come in handy one day, little did I know then that it would be at Hereford and on the Bluebell Line), and of course I did need the new jacket and overcoat. The rest was handed in and checked off and such is administration that I never did pay for those items I kept.

The prospect of receiving that letter had been tucked away in my mind for months, since it had been the previous March when I had applied for a transfer. I could have hung on and perhaps reached the driver's side of the footplate, because after all, that is what I had joined for, to drive a steam locomotive, but at the most, I would have had only a few years with steam locos being phased out as the diesels replaced them, and I had no inclination to spend the rest of my days driving those diesels. An additional spur to leave the footplate was the fact that so many other lads had gone before me, and had not regretted it.

At one time, once a man was accepted into the Locomotive Department it became his job for life, but the best years were now over, and the lads were leaving for better-paid jobs in pleasant environmental surroundings. Harwell R.A.F. Station had been handed over to the Atomic Energy Research people, and they welcomed ex-footplate men who could work without supervision, and alas the post-war boom had begun in the motor industry. Morris Motors and Pressed Steel at Cowley near Oxford were paying twice the amount that poor old British Railways Western Region could manage, and they too wanted good reliable men who could get up in the morning and do a fair day's work.

And they got them, good conscientious men who without exception soon rose from the shop floor to become supervisors. Much later, when I joined them in factory life, I too became a supervisor.

With this drain of good men footplate life went downhill fast, lack of maintenance soon eroded the advantages that had been gained after the Second World War. For the older men it was a case of sticking it out, and as for the younger men who stayed, they raised the last few years of steam to new heights, but I had decided regretfully that I would not hang on.

I had thought for a long time about what I could do; I could push a barrow on the platform, or hump sacks of wheat in the goods shed, but the eventual answer came from a neighbour, Jack Drew, who was a good friend and a good railwayman, when we were talking railways one day and he came up with the answer by inviting me to spend a couple of hours with him in Didcot North Junction signal box. Why not become a signalman, I thought! I had been in signal boxes many times to carry out Rule 55, all part of a fireman's duties, and on the whole they seemed a good lot of lads; boiling water for our tea can was never refused, and we paid by filling their coal bunker. There were of course the odd times when we were routed down a Goods loop which took the run out of a heavy freight train, and if it was a wet miserable day we were inclined to shout out that the box would benefit from a wire netting roof, but such insults were accepted in good spirit, and a signalman always replied with that most British salute of two fingers pointing skyways. On the whole, this signal box suggestion was worth looking into.

Then some weeks later and by a sheer fluke of luck the Shed Foreman forgot to book this young single lad for a Saturday duty, romance was out of the question because my young lady love was working, mother had no shopping for me to do, the 'old chap' had weeded the garden the day before, and the dog was asleep, so I was free, with time on my hands to squander, and off I went to Didcot North Junction. I slunk the long way round, through the goods yard, well out of the way of shed foremen and up the steps into the box. Jack was pleased to see me, for a signalman's life is a lonely one, and after the usual pleasantries, he began to explain the box workings. Bell signals were a complete jangle to me, although I could begin to follow through the frame by studying the diagram. Sequential locking had me beat completely, but not to worry, this was a visit simply to assess a type of railway working new to me, and by eight in the evening I knew I had been bitten by this signal bug: I loved it, at last I had found my niche in railway work outside the steam world, it was a job I knew I could get my teeth into.

As I left the box Jack pressed into my hand the signalman's 'Bible', the red book of signal box regulations, which was a condensed version from the Rules and Appendix with all the up-to-date amendments stuck inside. I took this book home and spent every spare minute reading through it. There was so much to learn, a lot of it of course overlapping the footplate rules, but still a tremendous amount to take in. Should I apply for a transfer, would I be making the right decision? I pondered over this for some weeks, meanwhile finding out that there were half a dozen of my old school mates in signal boxes scattered all over the district, now firmly entrenched, so visits were made, questions were asked, and once I was satisfied in my own mind beyond all doubt I took the plunge and applied for a transfer to the Traffic Department with the view of training for signal box duties.

The senior Shed Foreman, dear old Bill Young, was dismayed and held the application back for a few weeks while he tried to change my mind, for he had lost a lot of experienced firemen in the last few weeks. He got Bill Snow and Jack Jacobs, the two shift Foremen, to have a go at me, and the third Foreman, Ralph Painton (a shrewd move here because I had been Ralph's last fireman before he was promoted). Then Bill tried another tactic, he waited until my old Dad was booked as Shed Pilot driver, took me off my booked duty and put me as Shed Assisting, now he had us both together and available. My old Dad had tried of course, saying that things would get better, steam would not go and so on, but in his heart he knew it would never again be the same as it was in his early days, so while Bill tried every argument to get me to change my mind the answer was the same. I think in a way perhaps Bill pushed me into refusing to withdraw that application when he pointed out that all my years on the seniority ladder would be thrown away, my service would count, but I would start at the bottom again, graded as a Porter. Well, we would see, it was a signalman that I wanted to become, and a signalman I would be, even a small box would do, then after a couple of years I would go after promotion and make up the lost years. If I had known then what was in store within those few years I think I might well have backed out, because I went straight into a main line box and within three years I had moved up to Class One District Relief Signalman with a district of twenty-two boxes under my hat, but here I am going ahead of the story.

The application went forward, through the misty channels of administration to Paddington via Swindon, and I waited and waited, through the summer months and the autumn, and still my name appeared on the shed duty roster, so I gave up and made the best of it, thinking that my application had been quietly put to one side, and that I would make enquiries in the New Year.

So when I opened that letter my emotions were all mixed up: shock, surprise, sadness and elation. I stuffed the letter in my pocket, climbed up onto the footplate of *Norton Hall* and set about raising steam, wishing that the suet pudding did not feel quite so much like a brick every time I bent down. After spreading the fire all over the box, I began to make up the fire with the excess coal that had been spilled all over the floor boards, and by the time my Driver Bill Darby arrived I had the cab clean and his oil feeder filled and laid on the ejector to warm, a little thing to do, but appreciated by drivers, who in turn would inspect the ash pan when underneath and so save me a chore, which was all part of working together as a team.

As we drifted up to the shed signal ready to leave, the doubts began to rise in my mind: six days to go, only six more engines to work on, no more Didcot, Newbury, Winchester, Southampton, no more Banbury, Swindon, Honeybourne, Gloucester, no more steam and the open road, for I would be stuck in one spot. The doubts began to ferment but as I wiped the sweat from my forehead, other thoughts began to work; no more dirt, no more 1.00a.m. starts, no more wondering if I would finish in time to meet my young lady, and the fact that I was leaving a failing world for a new life. In the last nine months I had spent countless hours in various signal boxes and I knew that given the chance I could cope with that kind of work; well, now I *had* been given the chance, and this time next week I would be in up to my neck. There was no time for brooding, I had burnt my bridges, and *Norton Hall* would be in no fit state if I didn't get cracking. I had a lovely fire burning through, about two feet thick all over the box, with three-quarters of a glass of water and the boiler pressure on the point of blowing off; I put on the live steam injector and knocked her back to 180Ib, just long enough to keep her quiet in the station, because tannoys were not built to compete with Swindon safety valves blowing off. Then I began to fill up the back corners with the biggest lumps of coal I could find, knowing from experience that Bill drove in the Churchward manner, regulator up in the roof. We backed on to our ten coaches standing at number five platform and Bill eased up the pressure on the buffers so that I could lift the tender coupling over the coach hook, then I clamped together the vacuum and steam heating pipes, slid in the locking split pins, and returned to the footplate and opened up the valve to heat the coaches.

At 3.44p.m. the signals began to tumble off, one after another from the platform, over the Up relief, and up the Main Line. There was a shrill whistle from far down the platform, Bill yanked at the whistle chain sending a tall column of steam into the frosty air as *Norton Hall* responded, then up into the cab roof went the regulator, and *Norton Hall* marched out of the station.

As we clattered over the points I could hear the faint 'ting! ting!' on the block bell, a sound that I had heard many times, but now I knew what it meant, we were 'On Line' to Moreton. The shadowy figures moving high up inside the signal box at Didcot East Junction were signalmen, and soon I would be one of them. Once clear of the junction Bill began to wind the reverser back, two turns only, and *Norton Hall* eased her strident bellow and settled down to an angry barking. The fire was roaring away, my big lumps dancing in tune; as I fired her, there was no need to aim for the front of the firebox, for the coal was snatched off the shovel as soon as the tip of the blade reached the fire hole ring. Bill had a reputation for fast hard running, and a 'Hall' being worked this way with ten thirty-five tonners tied on behind could scoff coal at an alarming rate. I worked hard to Southall, then it was time to let her go, because I would get no thanks for coming into Paddington with the engine blowing off. It was not until we ran in that the sound of the Great Western Band playing carols on the Lawn reminded me that it was Christmas Eve, since that letter had completely taken my mind off the Festive Season.

As we waited for the Pilot to take away our coaches, the rasp of my shovel sounded almost indecent as I shovelled coal forward for the return journey.

We followed our coaches out, pausing only for the signal to be changed to allow us on to Ranelagh Bridge and the turntable. *Norton Hall* was quickly turned, we backed off the table, then while Bill squirted some oil round the motion I filled the tank, topping her up with a few hundred gallons of water. We now had half an hour to have a cup of tea and a sandwich, and to watch the world go by.

On the return trip, the 7.40p.m. out of Paddington was packed to capacity with last-minute shoppers and people going home for Christmas, and we were pulling twelve coaches, fast as far as Slough, then stopping at all stations. Those extra coaches made our engine rattle and vibrate, finding all the loose bolts holding the cab down, so it was a relief to run into Cholsey knowing that this was the last stop before going to shed, although we would not be spending Christmas at home like the passengers we had carried.

Bill and I studied the special duty roster when we had finished with *Norton Hall,* and thought 'what a come-down for a Christmas Day', as we discovered that tomorrow we had to go to Newbury. We both booked on that next morning at 11.00a.m. and prepared the old *Comet,* one of William Dean's old engines of 1899 vintage, but still going strong; she was in fact a powerful little engine, and one to be enjoyed, her only drawback for engine crews being the small cab, and the huge screw reverser that came so far back into the cab that the driver had to lean over the top of it.

We were off shed at 11.45a.m. and into the goods yard where we picked up twenty assorted wagons and a brake van, agreeing with our guard that there seemed no earthly reason for the good people of Newbury to need this train on Christmas Day, and as we punched our way over the branch we bemoaned our luck, the only consolation being a higher rate of pay for the day, and a day off in lieu at another time. However, when we shoved our little train into the yard at Newbury the reason for our trip became clear, the signalman knew what the return working was, a train of empty coaches in the bay platform which were needed at Didcot, and although we could have come over light engine to pick them up, bringing that goods train over meant that the early morning goods the next day which was double-headed with two Collett 'twenty-two's' was now reduced in loading, so that would be one engine and crew saved. Clever blokes, Shed Foremen! We ran down to Newbury Race Course and turned the little *Comet,* picked up the empty coaches and set sail for home, booking off at 3.30p.m. so it was a short turn and we still had part of Christmas Day left.

Boxing Day was another short turn, on duty at 1.30p.m. to relieve some Old Oak Common men with a Down stopper. They ran in ten minutes late with 5004 *Llanstephan Castle* leaking steam from every joint, being badly in need of a Swindon overhaul. We had to nurse her along, so for once Bill did not use full regulator, and she was steaming so poorly that I could only use the injector when Bill shut off for stations, but somehow Steventon, Wantage, Challow, Uffington and Shrivenham slipped by, and we were able to leave her on Swindon shed for a long-deserved rest.

The Foreman took kindly to us and told us to make our way home, so we caught the next Up train and were back home by five in the evening, both days having been messed about with short duties, a far cry from today's railway working, when the whole show shuts down. Friday brought a surprise when I arrived to prepare our engine for the 3.45 p.m. to Paddington. *Norton Hall* was at the rear of the shed waiting for attention from the fitters, then she would have a boiler washout, so, I had expected our other 'Hall' 6923 *Croxteth Hall* as that was the usual pattern, but instead, booked on the Duty Roster was 6973, a Churchward 'Mogul'.

I knew that she had been missing for a couple of months, and when a regular shed engine disappears it is usually because it has been lost in the pool of engines, and could be anywhere on the Great Western system, or might even have gone to Swindon for overhaul, and indeed this was the case, for I found her on number four road, gleaming with new paint.

I climbed up onto her footplate and just savoured her bright new cab; everything shone, the floorboards had been renewed and fitted tight, she even smelt right, all new and unsullied, a fireman's delight.

I had the fire burning up nicely and the new floorboards hosed off by the time Bill arrived, even he was excited about working on this new locomotive, although he was to change his mind before long. The first indication of difficulty came as we moved quietly up to the shed signal, her regulator was stiff, and it was a quiet departure, valves, piston, motions, axle boxes, all back to the original specification, with no wear anywhere, she rode like a Rolls, each rail joint sending up into the cab a distinct 'clunk, clunk'. We blew up over the points ready to set back on our coaches, then Bill placed his left foot up on the reversing quadrant foot support and heaved at the big lever. He got it halfway and dropped the clip down into the ratchet, his face turning red, and I had to give him a hand to place her into full reverse. Even I began to have doubts now, Bill was not a driver given to linking an engine back far anyway, what if we had full forward gear all the way? But I need not have worried, Bill was a canny bloke, and while I was busy coupling up, he was at work with the sight feed lubricator, so when I returned to the footplate those little oil blobs were going up the glass tube at a fair old rate.

We pulled away over the junction and up the Relief line, Bill shut off steam and together we linked her back just three notches, then Bill gave her half regulator, since he couldn't get any more. Then we began to fly, roaring through the two Moreton bridges like the 'Bristolian', and she rode like the coaches behind, straight and true, no dancing, jumping, or swaying, the red needle on the steam pressure gauge rock steady at 200lb, just, but not quite, at the blowing off stage.

I was enjoying myself now, this was a locomotive to appreciate, and I wished that they were all in this condition, what a pleasure it would have been to come to work. Leaving Cholsey, Bill was able to link her up himself as the extra oil reached her valves, then he adjusted the lubricator feed, cutting back the supply a little, and by the time we reached Reading she was much easier, and steaming so well I was able to allow her fire to go, in fact when we arrived at Paddington her firebox was down to the extent that I could see the fire bars.

The return trip with the 7.40p.m. was just as enjoyable, it was one of those trips, few and far between, where everything goes so perfectly it was a shame to come to the end of the duty, all that I could wish for now was to have the same engine tomorrow, my last ever trip as a Great Western fireman (there would be the odd occasion, all unofficial, but not as a registered fireman). When I booked off, there was a message for me, I was requested to come on duty the next day and report to the District Inspector's office on number five platform before coming to the shed. I wondered what this was all about, well, tomorrow would see.

Somewhere in the passing-on process the message had got a bit altered, for I found the District Inspector's office was on number four platform, but told myself to knock at the door and go in, as he probably wanted to welcome me into the Traffic Department and there was nothing to worry about. A gruff voice bade me to enter, and I walked in to be confronted by District Inspector Stacey, a big bluff man with a heavy white moustache, wearing Inspector's uniform with a peaked cap loaded round the edge with black braid. So, this was the big boss man in charge of all the signalmen and boxes in the district. I stood there, all dressed up to do battle with a locomotive in an hour's time, my 'Grimsby' box in my hand, and he just sat there, clean, smart, the very last word in authority, eyeing me up and down. He made me bridle with his remark as to why I should think that I was good enough to be considered as a budding signalman (the old rivalry between Traffic and Locomotive Departments again!), but before I could think of a suitable answer he asked me to sit down, as he could see that my feathers were ruffled.

The questions began; how long had I been a railway man, did I think a signalman's life was an easy one, what was it that made me dissatisfied with engine work, why did I want to be a signalman? To that last one I gave him an answer that seemed to please him, for I told him that I thought that to be a signalman was one of the most rewarding jobs on the railway, and after that I thought the interview was over, but as I made ready to go, he motioned me to remain seated. Then the serious business began, as Tom Stacey began to put me through the rule book as it applied to footplate work. For three-quarters of an hour I was bombarded with questions, each of which I answered as well as I could, then he got up and came round his desk, shook hands with me and welcomed me into the Department, with the passing remark that the Locomotive Department had provided the rough casting, and that his Department would put the polish on.

Tom gave me a letter addressed to a Mr. Blackhall in charge of the Signal School at Reading, a Free Pass valid for one month, and instructions to report there on Monday morning at 8.00a.m. So, I was over the first hurdle.

I made my way down the path to the shed and booked on duty for the last time, my feelings a mixture of sadness and elation, as I realised that this was the last locomotive to prepare, the last time off shed, and each time I picked up the shovel or put on the injector it was with a new perception. We had our new engine again, 6973, a fitting end to what I had once thought would be a career. When we ran in to Paddington and those big buffers loomed towards me for the last time, everything seemed to move at twice the speed as if the day and this final duty was in a hurry to be rid of me.

I enjoyed the run home, savouring every second, with no doubt in my mind now, just implanting in my memory the joys of locomotive work; Bill hammered away and I shovelled the coal in, knowing that I was soaking it all in to be stored away for another day, the experience of working on steam locomotives that could never be taken away.

When I climbed down from the footplate for the last time it was with a very deep feeling of regret. I handed in my overalls, even the pair I was wearing, with just a sideways glance at our engine on the ash road; I had burnt my bridges, it was all part of the past, tomorrow was Sunday, a day off, and Monday would bring another battle.

Chapter Two
Back to School

Monday morning found me boarding the 7.05 a.m. from Didcot, on a bitter cold day with snow on the ground. I was going to work, for the first time in many years, without overalls, and I even had a white shirt on. It was with a bit of a smirk on my face that I looked towards the engine, 5935 *Norton Hall* back in service again after her boiler washout - but someone else could shovel her to Paddington from now on. I heard her blow off running into Pangbourne, and I gave a sniff of disdain, but told myself 'forget it boyo, that is behind you now'. I walked down the platform at Reading without looking back, the sound of *Norton Hall* marching out keeping step with me, then round the corner into Caversham Road towards where I thought this Signal School ought to be.

I went through a gateway and into a yard full of every kind of signals imaginable: gantries, stop and distant signals, all laid down: there were piles of pulleys, coils of signal wire, and more loose semaphore arms, and at the far end of the yard a low blue brick building with a slate roof and four small dingy windows set back into the brickwork to allow room for the iron bars that protected the glass. It looked like a seedy run-down prison. There was one door into this building, painted in chocolate and cream about 1885 by the look of it, the paint being held in place by a cast iron plate which bore the words 'SIGNAL SCHOOL', and I recall thinking this was the most depressing place I had ever seen.

I knocked on the door and walked in, resplendent in my new footplate overcoat and jacket, both garments matching my flannels well. (Hand in all my uniform they had said last week, not likely, I wanted to have some railway uniform to start this job with just to show that I belonged, but it was to be my undoing in a moment.) Once inside I began to see that this building was something like a village hall, with a wooden floor, tables and chairs laid out in a row, and an old friend in the middle, one of the cast iron stoves supplied in enginemen's cabins, the whole place soaked in an atmosphere of decay and damp for the fire was out after the Christmas break. Six low-powered bulbs, suspended through the length of the room, were on, so somebody had been in, but as far as I was aware I was the first of the students to arrive. At the end of the room was a sight that drew me like a magnet, a two-inch gauge model railway about fifteen feet in length, with a junction, cross-over, four running roads and a 0-6-0 tender engine sitting in the middle. The whole lot was fixed up with signals and wires connected to a miniature frame with block bells and instruments at either end, so thinking that the loco might be powered I made a move to pick it up, when a sharp voice told me to leave things alone, and I looked round in the dismal light to see a small man emerge from a cubby-hole in the corner, wearing an overcoat, scarf, and stained once-grey trilby hat. I had come into contact with Freddie Blackhall, Assistant District Inspector, and the Tutor of Reading Signalling School.

I gave him the letter and stood still as he walked round me, eyeing up and down my footplate overcoat, then he said five words, 'I don't like footplate men'. I kept my mouth shut, as it was quite obvious that I was the enemy. I had met drivers like him who didn't like firemen, in fact some of them didn't even seem to like themselves, so I waited and waited, until at last he read the letter which must have confirmed his worst fears, that I was indeed a footplate man, then he instructed me to exercise all my skill in getting the stove alight.

I scouted round that snow-covered yard for some wood, found a drum of signal oil propped up on a trestle, and a pile of loco coal. Within half an hour the rest of the budding signalmen trainees had arrived and Freddie was glad enough to take off his overcoat, because I had certainly exercised all my skill on the fire, and the mixture of wood blocks, signal oil and loco coal had that old stove roaring like a 'Castle'. That first day was spent learning the rudiments of signalling and block working, Freddie ignoring me completely, which I found hard as I was used to the warmth and comradeship of the footplate, but it was a case of sticking it out and seeing what transpired. Looking back now I can see that it was a wise decision, and the situation was to change, but that first day certainly seemed a long one.

We finished at 6.00p.m. which allowed plenty of time to catch the 6.30p.m. from Reading, so I returned home fairly elated, for with the dinner break of three-quarters of an hour it gave a working week of 46¼ hours, so I was gaining an hour and three-quarters in each week and going home clean.

Nowadays, with a working day from eight to five, an hour for lunch plus morning and afternoon tea breaks, those old conditions seem ludicrous, yet at the time the new arrangement seemed wonderful to me, for there had been no set meal breaks or hours on the footplate. Tuesday came and the tension eased a little, Wednesday morning Freddie greeted me when I came in, Thursday was even better, he called me by my first name, but Friday was to clear the air once and for all.

When we arrived that morning Freddie had been busy, all our places had been set out with paper and pencil, for us to sit a simple examination. I wrote for an hour, answering each set question, then I laid down the pencil and sat back, while all around me a lot of whispering and pencil-chewing was going on. Freddie peered over the top of his glasses at me, and beckoned me to bring my papers to him, which I did and then returned to my desk. He began to read, going over each paper for a long time, until the rest of the lads had finished and it was time for the dinner break, and naturally the discussion between all of us was how we had answered those questions.

The rest of the afternoon was back to rules and regulations, not a word as to how this examination had gone, then when it was time to leave Freddie asked me to wait for him as he was coming back on the same train as me. Not a word was spoken as we walked to the station, but I waited for him to make the first move. Freddie was obviously pondering something that had him beat, and as we pulled away from Reading he told me that I had answered every question in that examination correctly, but how *could* an ex-footplate man acquire such a knowledge of the basics of signal box work? As he questioned me, he found that I had become so enthusiastic about this type of railway work that I had spent every minute I could spare over the last nine months in signal boxes. Of course he wanted to know which boxes, so I told him, then which signalmen, but he had to grin when I wouldn't tell him that, and said that no way was I going to land those chaps who had helped me in trouble for having an unauthorised person in the box. This last statement was appreciated by him, and he held his hand out and admitted that he had weighed me up all wrong and that he had started off on the wrong foot, and from that moment on, Freddie and I became friends. He told me that the course was a three month one, with visits to signal boxes playing an important part of the last month.

The second week fairly flew by. Freddie would set out the work and as soon as I had finished he would come and sit by my side pointing out various small slips until the other lads had finished. In the evenings on the train going home he would talk about incidents during his time as a signalman, and how he had dealt with various situations, and now he was passing on all his knowledge on to me.

During the third week things really began to happen. Freddie took me into his little office and put me through a mock oral examination such as a regular signalman would take each year. He must have been satisfied because he called me in again on the Thursday, and told me that he could teach me no more, and that I was to report to District Inspector Checkley on Monday morning.

The real surprise came with the next bit of information, that there were two vacancies, one at Kingsworthy on the Winchester branch which was a Class Five box, and one at Milton on the main line which was a Class Three box. I could reasonably expect to be successful with my application for the Kingsworthy job, which would mean lodging, or a fast sixty-minute run each way on my AJS motorcycle. I had found out from experience, that faint heart never won fair lady, and so I applied for both vacancies, with Milton as first choice.

Sunday was a day off, and I put the rule book to one side, being full up to the brim with it in any case. I collected my young lady from the Great

Western Hostel where she both worked and lived-in, and took her for a morning walk. The snow had gone, leaving everything wet and muddy although it was still bitterly cold. We walked for a couple of miles enjoying each other's company, my hands turning blue, not with cold, but from the dye in the woollen gloves which my young lady was wearing — ah, the passion of youth! When I took her back to the Hostel she informed me that I would not be seeing her any more that day as she had to wash her hair, a ritual all ladies go through which seems to last for hours.

Sunday afternoon in Didcot was scarcely a riot of activity. I could look at the ten shops, wish it was seven in the evening when the Coronet cinema opened, or I could get on the bike and go for a spin. There happened to be a motor cycle trial on at Aldsworth on top of the Berkshire Downs, so I set off to see if I could learn a few tips from the experts. They had 'observed sections', a familiar word, as I had been bashing 'sections' into my head for the last few weeks, but these sections were a little different, great patches of mud, around big rocks, and up banks of one in one. I stood at one mud patch and watched the Six Day Internationals go through. Fred Rist, on a BSA was first, straight through and no messing, then came Alan Jefferies, roaring through, with mud flying everywhere. My hero, Hugh Viney, was next, riding an AJS like the one I owned, so I positioned myself behind the section to watch his line through. He came along, lined up to a tree the other side of the section, the big single cylinder engine turning over with a slow steady 'plonk plonk' then he was through and away. There seemed nothing to it, it was just like taking a 'twenty-eight' up a bank, and after all I could do that. After the last rider had gone through, the Section Marshall allowed me to have a go. I lined up with that tree, put the bike in second gear, and in I went, 'plonk plonk' just the same as the expert, only I hit a rock in the middle that didn't seem to be there when *he* went through. The laughter from the spectators was genuine as they lifted the bike off me, and I rode home covered in mud, my beautiful black gleaming bike now a sorry mess, thinking, everyone to his own trade. It took me months to clean it all off, but, for a few hours my mind had been clear of block bells and signals.

Monday morning came, and I set off for the interview with Bill Checkley. I had never met him, but not many of the lads had, because during the three weeks that I had been at Reading, Tom Stacey had retired and Bill Checkley had taken over. When I first met him that morning, I didn't quite know what to make of him. He was a big, tall smart man, ex-Household Cavalry, still with the spit and polish about him. His bearing was very cold and clinical, and he came out with probing questions the sort one would have expected from a police inspector. Freddie must have briefed him about me, because he made no attempt to question me on the rules and regulations. He told me to report to Milton signal box under instruction, until he contacted me again, but he did emphasise strongly, that this did not have anything to do with my application for the vacancy at that box. I thanked him and left, and later when I got to know him better I found that he was a great chap, his hobby was growing roses and he was good enough at it for him to be an acknowledged expert.

Although I was told that this move was nothing to do with my application, I naturally had hopes, and there was one part of the overall picture that was in my favour, for no one had ever gone through the school at Reading in only three weeks, and certainly no one had started in a Class Three main line box. Now I had accomplished the first part, I would go all out to finish the second half, telling myself that there was a first time for everything. I would pull out all the stops, and if I didn't make it, it wouldn't be for want of trying.

I rode my bike down the footpath towards Foxhall Junction Signal Box, and as I drew near to the box, Bill Ackrill slid the rear window open, and wished me all the luck in the world. I had gone to school with both his sons, Frank and Bill. Frank had made a career in local council work, but Bill had come up through the ranks of engine cleaning and firing with me, and he was one of those who had left the service for a better job. So Bill in the signal box knew first hand of the change that I had made. The conversation was mostly leg-pulling, but Bill was pleased that I had managed this transfer, and, that I was going to be at Milton. He also pointed out one thing that I had not even thought about. Bill Checkley would certainly have briefed the man at Milton and a report of my progress would be required every week, which was more food for thought on my part.

I cycled on down the path which ran alongside the Up loop. This was familiar ground since I had spent hours in this same loop during the last winter, in charge of six freight trains blocked back by Control. Keeping the fires and boilers up on the six locomotives had been like painting the Forth Bridge, as by the time I had dealt with each one and worked my way back, it was time to start all over again.

As I cycled round the gentle sweep of the curve past Foxhall Down Main advanced starter signal, Milton Box came into view, a box that I had passed many times on the footplate taking little notice. It had been built in 1942 to replace the old wooden box that was situated on the Steventon side of the road bridge, and it was exactly half way between Steventon station and Foxhall Junction. In construction it was a standard ARP box, as was to be found all over the system, built of red brick with a flat concrete roof and like many of those on my beloved branch to Winchester.

I had no idea who would be on duty, but as I approached, the end window was pushed open, and it was with relief and pleasure that I saw Bert Vokings beaming down at me, a chap I had known for years. I placed my bike beneath the box and climbed the stairs to meet him. He had a cup of tea waiting, and also held out his hand to greet me. This was the kind of welcome that I was used to; the footplate kind. I decided that the

Traffic Department lads were not so bad after all, and now that I had joined them, I was fully accepted.

From that moment onwards, Bert took me under his wing and gave me every encouragement and help that it was possible to give. So much so, that in similar circumstances, where I had been in the position to help somebody, I was always reminded of Bert Vokings, and did my best to uphold the old Great Western tradition and help give a 'leg over the stile' to someone in need.

Bert sounded me out, learning all about my visits to other boxes, and the progress that I had made at Reading. He explained every detail of the workings of the box to me, and I just sat and watched him operate the box, gradually taking in all the procedures. On Tuesday morning I was up early, and back at Milton at 6.00a.m. to start the shift with Bert. I began a type of sound practical training that was to prove invaluable. Milton box was equipped with 38 levers covering the Up and Down goods loops, each with a lead in and out, the Up and Down main lines, and a cross-over. The box dealt with an average of sixty trains each shift, and during the eight-hour duty, the block was always occupied. I quickly decided that perhaps it was a good thing after all that I had been sent to Milton, instead of a small country box with one train each hour, as it altered my perception, and I became used to dealing with heavy traffic as normal working practice.

Bert's training began by allowing me to take care of all the Down traffic for the first few days, then I dealt with all of the Up traffic, whilst he took care of the telephones and bookings. This first early turn was made easy by the chaps in the signal boxes on both sides of me; Bill Ackrill at Foxhall Junction and Arthur Stoner at Steventon who had both been warned that a novice was in the box between them.

Bell signals are laid down in the regulations as distinct sounds. A goods train was coded as 3-4-1 with a pause between each beat on the block bell. I therefore sent the codes in this manner, and received the reply in a similar manner. Under normal practice, however, that would have been sent as eight bells, rattled out as quickly as the signalman could operate the key, and I soon learned how to work this way. It was surprising how, in later years, I could always tell if a Relief man was either side of me, as each man had his own distinctive way of operating the tapper key and it was instantly known when the regular man was missing. I completed that first week, confident that I was making good progress, and then the following week introduced me to my first period of night duty from 10.00p.m. to 6.00a.m. I soon found that the track circuits, signal repeaters, and the illuminated diagram were essential for night working, but, by the end of the week, Bert was allowing me to work both Up and Down traffic whilst he sat back and passed on advice.

On Sunday morning just before 6.00a.m. we banked up the fire and switched the box out, which was a simple matter providing that the block instruments read the same, either 'line clear' or 'train on line'. We sent the

5-5-7 bell signal to indicate switching out to the two boxes on either side of us and went home, ready to return at 2.00p.m.

On our return, we telephoned the boxes on either side to see what was on the block, and then we switched back in. We were now back in business again until 10.00p.m. On that Sunday, traffic was quiet, so Bert took the opportunity of going through the rules with me, which he did regularly, and after eight hours I went home feeling tired out. I began to wonder if it had been worthwhile. Footplate work had been tiring enough, but with all that I had crammed in during this last four weeks, I was dead-beat.

On Monday afternoon, I was back at 2.00p.m. ready to start the late turn, and Bert sat back watching me operate the box, since I was now able to cope with the booking and the telephone. Bert was always there in case I got into a tangle. I was unaware what he was reporting back to Bill Checkley and was far too busy even to think about it. What I did not know was that Bert was making certain plans, which was perhaps just as well, if I had known, I would have flunked out with sheer fright.

I realised on that Monday afternoon that I could deal with up to six trains, glancing at the clock for the times, booking it all in the register when the busy period was over, so I must have been making progress. At nine in the evening, I found to my surprise that I had dealt with everything; signals, booking and telephones, and made decisions on routing trains either up the loops or turning out on to the main line without once having to confirm with Bert. I went home tired; as tired as ever I had gone home from the footplate, the physical effort not being far short of shovelling. In addition there had been the mental concentration, but I went home happy as well as tired, as a little bit of satisfaction was beginning to sink in.

Tuesday came, and with it, Bert's well-laid plans. We had a cup of tea, and at about three in the afternoon he casually mentioned that he was going to check on the coal bunker. I knew that we were getting low, and I had made arrangements with the driver of the 'Up Fly' to drop off a couple of tons later on, but Bert was insistent that he had to have a look. I thought nothing of it at the time, and carried on with the work. First I dealt with an Up freight, and then pulled off the signals for a Down fast, and it was only when my advanced starting signal came off in the distance that I saw a small figure on a bike disappearing under Steventon road bridge. Was it Bert? It certainly looked like him, so I clattered down the stairs and found that the coal bunker was still there, but no Bert! He had obviously sent me solo!

Since that time I have always had the utmost sympathy with the trainee aeroplane pilot who is going solo for the first time. I began to imagine that every kind of emergency was going to happen, but the trains went by, I booked them in, dealt with others, and in between prayed that Bert would return soon.

A 'twenty-eight' stuck her nose under the bridge, turned her front end into the loop, her long rake of wagons snaking behind her, and as she passed under the window, I could hear the slap, slap, of her vacuum pump, and the usual shouted remarks about wire netting roofs. It was now my turn to give the sign of two fingers up in the air, for the wheel had turned full circle.

Bert rang me up from Steventon a couple of hours later to say that he was on the way back and would I please put the kettle on. He came up those stairs with a funny grin on his face. He knew as well as I did that I had coped all right and in those few hours I had aged a few years and become a signalman in the process.

This pattern was repeated for the next couple of days, Bert riding over to Foxhall on Wednesday, and to Steventon again on Thursday, leaving me for longer periods each time, but on Friday afternoon he stayed at Milton, so perhaps something was in the wind. The wind, in this instance, took the shape of District Inspector Bill Checkley cycling towards us, but we had received prior warning, by telephone, from Bill Ackrill at Foxhall, and I am sure that Bert already had an idea that this visit might come off.

Bill Checkley sat in the chair and watched. I will admit I found it very unnerving to be under his scrutiny, but I carried on putting into practice what Bert had hammered into me. Bill asked me a few simple questions on the rules, then at four o'clock he made a move, with the parting remark that, on Monday morning, I was to report to Chief Inspector Honeybone at Paddington for my final examination. Bert was jubilant at this news, which made it look as if I might, after all, get the appointment at Milton; this would then allow him to achieve his ambition of moving on to Didcot West End, as the only thing holding him back was someone to replace him at Milton.

In the few short weeks I had been in the Traffic Department, I had heard the name of Chief Inspector Honeybone referred to many times, he was a gentleman who had the reputation of being a 'holy terror', sending signalmen back for further training at an alarming rate. He was reputed to be rough, tough, and the ultimate expert on all signalling matters, and he expected those who came up before him to be on the top line. I managed to get through the Saturday somehow, with Bert coaching me, trying all the rules and incidents he could think of, and I managed to find answers to most of them, I also learned that Mister Honeybone was all that he was reputed to be. When Monday morning came, I walked down to the station with a quaking heart, collected my free pass from the Booking Office, and caught the familiar 7.05 a.m. up from Didcot. It didn't seem possible that six short weeks ago I could have been working this train on the footplate, and yet now, here I was with three weeks of signalling school behind me and three weeks of signal box training under my hat, going to Paddington to meet this terrible man.

The old well-remembered landmarks slipped past, the biscuits at Reading with the pot-bellied little fireless locomotive puffing out from the dark confines of the factory, and at Slough, the tang of Horlicks, Mars bars and Exlax (not that I needed any of that, the very thought of this meeting had seen me in the toilet enough times). When I arrived at Paddington I was in a real state, wound up tight and feeling sick. It was a period of exquisite torture indeed, and I still get the same feeling before going to do a talk to various railway clubs.

I stopped to have a word with my old mates on the footplate of 6923 *Croxteth Hall* simmering quietly after her run. As I swung up on to the footplate and sat down on the fireman's seat, I watched my friend Roy Saunders pull some coal forward. At that moment I would have given anything to change places with him. His driver, Roy Frewin, gave me a cup of tea out of the can, and I had a cigarette. *Croxteth Hall* began to simmer at the safety valve, so with a nod from Roy, I put on the live steam injector, and that simple act took some of the tension out of me. I still knew how to handle a boiler, but all too soon the pilot engine pulled the coaches away, and I had to leave the footplate.

I walked over the 'Lawn' and up the stairs towards the offices. I knew Paddington well, but not this part, and, feeling like a condemned man, I went down a dingy passage, turned a corner into a highly polished corridor and knocked on a heavy oak door thinking that, somewhere, there must be someone who could tell me where to go. There was no answer to my knocking, so I turned the big brass knob and walked into a room that looked like the Number One Court of the Old Bailey, with oak panelling all round the walls. I saw a gigantic oak table, running almost the entire length of the room, its surface polished like glass, and heavy oak chairs spaced all round, not an inch out of place. The oil paintings on the wall were also spaced out with precision.

I walked round this room looking back into the eyes of Gooch, Armstrong, Dean, and Churchward, as they stared at me from their portraits; they were all there, the great men of the Western, but I remember that Sir Felix Pole did not look amused. It was obvious to me that I had walked into the Great Western Boardroom, so I thought that while I was here, I might just as well have a good look around, since I had a quarter of an hour to spare. On the big sideboard at the far end of the room I could see a model of a 'King' locomotive inside a glass case, but I never got that far as there was a half-strangled screech behind me, and I turned round to be confronted by a stout little man dressed in a uniform which looked like that of an Admiral of the Fleet, but without the cap. He was most upset and wanted to know who I was, where did I come from, what was I doing in here, and so forth. I then noticed a little word embroidered on his collar, it was 'Messenger', so I realised that there was no need to call him 'Sir', and he wasn't a railwayman. It took me five minutes to quieten this excitable little man down and get him to address *me* as 'Sir'. After all, I did have my best suit on, and I had explained my presence and where I wanted to go. On the way out he breathed on that big brass door knob and gave it a polish with his handkerchief, as if I had contaminated this inner sanctum of power. He then took me along other corridors until we came to a door marked 'Chief Inspector', and I had arrived. I knocked on the door, and walked in to find myself inside a small room with a bench down the length of one side, and a door to an adjoining office leading off. The bench was full of pale, twitching nervous lads, all cramming out of the red signal book, just like a Swindon examination room, and I joined them on the bench after a shuffle-up to make room for me.

From inside the other office we could hear murmurings, followed by shouting, then the door opened and a lad crept out, his face burning with shame. A voice barked 'Next', and the lad at the end of the row went in. There was more shouting, and out he came, and so it went on until I was left on my own. I was welded to that bench, my toes digging into my shoes, my fingers gripping underneath the padded seat, waiting for that shout, and when it came I would be out of the door and down the platform as fast as I could go. I waited and waited, and gradually began to relax, until I was on the point of chancing a cigarette when the office door opened, and a quiet voice bade me enter. Perhaps the Good Lord had taken pity on me and Chief 'Executioner' Honeybone had gone out of another door and that this gentleman was the kind one. When I had a good look at him I saw that he was the one, sure enough. He sat there behind his desk, a small man, slightly built, stern looking and cold, with his cap and its gold-leafed brim set square on his head, peering at me over the top of his spectacles - if he had put on a wig and gown he would have assumed the proportions of a High Court Judge.

He studied the papers before him, and commented on the fact that I was an ex-footplate man. So he had my records, but there was nothing in that to be worried about, as I had never been late, ill, or in any scrapes — none that they could prove anyway. Then the inquisition began, and to my surprise it was on footplate rules, put in a gentle manner and I began to unwind. He then turned to the signalling rules; first the emergencies, these he expected to be answered correctly and without hesitation, because if such an emergency occurred, the reaction of the signalman had to be instant — there would be no time to fumble through a book of rules to see what had to be done.

I got through these without any trouble, because thanks to the coaching by Freddie Blackhall and Bert Vokings, and to my own study of the regulations, I knew them off by heart. Indeed, I still do, twenty-two years afterwards, they were like the multiplication tables at school, once hammered in they were there forever.

The complicated questions came next, dealing with those situations which make one think before answering. The odd sneaky one was thrown in for good measure, such as: what would I do if the platelayer came stumbling through a thick pea-soup fog to tell me that the wind had just blown down a large tree across the main line? I thought about that for one a minute, and then I replied, somewhat flippantly, that I would get him to jack up the tree while I shovelled the fog under it, just enough to lift it higher than a locomotive.

He took off his Chief Inspector's hat at that one, and tried a question on single line working: what would I do if I had two trains on the same line in the section? I told him that I would resign. Mr. Honeybone gave me a smile, looked at his watch and said that he had heard enough. He came round from behind his desk, placed his hands on my shoulders, and told me that he had heard all about me from Freddie Blackhall. Bless dear old Freddie, I thought, he had opened the door for me after all. As I was thinking this, Mr. Honeybone gave me the biggest surprise of all, when he said that, providing Bill Checkley, my District Inspector, agreed, there was no reason why I should not fill the vacancy at Milton.

I shook hands with him and went out of that office elated to the extent that I hardly knew what day it was. All the tension drained away to be replaced by such happiness that I was in a state of euphoria such as I had never known. After all, in six weeks, I had gone from a fireman's job to a Class Three main line appointment. All that I had heard about this man was untrue, and although our paths were to cross again many times, I always found him to be a gentleman. I walked out of Paddington, up Praed Street and into a pub for a couple of pints: I'm not normally a drinking man, but I reckoned that I had earned those. I still remember those two pints, and, at the risk of offending the lads 'up the Smoke' I must say it was some wishy-washy stuff, not a man's drink at all. I can remember even after all these years, wondering how they could fire a 'King' on such stuff!

When I got back to Didcot, I made my way to the office to report, and as I walked in, Freddie Blackhall bounded round the desk and shook my hand, as he had heard the result by telephone. I was delighted to see him, and to hear that he had finished with the Reading Signal School and was now working the district as assistant to Bill Checkley. Bill was out at the moment, so Freddie told me to carry on at Milton for the rest of the week, then he gave me a wink and a playful punch on the arm and told me to get off home. My 'old chap' was delighted to hear my news. While I had been training, I had been down on porter's money, but with this new rating, I would be up to a fireman's wage again, plus the added bonus of regular night-shift pay, and one Sunday in three at that special rate of pay. It was still not a lot of course, because railway pay was never as good as that paid in the factories, but it was enough to make me think of a settled future and to allow me to ensnare a certain young lady before someone else beat me to it. After all, I could hope for promotion once I had got to grips with this new job.

When I returned to Milton the next morning, I found that the 'jungle telegraph' had worked in the Traffic Department just the same as on the locomotive side. Bert's pleasure was beyond bounds, as all the hard work he had devoted to me had paid off. All that morning the phones rang with congratulations, and one call came from Bill Ackrill at Foxhall, warning that Bill Checkley was on his way. Cups, saucers, teapot, and most importantly, the forbidden portable radio were hidden away so that when he arrived, the box would be the picture of decorum. Bill came into sight, a small figure pedalling away far up the line, and as he came near we could see that he was going to miss the small wooden bridge over the point rodding, as he was too busy looking into the goings-on in the Army Depot at the other side of the fence. There was nothing to see really, just a lot of old wheel barrows, and when Bill picked himself up, we were looking the other way, as we had no wish to let him see us laughing, because this was the moment of truth for me, the final test had come. Bill came up into the box breathing hard, and with a cut on his hand, which we bound up for him: sooner or later he would let on what had given him so much interest in that depot. He sat there watching me work the box for an hour, and then told me that I could take over on the night shift the following week, and that Bert could go to Didcot West End and begin to learn that box. The next step was to get Bert to sign the form, the form which became a statement, that in the opinion of the signalman handing over I was fully competent to discharge my duties correctly at Milton. Bert signed, and was pleased to do so, a duty which I found pleasing in later years when signing the form for other lads.

Bill shook hands with me, and a frosty smile crept over his face; those stony features took on a new dimension with that smile, but looking back, I can now see why Bill had been so wary to begin with. He had just taken over the district, his first, so he had been feeling his way and, then, just as he thought that everything was perfect, this ex-footplate man had come roaring through. He had every right to feel a bit uncertain about me, for in those six short weeks I had broken through all known procedure, but I made a promise to Bill that I would never break, I would not in any way let him down.

I cycled up the path towards Foxhall with Bert that last Saturday afternoon, knowing that the next time I came this way it would be to take over. I had a long weekend ahead of me, which came round regularly, and was looked forward to by every signalman because one did not have to return to duty until 10.00p.m. on the Monday night. I was at a loose end. My darling Betty had gone home to Wales on the first of many forays which young ladies make once a wedding date is fixed. (The wedding was not until August, but already in mid-February the ground-work had begun.) That Saturday afternoon I was very preoccupied with my thoughts about the responsibilities of the coming Monday night. My old Dad could see this, and with the typical ease of a father understanding his son better than he did himself, he knew that I would be all right once I had got over that first night, but until then I needed to be taken out of myself, and given something different to do and to think about, which Dad set out to achieve.

The first step was to get me to go down with him to the Staff Association Club that evening, for a couple of pints and a game of darts. We were both good players, and a near miss on a double was just not tolerated. There would be gentle jibes such as 'amateur' and 'you're supposed to hit the double not the wire' or considerably stronger comments passing between us, but we were pretty evenly matched, and the remarks were all in good fun and certainly helped to take my mind off my worries. After the game we sat down to enjoy our drink, and then Dad leaned over and touched me on the knee, and in his crafty way, came out with a remark which he knew would make me rise to the bait he had prepared in his mind. Now that I was occupied with a job in a 'greenhouse' with a table and chair, a toilet, regular hours and even wearing a white shirt, just like the gentry, perhaps I considered myself just a little bit superior, and perhaps my hands had got too soft to handle a shovel?

My 'old chap' had a way of being deadly serious when he was pulling my leg, and every time he tried it I got caught, this time included. I replied rather indignantly, that my hands might be clean, but they were not soft, and I was every bit as skilled with the shovel as he had ever been, and I could fire any type of locomotive he cared to put in front of me, whereas he had been a driver for so many years that he was beginning to lose touch with firing. The conversation was going just the way he had intended: 'Right' he said, 'if you're so good you can come with me tomorrow, to give my fireman a rest. We've got a nice little run to Eastleigh with a farm special'.

I must have been made to fall for it, but it happened that a farm special was one type of train that I had never worked on during my firing days. This one would be coming through from Yorkshire, consisting of the farm machinery and household goods, while the cattle would be following by another special later in the day.

Father was due off shed at 9.00a.m. that Sunday morning, so I arranged to be on the platform soon after then, thinking that there was no point in letting the Foreman know what was going on by going into the shed myself, although he probably would not have minded anyway. I climbed the steps to the platform, my footsteps sounding hollow on this quiet morning, and found the farm special standing alongside number five platform. It was quite a sizeable train, with a dozen flats loaded with reapers, binders, ploughs, tractors and various odds and ends, and then came two containers and finally a third brake coach with the family and employees aboard.

As I got to the end of the platform I looked back towards the engine shed, expecting to see a 'Grange' or a 'Mogul' poking her nose out, since father had assured me that a good engine was booked for this job, but then

I found he had delivered a blow right under the belt as he came sliding quietly up to the shed signal with the little Didcot Dean Goods No. 2573. Poor little old lady, she had been built back in the eighties, with a boiler pressure of only 180lb., and now with the flap of her spindle glands pegged up over the front buffer she looked as if she was grinning at me, just like the 'old chap' was, as she chuffed up over the points and then set back on to the train. My hands were clean at the moment, but it looked as if I would be getting them dirty in a few minutes, so I might just as well start now, and tie her on. I slipped down between the platform and the tender and coupled her up, then climbed up onto the footplate, looking deadly serious, and not allowing either my father or his fireman any satisfaction in their smirking.

Tom, the fireman, climbed down and went back to install himself in the coach with the Sunday newspapers, being only too pleased to spend the next couple of hours relaxing on a comfortable seat. I hung up my jacket, took off my tie and rolled up my sleeves, determined to show the senior member of the family that I had not forgotten my old craft in a few short weeks. The timing of this train was so easy that it would be a doddle in any case. We had an hour to get to Newbury, another hour to Winchester, then half an hour to Eastleigh. Her fire was burning through nicely, so I packed some coal in the back corners of the firebox, which would last until we were on the branch. The guard blew his whistle, father placed the reverser in full fore gear, opened the little push-over regulator two inches off the guide stop, and we were away, drifting over the junction, round the curve and onto the branch.

As soon as she began to tilt her nose up, he linked her back with the pole reverser, and gave her half a regulator and left her there, letting her set her own pace. I fed the fire, in the back corners, front corners, round the sides of the box, and then a couple of shovelfuls sprayed into the middle, each shovelful of coal tingeing her exhaust with a slight brown stain. Half a mile further on, I went round the box again, sliding the underneath of the shovel on the fire hole ring, angling it round until the fire took on the shape of a big saucer. This was really expert firing, turning the fire into a sculpture, just as William Dean had designed the firebox to accept! The 'old chap' had a look inside, sniffed, then knocked his pipe out on my newly swept floorboards, but even if father was pretending to be unimpressed with my fire, the little engine loved it, and began to sing as the steam pressure needle hovered on the 180lb. red line. Her old flower pot safety valve perched high on top of the boiler just ahead of the two small cab windows, began to lift, and there was a soft mellow whisper of steam, as if she was purring with contentment as the white flower of steam drifted back over the tiny cab roof. I opened the tender water feed and turned the wire wheel of the right hand live steam injector two turns, then I tapped back the water feed until the overflow was gone, and the injector settled down to a quiet singing, as she drank gently from her water supply.

I turned on the coal watering pipe and hosed down the pipe ash and a pair of shining boots, the water in the gauge glass bobbing up and down, each rise a little higher up the glass than the last, and when it reached three-quarters full, she had lost twenty pounds of steam pressure, so it was time to shut the injector off for another mile or so.

It was a pleasure to be back, to feel the pulse of this little engine as she lifted the train up the bank towards Upton, and I realised that I had missed the warmth of the cab, the aroma of hot oil, steam and the whiff of good Welsh coal burning as the smoke rolled back from the chimney. Looking over the side I could see her small side rods going up and over, and hear her little heart beating, 'chuff, chuff, chuff, chuff' four little beats out of the chimney for each revolution of her driving wheels, her stubby boiler sniffing out the line ahead, lining up to go through Upton station bridge.

I began to fire her again round the box, dropping and lifting the flap between each shovelful. As she tackled the bank, the lever was dropped forward a couple of notches and her exhaust deepened, the tall chalk walls of the cutting throwing back the echo, and the lineside rabbits began to run, tumbling over in their haste to escape, or scampering up the sheer cliffs, scrabbling their way up to the accompaniment of a miniature avalanche of chalk rubble. The cutting began to drop away and we were clearing the top, out over the beautiful rolling Berkshire Downs, the reverser was linked back and the regulator eased down. I dropped the firebox flap and put the injector on again as we rolled through Churn Halt, then down through Compton with a cheery wave to the signalman, down the dip at a rush, putting a little steam into her cylinders to Hampstead Norris. Next came the long climb up through the trees to Hermitage, her little chimney barking away until we shut off going through Pinewood Halt, and rolled down to Newbury with the wheel flanges squealing as they bit into the sharp curve on the approach to Newbury East Junction. Up the middle road we went, and stopped at Newbury West to fill the tank at the water-column; I clambered over the coal to lift the flap and catch the chain as the column was pulled round, and just then I could see Jessie Barnett, the Newbury Relief signalman coming down the box steps with two empty coal buckets. Now Jessie was quite a character, a stout bluff ruddy-faced man, bubbling over with good nature and fun. He didn't ask the fireman to fill his buckets, up on the footplate he came and helped himself, pulling my leg about firing to father. It was the 'old chap' who let the cat out of the bag, by telling Jessie not only that I had become a signalman, but also that I was off duty and doing this turn just for the fun of it. Jessie began to laugh, and he was still at it when we pulled away, and I saw him lifting the telephone ear piece, the news was evidently going ahead of us.

We chuffed along gently down the Berks and Hants main line, then swung onto the Winchester branch, passing Enbourne Junction where we caught sight of Dare Warwick, the signalman, leaning out of the box window holding up his coal shovel in one hand and the red signalman's book in the other, which was all that he could think of by way of a joke in the short time that he had. We pulled strongly up the bank to Woodhay where we joined the single line, thinking it curious that there was no sign of a signalman, but when I collected the token from the carrier the steel hoop handle was covered in wet red paint, which showed that the vendetta was beginning.

At Highclere, I dropped the Woodhay token on the platform and with the ease of one who had exchanged tokens before, I collected the Burghclere one from the outstretched arm, only to find the hoop covered with wet tea leaves! Down the dip, through the bridge and round the corner into Litchfield, where the exchange was made, apparently without a hitch, until I realised as I hung the new token on the hook in the cab, that this one was smeared with sticky condensed milk. My old Dad had a lot to answer for, but he just sat there, arms folded, sucking away at his awful pipe, grinning wider and wider as we progressed south.

As we ambled down the bank into Whitchurch, I was sitting on the seat removing the remains of paint, tea leaves and condensed milk from my hands, with some paraffin-soaked cotton waste. I was reckoning on being safe at Whitchurch, because there was a lady signalwoman there who exchanged tokens by the rule book, the old token being hung on the catcher and the new one being taken out of the rack. Father was giving our little engine a whiff on the vacuum brake, just enough to slow her down a little, but still fast enough to give my hand a healthy smack as I picked up the token. A little steam was put into her cylinders now, and I began to fire her gently for the climb out of Sutton Scotney and over the top. We rolled down into Worthy Down, the lovely Hampshire Downs looking wonderfully soft in the sunshine. It was time to sit down and enjoy the view, with the regulator shut and flap down, as we coasted through Kingsworthy, through the tunnel and into Winchester.

We waited for ten minutes until the Southern T9 came up and clear with a train of empty coaches, then we were away again, over the long sweeping curve of Shawford Viaduct where we handed over the Southern tablet in its little leather pouch, and down the main line, enough steam being fed into her cylinders to keep her rolling into Eastleigh. On reaching our destination, I uncoupled, and we cleared the main line into the shed, while the Southern pilot engine collected our train and pulled it clear of the station and into the sidings. We turned on the triangle, then dropped back on to an empty shed road where the guard and the now well-rested fireman were waiting. It was agreed by all concerned, that I could still fire a Great Western steam locomotive, indeed, so good was I at it, and so skilled in boiling enough water to get us here, that the vote was passed that I should be able to make the tea without supervision.

While they were drinking their tea and chatting to the few Southern men who were about on this Sunday, I took the opportunity to have a look round, because to be let loose in a big Southern main line shed was too good a chance to miss, particularly as this was, in all probability, the last time I would ever be on Eastleigh shed. I had fired Southern engines, the 'Remembrance' class, and Urie's 'Moguls', and my feelings towards these locomotives was one of very happy memories, from the time when the Great Western had them on loan for about a year during the war to ease the engine shortage. Later, when the Swindon-built L.M.S. 84XX class came into service, together with the 'Austerity' class, we lost these fine engines, because the Southern naturally wanted them back, and I for one, was sorry to see them go.

As might be expected with a main line next to the Works, Eastleigh was similar to Swindon, there was plenty to see, and on a quiet Sunday, there was a chance to see it without getting in anyone's way. I had a good look round a 'Merchant Navy', and was surprised to look into that big square firebox after being used to the long narrow fireboxes of the Great Western. The 'King Arthur' class was big and powerful, but it was a little bit disconcerting to find that the cab seemed so small after our Collett cabs. I could never have got used to that small Southern shovel, it was so heavy and narrow, without the fine balance of the Swindon product, but I suppose it depends on what one is used to.

There was one locomotive on the railway that I really did want to see, and to climb all over, and that was the 'Schools' class. In the end, I found one at the rear of the shed, tucked away in a line of other locomotives, and if she was in for repair, but she didn't look like it, because she shone brightly. Her home shed must have thought the world of her, and I was all over her, and underneath her, just looking and admiring. The slant of the inclined cab gave her a racy look. On the footplate she seemed to have plenty of room, all her cab fittings and copper pipe work gleamed, the reversing wheel had been burnished, and the boiler front paint-work reflected the long double regulator handle, painted deep red, the driver's end shut tight down on to the stop, the other end up in the roof. Out of all the locomotives that I had fired, this class had eluded me, and, it was the one class that I would have given anything to work on. Had she been in steam then I would have gone to find the Foreman, for even a trip round the triangle would have been better than nothing.

That was the last time that I saw a 'Schools', until thirty years later, when I was on a visit to the Bluebell Railway in East Sussex. One Sunday, as I turned the corner of the repair shop, there inside stood a 'Schools', 928 *Stowe,* looking just a little bit tatty after her many years outside. Perhaps one day before I become too feeble to lift a shovel, my Bluebell membership may allow me to see her in steam.

It was time to go home, our little Dean Goods looked ludicrous parked between those big Southern 'Merchant Navys', and so with the footplate filled now with two extra bodies (the fireman and the guard) we chuffed gently up to the shed signal. I operated the old indicator instrument which told the signalman where we wanted to go, the points came over, the ground signal clanged off and we were away. Up through the station, past Shawford Junction, until at Winchester Junction, it was over the fields on the new cut-off, back on to the branch and set sail for home.

For a day's work that was the result of a bit of kidding from my father, it had been worth every penny, figuratively speaking, because of course, I was not being paid for this, but I wouldn't have missed the trip for anything. It had completely taken my mind off my first duty in a signalbox, and proved that I could still handle the shovel, so all in all it had been a very satisfactory day.

Chapter Three
Playing My Way In

Monday gradually passed, as I waited to go on that fateful duty at 10.00p.m. During the afternoon I went to bed for a couple of hours but I could not rest, and it was a relief when the clock said it was time to go. It was a beautiful evening as I cycled down the road towards Foxhall, the moonlight lighting up the old Provender Stores like the battlements of some border castle. Through the gate I went, and free-wheeled down the path, over the crossing of West curve, with the lights of Foxhall Junction box casting a warm glow as I passed. I crossed the Up loop, then cycled along the path, the Down advanced starting signal with Milton's distant beneath it coming off just then as if to give me a clear line.

As I mounted the steps of Milton box, the 9.40p.m. Oxford parcels train came pounding down the main line working hard, building up speed from the West curve restriction. Jack Gardner, the late turn signalman, was pleased to see me, as we were old school mates from years back. We had a few words on the changeover, before Jack had to go, his cycle rear light bobbing as he crossed the wooden bridges over the point rodding. I was at last alone, ready to start my first ever duty in my own signal box. At 10.20p.m. the Up main block bell rang, making me nearly jump out of my skin. It was the Swindon parcels train, then the Down main block bell rang for the 8.55 p.m. out of Paddington. I got 'line clear' from Foxhall and from Steventon and pulled off the signals: 28, 33, 34 and 35 for the Up train, 8, 3, 2 and 1 for the Down train. Now I was really in business, I thought, as both trains roared by, their tail lamps dancing as they passed, then it was 'Train out of section' on the bells, and signals back to normal, nothing to it, really, I told myself.

I had my two regular mates in the boxes each side of me, Arthur Stoner at Steventon and Bill Ackrill at Foxhall, two railway gentlemen, who treated this raw new man in the middle with every consideration, sending bell signals so slow and precise that even an idiot could have understood what was going on. I was to work with those two chaps for the next three years, and I found that the comradeship that existed on the footplate was also in the Traffic Department. A good example was with my first emergency that night, when a goods train came up with a hot axle box, and Arthur rang me up on the 'phone and told me that he was going to send me seven bells for 'stop and examine train', but to send it on to Foxhall as the train was running safely, and that the footplate chaps were aware of it.

Being helped in this way, I could hardly go wrong! Such close collaboration between signalmen was an essential part of signal box life, for although each train was the responsibility of the particular signalman whose block it was in, we could help one another out considerably with information and collaboration. This friendliness and dependence on each other was just like that between a driver and his fireman, so I soon began to feel at home.

They continued to treat me with care, but of course, as I progressed so did the work, and in a few weeks they were back to sending bell codes in the normal way, and as I was learning the schedule and timetable and therefore what train was due next and so what bell code to expect. I could receive and send as good as they could; 1-3-1, or 3-1-1, or 5 and 2-3 on the bells were all rattled out in one long string. In any case, now that I knew the service, I knew which bell codes to expect. The only change came with an emergency bell signal, and that was always sent in such a correct manner there was no doubt by the recipient as to what it meant.

That first night I dealt with 56 trains during the eight hour shift, seven per hour, which was pretty easy going, but as it took nine minutes for a passenger train to be on the block instruments from start to finish, and sixteen for a freight train, the block was always occupied. It was not all through traffic, however, some were turned out from the loop to the main line (which meant fingers crossed that I had allowed enough time margin for the train to clear the section without any delay to a following train) and some I turned into the goods loop from the main line.

My last train on that shift was the 6.05 p.m. fitted vacuum freight up from Fishguard, then I emptied the ashes, filled the coal buckets, and swept up. It was with relief that I saw the cycle lamp of my early turn colleague, Pat Ware, bobbing up and down as he came towards the box. The kettle was boiling on the fire, and it was only a matter of changing over, signing the train register and going home.

The weeks passed without any problems, and I came back on the Sunday afternoon, after a couple of hours in bed, to take over the box which I had left eight hours before, switching in expecting a quiet easy afternoon and evening, with time for the weekly polish of the floor and levers, and also to clean the windows. These 'housekeeping' duties were always the responsibility of the man on the late turn Sunday shift. Then, I heard a noise which was quite out of place compared with the normal sounds of a signal box, a faint plaintive squeak from downstairs. At first I thought it was a dry signal wire riding over a dry pulley, but when the frame had settled down from my reversing signals after switching in, it came again, and I began to be concerned that I might have a signal wire on the point of breaking. When a wire did break, as I was to find out many times in the future, it would not be a slow affair with plenty of warning, it would go with a bang and send me flying across the signal box. I slid back the window and had a look outside. The squeak came again and I was able to narrow it down to under the wooden boards covering the point rodding. I went down the stairs, lay down full length on the path, and looked under the boards, where I found a friend, a tiny grey and white kitten, dirty, wet and almost dead. As I lifted it out it curled up into the palm of my hand like a little sodden ball of dirty wool, chilled through almost to the point of extinction.

I took the kitten up into the box, but had to leave it for a moment laid on the polished lino, as I dealt with a train. I pulled off the signals, booked the train in the register, then went back to the kitten, which had not moved or cried out. I sorted through the cleaning cupboard and found some dry rags which I made into a pad, then I placed the kitten on it and laid it in front of the fire. There was no movement for the next hour, then as the warmth crept through that small body, the remaining spark of life began to flicker into a small flame, the kitten opened its eyes, opened its tiny pink mouth and let out a faint cry.

That day I was to go without any milk in my tea. I had brought enough for a couple of brew-ups, instead I poured the milk into a saucer and stood it on top of the oven. When it had warmed through, I began an operation that was to last for days and to be shared by my mates on the other turns of duty. Picking the kitten up, I dipped my finger in the milk and began to dribble some into its mouth — a long laborious job, until eventually it was all gone, then I mashed up a little corned beef from my sandwiches and managed to get some nourishment into that little cat.

When it was time to switch out at 10.00p.m. it was with some concern, because my mate coming on in the morning would have no knowledge of our new recruit. I left him a note and placed the kitten in a cardboard box behind the stove, where it promptly went to sleep, not even knowing that I was gone.

When I came back on duty the next afternoon I brought food and bedding for the kitten, but I could hardly believe my eyes when I climbed the stairs into the box, for that kitten was dancing and charging all over the floor chasing its shadow and anything else that moved, and it was clean too, for my mate had gently washed it in some warm water in the hand basin, and he too had given up his milk. I had brought enough to last until the next day, because, of course, the night man would be unaware of the kitten.

Looking back on it now, it must have been a laughable sight in Milton signal box, three grown men spending every minute between trains crouched down, or sat in a chair, concentrating on getting the kitten to lick their milky fingers. One day, after several weeks of nursing and constant devoted attention, it began to lap up milk and eat on its own. We had won.

'Susie', as we named her, grew sleek and fat, and she had the best of everything. When Harry Payne, the ganger, hit a key a mile away, she would be up on her hind legs looking down the line with the sure knowledge that he would have some titbit for her, and in the summer she would sit out in the sun on the window-sill, sedately watching the trains go by, aloof from it all, queen of all she surveyed.

She became a familiar figure to the train crews, and when the summer holiday traffic started, excited children would see this cat perched up on the window-sill and tug at their parents' arms, pulling them urgently towards the window to see her. In time, she grew wise of the way of train movements, and would cross the running lines to hunt in the fields opposite only when the signals were back in the frame. She remained with us for three years, then within a short period of time we too all moved on and left her, and so she went too; her three 'mums' had gone and there was nothing to keep her, so one night she slipped away and never returned.

Meanwhile I had settled in at Milton, and apart from the day-to-day working, various emergencies arose as they did at every signalbox, mostly little things that were dealt with as they cropped up: hot boxes, tail lamps out on the last vehicle, and failures in the section. Then one afternoon there was a fault on my block instrument. It occurred when the 1.18p.m. from Paddington was offered to me by Bill Ackrill at Foxhall. Despite turning the knob of the commentator on my instrument to 'Line Clear' this was not repeated with Bill, which meant he could not pull off his advanced starting signal because it was locked by my instrument.

There was nothing I could do except send for the signal lineman. I could get 'Line Clear' from Steventon and so pulled off my signals, but poor old Bill had an awkward time of it, as until the block had been repaired he had to stop every down train and verbally instruct the driver to pass the advanced starting signal showing 'On' under rule 38 (b). 'Instruct' under these circumstances is something of a misnomer. The drill was to go to the window with a megaphone and bellow one's lungs out against the roar of a 'Castle' or 'King' with a nice big fire in her box blowing her head off from the safety valve as she had come to a stop, after which the fireman had to come to the box to sign the register, which meant further delay.

The next train down was the 1.55p.m. from Paddington, which ran fast to Reading, then non-stop to Newport; she took six minutes to pass me from Foxhall instead of the usual one, with 5020 *Trematon Castle* blasting her chimney almost off to get some run into thirteen coaches again. However, the signal lineman was quick on the repair job, he cycled down from Didcot and had my instrument repaired by 3.40p.m., so Bill could rest his voice after that.

We notified District Inspector Bill Checkley, and the local controller at Didcot East Junction that no more delays were forthcoming. The controller was relieved because he had a very onerous job, and one that I would not wish to do. The man on my shift was Bill Churchman, one of nature's gentlemen, who had been a signalman for some time but with the build-up of traffic it had become necessary to create this controller grade to take some of the load off the signalmen in the district. Bill's job saw him based at Didcot East Junction and gave him supreme control and decision making responsibility over all movements. Didcot East could never have been said to be a quiet place either for in addition to Bill there were two signalmen and a booking boy. Bill had the overall picture of all trains on the main lines, relief lines, the Oxford branch avoiding loops, the Newbury branch, the goods yard and locomotive shed, plus all the station movements, so if necessary a priority of movement could be made.

Bill worked in close contact with all the signalmen in the district as well as Reading Control. For instance, he would advise me of the routing of Up goods traffic with suggestions as to how it should run and in what sequence. He could have given a direct order, but that wasn't Bill's way, because with the running of an Up goods there was sometimes a chance to run one main line but on a tight margin in front of an Up express. Bill would have been given the departure time of the goods from Swindon, so allowing for good running he would ring me up for information, and I would check back down the line to my mates in the signal boxes at Wantage and Challow. Sometimes we knew the drivers and their way of running, then I could go back to Bill and inform him that this train was running well and that we could allow it to carry on, and Bill, knowing of my experience of footplate working would take my word and allow a run-through.

Both Foxhall Junction and Didcot East Junction had the passing times of all Up trains wired to them, so we could see how things were brewing up and act accordingly, and of course, it worked the other way. Highworth Junction and Challow would enquire about the running of Down trains and work their margin out the same way. My standard telephone duties were in advising Reading Control of all Up trains, and with special attention made on Down passenger trains clearing Steventon, for this was leaving the London division, and as long as they cleared Steventon on time, any delays could not be blamed on London – it would be the turn of Bristol's to sort it out! My mate at Steventon had the reverse of this, any trains clearing me were out of the Bristol area and became our responsibility, so we were very much in demand from Reading and Bristol Controls.

My first real emergency came after three months at Milton, and it was one which could have had serious consequences but for the skill and correct handling of the goods train involved by the driver. I had come on duty for the late shift at 2.00p.m. and my first Down passenger, the 1.15p.m. from Paddington, was running on the Down main line while a train of empty coal wagons, from Old Oak Common on their way to Aberdare, was running alongside on the Down loop, both trains approaching my signals together. I stood at the frame ready to place back the signals once the trains had passed, and as I looked back towards them I could see the goods train behaving in a most peculiar manner, with wagons jumping about sending up a cloud of coal dust, then the passenger train drew alongside blotting out the goods. When the passenger train was past, I could see what had happened. The goods train had half a dozen wagons off the rails, but the driver had spotted this and kept them going with a tight coupling until the passenger was safely past. Had he not there could have been the risk of the wagons piling up and possibly blocking the path of the passenger train alongside.

Now the rules and regulations came into action, I placed the signals back, cleared the block back to Foxhall for the Down passenger, then sent him the six bells 'Obstruction Danger' and placed the instrument to 'Train on line', so that no more could come that way. However, a situation was also arising on the Up main line while this was going on. An Aberdare coal train was hammering up the main line towards me, and if I slapped the signals back into the face of this lad, he had no chance at all of stopping in time, and although he might have a try, he would most certainly knock the guard flying in his van. My experience as an ex-footplate man helped me in assessing the situation in a case like this: I could see that the Down goods with the derailed wagons was coming to a stand with the wagons upright, so I let the Up train run, judging that there was no likelihood that the derailment would foul the Up running line.

I notified Reading Control, Bill Churchman at Didcot East Junction, and Bill Checkley my District Inspector, and the latter told me to start making arrangements for using the Up main line for single line working. I replied, with all of three months experience, that I thought we could get away without resorting to this and avoid the consequent heavy delays. He went quiet for a minute and said he would be with me soon, and I wondered if I had put my head on the chopping block with my last statement. Single line working with all its attendant delays, was a long drawn out affair, and I had the 1.55p.m. out of Paddington to come, first stop Newport, then the 2.30p.m. for Gloucester, so I hoped we could avoid single line working. Ten minutes after I had rung him, Bill Checkley arrived on the station pilot engine, which I signalled down to the box and over the cross-over, then sent him back to Didcot; Bill had dropped off at the home signal with a District Relief Signalman, so he had taken some notice of what I had said.

Bill took a long hard look at that derailment, those half dozen wagons sat there squarely with their wheels on the ballast, in no way were they going to tip over, although half a mile of the Down goods loop was chewed up behind them where the wagon wheels had ridden over the sleepers. Bill came to the box and agreed that I could clear the 'Obstruction Danger' from the block instrument and accept trains down the main line again. He telephoned and made arrangements for the breakdown gang to come, and left the Relief Signalman at my Home signal, all trains being slowed down to walking pace past the derailment on the instructions from my mate on the ground.

The goods train which had caused all the trouble was quickly dealt with. The guard uncoupled behind the last wagon that remained on the rails, and the engine and wagons pulled forward, clear of my outgoing loop points. By now I had the breakdown train on the Down main line, then backed it in to the derailed wagons, and with the use of jacks and plates those wagons were back on the rails in no time. Out came the breakdown gang, through the cross-over and up the main line back to Didcot, while the goods engine backed on and completed his train again. Once coupled up, he was allowed to proceed slowly to Steventon and detach the defective wagons for examination. It was all over by 5.30p.m. leaving me and our normally highly polished floor now looking like a ploughed field, but, I had been blooded, now I really was a signalman, and Bill Checkley had seen me operate under pressure and was satisfied.

All it needed was for me to get a uniform! Events had moved so fast between leaving the footplate and joining the box that the uniform issue just hadn't caught up with me, and whilst I had been measured three weeks ago it had yet to arrive. But before the late turn came round in three weeks' time I would indeed be kitted out, because an important event was to take place.

On the Monday of that week, I collected my uniform from Bill Checkley's office, and somehow managed to carry it on the handlebar of my bike back to Milton. It was a lovely issue, pure Great Western with brass buttons everywhere, and included two pairs of trousers, two long-sleeved waistcoats, two jackets, one heavy overcoat, and one stiff-peaked cap. This cap was the only item that seemed superfluous: it was placed in the bottom of my locker and remained there gathering dust, indeed, I can't remember any signalman wearing one. Relief men had to wear one when carrying out the duties of Pilotman for single line working, or during the relaying of track or renewing signals, when they were acting as ground signalmen. The remainder of the uniform was good stuff, a far cry from my old footplate overalls and cap, and most of us took a pride in it, brushing and pressing, and polishing the GWR buttons until we would have done credit to a Guardsman. I still have a tin full of those buttons, a little tarnished now, but genuine Great Western brass, and something to hang onto as a reminder of those golden days.

I took the trousers, jacket and waistcoat home with me that evening, so that on Tuesday when I arrived on duty I would look every inch a signalman. When a 'Royal' was booked through, I belonged, not that I would be noticed any more than Harry Payne, the ganger, who kept me company, or the relaying gang stretched out along the section, spaced out half a mile apart until the 'Royal' had passed. But there was another reason for getting me kitted out on this late turn. It was discovered that Milton box had never been passed out by the Ministry of Transport, so the official passing-out was to be performed on the Thursday, and I just happened to be the signalman on duty.

My mates on the other turns were pleased to be clear of all this expected 'top brass', and I was not too happy about it either, not being exactly scared, just having the wind up a bit. On that afternoon when I relieved the early turn man, he was out of the box and gone in a flash although the Inspection train wasn't due until after the 1.15 p.m. from Paddington had gone through. As this passed, I cleared the section and accepted the Inspection train, stopping it dead at my home signal before changing the points over for the loop line and allowing it to clear the main line.

The little 14XX class tank engine with its one coach came to a stand opposite the box, and I could see down into that Inspection coach where there were tables laid out with white linen, silver cutlery, glasses and bottles and a white-coated attendant. These Inspection blokes certainly were doing themselves all right, I thought to myself. They all piled out with not a backward glance at the bulled-up little locomotive (perhaps they imagined it always looked like that?) and came towards the signal box.

I began to tick off the people that I knew. There were some familiar faces, Bill Checkley, Freddie Blackhall and Chief Inspector Honeybone, all resplendent in their number one uniform, gold braid and gleaming brass buttons in every direction. Then came Mr. Grand, the General Manager, looking very smart in a well-cut suit and bowler hat, and trailing along behind came a civilian gentleman wearing a trilby hat, whom I had never seen before.

I had a last quick look around the signal-box, the windows were clean, the floor highly polished, the levers gleamed like chrome plating, the brass release plungers shone, the stove had been black-leaded, even the coal buckets too, so there was nothing left to bring discredit to Milton box.

Bill Checkley introduced me, Freddie Blackhall winked, Mr. Honeybone whispered that everything was all right, and then I met the General Manager whom up until now, I had only seen in photographs in the Great Western magazine, naming locomotives. Then he introduced me to the man in the trilby hat, Lt. Col. Wilson from the Inspectors Office of the Ministry of Transport. To say that I was surprised would be an understatement, for this civilian that I shook hands with was not my idea of a full-blown high-ranking army officer. I had met enough of these gentlemen when firing the many troop trains, and they had all been big men, usually with red tabs on their tunic collars, and a host of lesser officers hovering in the background. This man though was slightly built with a little sandy moustache under his nose. He stood watching me deal with the trains on the block, gently asking questions as to my railway background and was most interested to learn about my footplate experiences. Once the block had been cleared, he asked my permission to take over and I stood back to see him pick up the lever cloth and go through that frame so fast, testing locking, signals, points and instruments that even I would have been hard pressed to keep up with him, so I was obviously in the presence of an expert.

Satisfied with the result, he gave me back my signal box, and the others began to prepare to leave, but this great man would have none of it. He pressed me more about footplate work, then he wanted to know about my transfer and my rapid progress through the Reading School into this job, turning to Chief Inspector Honeybone for confirmation, and he made the point of remarking that it would be a good thing if there was an interchange of jobs on the operating side.

There was a general discussion up in the corner, and handshaking all round, then they went clattering down the stairs and back to the little train, leaving Bill Checkley behind. I turned the train out on to the main line, 'right away' to Swindon.

Bill sat down and had a cup of tea with me, he was glad that this inspection was over, and that it had gone off correctly, and now he began to open up and reveal that behind those frosty features was a real nice bloke. He talked about his time in the Household Cavalry, and the spit and polish that went behind the ceremonial troopings, and of his railway years in a signal box, and of course his pet subject, growing roses. It was a good job that he mentioned that, because a few weeks later his hobby almost became his undoing; I was cycling up the path on the way home when I heard a cry for help across on the Down loop side, and laid down my bike and crossed the running lines to find Bill trapped face down in a bramble bush. He had gone in after a briar that he had been training for months to grow in a straight line. He had dug it out by the roots when he became tangled up, unable to move. I pulled him out by his feet, leaving bits of his skin here and there, but he emerged triumphant, clutching that briar with such a pleased look about him.

At Milton, (at the time) stuck out in the middle of the countryside, it was surprising to see that there was always something going on if one used one's eyes. Through the rear window I could look out over Didcot Depot, which has now been swept away to make way for the giant power station. It was worth a look through that window now and again, over the vast expanse of railway network stretching for miles between the various storage sheds, with pannier tanks bustling about, I knew every inch of those tracks from my firing days, knowledge that was to come in handy at a later date to overcome a very big problem.

The activities of one of the depot staff kept me interested for weeks. Behind the shed opposite the signal box was a large stack of wooden wheel barrows, and each morning this chap would come out with a little compressor and a paint spray gun, and spray the barrows army grey, working his way quietly through the pile. During the dinner break, he would change the colour of the paint in the spray gun to black and get to work spraying a new grey army bike which would dry off during the afternoon. At five in the evening he would mount it and ride off.

One of the War Department police officers came round the fence one day, and exchanging the state of the weather with him the policeman happened to mention that army bikes were being pinched; I kept well out of the matter, just wishing I could have had one of those bikes myself. They did catch him of course, months later, with a pound of nails in his dinner bag, and they took the nails off him and then watched him ride away on a shiny black bike...

The best friends that a signalman could have, apart from his mates in the other boxes, were the permanent way ganger and his men, and in this respect I was lucky as my district ganger, Harry Payne and all the platelayers were the best bunch of men you could wish to meet. I would see Harry every day except on the night shift, he would come out of his cottage at Steventon each morning, rain or shine, a bag full of wooden keys and liners on his back, and his big key hammer over his shoulder. He would walk his length, up the Down main facing the traffic, looking for cracked or broken rails, driving keys back into the rail chairs if they were out, and replacing those that were missing. In the afternoon he would walk back on the Up main line doing the same, joining the platelayers wherever they were working in the section. He had immense pride in his job, and as a result, had a prize section, the examination train never dropped a dollop of whitewash anywhere on *his* sleepers. On a hot summer morning I could tell that Harry was on the way just by listening for long before he came into sight under the bridge, I would hear the 'wang' of the rails as he drove in a key, and by the time he reached me, it was time for a sit down and a cup of tea, but not for long, because Harry would soon be itching to move on, never wasting a minute of the company's time.

It used to be a source of wonder to me to see some of these old gangers at work. Although they had no formal engineering training, they could measure up a complicated junction that was due for renewal, send off the measurements, and a couple of months later an engineering occupation on a Sunday would see the old track lifted out by a steam crane, and the new section go in without a change even of half an inch.

Occasionally Harry might come up into the box and inform me that he had found a broken rail in the section, and it was a case of us both working closely together so as not to cause any undue delay to trains. I would give Harry a time between trains (usually he would require about half an hour) then, waiting until that time came round, Harry would round up his gang, place a new rail on the platelayer's trolley (I had previously given him occupation of one of the lines and confirmed this with collars on the levers and an entry in the register), and they would all go post-haste to the breakage, pushing the trolley loaded with rail, shovels and picks, where they would then commence to slack off the fish-plate bolts where necessary.

If Harry was close to one of the loop line telephones, he would ring me to see if it was all right to start the job, but, if he was way out in the section, we used our pre-arranged system of communication. I would lower and raise the nearest signal to him, and Harry would go into action and the gang, spread out along the affected rail, would swing their key hammers knocking out the keys, lift out the rail, and replace it with the new one, and as soon as it was resting inside the chairs, the keys would be hammered back in, and the fish-plate bolts tightened up. I always gave Harry a good margin to complete this operation, and always with a proviso that should he be running tight on time, I would raise and lower the signal five minutes before I needed the section handed back, but in fact, I never once had to use that five minute reminder.

The platelayers in the gang of course spent all their time out in the various parts of the section, and months might pass before I saw them, while at other times, the area of maintenance would be within the signals, and I would have their company for some time. Three of them had duties connected with my signal box, and these chaps were my fogmen, but the whole gang turned out in the snow, to keep the points and signal free of ice. Fog working was one of the worst aspects of signal box work, throwing an immense strain on the signalman. With all visibility gone, particularly at night, we would 'fly on the instruments' as an airline pilot would say, watching the diagram, track circuits and signal repeaters, and, as a double safety measure, we would introduce double block working — that is to say, we would not give 'line clear' to the box in the rear, until we had received 'line clear' from the box in advance. We had our terms of reference (fogging-point) before introducing this system of working, namely if we could not see our home signals, but we also consulted together by a telephone call to our mates all up and down the line, and then we would all send for the fogmen together. If the fog came down during normal daylight working hours, they would report to the box anyway, but at night or during the early hours, a porter would be dispatched from the nearest station to knock them up.

My three chaps would report to me and I would enter their names and the time of reporting in the train register book, and off two of them would go. Harry Woodbridge went to my Down distant signal and Bill Strong to my Up distant, and providing that the distant signal was in the off position for oncoming trains, they would take no action. But if the Distant signal was at the caution position, they would place one fog detonator on the rail to be exploded by the wheels of the train, and also at the same time exhibit a yellow light to the driver, from a hand-held oil lamp.

It was a god-forsaken job on a dirty night, stuck miles out in the section in the fog, working from a little wooden but for shelter. Admittedly, they had a little stove inside, but for months at a time these huts were out of use, and so became damp and most uncomfortable. I always made a point of having some dry wood and a lump of paraffin-soaked cotton waste ready for my fogmen to take, plus a small sack of dry coal, which was only a little thing to do but much appreciated by my lads.

The third chap had the most enviable of jobs. His duty was to stay in the box with me and look for tail lamps, because in the fog it was a very difficult job to see a tail lamp on the last vehicle, and without seeing it we could not clear the section behind and accept another train. If, by chance, the tail lamp was out, then it meant waiting until the train had been stopped and an examination made to make sure that the last vehicle on the train was indeed there, then the message was passed back to the last signal box before 'train out of section' could be given.

Goods trains were no problem. By the time 70 odd wagons had passed by, the smoke and steam had cleared and the three lamps carried on the brake van could easily be seen, but with passenger trains it was very difficult. Many drivers were loath to run hard, so with the regulator eased down, the smoke and steam from the chimney would roll back along the coaches, mingle with the leaks from the steam heating pipes on the coaches, and tuck up behind the last vehicle, which was already becoming invisible as the fog swirled in behind. My chap out of the gang for this duty was 'Pecker' Strong, and I could not have had a better bloke to help me. He was quite within his rights to remain in the box and lean out of the window looking for tail lamps, as we both did in any case to confirm our sightings, but, if the fog was very thick, 'Pecker' would be down on the ground making sure, shouting up his confirmation to me so that I could clear the section with the least delay. None of these lads complained about the job, although sometimes after a hard day's work out in the section they would get home and only have time to snatch a meal before they had to be back again for a full night's duty. They were all professional railwaymen, devoted to keeping the trains running, and to this end they used to put up with the most atrocious conditions.

Fog was certainly an inconvenience, but it was the snow that caused the real problems. When the airlines shut down, and the buses stopped running, there was still one way of moving people and goods, and that was the railway. I can never remember the railways coming to a complete halt, but it was only because of the platelayers working until they dropped to keep the points and signals free from ice. It was heart-breaking to see them hunched up over a pair of points, scraping and brushing snow out of the slides with a blizzard blowing up their tail, then standing back to let an express pass, and finding afterwards that the rush of air from the train had blown the snow back in again. I used to help from the box as much as I could by keeping the points and signals on the move to prevent them from freezing, and I insisted that one at a time they came to the box to thaw out, and have a hot drink, every half an hour or so, and in return for those small considerations, hardly a week went by without my receiving a gift of a rabbit or a cabbage, and in the spring, young onions for the salad.

During normal weather conditions, the gangers had a short shift on a Saturday morning, oiling the points and locking bars, and we in the signal box, would help in this operation, by moving the parts to be oiled as they requested. One side of the point slides would be oiled, then they would wave their arm slowly from side to side in front, as a sign to change the points over so that the opposite slide could be dealt with. For the locking bars, the arm was raised up and down; the system worked beautifully, and it was always a delight to find how easily those points worked after the Saturday treatment.

One little game we used to play on them was when they came to oil near to the box. It had to be near so that we were on top of them and could see what they were doing. The oil feeder for this job was a big one with a very long spout, so we would watch the spout go into the open points, then a quick snatch on the lever would squeeze the end of the oil feeder flat before they could get it out, and they were obliged to go over to the platelayers' hut and get out the hacksaw to take off half an inch from the spout before they could start again. Every platelayers' hut carried a large stock of short-spouted oil feeders, but they took it all in good spirits, providing that this bit of fun was not carried out too often.

At the start of each period for which a new timetable was issued, one of us would pick out the trains relevant to our particular box during the full twenty-four hours, and stick a list of them on the wall over the register, but constant use and so familiarity over the first few weeks quickly made this list superfluous until the next change of timetables. My first experience of this came with the change from the winter service to the summer service, which always began on the first of May. I was introduced to it by the time-honoured method of delivery to out-station signal boxes on the Great Western. I was on the 6.00a.m. early shift when the first Down stopping passenger train came towards me blowing the whistle, so I slid open the window to see the guard fling out a bundle that went bouncing along the Up main line. When I had collected this bundle and opened it up, it proved to be the new service timetables for the summer months. It took me several hours to re-write our list, checking with the other lads down the line to see if we had missed any trains out, and when it was completed I could see that this was going to be a busy time. There were many extra trains, particularly on a Saturday, holiday trains from Newcastle to Bournemouth, Poole, Weymouth and Weston-super-Mare, and, of course, the returns, with the normal Up traffic booked to run in two or three parts. When the summer service started, the West Curve at Foxhall was a very busy place, and many goods trains were either blocked back until the night hours, or cancelled, for with all the extra trains mixed up with the ordinary booked service, there was just no margin for goods traffic.

I doubt if there were many locomotives or crews available either, all the 'Halls' and 'Granges' being in use, and even the old Churchward 'forty-threes' sported 'A' headlamps for a change.

To an outsider it would have seemed an impossible situation to sort out at junctions, and 'boxers' were flying about all over the place. 'Boxers' was the name for box-to-box messages, an example would be 'the first part of the Fishguard preceding the second part of the Weston'. When such a telephone message was received from Steventon, I would pass it on to Foxhall Junction, and so it would go on, all the way up the line to Paddington, and it would apply to the Down line as well, so a tight watch on the timetable had to be kept to sort out the confusion. It was up to the junction signalman to sort everything out, and at times it proved impossible, so trains got mixed up by running out of sequence. If there was any doubt, the signals would be pulled off for the main line and if the driver stopped we would change the points over and try him that way, working on the theory that the driver, at least, should know what train he was driving, and which way he wanted to go! One of these 'boxers' was a regular one, even in the winter, and this was the one about the 8.00a.m. up from Cheltenham, because it regularly carried the Chairman, General Sir Brian Robertson. He would get in the train quite unaware that the signalman was looking out for him, then the message would go ahead from box to box, and we all made sure that this express had a clear run. When Sir Brian got to Paddington he made a point of thanking the driver for a good run, little knowing how it was achieved, but the drivers did however, and always gave a 'thumbs up' sign to thank us.

The telephone system was one of the most simple systems devised. In the big boxes there were banks of them, but I only had six in Milton box, four on the wall and one on each side of the block instrument shelf, the latter direct lines to the boxes on either side of me. The through or omnibus 'phones worked on a code with a centre selector set in the cabinet. All of the boxes were listed with their code, so if I wanted to ring down the line, I would turn the selector to the appropriate number on the dial and press the selector the correct number of times. An advantage was that this system was an open line so that every signalman right down to Swindon could be on the line at the same time, and that way we were able to keep tabs on the running of every train. It could also be a bit of a giggle at times, for instance we might all be linked up having a chat in between trains, and then perhaps a goods train could be heard rattling through Shrivenham with a hot axle box squealing away, so Shrivenham would tell Uffington, he would have a look and decide that it was not too bad and inform Challow, who would pass it on to Wantage, nobody wanting to stop this train with all the attendant work of detaching a wagon and writing out a report. By the time it reached Steventon my mate there would decide that as it had come so far another few miles wouldn't hurt, so Didcot would have the job.

There was no safety risk involved, as we were all aware of the running powers of a hot grease box, and the driver would be keeping an eye on it, as he didn't want to stop with a heavy goods train, but when a grease box became a 'flamer' then action was taken at once. A 'flamer' was quite a show at night, flames whipping out from the axle box with red drops of molten grease splashing out all over the sleepers, and when this happened, the bell code for 'Stop and examine train' would be sent to the box ahead, and this signalman would stop any train going into the section until the defective train had come to a standstill.

Every morning we would all be on the telephone from just after five minutes to eleven waiting for the time signal, which was when the young lady in the exchange would be linked up with both us and Paddington. It was most important that we did not miss this appointment, because the moment the clock at Paddington reached eleven o'clock, the young lady would call out over the telephone, 'it's eleven o'clock' so that every signal box was operating on Paddington time. This signal had to be entered in the register with any alteration then made to the signal box clock. So much importance was placed on the ritual, that each month when the District Inspector made his routine visit, he would check back through the book to see that the clock had been booked every day.

All guards on passenger trains were also expected to correct their watches with the Paddington clock so that those country stations that were without a signal box could obtain the correct time from the guard on the first train out of Paddington that stopped at the station. In that way, the whole of the Great Western ran on Paddington time, the accuracy of times when trains passed in and out of the various divisions were confirmed, and in the unfortunate event of an accident, the actual time of occurrence could be recorded. Such was the importance to me of this standard time, that even today, thirty years later, I cannot tolerate a clock being wrong, the time has to be the correct time. In fact, when we were newly married, it used to drive my dear wife 'up the wall' if our clocks were slow or fast at home, because I would fiddle for days with the regulator until I was satisfied that the time was correct. Dear girl, she has got used to it now, and accepts it as one of my little ways that I cannot get out of.

As that first summer at Milton wore on, I began to settle down and enjoy life, and I found that I did not have to stop and think or work out margins for freight trains; the job became easier, I was in fact dealing with it in an unhurried way and fully confident. I had seen my share of ordinary emergencies and I had dealt with a derailment, so now I began to plan for the long term. I had the rule book out and the appendix, laid on the desk so that I could go through it at every opportunity. In any case, we all had to keep on top of the operating rules so as to pass the yearly examination by the District Inspector, but I had plans for the future, and any small alteration that came along, I carefully stuck inside my book so that it was always up to date. On the telephone, I would discuss rules with any of the other lads who were interested, wanting to be sure that I could answer any question that was thrown at me, but there had to be an incentive for all that knowledge I was cramming in, and there was, because I was getting married, and I wanted promotion to a higher class signal box, with the extra money, just as soon as I could.

The wedding was all fixed up for August, and as the time drew near I had so much advice about married life from the lads all down the line that I could not possibly fail to be a good husband. My young lady went home to Wales a month before to prepare for the wedding, and I had a lieu day owing to me for working on a bank holiday, so that would give me the Friday off in addition to a week's holiday for our honeymoon.

On the Friday afternoon I caught the train from Didcot, heading for Swindon and Newport (changing trains at both places), then on to and the church. I stood in the corridor as far as Swindon, as I had promised the lads that I would, and they were waiting for me, standing at the windows of their boxes all the way from Didcot West End. Some were swinging small axes, to signify that I was going to get the chop, some were wiping dry tears from their eyes, and some were pointing their thumbs down, the Roman sign to the gladiator, to show that I was doomed.

Changing trains at Swindon brought back many memories of steam days. As I waited for the South Wales express to arrive, a dirty old 72XX class tank came knocking her way through the middle road, with a long rake of wagons, her fireman pulling the fire through with the pricker, sweat was pouring off him as he struggled in the enclosed cab on that hot afternoon. I felt sorry for him, reflecting that, but for my transfer, that could have been me. As soon as the brake van was clear the South Wales express ran in, a scruffy 'Castle' at the head of thirteen coaches. The blower was on, and this fireman too was sweating hard as he leaned out of the cab, his face black with coal dust, a weary look about him. I climbed into the coach behind the tender, and as I sat down I could hear the scrape of the shovel as it rode on the tender plate. Poor blighter, he was firing in the station, and with the blower on it implied a rough trip. I sat back with a feeling of smugness, secure in the knowledge that I had left all that behind, and yet I was wondering in the back of my mind if I should go and offer him a hand. However, before I could talk myself into it, the whistle blew and we were off. Rough engine or not, we made good time to Newport, and when I got out of the coach the fireman was pulling the pricker through the fire, ready for going to shed at Cardiff. With my case in my hand, I crossed the footbridge to the opposite platform, then made my way back towards the end of the platform where the valley trains stood.

There were always two trains waiting, one for the Eastern valley and one for the Western valley, and not always in the right order, so it was as well to check with the driver. I had learnt that the hard way a few weeks before, when with the superiority of a railwayman who thought he had no need to ask questions, I got in the wrong train and landed up at Ystrad Mynach. It had taken two bus rides and a taxi to find my way to Abertillery, quite a feat for an Englishman stranded in the depths of rural Wales. So this time, I walked up the length of the rear train that was buffered up to the train in front, and spoke to the driver, whose reply was 'noo, mun, I'm Eastern, the boyo in front is for the Western valley'. I thanked him and walked on towards the head of the train, looking for a compartment on my own. There were four coaches this time, quite a load for the little 57XX class pannier tank, and finding a compartment next to the engine I climbed in and was about to place my case in the rack when a voice came in through the open window. 'Arrald, bach, what are you dooing yearrr?' I turned round and found myself looking at Jim Bevin, one of my old mates from my footplate days. During the time since I had become a signalman, Jim had returned to Wales and was now a driver, so it was a pleasure to meet an old comrade out of the blue like that. Jim pulled my leg unmercifully about going up the valley to be married, then he dared me to ride on the footplate with him to Abertillery, and I thought why not, because I could ride in a coach any time, but I hadn't been on the footplate for months, not since firing that farm special back in February.

Now it occurred to me that a 57XX class pannier tank is not the roomiest place to be on a hot August evening, and I now came out with a suggestion that was stupid, but it was done on the spur of the moment, never dreaming that it would be taken up. Why ride on the footplate as a passenger, why not fire the engine and let the fireman ride in the coach? Jim agreed, it would give me a chance to see what valley work was all about, so off came my jacket to join the case on the rack, and I jumped down on to the platform again. The fireman didn't need to be offered this opportunity twice, he pressed a ball of cotton waste in my hand and was in the compartment in a flash.

I rolled up my sleeves and tucked my tie in my pocket, then tucked my trousers into the top of my socks. There was just time to have a look at the enormous fire in the fire box, it must have been a couple of feet thick, then doors began slamming and whistles blowing. Jim blew off the brakes, placed the lever in fore gear, and at 6.50p.m. we were off, clattering over points and crossovers, and under the road bridge. I had just lifted the bunker flap when we plunged into the darkness of Newport tunnel, the light from the fire showing the coal pouring down to cover my shoes, and filling my socks with small coal, which I could feel between my toes, just like being at the seaside with a shoe full of sand. We came bouncing out of that tunnel into the sunshine, so I began to fire her, then there was an almighty lurch as we turned right and headed up a bank towards Bassaleg, causing me to stagger and scattering the coal from my shovel all over the footplate. I got up from my sitting position on the floor boards, and scraped the coal up, then it was time to put on the injector, and leave it on, for that little engine was using up water faster than I was used to.

Jim linked the valve gear up a couple of notches and gave her a bit more with the regulator, and I began to fire again, wondering whether I was ever going to see what was going on, as the firing seemed to be non-stop. Then Jim shut the regulator and we ran into Bassaleg, seven minutes out of Newport.

One minute of station time and we were off again, and I began firing, down with the flap, in with the coal, up with the flap, over and over again, that little tank engine scoffing up the coal as fast as I could put it in, without even the chance to shout a few words to Jim over the chattering of the exhaust. Then he shut off again and we were running into Rogerstone, sweeping past the great yards full of loaded coal wagons, and Rogerstone loco shed, packed with big 72XX, 4XX, tanks, and dozens of Churchward 'twenty-eights'. We stopped for one minute at Rogerstone and then we were off again, climbing now up into the mountains, the sun casting shadows, covering the sides of the valley with a soft green and brown hue as the fern growth changed colour towards the coming autumn. Now that the boiler was at a respectable level, and the fire burning well, I could spare the time to look outside the cab, to hear the chimney chattering away, and to see our silhouette reflected back. It was all so new to me; the view from the coach was appreciated and then forgotten, but from the foot-plate, that little pannier tank engine began to show me another aspect of the valley, something I could not appreciate when riding in a coach, the nature of the line ahead, twisting, turning, climbing, passing whistle boards every hundred yards, now having to slow down for a subsidence, now to open up again, the engine responding like a fussy little terrier, but still climbing ever up and through the valleys between the mountains. I could look down at the rows of miners' cottages, rows and rows of terraces, each home a couple of feet above the next one, all with slate roofs and dingy stone walls, each with a line of snow-white washing fluttering in the soft breeze, and I could see the dark River Ebbw tumbling over rocks and boulders as it hastened down the valley towards the sea.

I returned to my firing, the injector still on and forgotten, that little engine needing every bit of coal and water that I could put into her. We tore on with the urgency of the tightest timing that I had ever come across, scoffing coal and water at an alarming rate, equal to that of a 'Hall' on the main line with ten coaches on. We stopped at all stations, Tynycwn Halt, Risca, Cross Keys, Cwncarn, Abercarn, Newbridge, wasting no time at any, and eventually ran into Crumlin Low Level only thirty-three minutes after leaving Newport, to stand at the end of the platform under the spindly legs of the viaduct striding over the valley above us. I just had time to bend down into the corner of the cab and shut off the injector water feed and we were off again, the urgent blast of the whistle confirming the guard's 'right away'. Five minutes to Llanhileth, sweeping past the signal box in the lee of the mountain which towered above it, while the loco shed was tucked up in the corner between the main line and the mountain on the other side of the valley. Round the corner ahead, I could see the outskirts of Abertillery, and yet there were two more stops before I could leave this fussy, brave little engine. It was a three minute ride to Aberbeeg, and a booked stop for water, and here the line to Ebbw Vale curved away to the left of us, to disappear in the shadow of the mountain. The fireman came out of the coach and clambered up on to the tank, the lid clip was knocked back and the leather water bag dropped in, then water began to gush into her tanks, all done with the slick practice of familiarity. Five minutes later we were away again; I had finished with the shovel now, and could stand in the cab doorway to allow the cool air to dry the sweat which was streaming down my face. Two minutes brought us to Six Bells Halt, rows of sidings covered with coal dust and stretching back to connect with the colliery, where the tall winding gear overlooked the whole area, and the spinning winding gear wheels were accompanied by the soft 'puff, puff' of escaping steam from the engine house. The rows of terraced houses in serried ranks curved round the side of the mountain and looked down into the town below, down even into the top of the blackened chimney of the foundry, and overlooked the bridge crossing the dirty river, still tumbling its way down the valley. Jim closed the regulator and began to apply the brake. There was just time for me to shake his hand and jump down on to Abertillery platform, grabbing my suitcase and jacket out of the compartment, before he was away again, hammering his way up towards Brynmawr, the echoes of that chattering chimney coming back to me as he rounded the curve and disappeared out of sight. I saw him go, and felt satisfied that I had fired an engine up the valley and now I had some idea of what valley work was all about; it was a rough life, and one that I was thankful was not mine.

The other passengers were making their way over the footbridge and I picked up my case and made my way towards the bridge, to see a shapely pair of legs come down the steps, which could only belong to my Bet, my beautiful young bride of tomorrow who had come to meet me. I put down my case and opened my arms to sweep her off her feet, confident in the knowledge that she loved me, but when she saw me, her features were a mixture of emotions. She had been laying a plan of which I was quite unaware, of walking up through the middle of the town to show off this Englishman that she was about to marry on the morrow. It was to be a slow walk, so that all her friends could see the smart young man that she had spoken so much about, but when she set eyes on me, she had to change her plans. I was black with coal dust, my shoes covered in it, the trousers of my number two suit were crumpled and wet at the knees, and my tie was dangling out of one pocket, my white shirt was filthy, with two large damp sweat stains under my arms, and I had lost two shirt-buttons somewhere, so that the sweat and dust had congealed into a mess of slurry on my chest, and under the coal dust, my face was brick red from the heat of the fire box. She ignored my outstretched arms and backed away; this was no young knight in shining armour riding a white horse, neither was he a clean young off-duty signalman, but looked like a collier just up from the local mines, and it was as well if she stood up-wind of him. We walked in stony silence through the town via the back streets, up through back alley-ways and out into connecting roads. As we passed the 'Lamb' public house, the open door looked most inviting, and a sign on the wall advertised Webb's Golden Ale, cool and fresh from the barrel, and I could have drunk a gallon of it, but now was not the moment. We then began the one in three climb up to Darran Road and her home, conversation being impossible on this steep road in any case.

It took her mother only an hour to get over the shock, long enough for me to climb into a tin bath in the back kitchen with a bar of soap and a scrubbing brush, and while I was in the bath I could hear through the closed door some comments being made about marrying a local collier. Time though is a great healer, and when I emerged from the kitchen, the repairs had been made, and I was pink, clean, acceptable, and most important I did not smell any more. She married me the next morning at twelve in the Congregational Church to the ringing of bells, and the sound of the packed ranks of the Male Voice Choir, mixed up with much weeping from the ladies. The congregation included my father, mother, sister and my best man, Roy Saunders, all looking so solemn as the sound of the choir swept over them. Father caught my eye and winked. He had apparently laughed until the tears ran down his face when he had been told of my condition on arrival the day before, and it was only when mother heard the story, that she let out that on *her* wedding day my 'old chap' had been down in the pigsty with her father, which was where he had hidden the beer, because her mother was dead against drink, although it was said that she wasn't against a drop of her 'one hundred per cent' parsnip wine.

That afternoon, my new wife and I went to catch a train to Weymouth for our honeymoon, and when the little pannier tank swept in and stopped, Bet clung to my arm and pushed me into the compartment before I had a chance even to take note of the engine number, let alone have a word with the driver. At Newport I was hustled over the bridge and with much more haste, pushed into the train for Bristol, almost as if I was going somewhere under escort, and I found myself packed in with a dozen other people, with no chance at all of escaping on to the footplate. At Bristol we had a wait of half an hour, during which I had to sit quiet and behave. We boarded the local train to Westbury, and Bet began to relax, knowing that I was now in a district where no dirty old drivers or firemen knew me, and when we got to Westbury and our last change, we were almost down into the West Country.

Our train came in and I ran back to see the guard, showing him my free railway pass and explaining that I was with my bride, whereupon he unlocked a first-class empty compartment in the coach next to the engine for our benefit. As a good husband should, I stood back to allow Bet to enter first, and just at that moment, from the footplate, came a shout of 'Hey, Harold'. I had no chance to reply, as Bet was out of that compartment and down on the platform in a flash, then she pushed me up inside and the guard locked the door before I fully realised that someone knew me. She was determined not to let me anywhere near the engine on this trip: one would think that my first love was a steam locomotive, and, admittedly, it had been at one time, but now I had another love to keep me warm, and I was a signalman with a nice clean job, I did not smell coming home from work, and it was going to stay that way.

That evening, however, it was my turn to take a firm line, with all the experience of a husband of six hours, as we were walking along the front at Weymouth. Bet looked gorgeous in her going-away clothes, a bloom on her cheeks and a sparkle in her eyes which was enough to make other young men look at her longingly. They would then notice me looking 'daggers' at them and would hastily imply that it was something beyond my wife that they were really interested in. I really should have known better than to leave her for a few minutes. But, being trained on the footplate, I was used to six cups of tea, which resulted in me disappearing for a while. Five minutes I was away; just five little minutes, and when I came up from underground, my lovely girl had moved away. However, there was a smashing girl leaning up against the sea-front railings, but she was obscured from me by a group of American service lads, who were clearly chatting her up. Eventually, one of them moved to one side and I could see that it was MY WIFE who was being chatted up! I said two words, spoken very softly in the ear of one American, such as the Mafia would have said, to get the response that I wanted. He understood English all right, and vanished into the walking crowds with his friends, as quickly as he had appeared. My wife was relieved at their departure, fortunately convinced that the husband-to-be of yesterday was worth a bit more than those four well-heeled Americans.

During that week, we were in the same situation as hundreds of other young couples walking along the sea front. We explored, and sat in the sun, and for five per cent of the time talked about the future, while the other ninety-five per cent introduced me to the harsh realities of married life. This brand new husband was quickly transformed, in that short week, into an old married man. It was done so subtly with all the inborn perceptiveness of a young girl transformed into a married lady, already equipped with plans for a successful marriage. We had been fortunate enough to rent a house to return to; a broken-down old place, it is true, but nevertheless something that we could turn into a home. I knew that when we got back, there was going to be a spending spree, and we had the pick of all the furniture shops of Reading, Oxford, Swindon, Wallingford and Abingdon, plus a couple of local shops in Didcot, but with the stealth of a huntress, my nice new missus steered me into every furniture shop in Weymouth, not to buy, but as a rehearsal for that operation. This was the reconnaissance patrol to compare prices and to start my education, and in the process I was shown three-piece suites, wardrobes, sideboards, dressing tables and chairs of every shape, size and colour. When these shops were exhausted, it was the turn of the fabric shops, to look at bed linen, tea cloths, towels, carpets and curtains, then on to china shops to examine dinner sets, tea sets, knives, forks and saucepans. I was shattered, and thought 'Ye Gods, what could the real thing be like'. On our return home I soon found out, for our hard-earned savings went like snow in hot sunshine, together with the motor bike.

I can now look back on that period, knowing that it was a definite turning point in my life: all the rough trips on badly steaming locomotives, and the hectic time I had been through in the last few months, had all failed to do what one very sweet young lady had managed to do in a couple of hours. She had turned the boy into a man, and like all happy couples, we are still cementing the relationship. The colour of curtains, wallpaper, and any replacement to the household equipment is still a topic for debate, but now I can converse on equal terms, having become a very mature wise old married man, highly skilled in the art of agreeing, with the experience of over thirty years behind me to prove that I am right. Doctor Samuel Johnson summed the situation up very nicely, when he said, 'Marriage has many pains, but celibacy has no pleasures'.

We came home after that week, and I returned to Milton on the night shift. I also returned to the comments and well-meant advice from my mates in the other signal boxes. As soon as there was a lull in the traffic, the 'phones began to ring, and the congratulations were given. Advice on how married life should be dealt with swamped me, and everyone was an expert, all being eager to pass on their tips on how to make it a success, how to deal with tap washers, fuses, gardening, laying lino and carpets, and how to stand firm, when to back off, and, of course, the inevitable advice on how to change a baby's napkin. The last piece of advice could only come from one person, Jack Drew in Foxhall Junction box, who had moved round from Didcot North Junction while I had been away, so we now had the 'king' of leg-pullers on our shift, or so he thought at the time.

Jack's reference to nappies was just a start, he had other plans as well. He knew my address, and he passed it round the district. The postman began to call, filling up the hallway with catalogues from every manufacturer of prams, cots and baby clothes in the country; I found out that every signalman had filled in coupons or answered advertisements from every publication that they could lay their hands on!

When this flood of paper work eased off, it was time for me to have my turn, remembering the old saying 'vengeance is sweet'. I gave up spending my spare moments on study of the rule book for a little while, and began to spend a few hours planning revenge, sweet hours they were too, because this had to be something very special. I knew that Jack was partial to a bit of rough shooting, and he had every chance at Foxhall Junction because the box backed on to a small bank with a thicket on the top, a bit of waste ground dividing the West Curve and the Hump shunt spur in Didcot depot. I knew that when Jack was on the night shift, he would tie a torch underneath the barrel of a .22 rifle, and in the early hours when the rabbits came out to feed, he would poke that rifle through the open rear window, switch on the torch and aim between the rabbit's eyes. It was a successful method and he rarely missed, and I was determined not to miss a good opportunity either.

Before one period of night duty, I spent a few minutes of the afternoon in my shed with a milk bottle and a hammer, breaking that bottle into pieces which I collected up and then I set off to work half an hour early. When I got to Foxhall, I propped my bike against the box and swore the late turn signalman to secrecy. I then put that half an hour to good use, as I covered the bank with my little bits of glass, all carefully spaced two inches apart.

My revenge came soon after midnight; I had the Foxhall end of Milton box window open, and in the soft stillness of the night, I could just hear the 'pop, pop' of a rifle, as Jack banged away for hours, because everywhere his torch shone, he could see eyes. At one point he came on the 'phone and said that he had never known so many rabbits about at one time, and he even talked about a contract with the butcher! Poor Jack, when daylight came he could hardly believe his eyes, there were no rabbits, not a single one, but he found the glass, and near each piece a neat round bullet-hole in the bank. The bullets had gone home alright, and so had the message. Neither of us spoke of this incident afterwards, but honour was satisfied, and the next night I received a matchbox full of empty shell cases, so Jack had recognised an equal adversary.

That first summer in Milton box was a happy one. On the night shift the work could be carried out in daylight almost the whole time, the hours of darkness were so short, and on the early and late shifts I began to learn about the intricacy of signal wire adjustment, to allow for temperature changes, the adjustments using those tall derrick-like contraptions standing behind the frame and coupled to the signals, each with its own winding gear slotted on to the long threaded spindle. On the early turn, as the sun began to climb and heat up, the sharp tang of creosoted sleepers would waft up and into the box, and the rails would begin to 'whang' as they expanded, and that was a sure sign of a lot of work ahead. The wire would begin to sag between the pulleys and the signals would not respond to the lever movements, so it would be time to start winding in the slack, turning the winder on the derricks perhaps fifty times before the signals would begin operating again. Before long, a cloud might pass over, and the slack would have to be let out again, and this would go on all day, winding in and out, an additional chore to the normal box working. Points were not affected by this expansion because the blades were not coupled and so had a 'run off' but the locking bars to the points were very prone to give trouble because the signal detector blades that passed through the locking bars would expand at the wire end and would not engage in the slotted blade. Although the points could be changed they could not be locked, but as with most problems, this could be overcome without much trouble, with a little bit of knowledge not shown in the rule book. It was a way out without affecting safety standards or delaying the trains, and it was all done with a little bit of wood, in fact, a matchstick. The first indication that the heat had caused expansion was when the points were changed, and it was found that the locking bar would not go in, which meant that the signal could not be pulled off, so the signalman would go down the stairs to the affected point with a box of matches. All locking bar detector blades are drilled with a series of holes so that the signal linesman can take up any adjustment necessary, so it was possible to pull back the blade, by hand, until one of these holes cleared the locking slot, and then the matchstick could be inserted in the hole and the blade eased back on the stop, the matchstick being just strong enough to hold it there. Then came a quick dash back up into the signal box, to change points, and push home the locking bar, breaking the matchstick in the process, and off came the signals.

That little dodge helped us out of heavy delays very often until the repairs could be done, but it was only possible, of course, where the points were close to the box. If they were some way away, then it was sometimes possible to clear the defect by slamming over the points in the hope that the detector could be jumped in, and if that didn't work, then trains would have to stop at that signal until the signal lineman came and attended to it, and, in fairness to them, they were a good lot of lads, turning out at once on receipt of a telephone call.

As with all kinds of transport it was not so much the traffic that became a problem, but the weather. Fog meant delays, gales would blow out signal lamps, snow would block points and freeze signals and cover up the signal glass, and thunderstorms would discharge electricity and affect all the signal box circuits. My first experience of a thunderstorm was very spectacular. At eight in the evening as I had the last look round my garden, the atmosphere began to get heavy and the sinking sun had a copper tint about it. When I left home at half past nine there was a dullness on the horizon, not the sort of evening to leave my wife alone, but I had to go to work and hope that she would be all right. In the Swindon direction a blackness was beginning to sweep across the sky, and outside the quietness was unbelievable, the birds had stopped their twittering, there was no gentle evening breeze, everything was deathly still. I rang Highworth Junction, and my worst fears were confirmed, because they were in the middle of a severe thunderstorm, and it was creeping up the line towards me.

I had all the windows of the box open to allow what little air there was to circulate, and I stood at the open window and watched the 9.40p.m. parcels train from Swindon pass on the Up main line, the locomotive gleaming, the paint washed clean, and water cascading from the van gutters, and yet there was no rain here, just this dry stillness. The driver and fireman pointed back towards Steventon, and now I could see that the darkness was speeding towards me, a solid blanket of heavy cloud rumbling with anger.

The parcels train swept on towards Foxhall, its tail lamp light dancing and flickering on the last vehicle. I began placing the signals back, then went to the shelf and knocked out on the block bell 'train out of section' and as I did so, a great blast of wind came roaring through, sending notices flying off the hooks on the wall. Long-forgotten ash came billowing out from under the stove, and the trees opposite bowed towards the east, the leaves stripped off altogether in that great powerful draught. Then equally suddenly, came the rain, not a steady rain, but a great slamming deluge pouring out of that heavy cloud as a solid wall of water advanced up the line. It hit the side of the box with the open window, and drove a sharp distinct line across the polished floor, so I ran over to shut the window, and keep out the tempest. As the Down freight passed I could see the visible effort being made by the locomotive punching its way forward and saw the driver and fireman squeezed up in the corner as they tried to obtain some protection. Although I had never been in such a storm as this one, I could well remember what it had been like on the footplate, with the rain whipping past the cab, hissing and spitting where the suction from the firebox drew it in to hit the hot firebox flap, and the lightning striking the wet rails a mile ahead and racing up the line. Even so, I was not prepared for such fury as the storm was about to release. When the first strike of lightning came, it was with a jagged whiperack of angry red flame, ripping down from the black cloud to strike into the field opposite, lighting up the whole area for a split second, the trees and signal posts standing out stark in that sudden blinding flash, while the stench of sulphur filled the box.

Immediately there was a colossal crack of thunder directly overhead, obliterating the clanging of all the block bells and telephones, and I was plunged into darkness. The sudden discharge of all that electricity activated every bit of box equipment as I groped my way over to the locker, found the hand lamp and lit it. I lifted down the emergency oil lamps with tall chimneys, only to find them covered in dust and empty, the wicks dry and unused, which did not help the situation.

I now had another lesson to learn in signal box work, how to decipher block bell codes from the constant jungle of interference caused by each lightning strike, and how to pull off signals and book trains in the register, with the aid of only one hand lamp. It was half an hour before I managed to fill the empty lamps with oil and re-hang them from the ceiling, in between scrabbling round dealing with trains. Once they were hung and lit, I made up my mind that I would never be caught out again, realising that those lamps were there for an emergency such as this, and in future, they would always be ready for use.

As the storm raged, we had to resort to the telephone instead of block bells, because it was quite impossible to understand any kind of bell code, with the constant interference from the lightning making the bells ring continually. I also came across another phenomenon new to me, as the electrical discharge built up in the air, so did the static, and it was transformed into St. Elmo's Fire, dancing and flickering along the top of the shining signal levers. I had been told to expect this during a thunderstorm, and I had also been told that because of the excellent earthing properties of a signal box, it was one of the safest of places to be, but nevertheless it took some courage on my part to handle those levers. That storm became trapped inside the Thames Valley, rolling and rumbling round until two in the morning. In one brief instant during a particularly bad lightning flash, I can remember glancing out of the rear window across Milton depot and seeing very clearly the white lines of a church tower miles away across the countryside. Later in the week in daylight, I had a look through a small telescope, and realised that what I had seen during the storm was the tower of the chapel attached to Culham College, a lovely view not possible today, because, in the way, stands the giant Didcot Power Station, on the site of the depot.

For a Class Three main line signal box, Milton would take some beating for a newcomer to be weaned on, as it was new and modern, it had running water and a wash-basin inside, large windows for a perfect all-round view, and a flush toilet in the downstairs locking room. Every kind of traffic was dealt with, from light engines to the expresses, and the traffic was heavy enough to keep one busy, yet light enough to enable one to enjoy a cup of tea and a sandwich between trains. It was gentle going compared with some boxes, there was time to study the rules and regulations and hold quizzes with the other lads on the phone, each of us trying hard to catch out the other chap, and without realising it at the time, I was soaking up all this knowledge until the time came when I was able to give as good as I got, and I felt that I was now right on top of this job.

The time came round for the yearly examination by the District Inspector, which was not a sudden spot check; we all knew that he was on the trail after he had visited the first box, because the news went through the district at once. So I was not surprised when one day I saw Bill Checkley come cycling down the path towards me, a Relief signalman trailing along behind him ready to take over my duties while Bill put me through the rules and regulations. Soon he was at me, to the background of bells, lever movements, and trains rattling past, not an ideal situation to sit an examination, but that was the way it was done in those days. Bill was never the one to ask the odd question, he started at the beginning of the book and worked his way through, missing nothing, headlamp codes, bell codes, emergencies, standard block, permissive block, fog working, single line working, and station limits, and although we were in a main line situation at Milton, he even included questions on working a single line with tokens.

While the District Inspector was downstairs in the toilet, the Relief signalman confided in me that Bill had given me the hardest examination so far, he was still clearly a little bit wary of this ex-footplate man in one of his boxes. The average session was only half an hour, and yet I had been ploughing through for an hour. Thank goodness I had got through without any trouble, as the Relief signalman had been sweating on some of those questions, because if I had fumbled on any, Bill would have expected him to give the correct reply, being a senior man. However, that long session was to stand me in good stead in a couple of years, and went on my record, and to Bill's credit, in future examinations he never again put me through the hoop like that.

The summer service came to an end and the new winter timetables gave a much reduced service on the passenger side, so now the traffic ought to drop off a bit, or so we all thought, but the increase in freight trains gave us plenty to do. With the football season in full swing, the special notices became thicker, and as each cup round was played, so the number of specials began to increase. They would begin in the early mornings each Saturday, Cardiffs, Swanseas, Bristols, Arsenals and Evertons, all flying about the system, and one weekend it came to a head with such volume as will probably never be seen again. Cardiff and Bristol were in a cup replay with two of the London clubs, and Swansea were playing a league game, Wales were playing at Twickenham, and to top that lot, the American evangelist, Billy Graham, was holding a meeting in the Albert Hall. I knew that the Welsh nation had a liking for football and were known to be partial to a little rugby now and again, and that the remainder would turn up for a bit of Bible-thumping, providing that there was a small portion of the time set aside for some singing, but I had no idea what the mass evacuation of an entire nation could be like until that Saturday.

The whole freight programme was cancelled that weekend, and all those signal boxes such as Milton, which were normally closed on Sunday mornings, were booked to remain open. Each man on every shift throughout that weekend worked as he had never worked before. The football and rugby specials started in the early morning, by five o'clock the first were going through, one behind the other, clearing by eight o'clock for the normal passenger service, then in the afternoon the Billy Graham specials began to follow on, mixed up with the afternoon and evening expresses, the train register on the Up side page showing row upon row of 'A' headcodes. The locomotive power for all these trains was also something to see, 'Castles', 'Halls', 'Granges', 'Manors', and battered old 'forty-threes' that had not been at the head of a passenger train for years, let alone pulling an express, and each batch of specials dropped down the range of locomotives as the shed foremen scratched around for suitable power. Even two of the 'forty-seven' class, not normally used in the winter because of the lack of steam heating, were pressed into service, and one train towards the end of this mass exodus was headed by a grand old lady, a 'twenty-eight', her side-rods flashing round with the steam as it whipped back from her safety valve giving the impression that she was flying by at eighty instead of fifty, whilst the fireman leaned out of the cab with the slack of the coal-watering pipe in his hand, beating the side of the cab with it, urging her on, just like a jockey nearing the finishing post. When they were all gone, the Up main line was cleared for the delayed freights to run, and they too were one behind the other, hour after hour, at the expense of the Down traffic, which had, in turn, been held back, because just as the last Up special arrived at Paddington, the first of the returns began. Football specials started hammering away for home, dripping with paper streamers, and passengers littering the countryside with empty beer bottles and seat cushions. After these were gone, the Albert Hall returns began, lasting until the early hours, running so tightly behind each other that it was rare for any of them to see a distant signal off in its favour, but these were quiet trains, with compartments full of sleeping people, as they were hurried back to the valleys. It took a week for the normal freight traffic to recover from that weekend, and for days afterwards engines were running light back from South Wales to their home sheds.

One aspect of my signal-man's job I did enjoy, was the first-hand view that I had of locomotive testing. Weeks beforehand, we received the special notice and the timings for this programme and when it came it was well worth waiting for; to the other lads it was, admittedly, something out of the ordinary, and a little bit interesting, but to me it was real meat and drink.

It started with 6001 *King Edward VII* running up from Stoke Gifford to Reading with the dynamometer coach and twenty-five coaches tied on behind running at 60mph, and when that engine stuck her nose under Steventon bridge coming towards me, I could hardly believe my eyes. It looked as if there was the side of a garden shed stuck on the front, and, as she drew near, I could see that there was indeed a wooden shelter built on to the front frame and nailed back to the smoke box, with two little round windows let in at each side. Amazingly, there were people in there, because I could see two faces peering through the glass, but what it could have been like in there I can only imagine, as the roar from that chimney was like a volcano. The engine passed with the footplate full of people, then line after line of coaches, it was the longest passenger stock train that I had ever seen.

The trials went on for several weeks using other engines, all with these great loads. No. 1000 *County of Middlesex* was one to be hammered up through the section, then came No. 1009 *County of Carmarthen* now sporting a horrible little stove-pipe chimney, but the end of these trials was achieved with a run that was most interesting. In April, No. 6003 *King George IV* ran a test train from Paddington to Bristol with only eight coaches on, leaving Paddington at 10.55a.m. and passing me at Milton at 12.03p.m. going all out, so that she was through Steventon bridge before I could put all the signals back and past Steventon box in one minute, halving the normal express passenger time; this was the prototype Bristolian giving us a taste of things to come.

The next lot of tests that came my way were a bit of a shock to me, as I was used to the clean lines of the Great Western locomotive. That was when the first of the 'Britannias' came on the scene, great big powerful brutish-looking engines, running through with twenty-odd coaches on, and when they did take over regular services, it was to knock the beautiful 'Castles' out of the picture. One train, the Red Dragon up from Cardiff, was always run with a 'Castle' from Canton shed, a shed that took a pride in turning out the locomotive in showroom condition, but one Monday morning the train came up with a new 'Britannia', and we never saw the 'Castles' again on this train, but, to be fair to the new class of engine, they kept time, even if they did seem to be working hard at it.

The sequel was the introduction of the ten-wheel coupled 9Fs, and on the first test, this ugly locomotive came exploding through the bridge, tearing towards me, the exhaust climbing into the sky in a tall column before spreading out over the twenty-six coaches behind. Between the Down starting signal and my Up home signal the special brake test took place. The exhaust was cut off instantly to be replaced by the roar of steam from the safety valves and I could see smoke pouring out from the wheels as the brake blocks bit into the tyres, then the coaches began to shudder and they disappeared in a cloud of dirty brown rust, as all the accumulated rust and dirt was shaken out from under the frames.

They stopped for the booked five minutes at my home signal, people in white overalls swarmed out of the dynamometer car to look round the engine and the train. I could hear the ejector roaring up through the chimney, fighting to release the vacuum brakes, then the train began to move forward, the engine working hard to drag all those coaches against some of the brake blocks, which were reluctant to free from the wheels. As the engine passed me, I looked down into the cab, the air in the box whistling past as it was sucked out by the displacement of the engine exhaust, rattling the windows in their window-frames with each beat from the chimney. As the engine began to get to grips with that load, the driver pulled back on the regulator giving her more steam, then looked up at me and grinned, pointing over his shoulder towards the inside of the cab. I nodded my head and grinned back, to see two firemen, stripped to the waist, both as black as any coal miner, one opening and closing the fire hole doors, the other shovelling the coal in. No wonder lads were leaving the service, that was not just work, it was hard labour, without the benefit of having committed any crime.

It took that train as long as any goods train to clear the section, but there was no doubt as to what I had seen, those 9Fs might be freight locomotives and perhaps replacements for the ageing twenty-eights, but they were certainly capable of running a passenger train too. I never had the chance to fire or drive one, or indeed to go on the footplate while they were in service, but when *Evening Star* arrived for preservation at the Great Western Society's depot in my old shed at Didcot, I had a look round the engine, and a good long hard look on the footplate, and as an ex-locomotive man I could appreciate what a fine locomotive this was.

Chapter Four
Promotion

When promotion came, it was far in excess of what I had expected. My three years at Milton had been happy ones, but they had made me very used to routine; twenty-five minutes to get to work, cover the duty, then twenty-five minutes back home again, day after day. I was now conditioned to a sedentary job, and expecting to obtain promotion one day, into one of the bigger local boxes, but in the back of my mind I still missed the open road that I had enjoyed in the Locomotive Department. Then, out of the blue, there came a change in the working conditions, when the basic week of 48 hours was reduced to 44 hours. This caused some complications because now we were all working an eight hour day for a 48 hour week, so implementation of the new arrangement took some working out. The difficulty was surmounted by both the management and unions agreeing to an 88-hour fortnight, and so introducing a 'rest day' every other week, but before anyone could have this day off, there had to be someone to cover these duties. There were not enough Relief men to do it, as previously they were only intended to cover holidays and sickness, so a new grade was created, Rest Day Relief Signalman.

I didn't stand a chance of this new job, as there were dozens of higher grade men far ahead of me in class 2 and class 1 posts. Above that were the relief men and it took years to achieve that grade as it was *the* top job, equal to that of a top link engine driver, but I did stand a fair chance of getting into a class two box to replace one of those men if they went into relief work.

The notice came round inviting signalmen to apply for one of the new posts. It was advertised as Rest Day Relief as distinct from the normal Relief man, and to my surprise, it was a class one job. We all put in applications for these positions, as it was not often a class one came on the market. The reason for this was that signalling was much like a pyramid, and as you climbed upwards the area available to you became ever smaller. The signalling equivalent being just that there was just the one Class 1 box at Didcot – East Junction – the others in the area being either Class 2 or Class 3.

The class of a box or grade was based on a system of marks, one mark being awarded for every movement or action the signalman had to make; lever pulls, sending or responding to a bell, operating an instrument, even answering the telephone. The more traffic, the more he had to do, the busier the box, the more marks and so the higher the grade (and the more pay). A signalman could apply for 'the marks to be taken' whereby a bod would arrive with clipboard, sit in the box and record every time we did anything. Unfortunately making tea was not included. We would tell our mates either side in advance and they would help by sending us additional codes or making telephone calls that were not strictly necessary but all added to the numbers recorded on the sheet. Of course what we really needed was some extra train workings just for that day – and similarly hopefully no cancellations!

The management were in a hurry, being bound by the agreement to implement this reduction of hours as quickly as possible. When I pushed my application through Bill Checkley's letter-box, I knew full well that as a class three man with only three years of service in a signal box I stood little chance of being considered for the new grade. Within a week I received acknowledgement of my application from the District Operating Superintendent's office at Paddington, and a week later to the day, I received the following letter:

'List No. 45 Vacancy No. 1769 District Relief Signalman CI.1 Didcot (mainly Rest Day Relief)

I am pleased to inform you that you have been approved for the above vacancy with effect from 31.1.52, subject to competency not being delayed beyond a reasonable period of training.

I will advise you later regarding date of transfer.

Will you please note'

Would I please note! I would indeed, I could hardly believe it, and I still have that memo along with my other bits of railway history. The next letter was from Bill Checkley and it read:

'In connection with the above will you please commence learning duties as from Monday next 28th inst, reporting to this office after taking rest.'

I finished my last shift at Milton on the Saturday, clearing out my locker with a feeling of sadness. Again I was filled with the same doubts as three years previously when I had left the footplate, whether I had bitten off more than I could chew, and I wondered how my application had come to be approved. The answer to that question came when I reported to Bill Checkley on the Monday morning, because both he and Freddie Blackhall had recommended me.

That Monday, I was in a bit of a dream. I spent the day at Didcot West End, filling in time really, because I was booked to go to Paddington the next day, travelling on the familiar train, the 7.05 a.m, to visit Chief Inspector Honeybone, but this time without the worry and concern of the previous visit, although I did have a few 'butterflies in the tummy' nevertheless.

This time there was no messing about, and I didn't end up in the Board Room, but went straight into the little outer office, and finding it empty, I knocked on the door of the inner office and walked in. Inspector Honeybone was on the telephone, so he gestured to me to sit down. Whoever was on the other end was receiving a real rocket, and I began to have some doubts as I really didn't want this particular gentleman to be upset today, but I need not have worried. When he put the phone down, he shook hands and said how pleased he was to see me. He had been through my record, and said he had no intention of giving me questions on rules to answer, and that this visit was a formality, just to say that he had seen me, and that he thought I was suitable to take up relief work.

There was then another handshake and I was outside again, down on the familiar platform with honking taxis, echoing tannoys, and the bustling background that makes up Paddington station.

I was back at Didcot by 10.40a.m. reporting to Bill Checkley, and feeling very pleased with life, to think that I had made a top job in just three years, and I had a head start with it, having an intimate knowledge of the box at Milton. What the future would bring, I didn't know, but I would cross that bridge when I came to it.

Bill and Freddie were struggling, trying to work out a roster to give every signalman, including the relief men, a day off once a fortnight, and as there were 72 of them altogether, they were having a right old headache. They were also trying to find time for the new men such as myself to learn a big district, but Bill did have a job for me, and asked me to go and cover the vacancy at Milton until he could release me. As he gently pointed out, I would be covering my old job, so within two days I was back there, and likely to be so for a few weeks, so I opened up my locker again and settled in, but this time, I was on a higher rate of pay. I was also being paid walking time from Didcot, twenty minutes to the mile, two miles each way, which made an hour and a half extra each day, although in fact, I still rode my bike.

After two weeks covering my own vacancy, my replacement turned up. Granville Burt, one of the nicest chaps I have ever met, from Upton & Blewbury on the Newbury branch, was not a 'sprog' of a signalman, as I had been, but a chap with some service behind him, so we got on like a house on fire.

Granville was already used to double line working (but not in any volume) but he had no experience with permissive block working with goods loops. To Granville, it seemed against all nature to allow two or more trains into the section on the same line, and as it happened, freight traffic was heavy at that time, and the goods loops were in full use, both Up and Down. I was therefore able to show him the procedure, of how to bring a train to a stand at the loop home signal, then allow it to pull forward, instruct the driver as to how many were in front, then obtain the permission from the box ahead to allow the train in and allow it to proceed. The one thing to be careful of was to turn the loop block indicator to the correct figure, either one, two or three, and to make sure that this figure was reduced when one of the trains cleared at the other end.

On the Down side, it was a bit difficult to shout across, so we would stand at the open window and show two or three fingers to the driver. If he gave a toot on the whistle, then we knew he understood, but if he ignored our gesture, then he was stopped at the signal entering the loop, then allowed to pull forward, and he would then know that there was another train in front of him. It was quite a safe and legal method of working, because the drivers and guards were all aware of the regulations regarding permissive block working, they too had to pass the examinations, and the only time the guard was involved was during fog or falling snow, when he had to go back behind his train and lay detonators on the line. During my time as a fireman, I had spent many hours with my driver blocked back in a loop behind other trains, and it was a very nice situation on a dirty night, to bank up the fire, fill the boiler, and then join the guard of the train in front in his warm guard's van.

Granville had three weeks with me, one week on each shift, and it gave me the opportunity to give him the help that I had received from Bert Vokings three years before. I even tried Bert's trick of clearing off down the line to Steventon, which was interesting for me, as I had worked with Arthur Stoner for three years and had got to know him well, and yet, he was just a voice on the telephone, and at last, I had a chance to meet him and have a look at his signal box.

On the Wednesday of the third week, Bill Checkley rang me and asked how Granville was getting on. I told Bill that I considered that he was ready to take over, so Bill got on his bike and came to put Granville through the hoop, but there was no problem there. While I ran the box, Granville answered every question on the rules that Bill threw at him, and I was pleased to sign my name on the certificate that gave him the key to go forward to Paddington. He went the next day, a bit worried about Chief Inspector Honeybone, but I had told him truthfully, that I had found this big man to be a gentleman, and when Granville returned the next day, it was with the news that he had passed and would be taking over on the following Monday. The wheel had turned full circle.

Bill Checkley sent me a letter giving me instructions for the following months, but before I had time to open it, he rang me and said he would like me to take my time learning the new boxes, but at the same time not to be too long about it, only to let him know when I was moving on to another box. I opened the letter after this conversation, and nearly fell through the floor. I had only seventeen weeks to cover the district in time for implementation of the new 44-hour week. He also gave me the list of boxes: Foxhall Junction, Appleford, Culham, Radley, Sandford, Kennington Junction, Hinksey South, Wolvercote Sidings, Wolvercote Junction and Kidlington.

I made a start at Foxhall, simply because I knew the service and it was a box that I took to my heart. If ever a perfect junction box existed, then it must be Foxhall, there was all the main line running such as I had known at Milton, plus the goods loops, the West Curve traffic, traffic into and out of Didcot depot, and the sidings into the Provender Stores.

Foxhall was good basic training, because that list that I thought was so long grew to include Moreton Cutting and yard, Cholsey, Aston Tirrold, Didcot North Junction, Yarnton, Didcot West End, Nuneham, Abingdon, Hinksey North, Oxford Station South, Oxford North Junction, Witney, Carterton and Fairford, twenty-five boxes including Milton. I would have thought it impossible for any person to hold the knowledge of all those boxes under his hat, but it was possible, and there were some chaps who knew even more.

There were three first class chaps at Foxhall to choose from, Bill Ackrill, my original mate, Arthur Ryman and Jack Drew. I chose to go with Jack, not because he was any better than the others, but because he was the early turn man, and if I was going to spend the better part of three months learning the district, I might as well be on the day shift, there would be enough night and afternoon turns when we got cracking.

Jack made me welcome, so much so, I thought he must have forgotten about shooting at those bits of glass a couple of years back. He called out the lever numbers to me as I started to learn the frame, and I was gaining confidence as the trains ran by; that was his method, for him to call out the numbers while I pulled the levers, but then, on the last one, there was an almighty explosion under my feet. Flame and smoke shot up my trouser leg and I stood there trembling with shock until I realised that Jack had played one of his tricks on me. While I had been setting the road from the West Curve into the depot, Jack had been down in the frame room, and while there he wrapped the lead straps of a fog detonator round a spare lever so that when I pulled that lever, I rammed it up against the stop and exploded it.

I sat in the chair with my heart thumping like a 'King' going up Dainton bank, deciding that somehow I would have to think up another trick for Jack, and it would have to be something good, as he was an adversary to respect.

After three weeks at Foxhall, I felt that I could handle the box, so I moved on to Appleford and it was now that I came on to the Oxford branch telephone system, I also found that there were two other relief signalmen about. Three of us had been appointed to cover the new work, and these other two chaps were working their way up from Oxford. One was Eddie Edwards, who had given up Appleford to come on the relief staff, and the other was Ken Finch, who had come from Wolvercote Junction. I was to find out later that Ken was actually better at leg-pulling than both Jack and me put together.

Appleford was a nice little box, just the Up and Down main line outside the box, then on the Didcot side a pair of facing points to turn Up goods trains in, and a Down goods loop to turn trains out. The box was built in the traditional Great Western manner with brickwork for the frame room and wood with a gabled roof for the operating part. Access was up a wooden stairway on the outside, the whole box being adjacent to the level crossing. The crossing was not a busy one, open only when the residents from Arkwright's farm needed to come across, or when Cyril Butterworth, the regular signalman who lived in the cottage behind the box, decided to get his car out, but with a level crossing it did make a change for me to be in close touch with the public.

The road ran, with a sweeping curve, from Didcot to the village opposite the box so there was always something going on. To obtain water, we would go to the cottage opposite and draw it from the well. Fred Tyler and his wife lived there, and Fred worked on the farm, but was retained by the railway to take care of the tilley lamps at Appleford Halt, so he was a frequent visitor to the box. I spent a week there, which was enough to learn that box, then I moved on to Culham, a little old-fashioned box tucked up against a low bank, due to be demolished as soon as the new box on the platform was ready. One day there sufficed, as I had spent hours in this box unofficially when I had first begun thinking about transferring from the footplate. The next day I moved to Radley where I spent two weeks in the company of Wally Turner, who had been at the Reading Signal School with me. Radley was an interesting place, where the box was on the platform, so we were always in the public eye, and we had the company of the porters and the station master, plus a new type of signalling to me, the Abingdon single line branch.

I was beginning to enjoy myself, coming and going to work by train, but the further from Didcot I progressed the longer between home it took, and for the next box at Sandford meant I had to take my bike with me. I was to find when I began to 'work the district' that bike rides would average out at a hundred miles each week. Sandford I found to be like Milton, two main lines with an Up and Down goods loop, except that the Oxford side between Kennington Junction and Sandford was an Up Relief, reverting to a goods loop on the Didcot side of the box. There was a lead into the Kennington cold store from the Down loop, but it was not used very often. I found that a week was quite enough here, not only because it was so like Milton but because right behind the box the Sandford sewerage plant was situated, and after eight hours on duty it was the fresh air that smelt queer when I left!

My next box was Kennington Junction, and here I briefly met Ken and Eddie working their way south. We were at the halfway mark, and soon we would be getting together to work the district. My tutor at Kennington was a little Scot, Bob Chalmers, and what a help he proved to be. He would come on duty frozen after riding a little motor cycle all the way from Chilton on the Berkshire Downs, and he was looking forward to moving into a new house in the near future, which gave me an idea; Kennington was right in the middle of my district, how nice it would be to live there also. Bob, bless him, introduced me to the local councillor whose garden backed on to the goods loop behind the box, and he told me that a programme had just been passed to build a new estate a mile up the line towards Sandford, and I ought to get my name on the list. I did this straight away, and within a year I had a home and had moved in.

Kennington was the classic junction box from the old broad gauge days, very tall, and perched right in the middle of the Up and Down main line with the junction sweeping down from the Princes Risborough branch to join the main line in front of the box. It was not long before the Oxford drivers and firemen found me there, and they knew that I was an old footplate man used to catching single line tokens at speed. Although the normal arrangement was to throw the hoop on to the catcher, which was some way from the box, if they saw me leaning out of the end window, they would come roaring down off that branch at forty miles an hour, knowing that I would catch the token, and save myself a walk. Two weeks at Kennington and a telephone call to Bill Checkley confirmed that I was keeping up with the other two lads and running to the estimated training time. I had only four more boxes to go, and Hinksey South came next, another of the brick and flat-roofed war time boxes, much bigger than Milton, with the addition of a great big goods yard to contend with. I spent three weeks there, knowing that I could afford the time if I reduced the duties at the next box. I found that I was picking up the working of all these boxes better than I had thought I would, and that was because of the advice one of the senior relief men had given me, which was simply to write down in a little book the numbers of the lever movements. That little book was to be invaluable when I started the circuit.

Leaving Hinksey South, the list omitted the Oxford boxes and picked up again at Wolvercote Sidings, just a small passing box which I mastered in one day. Wolvercote Junction proved to be quite a surprise, it was as busy as Foxhall, dealing with all of the Banbury traffic and that of the 'Old Worse and Worry' line together with Yarnton goods yard and the Fairford branch. I spent a good three weeks there before moving to the last box at Kidlington for a couple of days, and ended up the week all ready to go into action the following week. I had never known time to fly so, seventeen weeks after leaving Milton I now knew the workings of nine other signal boxes, and had been introduced to many different kinds of signal equipment. My head was filled to bursting point with all the differing details I had had to learn, so that looking back now, years later, I wonder how any of us managed to handle it, perhaps because we were younger then and better able to cope.

I was the first to kick off (it has always seemed in my life that I am chosen to be the first) and I started on this two-week cycle at Milton; no problems there back in my old box, and it was nice to fall into the pattern of a service that I was brought up on, and on my old regular turn, so that I was working with my original mates again, but I did have Foxhall Junction to face tomorrow, and it had been seventeen weeks since I had learnt that box. That Tuesday morning I relieved Jack Drew, and before going up into the box, I checked the frame for fog detonators, not wanting to get caught twice. I checked the saddle bag on his bike, yes, he was still carrying round the half hundred weight of old fish plate bolts that I had placed in there all those weeks ago, and I would soon have to do something about fixing him in a proper manner!

I had a sick feeling in my stomach as I took over from him, and watched him cycle up the path for home, wishing that he could have stopped for an hour while I played myself in. The block bells began to ring, demanding attention, and I got down to work, Up main, Down Main, a trip into the depot followed by the workmen's passenger train from Oxford, a couple of Southern engines down from Moreton yard to turn, sending them round the West Curve to North Junction, and by the time I looked round, two hours had passed, the register was booked up to date, and I had a clear block, with no trains piled up in a heap outside, so I realised that I was winning, and began to enjoy myself. At nine the Up fasts began to appear, the 7.00a.m. Weston followed by the Fishguard, the slip coach dropping anchor just before reaching the box, then came the Cheltenham and the Swansea with the Bristol on her heels, and so tight behind, the Weston slipped right outside the box after I had given her a distant signal check. I could see the coupling drop away, and the vacuum and steam pipes part. She should not really have slipped with the distant on, as it was against the rules, although I had cleared it about a coach length behind. My old uncle, Bert Edmunds, loved this train and, as he was one of the top link drivers at Old Oak Common, I would now be seeing him in action, and he never slipped at Didcot with the Weston unless he was over the ninety mark. That duty passed quickly, it seemed no time at all when Ken Finch came into the box to relieve me, but I left him to it, tired after so much concentration, knowing that tomorrow would be spent at Appleford, which was as good as a day off. I never looked back after that first duty at Foxhall. I had broken the ice and I could now settle down.

As the months rolled by, the job became routine. We would relieve each other early if that meant a train home could be caught, or stop on if it meant our mate being able to come by train instead of a long cycle ride. If a 20-mile ride was unavoidable, as it very often was, first-hand information about road conditions was important, since in the winter, snow-drifts were commonplace, and also floods. We were up at 3.00a.m.

leaving home at four to cycle twenty or more miles to be on duty at six, always sure in the knowledge that when we got there the fire would be burning brightly and a pot of tea would be on the table. The only gripe that we had was that we could bike all those miles in some of the worst weather this old country was capable of throwing, and be there on time, and yet, some of the regular signalmen who would be relieving the night relief man (and who lived so close we could see their homes) would be late, turning up perhaps ten minutes behind time, and often losing us a train home.

As we worked together we became close friends, and familiarity brought the fun, between Ken Finch and myself anyway. Eddie Edwards, although a very nice chap, was a bit less exuberant, but being an ex-Appleford man, he did introduce us to the farmer's wife, Mrs. Arkwright, which in turn brought us into the market for eggs, not the shop eggs stamped with a little lion, but big rich old-fashioned brown eggs with some real flavour.

One week when I was at Appleford I had a most exciting time. I had collected my eggs, when the good lady came over the crossing in her car taking the children to school, and I had beaten Fred Tyler's dog between the well and the gate without spilling any of my water, no mean feat to outrun a cross-bred greyhound. Fred Tyler, who was ploughing the field opposite, gave a shout and stopped the tractor, so I placed the water can on the crossing on the safe side of the fence away from that dog, and crossed the road into the field. Fred was scraping the mud from an object which looked, at first glance, like an unexploded bomb, but as the mud cleared, it began to take shape and we saw it was a mass of hundreds of Roman coins stuck together. All but two of these coins ended up in the Ashmolean Museum in Oxford, but Fred had one and I had the other, in fact, I still have it. The newspaper report said that the coins were 1,600 years old, and came from the period of Constantine the Great. To think they had lain in that field all that time just for Fred and me to pick up.

Apart from their care of the Halt lamps, Fred and his wife were thought a great deal of by the railway people, because some years previously when the Down Birkenhead express had hit the wreckage of a derailment outside the box, the first coach had sheared across the Up main and ploughed through their garden landing up against the front door. Despite this they were both soon out of bed and giving help to the injured. They both, in a way, were adopted railway folk, and later, when a similar accident happened, they were the first on the scene with help.

It was while I was at Appleford for the day that I found out how kind and considerate Ken Finch was. I relieved him early on the afternoon shift so that he could cycle down the line to Culham and catch the train back home to Oxford, and as he left the box, he mentioned that there were 50 young Brussels sprouts plants up in the corner for me, carefully wrapped in newspaper and soaking in a bucket of water. I gave 25 to Eddie Edwards when he relieved me at 10.00p.m. and the next morning with all the enthusiasm of a trainee gardener, I planted mine out. But this was to be a long-term joke of Ken's as those plants just grew and grew, in fact they turned into the finest patch of cow kale ever seen with stalks as thick as trees, and eventually, I had to use an axe to cut them down.

When we took over Culham, it was to be in the new box, which had been built on the Oxford end of the Up platform, so we were in the public eye and the windows were so low that people could look into the box, but it was a nice duty there, working with the porters and the Station Master for company. Culham was an interesting place as between the box and the bridge on the Oxford side and to the east of the cutting was an airfield, a Fleet Air Arm branch of the service, H.M.S. Hornbill, flying Sea Furies of 1832 Squadron but within a few weeks they began to change over to Vampires. It was quite a racket to hear the banshee wail of a jet engine as they took off and landed, that was after being used to the Rolls-Royce Merlins of the Sea Furies [the Sea Fury was powered by the Bristol Centaurus]. The flight path was right over the main line, so we had a crash bell fitted in the box and a telephone, and were in direct contact with the control tower on the airfield in case of emergency.

I only had one emergency while I was there, and that did not affect the main line. I watched the pilot come in with a Vampire, side-slipping as he flared in but he clipped the fence with his under-carriage, leaving a couple of wheels behind and an ugly column of black smoke drifting back over the railway. That telephone was mostly used by the lads on the airfield when they enquired about train times, which was very handy as they would ring up to see how the afternoon Up stopper was running (it connected at Didcot with the London train), then half a dozen of them would come over the fence, scrabbling down the bank, and underneath the box, dressed like sailors going in, but civilians coming out as the train ran into the station. At the last minute, when the guard was blowing his whistle, they would dash out and into the train. Time after time, just as the train cleared the platform, two beefy perspiring, angry-looking pickets with red armbands and white gaiters would run on to the platform and they always asked us if we had seen any sailors get on the train, but the answer they got was always true, only civilians had boarded the train. This procedure was reversed later in the evening when the lads returned, and we never split on them, perhaps because of the carton of duty-free cigarettes left behind for understanding signalmen.

Culham was full of fun, and we got on well with the porters. One of them was an old chap and he was fascinated by the new jet aircraft, so, with a straight face, I happened to mention that the 5.00p.m. stopper up from Oxford had some canisters of compressed smoke on board for these jet engines. When the train ran in, that dear old chap carefully unloaded two large cylinders of welding oxy-acetylene that just happened to be for the airfield and dragged them on a station trolley all the way round to the airfield stores, but after this leg-pull he soon learnt to be wary of Ken and myself.

We had an anxious moment one day when the Government were clearing out a dump of army vehicles from nearby Dorchester village and these vehicles were loaded into wagons that had been shunted into the cattle sidings behind the signal box. It used to break our hearts to see dozens of motor-cycles tipped into those wagons, all upside down with the handlebars of some rammed through the spokes of the wheels of those underneath, while we had to ride push-bikes just because we couldn't afford to buy a motor-cycle. On this day, however, there were low-loaders shunted in and they had been loaded with lorries, all except one which contained a Bedford lorry, but with rear end converted to hold a mobile crane. I relieved Ken, who stopped behind for a few minutes for the Down train to take him home, so being nosy, we stepped from the platform and on to the floor bed of the low-loader to have a look at this interesting vehicle. The crane was coupled up to a diesel engine, independent of the engine of the vehicle, and there was an impressive panel bolted to the side, full of switches and dials, and right in the middle was just one red button. As everyone knows a red button is there to be pressed, so we obliged. There was a snort and a cough, and that blessed diesel engine began to run, settling down to turn over with a very soft 'chug, chug'.

Ken's train ran in, so he left me, and after I had dealt with the train and the block was clear, I tried everything to stop that engine. I pulled down switches, pressed other buttons, looked for levers and even kicked it, but it wouldn't stop, it just kept on chugging away. At about four in the afternoon, Mr. Fouracre, the Station Master, came up into the box for a chat and a cup of tea. He sat there looking out of the window, and said, in casual conversation, that he could have sworn that he had seen the jib of that crane move. I had a look, and with a great deal of earnest effort, managed to persuade him that it was a distortion in the glass. That diesel ran all day and night, luckily stopping the next morning when the fuel ran out.

It was well known that Mr. Fouracre, the Station Master, was a bird-watcher, the feathered kind, of course, and the old broad gauge goods shed opposite the signal box was a haven for swallows, so there was nothing unusual in Mr. Fouracre propping up a ladder against the great oak beams that spanned the shed and settling down to watch for a couple of hours. I relieved Ken one afternoon, and off he went home.

At four in the afternoon Mrs. Fouracre came over to the station, and made enquiries about her husband, as he hadn't come home for his dinner. Together we searched the area, and eventually we heard him shouting for help. He was perched up in the goods shed, legs straddling a beam, and the ladder miles away from where he had placed it, for Ken had nipped in and moved it. Mr. Fouracre was too much of a gentleman to take any official action over that, but he could give as good as he got, and there would be another time for him to get his own back on Ken. There was, weeks later; he rang Ken up when he was at Radley, and putting on a voice very much like Bill Checkley, he asked for a complete list of all train bookings to be copied out of the train register, and sent to the District Inspector's Office, with a covering report of all shunting movements. Ken duly carried out this request, and sent it in, and Bill Checkley rang him up and said that one swallow does not make a summer, so Ken conceded that he had been rumbled.

Now all this might make the reader feel that signal box work was one long period of hilarity, but that was not the case, it was a rough, tough job and a responsible one to be carried out by young men like myself in their twenties. There had to be some relief in the normal working day or we would have gone mad. When the pressure was on, we were not lacking, we had a safety record to be proud of, but normal working is boring, and does not make good reading, so it is of the funny or unusual incidents in my railway career that I write about.

The next box down the line was Radley, which, like Culham, squatted on the Up platform, but with the Abingdon branch to add to the working. Once the little tank engine of the Abingdon branch had arrived from Oxford we did not have much to do with it, the branch was worked as a single line with one engine in steam, so once the single line staff was handed over, it was just a matter of it running back and forth, connecting with the various passenger trains that stopped at Radley.

By this time, Ken and I had become known as the 'terrible twins' but at least we did bring some life into the district. Bill Prior at Appleford added the spice with one incident. He pulled off a classic that is still talked about today wherever old signalmen gather together, and he managed it simply because he was a champion gardener. We were all linked up on the phone one afternoon in between trains talking about gardening, then Bill began to talk about a giant marrow which he had grown, feeding it on sugar water and beer. As a result, it had grown so big that he would have to borrow a hand cart from the farmer to move it, and he went on to say that a well-known firm who made soups was going to buy it from him for an advertisement. We took all this in, so much so, that the lad in Oxford Station South signal box called in at the *Oxford Mail* offices on the way home from work, thinking that it would make a news story, and they thought so too, and they sent a reporter and a photographer out to Appleford to see this wonderful marrow. Bill only got out of that one by convincing them that the marrow had already been collected by the soup firm, and telling them that there was far more going on at Radley, they ought to go there and interview the ghost.

Mr. Wright, the Station Master, believed in the ghost, the porters believed it and so did the regular signalmen, although nobody would admit to having seen it. Like all good ghost stories, this ghost was reputed to appear only at night, and then, only on foggy winter nights. Perhaps closing time at the pub opposite had something to do with it, but all the station staff pointed out that they would not like to be the signalman on duty all alone on a deserted platform when the ghost was due to appear. The regular signalman kept the door locked, and nothing would induce him to go out on to the platform.

This story had continued for years, so when Ken and I came on the scene it was too good to be missed, we had to do something about it, if only to keep a good story going - the ghost had to be 'resurrected'.

Ken started it off on the night turn. First he waited for the station to close down and to see the Station Master's bedroom light go out in the station house opposite, then he trundled a platform trolley from the Up platform over the crossing and on to the Down platform, keeping out of sight under the overhang of the roof canopy. Mr. Wright opened his bedroom window, and through the fog, he could just make out the barrow moving, without being able to see Ken, but there was no move on his part to go and investigate. The next morning the station was full of this incident, the ghost was about again, but stories feed on stories, and now that we had brought the ghost back to life, it was time to build on it, so I took a hand in enlarging the rumours.

I had to wait a couple of weeks until it was my turn to be on the night shift, and to have a foggy night, because there was no point in rushing things, after all, if a job's worth doing, it's worth doing well. During the afternoon, Ken set the stage, bringing the ghost into every conversation, priming the station staff so that their thoughts were orientated ghost-wise, hence by the time that I came on at ten, they were jumping at their own shadows in the station lights.

At 11.30p.m., after the last train had gone, the late turn porter shut off the station lights, and came up into the signal box with the keys. He did not notice the end window open, or the ball of cotton waste, which I had scrounged off the Abingdon branch engine driver, soaking in a bucket of water, he just left the keys and with a parting remark about locking the door to keep out the ghost, he made his way back up the platform towards the gate. I could hear his steel-heeled boots on the flagstones, regular steps, brave steps, he was not afraid of any old ghost, then I threw that ball of cotton waste, heavy with water. I could not see its flight, but I did hear it drop with a flop just behind him, and the result was most encouraging. There was a half-strangled shriek, then the gate slammed, and hob-nailed boots went like the clappers up the road, over the bridge, and down into the village. As I retrieved the cotton waste, not wishing to leave any evidence around and spoil things, I could see that water had splashed everywhere, and so another aspect was added to the story, the ghost came from the river. That porter is no longer a railwayman, but he still lives in the village, and he still recalls the night when the ghost nearly had him. I sit in the corner of the pub sometimes, and listen to this, and wish that I could put the clock back twenty-five years, I could really put on a show now, with a tape recorder and some organ music.

As the winter closed in, the couple of days I had owing to me for working on bank holidays came in useful, as my new house was ready at Kennington, so I had the time off and moved from Didcot, borrowing a railway lorry and container for the furniture, and returning to Didcot for my family. We were tipped out on to the platform at Radley on a dirty night, with fog, drizzle and a long way to go on the bus, and there was my wife with the two children, I had a budgie in a cage, a goldfish in a bowl, and a lively puppy on a lead, all of us cold and tired. I began to wonder what I had done to deserve this, just one week before Christmas, then the bus came along and we piled in. We settled down for the four-mile run, but half way along the road, the driver missed one of the twisting curves and put the near-side wheels into the ditch. We stepped out on to a muddy ploughed field and went home to find the fire had gone out. Only a railwayman used to roughing it could have got over that introduction to Kennington, but it would be worth it, in the long run, as I was now at the half way mark of my district.

The car factories at Cowley were now really beginning to attract away railway labour, so much so that it was impossible to continue with rest days, the labour was so short, and it was easier to pay the lads overtime for their day off, so rest day relief was broken up and our circuit with it, and we were all absorbed into the regular relief work. That did not mean that I would lose Ken's company, as we were to overlap, almost as much as before, and it used to please me to see him come puffing up the steps of a signal box to relieve me, knowing that, after all these months, he still had not found out about the two bricks I had put in his saddle bag, or that I had tightened down his rear brake blocks. I had to gain some satisfaction to make up for those cow kale plants.

My first job after moving house to Kennington was to cover a vacancy at Sandford, and very nice it was too. I could see the box from my garden, so it was just a case of hopping over the fence and up the line for half a mile, with the added advantage of being paid lodging allowance for it. The agreement was that any box under three miles distant was paid walking time, based at the rate of twenty minutes to the mile, but any box outside that distance was a lodging turn, paid at the rate of 7/6d or 37½p for each turn, and the tricks we got up to so that we got home and still drew that lodging money I will come to later. It was a tax-free bonus and we grasped it with both hands.

It was swings and roundabouts in my case, with lodging pay for boxes near Kennington, but nothing for the Didcot boxes, because that was my home station. There were drawbacks at Sandford, including tilley lamps for lighting, no water and no toilet, which was ludicrous really, and that sewerage works right behind the box. Then there was the dubious advantage of the filter beds, the aroma coming off them on a misty summer morning or during the evening at the end of a hot day, was very uplifting, and even more surprising that we were never bothered with flies or wasps, even they couldn't breathe it.

It was here, in the Sandford box, that I had the pleasure of training a new man: Chris Boyne came to fill the vacancy, and in much the same way as I had gone to Milton, but without the benefit of the Reading Signal School. Chris was brand new to railway work, so we had to begin from scratch, but <u>he</u> was a willing learner. I began very quietly with him, explaining over and over again, then setting studies for him to do at home. I had had the advantage of a railway background, but what seemed simple to me was hard for Chris. Week after week I hammered away at him, and then suddenly it all began to fall into place and make sense to him, and after that there was no looking back. He told me long afterwards that several times he had been on the point of packing it all in, but that I had been so patient with him, it would have not been fair to do so. Three months to the day, Bill Checkley came and gave him an examination, and Chris passed, and the next day he had to go up to Paddington, where he passed again. When he took over I was as pleased as he was, and he never let me down. He ran that signal box as if he had been born into signalling.

I now moved into Kennington signal box, and came up against the village bobby, P.C. Tony Hore. I knew Tony slightly through seeing him in the village, he was a good copper, one of the old school, who believed in a clip round the ear instead of juvenile court, for any youngster misbehaving, but what I caught him at one afternoon, was right outside police practice - or so I thought at the time.

My first sighting of him, on this particular afternoon, was of him on the river bank poking away in the water with a long stick. He was there for an hour, then he climbed over the fence and came up into the box, which was not unusual, as a lot of the city police used to come to the box for a warm and a cup of tea, but this was afternoon, not night-time. He changed out of his Wellington boots and into his shoes, as if it was an everyday affair that he had been up to, then he asked if he could use the telephone.

He rang Oxford city police and very kindly informed them that they had a body in the water on their side of the river, then he hung up and turned to me, grinning all over his face. As he said, it saved him a lot of paper work, and they had done the same to him a few weeks before. Tony was a man after my own heart, I could appreciate the situation.

Some weeks later at Kennington, I saw Bill Checkley go into action and also show just what a good railwayman he was. It was also the first time that I had a signal wire break. The weather was bad, the wind howling and the rain battering up against the window, and I had a 'Royal' booked up at 11.00p.m. from Oxford, so Bill Checkley (as was his habit when 'Royals' were about in his district) arranged to go to one of the signal boxes to see it go by and this time he decided to come to Kennington. He parked his little car in the lane tight up against the hedge and battled his way over the level crossing, content to sit in the chair near my roaring fire, until the train had passed.

I received the 'call attention' one beat on the block bell, then after I had acknowledged it back to Hinksey South, the 'Royal' train code came through, 4-4-4 on the bell. I repeated the sequence to Sandford then went to the Up starting signal to pull off and really swung into that lever as it was a heavy pull with the signal being so far away. As I lifted the clip and opened my shoulders, there was a loud bang downstairs, and I went crashing across the box to land up against the lockers on the other side, because the signal wire had broken.

The shocked look on Bill's face was something to see as I picked myself up. Bill shot out of the chair and even forgot his trilby hat. He went down the tall outside stairway sliding on his hands on the stair rails, grabbed my hand lamp and was off up the line on my bike, coat tails flying, and shouting over his shoulder 'repeater'. Then I understood, Bill was going to try to beat the train and hold up the counter balance weight of the signal so that it would be in the off position. The 'Royal' was blowing up for my distant signal when I saw the little signal show off in the glass case, I pulled off my home signal and heard a satisfactory toot on the engine whistle. The 'Royal' went thundering past under the window, the driver, fireman and inspector looking up at me with an enquiring look on their faces. Little did they know of our efforts to give them a clear road.

Bill returned to the box, wet through and wind-blown, his hands bruised and bleeding but he had done a great job and one that I admired him for. After he had gone, I had a rough couple of hours until the signal lineman had repaired the wire, as I had to stop all Up trains and instruct the drivers to pass that signal showing a red light, all part and parcel of railway work which the public never knew about.

The next week brought extra work to Kennington as a result of the disaster at Harrow and Wealdstone. We had heard rumours, news like that travels swiftly round signal boxes, even if it is in another district or another railway, but even we were not prepared for the magnitude of it until the details began to filter through.

Being signalmen, we could feel the anguish that the signalman there must be going through, to have seen that happen right outside his box. As a result of the disaster, some London trains were rerouted over the Princes Risborough branch and down through Kennington Junction, and it was a week before it slackened off, but now that bit of line is all ripped up, and a way of life is gone.

My next change came with a move to Wolvercote Junction for a couple of months, and it brought a bit of fun that we all enjoyed. The box here was situated under the bank of the Oxford to Witney main road, the A40, with the junction to Banbury curving away in front and the line to Yarnton, Worcester and Fairford cutting away behind. Across the other side of the main line was the Oxford canal with a most attractive lock-keeper's cottage sited near the tow path. Although we had water supplied from Oxford in cans, we did, at times go down to this cottage and draw water from the well for it was pure spring water and far sweeter than our official supply. But the lock-keeper there had a problem, undesirable tenants, and they were to give us several weeks of entertainment before they were dealt with.

Floating in the pound off from the canal was a converted war time landing craft made into a houseboat. It was a smart little job with a big bay window at one end, and we could see right down inside from the signal box. The problem was this houseboat was occupied by two 'ladies of pleasure', and, with a pair of binoculars, it was possible to see a lot. Binoculars, you may say, what would clean-living young signalmen require with those? Well now, Wolvercote canal backwater was a haven for kingfishers, and they formed a constant display of beautiful colours diving into the still waters as they fished. If they happened to be near the houseboat, then we saw other types of colourful birds. But the use of those binoculars was also official, since the lock-keeper wanted these girls moved on and so did the County Police, but because of some long-forgotten law dating back to Queen Anne's time, a houseboat was protected for such purposes providing that there were no more than two customers on board at any one time.

An approach was made to the railway by the police, which resulted in Bill Checkley issuing a pass for the police to use the signal box as an observation post, so we had the company of a police constable on the early and late shift, and it was he who was equipped with binoculars. So what was more natural than for us to assist him 'in his enquires', in between trains?

We would see the paying guests arrive in cars and they would park them on the grass verge up on the bridge, then they would creep down the tow path and into the boat. They must have known about that old law, because there was never more than two at a time on board yet in the evenings traffic was so heavy that the two coming out used to pass the two going in.

It went on for weeks, with the police becoming concerned, as not only was it wearing out the tow path, it was causing severe eye-strain to the officers and ourselves from those high-powered glasses. Steps had to be taken that were outside the law.

I came on one afternoon in the middle of the week to relieve Ken and take up my observation duties only to find the boat gone and also the policeman, but we both put on a brave face about it and blinked back the tears. Ken then told me what had happened. At ten in the morning, both girls had gone tripping up the path as young girls do, arms round each other's waists, gaily chatting away, their shopping bags swinging. It was a beautiful morning, business was good, so a trip into Oxford would do no harm, and they waited on the road for a lift, and it was not long before some kind person took pity on two innocent young ladies and gave them a lift.

Ken said that it was then that the policeman in the box went into action and was on the phone to Witney in a flash to report that the boat was empty.

Within twenty minutes a police van drew up on the bridge and the police driver came running down the path and into the signal box, where he began to strip off and put on a pair of swimming trunks. He then opened a bag which he had brought with him and took out a whacking great carpenter's brace with a two inch bit. His next move was to swim over to the boat, take a quick look around, a deep breath, and then he was under the water, coming up now and again for another gulp of air. It took half a dozen dives before he climbed out of the canal by which time he had returned to the box with the water already lapping at the bay window as the boat settled. Soon after then there was a lot of disturbance in the water and the boat gently slipped under the surface of the canal, leaving the roof outlined a foot below.

When those girls returned Ken said that even across the width of the canal, across four running lines and with the windows of the box closed he could still hear the language of those girls! They went back up the tow path and we never saw them again, and in October a farm tractor dragged the houseboat out and took it away.

Signal box work was full of incidents which still stand out in my memory. Wolvercote Junction was also the only place that I ever had the horror of horrors for a signalman, namely having two trains in the section at the same time, and to make matters worse it was on a foggy morning. Like all incidents of this nature it happened so simply.

Wolvercote Sidings box was switched out so I was working with Bert Allen, another relief signalman at Oxford North Junction. Bert's signal box controlled the exit from Oxford locomotive shed, where in the early mornings two movements were booked out close together. The first was a diesel railcar that went to Kingham, followed by a light engine for Yarnton yard. On this particular morning the diesel railcar came up to the shed signal out of sight of Bert in the fog, but instead of letting Bert know that he was there, the driver sat in the cab and started to make up his ticket. The light engine came up behind him, and the fireman telephoned Bert that the engine was there and ready to leave, so Bert asked me for 'line clear' on the block bells. I gave him the road, thus freeing the block so that he could pull off his signals – and away went both of them, down the main line towards me, each unaware of the other due to the fog.

Bert could see what had happened as they went past, a few hundred yards separating them, but all he could do was to phone me and keep his fingers crossed. There was only one course of action open to me and that was to watch the track circuit on the diagram and hope that I wouldn't hear a bang under the road bridge. The track circuit lit up, and a moment later the diesel railcar swept by. I slapped back the signals and changed the points over for the Banbury line, just as the circuit lit up again with the light engine.

It had been a nasty moment, but we got both drivers together and squared it up. Both Bert's register and mine showed nothing wrong so we had got away with it but the jungle telegraph worked and Bill Checkley knew that something had happened, but he couldn't get to the bottom of it, as we had closed ranks all round, both locomotive and traffic departments; we had to, or we all would have been for the 'chop'.

One Sunday morning, years later when Bert had retired and I had left the service there was a single line working on the main line at the bottom of my garden and Bill Checkley saw me in the garden and came over for a chat. We sat down in the kitchen and had a cup of tea and it was then that the whole story came out. It was still bothering Bill after all those years so I told him what had happened and he went away happy because he didn't like mysteries.

Kidlington box was our limit down the Banbury line and it was like having a day off to be sent there. It was a big box with a large frame tucked into the bank on the Up side about a hundred yards from the station, but the bigger frame was a left-over from more prosperous times nowadays, the booked service was light with only the Blenheim and Woodstock branch running in and out to connect with stopping passenger trains.

The cross-over was a sight to see however. I knew from my footplate days that the road was always rough there and now I could see the reason as the rails had been laid across a bog.

The ganger had packed tons of ballast under that cross-over but within a few weeks the mud and water would seep up and when an express came thundering over it the whole lot would lift up between the wheels, showering a thick yellow mud everywhere.

At times, as the engines lurched, it looked as if they would come crashing into the end of the signal box and I used to get a bit concerned about it but it didn't seem to bother the regular men, who had got used to the situation so I supposed it was safe enough.

Opposite the box was Campsfield, the Borstal correction school, and Kidlington airfield lay behind that, so there was always something going on to relieve the boredom.

One day, as the Down stopper ran in some of these Borstal boys arrived with their escorts to go to the school and as I watched them get out one of them make a dash for it running as hard as he could down the path towards me. There were people chasing him and shouting for somebody to stop him and I thought I had better do something about it. Down the steps I went holding out my arms, which was all I could think of on the spur of the moment. The lad came on towards me a hulking great kid with hands the size of footballs and I began to wish that he was going in the opposite direction and that I was chasing him. However, I stood my ground feeling that the honour of the Company was at stake. Then he saw me and stopped and with a look of complete despair on his face he burst into tears. Poor kid, whatever he had done to be sent to Campsfield it must have been bad, but I felt sorry for him and hoped that he turned out all right in the end.

Chapter Five
Consolidation

W hen the holiday period was over and all the lads were back in their boxes, Bill Checkley recalled me and I became 'spare' for a few weeks. It had been a tiring period for I had been on duty seven days a week for twenty-seven weeks without a break, but rather than sit about in the office, I asked if I could go out into the district and learn some of the other signal boxes. Bill agreed to this arrangement, because he knew where to find me if I was wanted. Hence I learned my way around Didcot North Junction, Moreton, Cholsey and Didcot West End boxes, then later I had a day at Aston Tirrold, and a few days down the Fairford branch. In that way I was actually doing myself a favour financially speaking, because the more boxes that I signed for, the less spare work I would do. 'Spare' meant just the bare hours with no allowance for walking or overtime, and with two children in the family I needed every penny that I could lay my hands on. It was while I was learning Carterton box that I got landed with the branch for a couple of weeks; Bill rang me up and asked me to cover the late-turn duty the next day and I agreed. The box was right opposite the big American air base, in fact, some of the big bombers were parked on dispersal pads behind the box having to cross the single line to return to the base.

It was full of take-offs and landings all day, a succession of big swept-wing bombers roaring over the top of the box so low that I could see the rivets in the panels, and as I was most interested in these big aircraft, the next day I brought a high-powered ex-naval telescope with me, through which I spent a happy hour watching close up the air activity. Suddenly, the box door burst open and I was confronted by two very large members of the American Air Force Police. They both held six-shooters and pointed them directly at me. It was like looking down the front of a cannon.

These colonials meant business, and explanations took time. Even when I pointed out that my family went back to 1066, long before the *Mayflower*, they still took away my telescope, and I believe they would have taken me too, that is if it had not been that a ground crew wanted to move a parked bomber across the line and I was the only one there able to take care of the railway side of the operation. I had to ring Bill Checkley and tell him what had happened as, apparently, a letter was on the way to him from the White House, containing objections to my close scrutiny of the U.S. aircraft. Bill sniffed and made remarks like 'What about going to Fairford for a week to keep out of mischief', so that is what I had to do, but the story has a happy ending, in that I got my telescope back a month later.

349

I worked the late turn at Fairford without having learned the box in advance but it was fairly simple, even if I had to do the jobs of the signalman, ticket collector and porter at times.

There was also a weighbridge at Fairford which was right outside my powers of comprehension so I used to trust the farmers and the coal merchants to weigh the loads and just give me the tickets. When the last train from Oxford had run in, the little tank engine went to shed, leaving me all on my own and it was my job to lock up the station and turn out the lights but not before checking the toilets to make sure that they were empty. It was the first time that I had been in the ladies' toilets and I was most surprised to find that the writings on the walls were far more interesting than those in the gents, quite educational in fact. It took me a week to read them all.

Once the station was secured, I put the keys through the letter-box of the early turn signalman's house, which was only just across the station yard, then I would mount my bike and cycle all the way to Swindon, catching the 1.40 a.m. parcels for Oxford, the driver very kindly stopping at the bottom of my garden to let me get off. Doing it that way, and catching the train from Oxford for the next duty, meant quite a long round, but it saved the lodging turn money, which was worth a couple of pounds a week and I would far rather have the money for my wife than hand it over to a landlady.

When Bill thought he had punished me sufficiently over the Carterton incident, he called me in and sent me to Milton for a week. Again, now that I was living at Kennington it meant a long cycle ride each day, but on this occasion it was worth it.

Once every twenty years or so, depending on the state of the passenger receipts, goods returns, wage increases and such-like, the company would discover, much to their surprise, that they had too much money so there would be enough to allow for redecoration of signal boxes.

When repainting was planned, signalmen hoped to be on holiday or off sick for a couple of weeks, because trying to run a busy signal box with three or four painters around was nearly impossible.

The first indication as to what was in store would come when a signalman was placing his cycle inside the frame room and would see two dozen one-gallon tins of chocolate and cream paint in the corner together with half-gallon tins of red, blue, yellow and black for the levers. There was enough paint to cover Paddington station, but the painter knew from bitter experience that once a tin of cream or chocolate had been opened unless it was used up that day it would evaporate mysteriously during the night, but it was only Newton's Third Law of Motion at work: 'for every action there is an equal reaction', and it was their cunning against our empty coffee jars.

There was now no excuse for any signalman to own a rusty bike and I decided that locking-bar blue was just the colour for mine, chocolate and cream fitted nicely into the colour scheme of the bathroom and toilet at home, while signal lever red came in handy for the window-sill tiles. The white was useful for the window frames, but I never did find a use for the yellow, so that particular can remained full.

These painters would travel down from Reading each day, big portly men taking an hour to walk from the station, and when they arrived it would be time for a cup of tea so they would be with us a long time. Once the battle began it would start with the removal of dust. All the windows would be opened and the brushing-off started removing dust that had laid an inch thick on the crossbeams. After two days, when this had either blown out of the window or settled back down, the rafters, beams, roof and walls - as far as half-way down - would change from blackened puce to cream, and the lower half together with lockers, table, chairs and even the broom handle would become chocolate, all giving off a heavy stinging aroma of good old-fashioned lead paint.

Our meat and cheese sandwiches would taste of paint and we washed them down with a cup of paint-flavoured tea. The next procedure was for the painters to go away for a couple of weeks and then return to paint the window frames, that is if there was any white paint left! Once that was done, it would be the turn of the levers, and it was not long before our hands, lever cloths and trousers were covered in red, black, yellow and white paint. Finally they would be gone, leaving us with another twenty years to scrape paint off the window-glass and paint spots from our, once highly polished, floor. They were not a bad lot of lads, they never reported the loss of paint and they had a job to do, so it was quite unfortunate for them that they were the only people not really welcome in a signal box.

I found that Sunday engineering working made a nice change and an interesting time acting as hand signalman clipping points under the direction of the signalman in the box or acting as Pilot-man during single line working when one line was occupied by the engineers.

It was very interesting to see miles of relaying in progress, with signal gantries and crossovers being ripped out to be replaced by new, and if there was a big job in another district we would be sent there to assist. Reading and London were the most usual places for us to be sent and I always looked forward to working with the Cockney boys.

They were a good lot of lads, and took good care of us, particularly where the underground electric lines ran because in the dark it was all too easy to step on to the live rail as we were not used to it. When they came to our district we would look after them too because they were not used to fast-running trains, as everything in their district was either just starting out of Paddington or slowing down to run in, but they did not like tilley lamps.

I was sent up to Old Oak Common East Box one Saturday evening with Gerald Massey, one of the Oxford relief men, both of us expecting to spend our time clipping points, as the job we were involved in was a big relaying operation that spanned the whole of the weekend. When we walked up into the box to report to Bill Odey, the District Inspector, he confronted us with 150 tilley lamps which had been lying dormant for years. In the London district if a signalman wanted a light he pulled down a switch and a light appeared, but a tilley lamp was filled with paraffin, it had a gas light mantle and you had to pump it up. The London chaps had tried one but once it started to spit and pop, spraying paraffin all over the place, they threw it into a bucket of water and sent out an appeal to Bill Checkley so we country boys were sent up to cope with the lamps. Bill Odey was more than pleased to see us as he badly needed those lamps outside hence Gerald and I set to work cleaning, filling and priming those lamps all night and the next night too, so in fact we never did get outside to see what was going on.

I also seized every available chance to travel on the footplate, so I caught the train at Didcot, joining Gerald who had got on at Oxford. He thought I was 'eleven pence short of a bob' because I obtained permission to have a go on the shovel and when the firemen saw that I could handle locomotive work, they would sit down to enjoy a break, in fact one fireman soon got into the coach when we stopped at Reading and left the firing to me.

I had four footplate trips that weekend, two Up and Down, and on the last trip home on the Sunday morning, it was with a 'County' a type that I had not had a go at before.

We had walked up to Paddington to catch this parcels train so I stopped when we reached the engine cab and asked the driver if I could come up on the footplate, and have a look, as I had never been on the footplate of a 'County' class locomotive. He was most pleased to let me have a look and when I told him that until four years previous I had been a fireman for years, the invitation that I was angling for was offered and for the first time ever I had a chance to fire a 'County'.

The engine was the first of the type built, No. 1000 *County of Middlesex* and it was a surprise to me to find that the cab and boiler front were as big as those on a 'King' and when I looked inside the firebox, I found that it was the same size as a Churchward 47XX. It seemed to go on for ever.

Had I lost touch with a big firebox, I wondered? Looking along that fat squat boiler to see the double chimney sitting on top of the smoke box gave me the feeling that this was a locomotive with power to spare, indeed it ought to have plenty with the steam pressure needle hovering on 280lb. I had never worked with such high pressure before.

The fireman gave me a few tips, such as keep the back corners tight and well up under the flap, and build her up to a thick wedge of fire that fills the box from side to side, leaving a gap under the brick arch, so that the coal can reach the front; he might just as well have told me to pack as much into her as she would hold!

The driver, Tom Evans, opened up the ejector and blew off the brakes, the ejector sounding harsh as the jet of steam roared up through the chimney. He placed her in full fore gear and we started off, those big cylinders taking the steam, then sending it back to exhaust out of the chimney, not with the crisp, short bark of a 'Castle' marching out, but with a sound very new to me, exhausting with a brutal beat, each one cut off cleanly, each one to slam up against the underside of Westbourne Terrace bridge as we pulled away. I pulled up the flap as Tom shut off to let her roll over the newly relaid section, looking down at the lads collecting up the tilley lamps, answering back the ribald comments thrown up at me, then once clear I saw the big counterbalance weight come down as Tom lifted the regulator half way over and the power began to show, slamming the flap up against the firehole. The fireman standing up in the corner looked over at the pressure gauge and began to look a little apprehensive as if wanting to say something but not liking to interfere, so I took the hint and picked up the shovel and began to fire her. She took the coal from the shovel almost before I could get it in, then Tom wound back the lever so that I could dig the shovel down into the back corners and under the doors. I began to fill her up, the memory of my firing methods all coming back to me as I packed the coal in, first dribbling it under the doors then straight down the middle, and the lovely bit of burnt Welsh coal mixed with the exhausting steam and drifted over the roof of the cab and onto the footplate.

Through Acton the exhaust injector went on and I was firing her again through Ealing Broadway and West Ealing. The red needle touched the 280lb mark and she began to sizzle from the safety valve. The fireman looked at me and grinned, seeing that I had her on the boil so he relaxed and sat on the seat, reaching over to drop and lift the flap between each shovelful. Tom eased down over Hanwell viaduct enough for the exhaust injector to blow out and then she lifted her safety valve, roaring enough to waken the sleeping town, so on went the live steam injector to quieten her, only for a few minutes though, which was just enough to return the glass full of bobbing water up out of sight, then we tore through Southall. Hayes and West Drayton slipped past, and I picked up the shovel again, firing her all the way through Iver and Langley.

She was certainly living up to the reputation that I had heard about the 'Counties' scoffing coal as fast as I could feed her. I wouldn't have cared to fire her on the 'Cornishman', firing nonstop for four hours and though I had heard that they were shy on steaming, this particular one wasn't. It was only the exhaust injector which was keeping her from blowing off, the needle was stuck fast on 280lb with just a whisp of steam coming out of her brass bonnet.

As we passed Taplow I could see the familiar piles of rusty barbed wire, still there years after the war was over, and it was obvious that they had not moved at all during the years that I had been away. We then tore over Maidenhead bridge, the sound echoing back from the sleeping town below through Twyford and once past the big power station. Tom shut off steam and we freewheeled into Reading for a ten minute booked stop. This gave us time for a chat and Tom and his mate chivvied me for leaving footplate work and urged me to go back, but I told them that was impossible as I had lost my seniority and I was well contented with a relief signalman's life. It was just that a little run like this kept my hand in. In real life one can never go back, only in books such as this.

I sat down on leaving Reading because I was so tired after having been up since the afternoon of the day before and having worked all night but I did ask if I could use the scoop over the water troughs at Goring. It had been so many years since I had used one but the water came flooding in as if it was yesterday, the float rising up until the water began to gurgle in the vents and we were full again.

We drifted around the Didcot avoiding loop towards Didcot North Junction and I sat on the seat peering out over my old engine shed to see the familiar locomotives that I had known for years; row upon row of them, the smoke drifting out of their chimneys as they waited for another day's work. We clattered over the points and swept down towards Appleford, the signalman with his hand on the Down distant signal lever ready to return it into the frame and I could see the look of surprise on his face as he spotted me peering round the side of the cab. We then flashed past over Nuneham bridge through Culham, pounding on to Radley, the clang of the shovel ringing out over the sound of this lovely engine hard at work. We passed through Radley and on approach to Sandford Tom shut off and allowed the engine to drift. I shouted to Chris in the box and as he slid back the window, I pointed forward with my hand. He nodded his head, understanding my charade of signs, so I shook hands with Tom and his mate and climbed down the foot steps, jumping clear on to the ballast easily from long practice. Tom gave a short blast on the whistle as I walked up my garden path. I was grateful to him and his fireman, for they had given me one of the most enjoyable Sunday engineering turns of duty that I had ever had. It had been the first time on the footplate for a long long time and I began to wonder if there would be another time, but if that was one of the best Sundays the next weekend was to bring the worst and one that I never want to see again even if I did return to the footplate for a few brief moments.

That week I was 'spare' for a couple of days, then I went to Foxhall Junction to cover the early turn for the rest of the week. It was in November, dismal days with just enough fog to make working difficult, but not foggy enough to call out the fogmen. I had a busy time with trains out of the

Didcot ordnance depot and engines coming from the Down relief into the depot yard and then finding margins to let them out, and the freight traffic from the West Curve came at awkward moments, they needed a long margin to cross the junction and over into the Down loop to Milton. In fact, if an express had left Swindon on the Up main, and another was through Reading on the Down main, there was no chance at all to move across the junction from the West Curve. Once I had cleared the curve, the transit traffic from Didcot yard via North Junction would be on the move and it was an involved operation for both of us to get this traffic into the depot.

My problem was with the War Department Police. I had to get on the phone to them usually at breakfast time and prise someone out of the mess room to walk down to the depot gate and unlock and open it, and that chap knowing that he could expect to be there standing about in the cold for perhaps an hour. This was because now the gate was open, I could let the signalman at North Junction know, and he in turn had to allow the transfer trip with 70-odd wagons propelled by a 57XX pannier tank to go from the yard across his junction and into the Appleford Down loop. After this he was able to change his points, obtain 'line clear' from me and give the little engine the chance to charge off. It had to be a full-blooded charge with the driver confident that the gate was open, because he couldn't see it from the other side of Foxhall bridge and once committed with those wagons on the move it was a fight between the weight of the train and the tight curve binding the wheels.

In the box we could hear the struggle but we could not see what was going on because of the trees and earth works so we had to rely on the depot policemen ringing up and informing us that the train was inside the depot complete with tail lamp, thus enabling 'train out of section' to be given to North Junction and another train accepted.

Depot policemen could not seem to understand the importance of that little oil lamp and they would close the gate and just clear off, leaving me stranded with 'train on line' on the block and North Junction tied up too. We had repeatedly tried to explain the situation and in the past we had phoned, written reports and asked Bill Checkley to look into it. Things would then improve for a couple of days before it was back into the old routine. I decided to take things into my own hands and rang the Commanding Officer at the Depot and by sheer luck I got through to him instead of some orderly clerk. I asked this gentleman if he could spare the time to come into the box the following morning to see the problem and he agreed.

It was sheer luck how it worked out on the following day as the CO came into the box just before the depot trip was due and he turned out to be a Royal Engineer who had been on the Longmore Military Railway. When the trip came round the curve the policeman cleared off as usual but we had a troop special booked for ten minutes later and there I was with the block tied up back to North Junction. The officer was as good as his word, he was out of the box and into the depot in no time and whatever he did must have worked for I had no further trouble from the depot policemen. However, I received a mild rocket from Bill Checkley for by-passing him and a request for me to work at Foxhall as groundsman for engineering work on the Sunday.

I accepted the extra overtime as it seemed a simple job to do and I didn't have to start until 7.00a.m; the engineers' occupation was near the Up main Home signal and all trains, including passenger trains, would have to travel over the Up goods loop from Milton, so all that I had to do was put a clip on the facing points and hold a green flag up. Considering the light Sunday traffic I should be home again by three in the afternoon.

The mist cleared as the 'Red Dragon' came sweeping up the main line, the gentle curve stretching back to Milton giving me a panoramic view of this greyhound streaking towards me, the smoke rolling back along the roofs of the coaches. As 'Britannia' No. 70026 *Polar Star* roared through the jumble of rods connected to the driving wheels seemed so mixed up when compared to the sleekness of a 'Castle'. She bucked a little as she rode over my junction, tucking the mixture of smoke and steam in behind the last coach and making me look hard for the tail lamp. She was a familiar sight on this train now that the 'Castles' had been moved on, sharing the run on the 'Red Dragon' with *Ariel*. Little did I know then that when I saw her the following day she would be in a very different position.

That next morning, Sunday, 20 November 1955, according to my diary, I went on duty and found Jack Drew in the box. I carried a point clip down to where I should need it, together with a red and green flag. Then I went up the path and over the bridge to Jackson's for the Sunday papers. As I left the little shop the mist began to clear and by the time the engineering train took up position on the Up main line there was the promise of the sun coming through. We had a leisurely morning, I had only eleven trains to deal with so I helped Jack to clean and polish, being glad of something to occupy my time between trains. At midday we stopped and had a pot of tea and some sandwiches as there was nothing due up until the Treherbert excursion just after one in the afternoon. I was able to renew my contact, by telephone, with Granville Burt, as he was down the line at Milton box and I had not seen him for some time. Whilst we were speaking his block bell rang calling his attention to the Up excursion, so I rang off knowing that it would soon be time for me to go down to the loop points and deal with this train, which was approaching the speed restriction.

Granville asked for 'line clear' from Foxhall and as the block bells rang I made to move down the stairs. As I reached the top step the loop and Down main bells began to ring out simultaneously, an urgent rapid beat as they were intended to 'call attention'. Jack acknowledged the call with one beat on the bell key, then from Milton came the worst bell signal of all, slow and distinct, so that there could be no mistaking it — 'ting, ting, ting, ting, ting, ting' meaning - six beats - 'Obstruction, danger'.

Jack and I looked at each other wondering what on earth had happened, then the telephone rang and Jack answered it. He listened for a moment, then turned towards me his face ashen with shock. He had just been told by Granville that the excursion had gone down the bank and into the fields. I tore down the steps, only stopping to snatch up my bike, and got to the loop points, where I quickly took off the clip in case Jack needed those points later and as I passed the engineering train on the Up main line, I shouted out to them what had happened. Then I was off down the path towards Milton as fast as I could pedal. As I got nearer to Milton box I could see that something was badly wrong. There were a couple of coaches standing on the main line and several more skewed over at an angle but no-one could have been prepared for the sight that met my eyes when I got to the signal box. The 'Britannia' *Polar Star* was down the bottom of the bank on her side, and I remember thinking that her 6 feet 2 inches driving wheels looked so thin, indeed she looked almost like a 'Hornby' engine that had jumped the rails and there were coaches piled on top of her.

I went straight up into Milton box to see if Granville was all right. He wouldn't let me relieve him, and said that if he walked out then he could never return to a signal box again. Later when it was all over he described to me the dreadful shock of seeing that engine tearing towards him, disregarding the speed limit and then seeing it come lurching through the points from the main line into the loop bucking and leaving the rails before plunging down the bank, taking the coaches with it.

When I left Granville he told me that the fireman had gone back towards Steventon with detonators to protect the derailment so I could now concentrate on rescue work. The scene was appalling. Out of the ten coaches, five were off the rails whilst the leading four coaches had followed *Polar Star* down the bank and were badly damaged. I crawled into the cab of the engine to see if the driver was still in there but it was empty, apart from coal scattered in a heap all over the cab side. One of the coaches was perched up over the side of the tender and cab and another was telescoped up behind it, the underframe and wheels sheared and lying across the loop and the Up main line.

As I crawled out of the cab, the Ordnance Depot Fire Brigade and police began crowding over the fence with ladders, propping them up against the sides of the coaches and pulling the dead and injured up through the doors and shattered windows. I heard a cry for help and immediately crawled under the underframe of the coach that had sheared off to find a young man pinned down by the coach frame lying across his middle. There was nothing I could do for him except to hold his hand and talk to him, and share several of my cigarettes with him. With the arrival of the rescue train,

Dr. Horan from Didcot crawled in alongside us both and gave the poor chap a shot in the arm to ease his pain, then he left to attend to others. I stayed with the young man until the jacks were placed under the frame but just as the pressure was eased the poor chap died holding my hand.

The next few hours were the worst hours of my railway career. I worked non-stop, helping to recover the dead and injured people, that is until two o'clock the next morning, when Bill Checkley found me, my uniform torn and filthy and covered in blood. He made me go home and I did so but reluctantly, and only on the understanding that I could come back as soon as I felt that I had rested enough. As I left the scene I could hardly believe that this was my beloved Milton, ablaze with portable electric lights flooding all over this great piled up heap of tangled wreckage, the Swindon and Reading steam cranes lifting and slewing as they sorted out the priority lifts to enable trapped people to be reached. My poor wife was beside herself with worry when I finally reached home at half past two in the morning as she had heard nothing of the disaster.

At ten the next morning I was back at Milton again after a fitful sleep. The passengers who had survived injury were gone, together with those coaches which had not been derailed; all that remained were the wrecked coaches, and they had been lifted clear so that the Up main line could be used again, although at reduced speed. I was very sorry to hear that Bill Checkley had been taken to hospital as he had stumbled down the bank during the night and broken his ankle, so Freddie Blackhall was in charge and I spent the day assisting him in every way that I could. *Polar Star* was still in the field on her side and she was to remain there for two weeks, sinking further into the mud as the water in her tank drained out long after the other debris of the accident had been removed.

Long discussions took place as to how to get her back up the bank, for a 'Britannia' Pacific weighing 146½tons with the tender takes some moving, but the simple way in which it was achieved was something that I was lucky enough to see and it was an education to watch when the operation eventually took place on Sunday, 4 December 1955.

During the previous week the relaying gang had been busy, all the damage to the track had been repaired and the signal department had renewed points, rodding and signal wires so Milton box was fully operational again. Now it was the turn of the locomotive and this was where the convenience of Milton depot came in. The gang built a track across the field from the sidings even building a small bridge from sleepers over a ditch. Rails were then bolted to the wheels of *Polar Star* and she was lifted up by a steam crane into the upright position, then the rails attached to the wheels were connected up to the temporary track, the bolts removed and she was carefully dragged out and into Milton depot, then back to Didcot depot where an engine was waiting to take her to Swindon for examination.

V

She had sustained some damage of course but not as much as I would have thought and that because the ground had been soft and she had not hit another vehicle. A rail had gone up through the left-hand leading bogie and the frame and then up behind the cylinder. The regulator rod was broken and she had lost her smoke deflector plate on that side while a buffer from one of the coaches had punched a hole in the tender and allowed the water to drain out. The boiler cladding was crushed and covered in mud, but all in all she got away with it fairly lightly and within a few months she was again pounding up the main line to Paddington.

This railway accident had been the first one that had involved me in death and injury on a large scale. As I had cycled rapidly down the path that Sunday afternoon towards the scene, I had steeled myself to expect the worst, and I had indeed seen horrors that I hope I never see again. I was so busy once I got there that having to handle shattered bodies had no effect on me at the time. Only my wife knew what I had really gone through as she would be woken by my restlessness in the early hours of the morning. Perhaps my colleagues thought me hard at the time but as a result of this outward bearing I was to be landed in another unpleasant task later, that of searching the line.

I had helped to carry this out many times when on the footplate but there had always been other people on the ground and the engine and crew were just a means of conveyance. A light engine would go through the section with a recovery team after any report of a door open on a passenger train. It was all part and parcel of working on the railway; a signalman would see that a door was open, so he would send to the box ahead the bell signal 'Stop and examine train' and telephone the reason so the line had to be searched between that box and the one behind. Nine times out of ten it was a faulty door lock but chances couldn't be taken so a search was made and I now became one of those on the ground, all because Bill Checkley thought that I was tough enough to go on such a job with him. Thank goodness I could only be called upon when I was 'spare' and available.

Once Bill and I searched the line between Didcot East Junction and Moreton on foot, Bill still limping from his injury at Milton. It was a dirty wet evening as black as a coal mine and we set off with only the flickering light of a hand lamp each to light our way, wondering what awful things we were going to find. All we knew was that the driver of a Down fast train had stopped and said that he thought he had seen someone fall off Moreton bridge. The first indication that anything had indeed gone wrong was a shoe, with the foot still in it, and then other bits and pieces of a body scattered over a hundred yards of track; a 'King' with thirteen coaches behind doesn't leave much.

The next step was for one of us to stop with the remains while the other went to the signal box and made arrangements for removal. To my discredit I made sure that it was Bill who stopped there, I was off!

Looking back on it now the things that we had to do for nine and a half quid a week were far beyond the normal call of duty but we accepted it then.

Cattle on the line could prove a real nuisance, holding up trains for some time. The first reports would come in from train crews pulling up at the signal box to inform the signalman that there were either horses or cows on the line, so I would pass this information back to the signal box behind me and the work would begin until the porters or relaying gang had cleared the section. My mate would stop all Up trains, and I would stop all Down trains, both of us acquainting the driver with the circumstances and they were then allowed to proceed at reduced speed.

It was rough luck on expresses, which would urgently blow up on the whistle for the distant signal, reducing speed until they were nearly stopped. Then the Home signal would be lowered to allow them to draw forward, only to be brought to a dead stop by a red flag from the box so that information could be passed on. It knocked the stuffing right out of a run but they were all good railwaymen and they understood, and it only happened now and again. Cows were not too bad, they could be rounded up fairly easily and returned to the fields, the gang then repairing the fence behind them, but horses were another matter. They would often gallop off down the line into another section so that two or more signalmen had to go all through the procedure of stopping trains until the horses were captured. Perhaps we should have had a special bell-code for (non-ironhorse) entering section?

Once at Milton I saw a pack of hounds crossing the line while the huntsmen on their horses were milling about on the other side of the fence shouting to those stupid hounds and helpless to avert what seemed a hopeless situation. The Up afternoon Pembroke train came tearing through under the bridge, the driver hanging on the whistle as he rocketed along in the eighties but those hounds just ran ran round in circles completely confused. Then the driver acted in a way I wouldn't have thought of; he opened up the regulator and the cylinder steam cocks and on a 'Britannia' it sounded as if the end of the world had come. Those hounds thought so anyway and they took off, some of them clearing the fence with one leap to vanish into Milton depot. When the train passed me the driver was leaning out of the cab with his fireman laughing at the sight of it all but at least the hounds had got out of the way.

One hound became a pet in the home of one of the platelayers simply because he refused to go home. When taken out for walks he would set off towards Steventon village away from the railway and if trains were running on his return he had to be dragged and carried back home.

Once at Culham I had the report of a lion in the section between Radley and myself so the usual procedure of warning trains was carried out, and it went on for some time because nobody from either Culham or Radley dared to walk through the section to find out. Then eventually through the bridge towards me came nothing more exciting than a Great Dane, plodding his way up the main line. The poor old chap was confused and exhausted so I caught him without any trouble and brought him up into the box, where he drank a bucketful of water, then settled down until the police van collected him. They told me later that he had a cell to himself until his owner collected him and he left behind two gallons of water over the floor!

No record about signal box work would be complete without a few pages devoted to a very important man rarely seen by the public and that was the signal lamp man. The lad in our district was a diminutive Pole called Stefan, one of the most cheerful little chaps imaginable although he had one of the roughest jobs on the railway.

In all weathers he would start going round the district each week beginning at Milton; we would all know that he was about because the copper coil in the signal lamps would contract when he took the lamp out and this would cause the contacts of the low voltage sensors to touch and ring the 'lamp out' bell in the signal box.

He would trim and fill his lamps in the small tin lamp hut near the box and then trudge off, his lamp stick loaded down with a dozen lamps suspended from it all filled with long-burning oil. He would climb up tall Distant signal posts whilst a gale was blowing hanging on for dear life if the signal was dropped. Sometimes, on a wet day he would be wet through to his underclothes and yet I never heard him grumble.

Milton and Foxhall would take a day between them whilst the big junction at Didcot East would take him all day for apart from the stop and distant signals he had all the ground signals to do, but he would beaver away, and by the end of the week he would be through to Sandford, ready to start the round again on Monday morning.

Now and again he would get a little overtime, a Sunday duty when signal box supplies were renewed and on these occasions, a pannier tank with two coal wagons and a brake van would set off round the district calling at each signal box with a drum of oil for Stefan, which he would unload, and ten hundredweight of coal for the signal box, which a loco shed labourer would shovel out. This was supposed to be our supply for six months, but in a twenty-four hour box it only lasted about six weeks, which was why we were always scrounging coal from loco crews. Then on Monday morning Stefan would be back singing one of his Polish songs, happy now that he had a new supply of oil and a Sunday duty paid at time-and-three-quarters.

I used to insist that he had his meal-break with me in the box so that he could get warmed through on a cold day, and I also liked to know that he had a hot drink inside him before he went out again. In this way I got to know him well and I began to find out why he was so happy. Apparently it was because a few short years before he had been hungry and cold working as a slave on fortifications in France after he had been shuttled back and forth between Germany and France, so although I thought he had a rough job Stefan knew what a *really* rough job was and he was just so happy to have survived.

After all the overtime I had done, I had saved enough money to get mobile again so I bought an old ex-army Norton side-valve motorcycle. It was a 500cc job and a great brute of a thing. As they might say, it would 'climb the side of a house', and I got it at just the right time. The porter came from Radley one morning and called me out of bed to tell me that Bill Checkley was in a spot because the day shift man at Moreton Cutting box had reported sick at short notice so the night man was still there and I was to go to Moreton as soon as I could. So I set towards a signal box that I had never worked, and had learned two years before. On thinking about it though perhaps that was the best way, to get pitched into a busy box before I could think about it. I relieved Eric Membery and he was gone in a flash, leaving me with a full block and it was a busy one with Up and Down main lines and reliefs carrying all of the traffic (that traffic I was used to at Foxhall), plus all the Oxford trains. Then I had an Up goods loop to contend with and behind the box the big marshalling yard with two pannier tanks blasting away all day. At least I was in good company, I knew all the drivers and firemen, the engines were the same ones which I had fired in this very yard, and I knew the yard Inspectors and the shunters. One of them was, in fact, my brother-in-law and I never had to fill a coal bucket or make a cup of tea, they looked after me so well. It was as well that they did look after me because I wouldn't have had time to do it myself. I thanked my lucky stars that I had kept my little book with the lever movements written down in it because I would never have had the time to work my way through the frame. My first move out of the yard was to dispatch a light engine back to Didcot shed, which meant turning him out of the yard on to the Up relief line through the cross-over and down the relief. When I asked for 'line clear' from Didcot East, they gave it to me on the Down main so I had another sequence of lever movements to go through, 26 to 30 levers, and at the same time I had to deal with other trains. It was no wonder that it took me several hours to 'play my way in'.

From the lofty height of the box, it was possible to see all over Moreton yard and to appreciate the work of the little pannier tanks. On four of the yard roads, the stop blocks at the far end of the sidings were mobile, each being a solid concrete block the size of a bungalow riding on skids on the rails. These blocks would be pulled up the siding by the engine and then left with enough room for a couple of freight trains to be built up against them, then perhaps the last wagon going into that siding would be foul of the next line, so the pannier tank would be called in to squeeze them up. It was a sight worth watching. The little pannier would come gently in to buffer up, then with the sand trickling down on the rails and the safety valve blowing, it would push up all the loose wagon buffers until they were all compressed up against the concrete block. Then the little engine would go down hard on her springs, her valves would groan in protest and inch by inch a thousand tons would begin to move slowly, like some great ocean liner easing away from the dock side. Today, such a feat would be covered by television and a vast crowd and yet we took the power of the steam locomotive to be an everyday affair and never gave it another thought.

I had two good weeks at Moreton and it was to be the only time that I worked there because the box is now long gone along with the yard but it had showed me that signal box work was as demanding as a hard-worked steam engine.

Chapter Six
End of an Era

The saddest time that I had as a relief signalman was when I had to see a signal box pulled down. The box was at Aston Tirrold, a signal box which I had learnt but never been called upon to operate. The box was an intermediate one between Moreton and Cholsey with only twelve levers in the frame, a Home and Distant signal for each of the running lines and a detonator lever for each. The signalman there was a much-envied man because the box was a day duty only, being closed between five in the evening and eight the next morning, but as with steam itself the writing was on the wall and the signal box was to be demolished as automatic signals had been installed.

A month after the new automatic signals had been installed, I was given the duty to act as groundsman at Aston Tirrold, protecting the Up and Down relief lines as the Signal and Telegraph Department had an occupation on the Up and Down main lines so that they could use a steam crane to demolish the signal box and remove the signals. I arrived at Aston Tirrold just in time to meet the train, which was pulled by a Collett 22XX class, taking up the occupation, which consisted of half a dozen low loaders and the steam crane with guard's van. My job was to make sure that when the steam crane began operating and the cab or jib was fouling the Down relief line it was safe to do so and I had to station myself well back towards Cholsey so that engine drivers could see me with my red and green flags.

The engine pushed the train back about fifty yards, then the van was uncoupled and left and the wagons and crane drew forward to the signal box and the gang began work. One section began disconnecting signal wires and rodding while the other gang began knocking out bolts in the wall sections and roof. With a soft 'chuff, chuff' the crane began to work. The jib came round and the hook was connected to slings on the roof and off it came in one section, scattering roof tiles all over the place. As soon as the roof was laid on a low-loader, the front section was lifted out, leaving the frame naked and bare, and within minutes that too was removed, leaving a gaping hole in the floor. The highly polished stove was next, ripped out without ceremony and thrown down into the waiting truck, to be followed by the table, chair and lockers, now just all so much junk. The train was then pulled forward so that an empty truck stood under the shell and the crane set to work again lifting out the remaining walls and steps; the coal bunker and lamp hut soon followed and then the site was laid bare, all that was left was a lot of churned up ground covered with bolts, tiles, glass and wood fragments. Aston Tirrold signal box was no more, and another little bit of the Great Western had been laid to rest.

It was almost indecent to see the way in which the signal posts were removed; a chain was slung round the base, the little piston driving the flywheel on the crane flashed up and down and the jib began to rise with the pulley spinning round as the cable was wound back on the drum. The chain tightened, scrunching into the post and it began to quiver, then with a loud sucking noise the post came out of the ground like a giant tooth, leaving a deep hole half full of muddy water. By three in the afternoon it was all over, the train had been coupled up and trundled down into Moreton yard, it had run round and transferred the brake van, then set off home to Reading, passing the empty site without so much as a glance.

The next day I was 'spare' and knowing that I would be called upon to cover Cholsey at the end of the week, I had a day there to refresh, which seemed necessary because it had been a year since I had learnt the box, and it was one job to which I did not look forward.

Cholsey signal box was part of the station. It sat squarely on the platform between the Up main line and the Down relief line. It also had control of the Wallingford branch, but this was no problem as the 'Bunk', as it was known, operated just the same as the Abingdon branch, that is to say, one engine in steam, so that once the single line staff was handed over to the driver, it ran like a bus service, connecting with all the stopping passenger trains calling at Cholsey.

The automatic signals had been installed on the east of Cholsey for a long time, replacing the box at South Stoke, so those at Aston Tirrold, on the west side, were an extension. The automatic signalling certainly speeded up train handling, but at the expense of the Cholsey signalman, for in addition to his own work, he was now covering for those two removed signal boxes, working directly with Moreton and Goring on the block bells and instruments. The diagram was fully illuminated and showed both the sections at each side, the automatic signals being released by levers in the box. These were full-size levers with the handle cut down but they still had to be pulled over to allow the electrical contact to be made, which in turn showed up as a green light on the diagram where the intermediate signals were located.

Tom Palmer was on duty when I got there and he was pleased to see me. The volume of traffic was such that handling sixteen trains at once all travelling at express speeds with only a minute between was classed as normal working. Indeed, so busy was it that the custom of booking trains in the register was dispensed with and only passing times were booked. I was able to give him a break by taking over the Up traffic while he dealt with the Down, but from what I could see I was in for a very busy time on Saturday.

I knew that day when I left my old Norton motor-cycle in the station yard that I would be mighty pleased to see it again after that duty. I took over with the block full and as fast as I could get to one end of the frame to pull off I had to be up at the other end putting signals back as the expresses roared through just a few yards away from me. Cholsey was the only signal box where I would have been glad to have been wearing roller-skates because there came one period in the afternoon when the trains were running so tightly between each other that I just could not work fast enough and they began to receive Distant signal checks.

Booking of any sort was out of the question, even the passing times; it was not the sort of place to come to full up with tea because a call of nature would have meant trains standing at signals and there was no time for such mundane affairs. No one was more pleased than me to see his relief come and I thanked my lucky stars that I did not work that box every day like the regular chaps. I will say this much for them, they were all thin lads so obviously it was not the place for some of those portly signalmen.

On Monday, I went to Didcot North Junction to brush up on the box. I had not been there for a long time and it was a pleasure to work with Jack Gardener again, who had been one of the original 'mums' at Milton with the kitten. Jack was a signalman worth being with. He had been brought up in that world, being the fourth generation to go into the box. His grandfather was one of the original Didcot signalmen and Jack was very proud of the document that he showed to me, where his grandfather had been awarded £2.10.0d on July 3, 1891 for running his signal box without making any mistakes, a bit of Great Western history indeed. Whether or not he was a practical joker like his grandson, I don't know, but Jack was, as I found out to my cost. During my brush up on the frame, I set the road out of the yard and into the Down goods loop ready for the transfer trip into Didcot depot.

Then I just had to go to the toilet and with it came the chance that Jack was waiting for. The toilet was in a little smelly dirty hut with a tin roof tucked under the outside stairway, and I had just entered when the wagons of the trip went rattling by outside the door. At the same time Jack taped the lead straps of a fog detonator on the handle of the fire poker and dropped it out of the window, and down onto the tin roof. I remember at the time of the explosion thinking that we had another Appleford on our hands because a few years previously a goods train had run through the sand drag in the loop at Appleford, and the wagons following had smashed down the box, pitching the signalman, Gordon Churchman, into the field behind together with the frame. But then I could hear the wagons still rattling by, the rust flakes from the roof began to subside and I realised that I was safe, but it was still half an hour before I dared come out.

I settled my nerves by having a cup of tea and sat down to read the special notices - after loosening the bolt holding the saddle on Jack's bike by way of retaliation. These special notices were always interesting, about things like out of gauge loads, and ships' boilers and transformers. They all needed special attention, but the one in particular that caught my eye was a very special train, *City of Truro* en route from York to Swindon.

I had never seen a 'City', although I had heard my father talk about them enough, as he had fired them for miles when he was a fireman. That was long before my time and I was a little disappointed when *City of Truro* came rolling past the next morning in the half-light of a dirty March day. She looked dowdy with her side rods stacked in the tender, along with wooden packing cases, just another 'Bulldog' with big driving wheels, but I had not made allowance for the expertise of Swindon Works where she was bound for and they did a splendid job on her. When I saw her next, a few months later, she was standing in the spur outside Didcot East Junction signal box. She was covering station pilot duties and I just had to wait for her to come into the station. When she arrived I was soon up on the footplate, having a good look at her; she had been painted, her nameplate was restored and she was as new as the day she was born. I would have loved to have fired her not just shunting up and down, but on a train running free as she was meant to, and from that casual remark I began to wonder if plans could be laid. It had been a long time since I had used a shovel and this little locomotive was no 'County'; her firebox was the same as a 'Bulldog', and her little tender was the same size as a Dean Goods. It should be easy, if only I could arrange it.

'In this world there is nothing for the dumb', that's what my old dad used to say, and I've found it to be true, but the way things fell into my lap was on this occasion a combination of circumstances. Firstly, with my being in Didcot instead of miles down the line and secondly walking into my old footplate mate Ted Hurle. From the conversation (after we had finished hugging each other) emerged the fact that during the next week, he was working the 12.42p.m. Didcot to Southampton, and the engine booked for the job was *City of Truro*.

With that information, it was up to me to do something. I was booked in Sandford box that week, but I did have a day owing, and also an understanding wife, thank goodness. What I was attempting was sheer pleasure, if I could pull it off, but a lot of arranging had to be done, and the first thing was to apply for a day off. Bill Checkley liked to have a good reason on any application for a day, so I gave it to him, namely that I was going to fire *City of Truro*. He didn't believe me, nevertheless he did grant me the day off. The next step was to go down to the shed and see the foreman and square him. He was most sympathetic; he would love to allow me to fire her, and if it was up to him I could, but (and there is always a 'but') I was no longer a member of the locomotive department, indeed, I hadn't been for years and neither was I still a member of the Footplate Union, so there was a problem there. However, he could give me a pass to travel on the footplate as an observer and once out of sight if I did just happen to pick up the shovel then he wouldn't know anything about it, so long as I didn't shout it about, and didn't turn up in overalls. So I arranged it for the Thursday, and brought my wife and children to my mother's house in Didcot, where we could all stop overnight and return home the next morning.

The next day I slid through the station entrance, turned right and ran up the steps on to number one platform and there, standing in the Newbury bay, were four coaches with *City of Truro* at the head. I saw Bill Checkley walking towards me and he told me that I must be mad to spend a day firing a steam engine. I agreed with him, I *was* mad, but so must he be to go crawling into bushes to get briars for his roses! At all events he was satisfied, but knowing that I was one for a leg-pull he had thought that my reason for wanting a day off was one; now he knew that for once I was genuine.

There was a short toot on the whistle so I began to run, as Ted was obviously ready to leave. I sprang into the cab just as the engine began to move, Ted beaming with pleasure at the sight of his old fireman from years ago back on the footplate with him once more, and I grinned back delighted to be there. Then I got up into the corner of the cab out of sight until we were past the pilot engine and the signal box.

Ted pointed to a carrier bag hanging on the cab hook and I opened it and took out an overall jacket and trousers, and by the time we were passing the milk depot and on to the branch, I was dressed ready to start work. I looked over the side, expecting to see the side rods flashing round as they would have been by now on a 'Bulldog', but they were going over in such a lazy manner it was hard to believe that we were keeping time. It was a situation which I found hard to accept, as I was on the familiar 'Bulldog' footplate but with the wheels of a 'Castle' going round outside, and there was none of the haste that I remembered so well. We seemed to be floating, and it was a surprise to see Ted shut off and wind down the screw reverser ready to run into Upton; a couple of brisk shots on the vacuum brakes saw her gliding into Upton station and with one final burst she stopped.

Ted's fireman was known as Johnnie; I can't remember his surname now, but I can remember what a good lad he was, and he suggested that the guard might like his company, which would give me a bit of room on the footplate, so he jumped off on to the platform and left me to it. After a break of ten years, the old combination was together again. Ted and I looked at each other, the look of sheer pleasure of two old mates enjoying the situation, as we felt that we had put the clock back and for those few hours we were going to savour every minute. There was a blast on the whistle back down on the platform and Ted hurriedly blew off the brakes. We had been so wrapped up in each other he had not noticed the time but now we were off, hitting the bridge with our exhaust then into the start of the chalk cutting, Ted winding her back slowly on the reverser so that she would not pick up her heels. My goodness, it was good to be alive on this beautiful summer day, to see the sun shining in a blue sky and the lushness of the green fields and to sense the warmth of comradeship which we had for each other flooding across the footplate. I dropped the flap and left it down as I fired her, just the same as a 'Bulldog', well up at the back end to slope down towards the front of the firebox, the tongues of flame rolling and curling up with each shovelful over the top of the brick arch. She began to whisper at the safety valve so I put on the right-hand live steam injector (she was steaming so freely there was no need to use the exhaust one). I lifted the flap, pulled down the tip-up seat and sat down to watch those slender six foot eight and a half inch wheels go round. She was not climbing up this bank in the manner that I remembered, she was striding, with the slow easy gait of a 'twenty-nine'. I watched the water in the gauge glass climb up out of sight, then I shut off the injector and fired her some more, the shovel matching my mood and that of this lovely old lady. Slow easy movements, sliding the shovel in the coal, turning round to slide it over the firehole ring, twisting my wrist in the old well-remembered way, scattering the coal all round the firebox.

I sat down again and had a good look at the boiler front. Swindon had really made a good job of her, with the deep green paint on the cladding, all the copper and brass pipes burnished, the gauge frame and the sight feed lubricator, up in Ted's corner, shot-blasted clean, the brass plate engraved with the valve cut-off on the reverser shining like gold. Even the ejector had been cleaned off, and the wooden handles of the brake and injectors had been varnished. I had never been on a footplate like it before, it was a show place. We cleared the bank with the water in the glass dropping half way down as we came onto the level and I put the injector on again; no more firing was needed for the moment. Ted tapped down the regulator until she was riding on the jockey valve and wound her back, nearly into mid gear, and then she began to fly, racing across the top of the Downs, leaning over slightly into the gentle curve through Churn Halt, flying gracefully with the wind running with the smoothness of a race horse. There was no rattling or bucking, every bolt in her frame and cab was tight. In other words, she was perfection.

With the bit between her teeth, *City of Truro* seemed to run for ever and this occasion was certainly the nearest that I had ever been to feeling that a locomotive was really alive, but alas she had to be held back as Compton station was growing larger with each turn of those slender tall wheels. Ted gave her a good long burst on the vacuum brake and as his hand grasped the handle and pushed it over the air roared harshly in and she reared back, almost as if he had reined in a galloping horse, then the vacuum pump took over and she rolled sedately into Compton.

City of Truro began to blow off gently as we stood in Compton station. Despite that leisurely gait up the bank from Upton, the run through Churn had made us two minutes early so she had to stand there, a slight blow from the cylinder drain cocks giving the impression that she was straining forward, eager to get moving again. Then we were away once more, Ted opening and closing the cylinder cock lever and sealing the blow, while I dropped the flap again and fired her all round the box. I packed the back corners and under the fire hole doors where it had burnt hollow, and as I slid the shovel back into the coal we were swooping down into Hampstead Norris, the blower on slightly to clear the smoke, and I realised that after the long lay-off I was beginning to forget the distances between the various stations.

As she pulled away she began to 'lose her feet', giving a quick 'cha cha' out of the chimney before Ted could shut her down, then she picked up and began to gallop up the bank towards Pinewood Halt, which was not an easy place to stop because it was on the curve and difficult for the driver, but I remembered the drill, and Ted let her drift in with the brakes just rubbing whilst he watched my hand as I waved him down. I leaned far out of the cab until the coaches were almost in the Halt, then when I gave my hand signal to stop there was a 'woosh' as the vacuum brake was applied and we had arrived.

No more firing was needed for a while, and after what seemed like just a few turns of the wheels we arrived at Hermitage for a one-minute stop. Then we needed a little bit of steam, enough to get her rolling, and it was then just a matter of letting her free-wheel down the long drop into Newbury, running level with the rooftops of the houses, drifting over the Bath Road and under the bridge, where we waved to the signalman at Newbury East Junction (he had come to the window to admire this resplendent lady). Then Ted brought her speed down sharply as we came off the branch and on to the main line, letting her run, just ticking over until we felt the kick of the facing points and a little steam brought us into Newbury station.

We were booked to stop here for thirty-five minutes, so as soon as the station work was done we pulled forward and filled the tank at the water column. Then we pulled forward up and over the points to back into the Down bay, leaving the platform clear for the next train. As soon as we came to a stand, I dropped the flap and the back damper down one notch and began to pull forward some coal. She stood there in the sunlight, gleaming in her red and green paint, the sun sparkling from the safety valve bonnet, the copper band round her chimney taking on a blue tint from the heat and the famous nameplate curving over on the frames, proudly acclaiming her name to her admirers, who were a dozen small boys all very excited by the sight of her.

At 2.00p.m. we were off again, and I lifted the damper and let the fire brighten up until the Lambourn branch began to climb away on our right, then I started to fire her again as she galloped towards Enbourne Junction. The vacuum siren gave a 'whoop' as we hit the A.T.C. ramp at Enbourne's

Distant signal. Ted lifted the cancel trigger and eased her down a bit, then there was a lurch and we swung away from the main line and on to the Winchester branch and she was working hard up the bank towards Woodhay.

It all came flooding back to me now, the engines that I had worked on this line so many years ago. The big American 2-8-0s, where were they now I wondered, and the L.M.S. 8Fs and the many 'Halls', 'Granges' and all the others? Now, by sheer luck I was firing *City of Truro,* an engine that had been tucked away for years while all my footplate years slipped by and I realised that my old dad had been right, these 'Cities' were good engines, and I asked myself why on earth were they ever done away with?

It was ironic in a way that time on the old Winchester branch seemed to have stood still while I had been away and yet Woodhay, Highclere, Burghclere, Litchfield, Whitchurch, Sutton Scotney, Worthy Down and Kings Worthy all slipped past so quickly on this particular day and in no time at all it seemed we were gliding into the tunnel to pull up gently to a halt in Winchester Chesil station. We stopped for only two minutes here, just enough time to uncouple the horsebox that had been coupled on at Newbury, leaving it in the station for the yard engine to collect, then we commenced the fifteen-minute run down into Eastleigh. That big busy station was simply bustling with movement, in sharp contrast to the sleepy country stations which we had just left. Southern locomotives burst through to flash by, their coaches roaring behind them, and the Up expresses fresh out of Southampton hammered up through the station; they were almost enough to make our little lady shy-off.

We stood shimmering in the station, posing for the numerous devotees with their cameras. Grown men serious with intent, not for them the schoolboy chatter, but soon the guard's whistle sent us on our way. I could afford to sit down now and bask in the tribute given by the Southern lads as they looked up and saw us marching by. Past the smoky engine shed, past the lines of tired dirty engines waiting to go through the Works and the half-dozen that had just come out, brilliant in their new colours, their wheels clean and sharp looking, side rods polished and buffers ebony black. They had been cleared of all the years of grime and were now waiting to go back into service and unfortunately to renew that dirty mantle. The lads waved as they enjoyed the sight of this grand old lady striding south in the sunshine.

As we ran down the main line between Eastleigh and Southampton I could see the changes that had been made since I was last this way. The rubble of bombed houses was gone, the bomb-sites had been cleared and new buildings had sprung up to replace the scars, and as we ran into the once dingy terminus at Southampton I found there too the station newly painted and everything was bright and cheery in the sunshine. Johnnie emerged from the guard's van and uncoupled while I was placing a lamp on the tender, then the station pilot drew off our coaches and pulled up over the points. The points were then changed to allow us on to the turntable, whilst the coaches were shunted back into the platform we had vacated.

Since we had arrived at 3.56p.m. and were not due away again until 4.55p.m. that gave us an hour to turn and top up with water and back on to our train, plenty of time for a cup of tea and a sandwich. By 4.25p.m. we had finished, so while Ted and I went round with the oil can, Johnnie shovelled some coal forward and I went round *City of Truro* with a handful of cotton waste, dry-wiping the dust of the journey from her boiler, keeping the sheen of her beauty from becoming soiled. I felt that I owed her this little bit of attention for she had given me more pleasure in these last few hours than I would have thought possible.

At 4.55 p.m. we began the long trip home and as we left I looked back towards the terminus, knowing that I would never again see Southampton from the footplate of a Great Western steam locomotive. We ambled back into Eastleigh for a two-minute stop, then at 5.12p.m. we were away, swinging right over the main line at Shawford and on to the branch up to Winchester and our home ground. I had stood behind Ted up from Southampton, just enjoying the sight of him handling this engine in the way that I well remembered. I didn't even watch Johnnie firing her, I was just content to soak in the enjoyment of being on the footplate again but realising that each time those great big driving wheels went round it was drawing my illicit journey into the past to a close.

Winchester was reached on time and we stood in the station watching the shop girls and workmen leave the train weary from the day's work in Eastleigh and Southampton. The tunnel mouth showed as a black hole in front of us and the tunnel itself curved away into the darkness as it burrowed under the big hill towering above us. Ted opened the ejector and blew off the brakes, then he told Johnnie to sit down and went over to the fireman's side to watch out for the guard. As the twin needles reached the 22Ib mark on the vacuum and reservoir gauge I stepped forward and placed the handle in the upright position, and as I did so Ted pulled the whistle chain looked over at me with a smile on his face and said 'Right away, mate'.

Without even thinking I opened the ejector again and lifted the regulator, the metal feeling smooth warm and friendly in my hand, and *City of Truro* began to move, gently at first as I could feel the power going from that shining handle into the wheels. As her exhaust hit the tunnel mouth I gave her a little more steam and instantly the exhaust deepened and she began to stride deeper into the tunnel. I snapped down the clip on the reverser, held the fixed handle loosely in my hand and very gently began to link her up, half a turn at a time with the valves floating enough for me to feel them in my palm. We cleared the tunnel with her running strongly, one more turn and I clipped her down the regulator, stopping in the same position, then up went her nose and she began to bite into the bank, but just as she was beginning to run freely I had to close her down for Kings Worthy.

I gave her a little shot on the vacuum brake just to get the feel of her braking and as the blocks began to rub on the wheels I gave her a little more and she sauntered into the station and stopped. She stood there almost sniffing at the long climb ahead to Worthy Down. Just then Ted came over and told me not to treat her so gently because she was built to take hills and dales in her stride. So when we set off once again I gave her half regulator and wound her back as she began her march, matching the turns to her demands, then when she told me in the way that all steam locomotives communicate to the driver (through the palm of the hand and the soles of the feet) that she was happy at this setting, I lifted the clip back in the ratchet and she was left alone to make her own way. I looked down at Ted doing the firing, feeding her with coal as he had taught me to do so long ago, little and often in the right place and at the right time, spraying and spreading, tucking it into the corner of the fire box, each shovelful darkening the plume of her exhaust. I felt a deep feeling of affection for this wonderful man who had enriched my life so much and he must have read my thoughts as he looked up at me and smiled. We were so close again we did not need to speak.

I shut off at the top of the bank and let her run, the gradient slowing her up for Worthy Down station. Leaving there was another climb but once out of the cutting beyond the station she could free-wheel again down to Sutton Scotney, Ted leaning over the side of the cab to catch the cool air on his face, before the easy climb to Whitchurch, followed by the long drag up to Litchfield and beyond.

It was a roller-coaster road now, swooping down into Burghclere, pausing here and then like the wind down the dip through the bridge and up into Highclere, where she stood waiting time almost panting with excitement until the time came to be off again.

At this point I handed her back to Ted, satisfied beyond words that I had handled the regulator again and happy to pick up the shovel and enjoy myself in feeding the fire. We ran into Newbury at 6.41 p.m., an hour and forty minutes out of Southampton. After the station work was over we pulled over the points and backed into the up bay for a rest until 7.22p.m. There was time to take water and have a last cup of tea. It was to be the last time for me when that tea can went into the firebox, the last one after thousands over the years, and the last one with Ted.

I rode on the fireman's seat when we left Newbury, watching the sun go down and our shadows flying over the fields beside us, past the old familiar stations, little homely country stations with a blanket of roses growing along the fences, the Great Western branch line in all its glory, basking in the warmth of a soft summer evening. As we ran down the bank from Upton I noticed that the fields of corn on the Didcot side were beginning to turn colour, a soft yellow haze, before the coming rich brown of harvest time reflecting back on the green of the polished boiler. As we swept under Hagbourne bridge the clock was put back nearly thirty years as my dear wife and children waved to me from the same spot as I used to wave to father on the old 'Skylark'. We then floated round the curve and over Fleet Meadow bridge, the flanges squealing on the tight curve, a little steam into her cylinders, enough to clear the points, and then she slid into the bay platform at Didcot and arrived at her journey's end.

I still see *City of Truro* now and again in the museum at Swindon, but she is now cold and silent, clinically clean, the tender vacuumed out, new fire irons in the tender rack, an unblemished shovel and coal pick clipped so neatly in the cab, no oil drips and no warm comforting smell of an engine in steam. She is dead, as dead as *Lode Star* and the little Dean Goods, but, perhaps one day they might all come out again. Perhaps it is wishful thinking to see a Churchward 'forty' marching out of Swindon station, followed by *City of Truro* and the Dean Goods with the 94XX tank barking her head off, but stranger things have happened and I can only wish that this may happen one day.

To have to go back to work in the signal box the next day was a bit of a comedown, and I was silent and withdrawn for a couple of days. Had it been a good idea to try to recapture the past or should I have left things alone? But then the demands of my signalman's training came to the fore but for how much longer it would assert its pull, I didn't know. Each week saw more resignations going in from the lads and it seemed that our old railway was dropping apart. I too was beginning to think that perhaps I owed my family a better life.

I finished up the week at Wolvercote sidings and took over the late turn at Didcot North Junction the following week, and that was when the die was cast. The only way to this big box from my home at Kennington was to go by road to Appleford and then walk up the line to Didcot. So on the Monday afternoon I parked my old Norton behind Appleford box and prepared for the walk, when Bill Prior of the marrow incident stuck his head out of the window and asked me if I was aware of the opportunities only a few miles away at the Morris Motors car factory. It seemed from his information that his son-in-law had joined the security staff there working the same hours as we were doing but for five pounds a week more, plus a pension and pay when off sick.

I had not been aware of this, in fact it seemed almost too good to be true. The sick pay certainly sounded interesting for I knew that at the moment if I went off duty sick my money would stop the minute that I walked out of the signal box, hence this information seemed to be worth investigating.

I wrote to the factory for an interview and a couple of weeks later I was called to attend, where I found everything that I had been told was true.

I left that interview to discuss things with my wife and although she knew that the railway was my life that extra money and the conditions that went with it were an opportunity not to be missed.

To cut a long story short, I accepted the job and gave Bill Checkley a month's notice. Bill was most upset to hear that yet another man with the district 'under his hat' wanted to leave, but he had to face the fact that £9. 8s. 0d a week was not much for the responsibility of being able to work all those signal boxes.

It was pure coincidence that my last three weeks as a signalman took me back to Milton where my career had begun ten years before. With the introduction of colour light signals and power signal boxes, it would not be long before there would be no more Milton or any other manual signal boxes. Progress had caught up with me again, and I could see that given a few years I would be either stuck in a power box where I would never actually see a train or land up (as so many lads did) on the platform as an inspector, neither position really appealing to me. The third alternative was to be made redundant so it was obviously time to get out while I was still young enough to learn another trade. My last turn of duty was on Saturday, July 26 1958 and the last train that I dealt with was the 9.18p.m. stopping passenger train from Didcot to Swindon, a fitting end for a Didcot signalman to pass on a Didcot-crewed train.

I cycled up the path towards Foxhall for the last time with sadness in my heart, thinking about nearly twenty years of railway work behind me. On the following Monday I began work as a security officer at Morris Motors at Cowley and in the years that followed I found that all the railwaymen who had gone to Morris's before me (and there were many) had not stood still but like good railwaymen had found that there is always another step to climb. Ten years later I was the supervisor and then the final avenue opened up and I became an engineering investigator and, for once, I reckon that I will stand still and settle for that.

Some time after I had left the footplate the other lads who had left said that they had no regrets and the same was repeated to me by the lads who had stayed in railway service. In reality of course, there must be regrets for the railway that I knew in my youth, although perhaps not for the railway of colour light signals and diesel locomotives.

It was a long time before I held a shovel in my hand again, on 26 May 1975 on *King George V* at Hereford, and several years were to pass before I would have the chance for a footplate run. Then one Sunday in August 1980, I had a day out and visited the Bluebell Railway and there I ran into a wonderful lot of understanding lads who quickly kitted me out with a cap and overall jacket, together with a footplate pass. Then I was escorted on to the footplate of the beautifully restored Adams' radial tank No. 488 and invited to 'have a go'.

It gave the lads a good laugh to see an ex-Great Western man firing a London and South Western Railway locomotive, but I fired her from Sheffield Park to Horsted Keynes in just the same way as I had always fired a locomotive and the injectors worked the same way, so nothing was really any different. The surprise came when we got back to Sheffield Park and I started to make my farewells. Those lads would have none of it as I had proved that I could fire this little engine, but they asked if I was still good enough to *drive* her? I could scarcely ignore this challenge, so I placed her in full fore gear, pushed over the regulator and marched her up the bank as if I had never been away.

I've joined the Bluebell now, and who knows, one day I might get the chance to fire the 'Schools'.

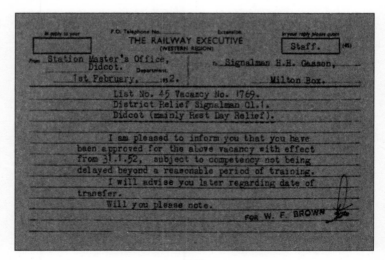

GREAT WESTERN RAILWAY.

(1406)

APPLICATION FOR SIGNALMAN'S BONUS.

No. 7871

Signalman _James Jardine_ having performed six months' duty in the _____ Cabin at _Didcot_ Station, without having made any mistake in working Points, Signals, or Block Telegraph, or having committed any other act, or made any omission, which might have led to an accident, applies for his Bonus, and is entitled to W in accordance with the conditions shewn on the other side.

The authorized Bonus for this Cabin is at the rate of £ _5-0-0_ per annum.

Half-yearly Instalment of £ _2.10_ due on _Jany 3rd_ 18 _92_

Previous Bonus was due on* _July 3rd 1891_

Jackson .... Sub-Inspector of Division.

Edmunds .... Chief Inspector of Division.

Murphy (?) .... Superintendent of Division.

* If the Bonus has been deferred from any cause, the particulars must be stated here, giving the date of the offence.

CONDITIONS.

1. If a Signalman is off duty for more than a month by illness, his bonus must be deferred for a period equal to the time of his illness.

2. The portion of bonus money earned shall be allowed in cases of Signalmen dying before the expiration of the bonus half year, as well as in the case of those promoted or transferred to other grades, or incapacitated and unfit for further duty, provided they have worked for three months without having any serious irregularity recorded against them in connection with the working of the Block Telegraph Points and Signals, and affecting the safety of the Line;

3. Signalmen, who are promoted during their bonus half-year from less important to more important Cabins, will receive a proportionate amount of the increased bonus paid at the more important Cabin, dating from the time of transfer, thus:—If a Signalman is one month at a £3 Cabin, and five months at a £5 Cabin, he will receive for the half-year £2 6s. 8d.

4. To be entitled to receive a bonus, a Signalman must have performed six months' duty, without having made any mistake in working Points, Signals, or Block Telegraph, and without having committed any other act or made any omission which has or might have led to an accident. Should he be guilty of any such act he will lose his bonus for the period between the date upon which his previous bonus became due and the date of the offence, from which latter date his next half-yearly bonus will commence to run.

Index